Cyber Criminology

Exploring Internet Crimes and Criminal Behavior

Cyber Criminology

Exploring Internet Crimes and Criminal Behavior

Edited by

K. Jaishankar

CRC Press
Taylor & Francis Group
Boca Raton   London   New York

CRC Press is an imprint of the
Taylor & Francis Group, an **Informa** business

CRC Press
Taylor & Francis Group
6000 Broken Sound Parkway NW, Suite 300
Boca Raton, FL 33487-2742

Visit the Taylor & Francis Web site at
http://www.taylorandfrancis.com

and the CRC Press Web site at
http://www.crcpress.com

To my daughter D. J. Mriganayani who questions, put things in different perspectives, and makes me think radically

Contents

Section III

DIGITAL PIRACY

Section V

LEGAL AND POLICY ISSUES OF CYBER CRIMES

Foreword

I am very pleased to be asked to write the foreword to this interesting book. I first met Dr. Jaishankar (Jai) at a conference in Bangalore in early 2009 and again some months later in November of that year when he visited the University of Leeds for 6 months on a Commonwealth Fellowship. While he was in Leeds, Jai engaged energetically in many fruitful activities, one of which was the compilation of this edited collection of chapters by international scholars.

I got to know Jai during those 6 months, and we had many lively discussions about cyber crime and especially the different ways that it has affected the people of the Indian subcontinent. I am very grateful to him for this knowledge because it has helped me to begin to understand just how ubiquitous the Internet has become and how this ubiquity has, in fact, begun to spiral in the new millenium.

Even today, some 20 years or so since the graphic user interface made the Internet user friendly and popular, networked technologies are still becoming further embedded in each and every aspect of our daily lives. Even if we do not use the Internet, much of our personal information will be stored somewhere on a networked computer, so in one way or another it affects all of us. Because of this reality, the potential for our data to be used maliciously is much greater, and it therefore becomes increasingly important that we study the impacts of the Internet, especially as the freedom it brings comes at the cost of the new risks we experience.

Regardless of whether you are a member of the academic community, a practitioner, a media commentator, or just someone who is interested—yes, you do exist—this book will provide you with a provocative and thoughtful collection of viewpoints upon which to develop your thoughts and strengthen your debate. So I invite you, the reader, to read on.

David S. Wall, PhD
Chair of Criminal Justice and Information Society
School of Law
University of Leeds
Leeds, United Kingdom
May 2010

Acknowledgments

From the bottom of my heart, I would like to thank Professor David S. Wall, University of Leeds, UK, for being kind in accepting my request to write a foreword for this book. My heartfelt thanks to Carolyn Spence, Patricia Roberson, Robert Sims, and Elise Weinger Halprin of CRC Press and the Taylor & Francis Group and Marc Johnston of Cadmus Communications for effectively coordinating and managing this book to print. I would like to thank the reviewers of this book: Gillian Dempsey, Gregor Urbas, Justin W. Patchin, Majid Yar, Marcus Rogers, Maura Conway, Peter Grabosky, Robert G. Morris, Russell Smith, Sameer Hinduja, and Thomas J. Holt. My special thanks are due to Susan Brenner, the chief editorial advisor of the *International Journal of Cyber Criminology* and Shaheen Shariff, the book review editor of the *International Journal of Cyber Criminology*.

I sincerely thank Prapon; the Bangkok Police Department; Bessie Pang, the executive director of the Society for Policing Cyber Space; and Steve Chon and Laurent Testard, the former moderators of Virtual Forum against Cybercrime (VFAC; http://www.cybercrimeforum.org).

I also thank Roderic Broadhurst, VFAC, and the Korean Institute of Criminology for being strong supporters in the development of the *International Journal of Cyber Criminology*. Mathew Grandy, the designer of the book cover, needs a special mention for agreeing to use his image without any fees, and I genuinely thank him for his generous nature. A. Ravishankar, the volunteer cover designer, played a vital role in making the collage design of the cover to bring out the theme of cyber criminology—my sincere thanks are due to him. My heartfelt thanks go to my research students, Sivakumar and Periyar, for their wholehearted assistance in the cover page design work. My earnest thanks are due to Dhruv, Samyuktha, Mili, and Megha for significantly assisting me in the editorial process. Last but not the least, I would like to express my heartfelt thanks to my wife Debarati for being a great intellectual support and for taking most of the familial responsibilities on her shoulders while I was tied up with this project. As I have completed this editing work, I hope I will now have time to support my wife.

Editor

K. Jaishankar, PhD, is a senior assistant professor in the Department of Criminology and Criminal Justice at Manonmaniam Sundaranar University in Tirunelveli, India. From November 2009 to April 2010, he was a Commonwealth Fellow at the Centre for Criminal Justice Studies, School of Law, University of Leeds, UK. He is the founding editor-in-chief of the *International Journal of Cyber Criminology* (http://www.cybercrime-journal.com) and editor-in-chief of the *International Journal of Criminal Justice Sciences* (http://www.ijcjs.co.nr). He is the founding president of the South Asian Society of Criminology and Victimology (http://www.sascv.org) and founding executive director of the Centre for Cyber Victim Counselling (http://www.cybervictims.org). He was awarded the prestigious Commonwealth Academic Staff Fellowship, 2009–2010. He was a member of the United Nations Office on Drugs and Crime core group of experts (15-member group) on identity-related crime (2007–2008) and a member of the International Scientific and Professional Advisory Council of the United Nations working group on cyber crime, Milan, Italy. He was recently appointed as a fellow of the African Centre for Cyberlaw and Cybercrime Prevention. He was a coinvestigator of an international grant funded by the Social Science and Humanities Research Council of Canada to develop a profile of cyber bullying, inform the current policy vacuum, and develop guidelines to help schools address cyber bullying. Among the recent books he has written and/or coedited are *Cyber Bullying: Profile and Policy Guidelines* (DOCCJ, Manonmaniam Sundaranar University, India, 2009); *International Perspectives on Crime and Justice* (Cambridge Scholars Publishing, UK, 2009); *Trends and Issues of Victimology* (Cambridge Scholars Publishing, UK, 2008); and *Crime Victims and Justice: An Introduction to Restorative Principles* (Serial Publications, New Delhi, 2008). He pioneered the development of the new field of cyber criminology and is the proponent of the space transition theory of cyber crimes. His areas of academic competence include cyber criminology, victimology, crime mapping, geographic information systems, communal violence, theoretical criminology, policing, and crime prevention.

Contributors

Adebusuyi I. Adeniran is a lecturer in political sociology, research, and development ethics at the Department of Sociology and Anthropology, Obafemi Awolowo University, Ile-Ife, Nigeria. He earned a BSc in sociology from University of Ado-Ekiti, Nigeria in 1999 and a MSc in sociology from University of Lagos, Nigeria in 2005. He is currently completing his PhD in sociology at the University of Ibadan, Nigeria. He has published widely in renowned local and international journals, periodicals, books, and encyclopedias. He is a recipient of cogent scholarship, sponsorship, and fellowship awards. He is a member of notable professional bodies, such as the American Sociological Association, Utopian Studies Society, Global Forum on Migration and Development, and Migration and Development in Africa Monitors. He presently functions as the African editor of Wiley-Blackwell's *Working USA: The Journal of Labour and Society* and as an editor of Wiley-Blackwell's *Encyclopedia of Global Human Migration*.

Michael Bachmann is currently Assistant Professor of Criminal Justice at Texas Christian University, Fort Worth, TX. He received his PhD in sociology from the University of Central Florida in 2008 and his MA in social sciences from the University of Mannheim, Mannheim, Germany, in 2004. He specializes in the investigation of computer and high-tech crimes. He is the author of several book chapters and journal articles on cyber crimes.

Adam M. Bossler is an assistant professor of justice studies in the Department of Political Science at Georgia Southern University in Statesboro, GA. He received his PhD in criminology and criminal justice from the University of Missouri—St. Louis in 2006. His research interests include testing the applicability of traditional criminological theories to cyber crime offending and victimization. His recent work has appeared in the *Journal of Criminal Justice, Journal of Crime and Justice, Deviant Behavior*, and *International Journal of Cyber Criminology*.

Roderic Broadhurst is a professor in the School of Regulation, Justice, and Diplomacy at The Australian National University, College of Asia and the Pacific. In 1994 he received his PhD in criminal justice from the University of Western Australia and an MPhil from the University of Cambridge. He is a chief investigator and deputy director of the Australian Research Council's Centre for Excellence in Policing and Security and leads projects on organized crime, investigations, and cyber crime. Professor Broadhurst has considerable international experience and has conducted UN crime victim surveys in China and Cambodia and taught at the University of Hong Kong. He serves on the steering committee of the Virtual Forum Against Cybercrime hosted by the United Nations Office on Drugs and Crime (UNODC)/Korean Institute of Criminology. He is an associate of the Australian Institute of Criminology and founding editor of the *Asian Journal of Criminology*. Recent publications include edited volumes *Cyber-Crime: The Challenge in Asia* (The University of Hong Kong Press, 2005) with Peter Grabosky and *Policing in Context: An Introduction to Police Work in Australia* (Oxford University Press, 2009) with Sara Davies.

Gregory (Chris) Brown joined the California State University, Fullerton (CSUF) faculty as an assistant professor of criminal justice, following a 1-year position as a full-time lecturer. In 1990, he received his PhD in social ecology from the University of California, Irvine, with an emphasis in criminology. He completed his undergraduate education at the University of California, Santa Cruz with a BA in sociology. His first teaching job was at the University of California, Santa Barbara. He next worked as an assistant professor of criminal justice at Chapman University in Orange, CA from 1991 to 1997. He also taught at the California Youth Authority in Whittier for 3 years and worked part time at CSUF. From 2003 to 2005, he taught as a full-time lecturer at California State University, Long Beach. He has taught at California State University, Fullerton in various capacities (e.g., part-time lecturer, full-time lecturer, and assistant professor since 2001). In 2003, he received a Certificate of Recognition as a volunteer for the Gang Class and Brothers Out-of-Trouble (BOOT) programs at the Fred C. Nelles Youth Correctional Facility. His teaching interests include gangs, corrections, minorities and crimes, and white-collar crime. His research interests include gang theory and practice, prisons, the death penalty, and corrections.

Kyung-shick Choi is Assistant Professor of Criminal Justice at Bridgewater State College, Bridgewater, MA. He also serves as a lecturer in connection with the development of the UN virtual forum against cyber crime. He received his PhD in Criminology from Indiana University of Pennsylvania. His scholarly interests focus on the study of computer crime, theory testing, and policy evaluation via quantitative assessment.

Jeffrey S. Crane is president of Simpex, a strategic international management company located in Miami, FL. Crane also holds academic appointments at the University of Miami, College of Medicine (2006–present) and Western Carolina University (2003–present); he is also a fellow at the University of Pittsburgh (2006–present), Center for National Preparedness. From June 2006 to August 2009, Dr. Crane was the executive director of John P. Murtha Institute for Homeland Security at the Indiana University of Pennsylvania, Indiana, PA.

Rob D'Ovidio is an assistant professor at Drexel University, Philadelphia, PA, where he teaches criminal justice and directs Drexel's research program in computer crime and digital forensics. His research and teaching interests lie in the intersection of computer technology, crime, and the criminal justice system. In the past, D'Ovidio has worked with the New York City Police Department and the Philadelphia Police Department on research projects involving computer crime. His work with the law enforcement community also includes training investigators on techniques to trace Internet communication and seize electronic evidence and cell phones. D'Ovidio is a past president of the Philadelphia/Delaware Valley chapter of the High Technology Crime Investigation Association. He is also a member of the International Association of Computer Investigative Specialists, the American Society of Criminology, and the United States Secret Service Philadelphia-Area Electronic Crimes Task Force. D'Ovidio sits on the National Governors Association's Strategic Policy Council on Cyber and Electronic Crime. He serves as an advisor to the Pennsylvania state treasurer on identity theft and is a consultant to BK Forensics, assisting with law enforcement outreach and the development of training curriculum. He provides regular commentary for media outlets on news stories pertaining to computer crime, Internet safety, identity theft, and surveillance.

Imaani Jamillah El-Burki is a graduate student at the Department of Culture and Communication, Drexel University, Philadelphia, PA.

Tina Freiburger is an assistant professor in the Department of Criminal Justice at the University of Wisconsin–Milwaukee, Milwaukee, WI. She received her PhD in criminology from Indiana University of Pennsylvania and her MA from Sam Houston State University. Her primary research areas include gender and racial disparities in sentencing, criminological theory, recidivism among sex offenders, and experiences of females in the criminal justice system.

Gilbert Geis is Professor Emeritus, Department of Criminology, Law and Society, University of California, Irvine. He received his PhD in sociology from the University of Wisconsin, has been president of the American Society of Criminology, and is a recipient of its Edwin H. Sutherland Award for research achievements. Other recognition has come from the National Association of Certified Fraud Examiners (Donald Cressey Award), the American Justice Institute (Richard A. McGee Award), the Western Society of Criminology (Paul Tappan Award), and the National Organization for Victim/Witness Protection (Stephen Schafer Award). His most recent books are *Criminal Justice and Moral Issues* (Oxford University Press, 2006) and *White-Collar and Corporate Crime* (Prentice Hall, 2007).

Whitney D. Gunter is a doctoral student in the Department of Sociology and Criminal Justice at the University of Delaware, Newark, DE, and a research assistant at the Center for Drug and Alcohol Studies. Her main research interests include criminological theory, research methodology, statistics, and computer crime.

Debarati Halder is an advocate and legal scholar. She is the managing director of the Centre for Cyber Victim Counselling (http://www.cyber victims. org). She received her LLB from the University of Calcutta and MA in international and constitutional law from the University of Madras. She is currently working toward her PhD at the National Law School of India University, Bangalore, India. She has published many articles in peer-reviewed journals and chapters in peer-reviewed books. Her work has appeared in scholarly journals, including the *Journal of Law and Religion, Murdoch University Electronic Journal of Law, ERCES Online Quarterly Review, TMC Academic Journal* (Singapore), and *Indian Journal of Criminology & Criminalistics* and, among edited volumes, *Crimes of the Internet,* (Prentice Hall, 2008) and *Trends and Issues of Victimology* (Cambridge Scholars Publishing, 2008). Her research interests include constitutional law, international law, victim rights, and cyber crimes and laws.

George E. Higgins is currently an associate professor in the Department of Justice Administration at the University of Louisville, Louisville, KY. He graduated from Kentucky State University with a BA in criminal justice in 1994, the University of Kentucky with an MA in public administration in 1996, and Indiana University of Pennsylvania with a PhD in criminology in 2001. He was on the faculty in criminal justice at West Virginia State University, Institute, WV. His research focuses on testing criminological theory and using advanced quantitative methods (e.g., structural equation modeling and Rasch models) to better understand crime and deviance (e.g., computer and cyber crimes and binge drinking) and racial and gender/sex disparities in criminal justice. Along with two graduate students, he was the recipient of the 2006 William L. Simon/Anderson Outstanding Paper Award at the Academy of Criminal Justice Sciences annual meeting in Baltimore, MD.

Dianne L. Hoff is presently Associate Dean for Teacher Preparation and Professional Programs at the University of West Georgia, Carrollton, GA. Previously, she was an associate professor of educational leadership at the University of Maine, teaching education law, policy, research, and finance. Her undergraduate and MA degrees are from Indiana University, and she holds an EdD from the University of Louisville. Prior to her academic appointments, she served as a principal in large schools in Georgia and southern California. She conducts research on the social/political context of schooling—specifically the ways law, policy, and practice intersect to create discrimination challenges for schools. She is currently conducting research on contemporary legal issues that schools face, including cyber bullying, charging students for activities (pay-to-play), and appropriate accommodations for students with peanut allergies.

Thomas J. Holt is an assistant professor in the School of Criminal Justice at Michigan State University, specializing in computer crime, cyber crime, and technology. His research focuses on computer hacking, malware, and the role that technology and the Internet play in facilitating all manner of crime and deviance. Dr. Holt has been published in various journals including *Crime and Delinquency, Deviant Behavior,* and the *Journal of Criminal Justice.* He received his PhD from the University of Missouri—Saint Louis in December 2005.

Kasun Jayavardena is a PhD student at Queensland University of Technology, Brisbane, Australia.

Richard W. Lovely is currently Associate Professor and Codirector of the Master of Science in Forensic Computing Program at John Jay College of Criminal Justice, New York, NY. Lovely arrived at John Jay in 1985. He earned his PhD at Yale University and a BA from the University of Southern Florida. His primary areas of interest are cyber crime, deviance and social control, organizational responses to technology, leadership and group dynamics, and computer applications in research. In the field of criminal justice, he has done research on search and seizure law, causes of serious violence, and organizational innovation. His current research concerns cyber crime, geographical solutions to stigma, and educational outcomes assessment. Currently he teaches seminars in criminology and data analysis.

Alaeldin Mansour Maghaireh is currently a lecturer in law at the Centre for Transnational Crime Prevention (CTCP), University of Wollongong, Australia. He is an expert in Islamic criminal law and cyber crime with considerable experience in the First Instance Court in Jordan. His doctoral research, completed in 2009 at Wollongong University, was entitled *Cybercrime Investigation: A Comparative Analysis of Search for and Seizure of Digital Evidence.* He also holds a graduate certificate in transnational crime prevention from Wollongong University. His primary research interests are cyber criminology, cyber terrorism, digital evidence, and Shariah law. He has published on cyber crime, Shariah law, and related legal issues.

Catherine D. Marcum is an assistant professor of justice studies in the political science department at Georgia Southern University, Statesboro, GA. She graduated in December 2008 from Indiana University of Pennsylvania with a PhD in criminology. Her most recent publications are in *Deviant Behavior; Criminal Justice Studies: A Critical Journal of Crime, Law, and Society; International Journal of Cyber Criminology;* and *Journal of Child Sexual Abuse.*

Tyson Mitman is a graduate student in the Department of Culture and Communication, Drexel University, Philadelphia, PA.

Robert Moore is an assistant professor of criminal justice at Troy University, Troy, AL. He obtained his PhD in administration of justice from The University of Southern Mississippi in 2003. His research interests focus on cyber-related crime and deviancy. He has published two introductory books on cyber crime and is currently involved in researching deviant relationships that involve the use of Internet-based communications and websites. His publications have appeared in *The American Journal of Criminal Justice, The International Journal of Cyber Criminology, The Journal of Criminal Justice and Popular Culture,* and *Policing: An International Journal.*

Michael L. Pittaro is currently the executive director of Community Prevention Resources of Warren County, Inc., Washington, NJ. He was formerly the executive director of the Council on Alcohol and Drug Abuse in Allentown, PA. He is an adjunct professor with Cedar Crest College's (Allentown, PA) criminal justice department. Earlier, Pittaro was the chair of the legal studies department at Lehigh Valley College. He is the author of several publications, including the United States' first and only criminal justice quick study reference guide, and has been the honored recipient of several awards for his teaching style and practice. Pittaro is coeditor of *Crimes of the Internet* (Prentice Hall, 2008) and a member of the International Editorial Advisory Board of the *International Journal of Criminal Justice Sciences.* Pittaro has nearly 20 years of professional criminal justice field experience. He holds an MA in public administration and a BA in criminal justice from Kutztown University and is currently pursuing a PhD in criminal justice from Capella University, Minneapolis, MN.

Henry N. Pontell is a professor of criminology, law, and society in the School of Social Ecology and a professor of sociology in the School of Social Sciences at the University of California, Irvine. He received his PhD in sociology from Stony Brook University in 1979. His academic work has spanned such topics as social deviance, punishment and deterrence, crime seriousness, health care fraud, international financial fraud, white-collar and corporate crime, cyber crime, and identity theft. He has testified before the U.S. Senate on financial fraud, has worked closely with numerous government agencies, including the FBI and the U.S. Secret Service, and has had his research on white-collar crime highlighted in the national and international media. He has served as president of the Western Society of Criminology and as vice-president of the American Society of Criminology and has been elected a fellow of both organizations. In 2001, he received the Donald R. Cressey Award from the Association of Certified Fraud Examiners for major lifetime contributions to fraud investigation, detection, and deterrence; he also received the Albert J. Reiss, Jr. Distinguished Scholarship Award from the American Sociological Association. He has held visiting appointments at the Australian National University, the University of Melbourne, the University of Macau, the University of Virginia, and Waseda University in Tokyo, Japan. His most recent books include *Profit Without Honor: White Collar Crime and the Looting of America* (4th ed., Prentice Hall, 2007) and the *International Handbook of White-Collar and Corporate Crime* (Springer, 2007). He is editor of the *Masters Series in Criminology* (Prentice Hall).

Marcus K. Rogers is the director of the Cyber Forensics Program in the Department of Computer and Information Technology at Purdue University, Lafayette, IN. He received his PhD in forensic psychology from the University of Manitoba in 2001. He is a professor, university faculty scholar, and fellow at the Center for Education and Research in Information Assurance and Security. Dr. Rogers is the International Chair of the Law, Compliance, and Investigation Domain of the Common Body of Knowledge committee, Chair of the Ethics Committee for the Digital and Multimedia Sciences section of the American Academy of Forensic Sciences, and Chair of the Certification and Test Committee–Digital Forensics Certification Board. He is a former police officer who worked in the area of fraud and computer crime investigations. Dr. Rogers is the author of books, book chapters, and journal publications in the field of digital forensics and applied psychological analysis. His research interests include applied cyber forensics, psychological digital crime scene analysis, and cyber terrorism. He has authored several book chapters and articles in the area of computer forensics and forensic psychology. Dr. Rogers is the editor-in-chief of the *Journal of Digital Forensic Practice* and sits on the editorial board for several international journals. He is also a member of other various national and international committees focusing on digital forensic science and digital evidence. He is a frequent speaker at international and national information assurance and security conferences and guest lectures at various universities throughout the world.

Kathryn C. Seigfried-Spellar is the cyber forensics research coordinator and a PhD research student at the Department of Computer and Information Technology, College of Technology, Purdue University, Lafayette, IN.

Shaheen Shariff is an associate professor and international expert on legal issues that have emerged in relation to online social communications such as cyber bullying, free expression, privacy, libel, and criminal harassment. Her research and teaching are grounded in the study of law as it impacts educational policy, pedagogy, and practice. Specifically, her work addresses the emerging policy vacuum on legal and ethical limits of online expression and the tendency of policy makers to react and overregulate as opposed to the need for increased education, dialogue, and awareness about the limits of free expression in virtual society. Her work identifies limits on student free expression in school and cyberspace—such as the line between joking and cyber threats—privacy rights, cyber safety, cyber libel, and school supervision. She has developed guidelines for school administrators, teachers, and parents regarding the extent of their legal responsibilities in addressing cyber bullying in various contexts. Her work also focuses on human rights, constitutional and tort law as they inform institutional responsibilities to provide safe and productive school and work environments, and censorship and diversity in schools. She was invited to participate on a UN panel on cyber hate chaired by Secretary General Ban Ki Moon and has served on an international advisory committee working with UNESCO and CIDA and the International Institute for Educational Planning to develop a toolkit for global use in drafting Teacher Codes of Conduct. She was also recently a panelist with the (US) First Amendment Center's online symposium, which featured her scholarship on the legal implications for educational institutions in relation to policy issues around cyber bullying. She graduated with a PhD from Simon Fraser University in curriculum implementation, leadership, and policy studies.

Wesley Shumar is a professor of anthropology and chair of the culture and communication department at Drexel University, Philadelphia, PA. He is a cultural anthropologist whose research focuses on virtual community, higher education, and ethnographic evaluation in education. Since 1997 he has worked as an ethnographer at the Math Forum, a virtual math education community and resource center. He is coprincipal investigator on the Virtual Math Teams project, a 5-year National Science Foundation project at the Math Forum that is investigating the dynamics of online and face-to-face collaborative problem solving and problem creation. He is also coprincipal investigator on Leadership Development for Technology Integration: Developing an Effective NSDL Teacher Workshop Model. This project is a 3-year NSF project to develop and refine a hybrid workshop model that supports teachers to integrate National Science Digital Library (NSDL) resources and technologies into their classrooms.

Russell G. Smith is currently principal criminologist and manager of the Global, Economic, and Electronic Crime Program at the Australian Institute of Criminology (AIC), having joined the AIC in January 1996 from the University of Melbourne, where he was a lecturer in criminology. He has an LLB (1980), BA (degree with honors in psychology, 1980), diploma in criminology (1982), and an MA (1986)—all from the University of Melbourne. He also has a PhD (1990) from the Faculty of Laws, King's College, University of London. He is admitted to practice as a barrister and solicitor of the Supreme Court of Victoria and the Federal Courts of Australia (1981) and as a solicitor of the Supreme Court of England and Wales (1991). He has had extensive experience in criminal justice research, including the publication of 7 authored, coauthored, or edited books; 22 reports/monographs; and more than 110 other publications. He has also given over 220 conference or seminar presentations locally and internationally. Russell's main research interests relate to financial crime, including identity crime and money laundering, technology-enabled crime, professional regulation, and history. His principal books are *Cyber Criminals on Trial* (Cambridge University Press, 2004, jointly authored); *Crime in the Professions* (Ashgate Publishing, 2002, edited); *Electronic Theft* (Cambridge University Press, 2001, jointly authored); *In Pursuit of Nursing Excellence* (Oxford University Press, 1999); *Health Care, Crime and Regulatory Control* (Hawkins Press, 1998, edited); *Crime in the Digital Age* (Federation Press/Transaction Publishers, 1998, jointly authored); and *Medical Discipline* (Clarendon Press, Oxford, 1994).

Orly Turgeman–Goldschmidt is a lecturer at the Interdisciplinary Department of Social Sciences, Bar-Ilan University, Israel. She earned her PhD in sociology and anthropology from the Hebrew University of Jerusalem. Her research interests include computer crime, hacking, digital culture, and gender differences in language.

Scott E. Wolfe is a PhD student at the School of Criminology and Criminal Justice, Arizona State University, Glendale, AZ.

Kimberly Young is an internationally known expert on Internet addiction and online behavior. She serves as the director of the Center for Internet Addiction Recovery (founded in 1995) and travels nationally conducting seminars on the impact of the Internet. She is the author of *Caught in the Net* (John Wiley & Sons, Inc., 2009), the first book to address Internet addiction and translated in six languages; *Tangled in the Web* (Authorhouse Library, 2001); and her most recent, *Breaking Free of the Web: Catholics and Internet Addiction* (St. Anthony's Messenger Press, 2007). She is a professor at St. Bonaventure University, St. Bonaventure, NY, and has published more than 40 articles on the impact of online abuse. Her work has been featured in media outlets such as *The New York Times, The London Times, USA Today, Newsweek, Time*, CBS News, Fox News, Good Morning America, and ABC's World News Tonight. In 2001 and 2004, she received the Psychology in the Media Award from the Pennsylvania Psychological Association, and in 2000 she received the Alumni Ambassador of the Year Award for Outstanding Achievement from Indiana University at Pennsylvania. She has served as an expert witness regarding her pioneer research, including the Child Online Protection Act Congressional Commission. She has been an invited lecturer at dozens of universities and conferences, including the European Union of Health and Medicine in Norway and the First International Congress on Internet Addiction in Zurich. Dr. Young serves on the editorial board of *CyberPsychology & Behavior* and the *International Journal of Cyber Criminology* and is a member of the American Psychological Association, the Pennsylvania Psychological Association, and a founding member of the International Society of Mental Health Online. She received her PsyD from Indiana University of Pennsylvania in 1994.

Introduction
Expanding Cyber Criminology With an Avant-Garde Anthology

K. JAISHANKAR

Since 2000, cyberspace has changed the ideological perspectives of criminologists (McKenzie, 1996). The paradigm shift created by the development of the Internet and its sophisticated forms of communication and its ugly offshoot, cyber crime, have broken the traditional barriers of research done by conventional criminologists (Thomas & Loader, 2000; Littlewood, 2003; Yar, 2005). New and old criminologists have quickly understood the gap in research that has occurred in the areas of cyber crime research (Nhan & Bachmann, 2010). Even though phase of research is slow in this area, it is gaining momentum (Jewkes, 2006; Mann & Sutton, 1998). There are now also a handful of edited collections and authored books on cyber crimes written by criminologists purely from criminological perspectives (Jewkes, 2006; McQuade, 2005; Schmalleger & Pittaro, 2008; Smith, Grabosky, & Urbas, 2004; Wall, 2001, 2003, 2007, 2009; Yar, 2006; Yar & Jewkes, 2010). These new developments in the field of cyber crime also opened vistas for a new discipline called *cyber criminology.*

In 2007, with the launch of the *International Journal of Cyber Criminology* (http://www.cybercrimejournal.com), an online open access journal, cyber criminology got its academic recognition. Cyber criminology is a multidisciplinary field that encompasses researchers from various fields such as criminology, victimology, sociology, Internet science, and computer science. I define cyber criminology as "the study of causation of crimes that occur in the cyberspace and its impact in the physical space" (Jaishankar, 2007, para 1). I academically coined the term *cyber criminology* for two reasons. First, the body of knowledge that deals with cyber crimes should not be confused with investigation and be merged with cyber forensics; second, there should be an independent discipline to study and explore cyber crimes from a social science perspective.

I developed a theory to further the discipline of cyber criminology. The theory is called *space transition theory*, and it explains the causation of crimes in cyberspace. I felt the need for a separate theory of cyber crimes because the general theoretical explanations were found to be inadequate as an overall explanation for the phenomenon of cyber crimes (Jaishankar, 2008). I have published this theory as a chapter in a book titled *Crimes of the Internet* (edited by Frank Schmalleger and Michael Pittaro and published by Prentice Hall, 2008). Space transition theory is an explanation about the nature of the behavior of the persons who bring out their conforming and nonconforming behavior in physical space and cyberspace (Jaishankar, 2008). "Space transition involves the movement of persons from one space to another (e.g., from physical space to cyberspace and vice versa). Space transition theory argues that people behave differently when they move from one space to another" (Jaishankar, 2008, p. 292).

The postulates of the theory are as follows:

1. Persons with repressed criminal behavior (in physical space) have a propensity to commit crimes in cyberspace that they otherwise would not commit due to their status and position.
2. Identity flexibility, dissociative anonymity, and lack of deterrence factors in cyberspace provide the offenders with the means to commit cyber crime.
3. Criminal behavior of offenders in cyberspace is likely to be imported to physical space, and criminal behavior in physical space may be exported to cyberspace as well.
4. Intermittent ventures of offenders to cyberspace and the dynamic spatiotemporal nature of cyberspace give offenders an escape.
5. (a) Strangers are likely to unite together in cyberspace to commit crimes in physical space. (b) Associates in physical space are likely to unite to commit crimes in cyberspace.
6. Persons from closed societies are more likely to commit crimes in cyberspace than persons from open societies.
7. The conflict between the norms and values of physical space and the norms and values of cyberspace may lead to cyber crimes (Jaishankar, 2008, pp. 292–293).

Because criminology has started viewing the emergence of cyberspace as a new locus of criminal activity, a new theory is needed to explain why cyber crime occurs. The space transition theory presented above provides an explanation for criminal behavior in cyberspace. There is a need to test the theory to see if it explains cyber criminal activity (Jaishankar, 2008). Apart from the theory, this book is also an effort to take cyber criminology to the next level. This book is an edited collection of chapters that focus on issues of cyber criminology. This book is divided in to five sections: Section I. Deviance and Criminal Subculture in Cyberspace; Section II. Perpetrators' Perspectives and Offender Use of the Internet; Section III. Digital Piracy; Section IV. Cyber Victimization; and Section V. Legal and Policy Issues of Cyber Crimes. The chapters that make up these sections deal with both empirical and theoretical perspectives.

Chapter 1 concentrates on the growing menace of cyber crime in Nigeria. The author aims to understand the emergence of the infamous *yahooboys'* (cyber crime) subculture among youths. In this study, both the multilinear evolutionary theory and Robert Merton's view are utilized to help analyze the yahooboys' subculture. The study was conducted in Lagos, the commercial capital of Nigeria, and the research method used involved both survey research and participant observation. The findings confirmed the author's hypothesis. According to the author, inactivity on the part of the political leadership, which has failed in giving needed direction and opportunities to the youths in Nigeria, has been the major factor facilitating the unwholesome utilization of the Internet platform in defrauding unsuspecting individuals across the globe. Moreover, poverty, unemployment, and deteriorating social standards of life have also resulted in the enhancement of the yahooboys' subculture.

The status of Internet gambling on the world scene has been notably addressed in the David and Goliath dispute between the United States and the small Caribbean islands of Antigua and Barbuda, which constitute a single nation. Chapter 2 discusses the dispute represented by the first attempt of the World Trade Organization (WTO) to examine cross-border electronic services, with the added ingredient that the behavior itself under review has at certain times and in certain places been regarded as criminal. This chapter attempts to trace the development of the WTO case, offering a view of what is regarded as the most sensible and probably the inevitable path that the trajectory of Internet gambling should and will take.

Hacking has been an old problem but has not been studied in depth. It is a global problem and is growing at a fast pace. Hacking has been difficult to interpret due to the lack of a solid definition and vague boundaries between computer experts and hackers, as well as those characteristics that differentiate various types of hackers. The author of Chapter 3 has interviewed 54 hackers based on the narrative interview technique to understand their lives, behavior, and beliefs, as well as their perceptions of how society treats them. The study is based on the *grounded theory,* a data-driven method that produces theoretical propositions and concepts and systematically processes them. The chapter attempts to explain the different types of offenses that a hacker can commit. The author has categorized the hackers as good or bad based on the basis of the hacker's perceptions of themselves.

The author of Chapter 4 on sexual addiction on the Internet argues that Internet anonymity promotes pedophilia within the otherwise normal populace. The study aims to correlate the association of sexually compulsive or addictive behavior with social isolation. Clinical research suggests that deviant sexual fantasies carried out online do not always originate from individuals with a preexisting disposition for deviancy, but cases document how once prosocial citizens will engage in this same behavior. Based upon a study of 22 forensic interviews, the chapter outlines a framework for understanding the psychology of the sex offender from a clinical perspective. The chapter outlines five stages from inception to incarceration that the virtual sex offender follows. The research attempts to provide insight in relation to it for use by treating professionals, academia, and the general public. New and continued research in the area of online sex offenders will also assist the courts in achieving learned, accurate, and just evaluation of such matters as they become presented with increasing frequency.

Chapter 5 is an attempt to understand the psychology of the child pornography (CP) consumer. It tries to distinguish between an Internet CP consumer and a non-Internet CP consumer using Bandura's theory of reciprocal determinism. The sample was drawn from a population of Internet users via an anonymous survey through an examination of demographic, personality, and behavioral characteristics for ascertaining the existence of any discriminating traits or factors between the users and nonusers of Internet child pornography. Subjects were voluntarily recruited via the Internet by publicizing or advertising the survey using various online resources, such as chat rooms, bulletin boards, and e-mail discussion forums. The analysis has provided valuable information regarding the types of individuals who utilized Internet child pornography, where there was previously a significant gap in the literature. Statistical analyses revealed a relationship between higher scores on exploitive-manipulative amoral dishonesty traits, lower scores on internal moral choice, and the viewing of child pornography. Furthermore, the study suggests women are engaging in Internet CP consumption more often than previously suggested. The author concludes that the consumption of child pornography over the Internet is likely to increase unless researchers decide to make this area of study a priority.

In Chapter 6 the authors discuss the online exploitation of children by using a novel methodology—a sting operation. This chapter provides an initial exploration of the role Web 2.0 network technology may play in providing access to underage victims who may be vulnerable to online sexual predators. They conclude that it is essential to empower children to police the Internet and to recognize their rapid absorption of the changes released by Web 2.0 and the relentless privatization and commercialization that is now increasingly apparent.

Chapter 7 on adult-child sex advocacy websites is one of the chapters in this book that received a high rating by the reviewers of this book. In the form of a content analysis, the study tried to find out how far the sites that encourage sexual relationships between adults and children are criminogenic in nature. The study also utilized various criminological theories such as differential association theory, social learning theory, and neutralization theory. The authors found that these sites are pedophilic in nature and should be banned. The authors also believe that courts should prohibit child offenders from visiting these sites.

Chapter 8 is a systematic examination of terrorist use of the Internet. The anonymous design of the Internet has made it a haven for terrorists to carry out their activities in an organized manner. This chapter seeks to present an appraisal of the existing literature on cyber terrorism vis-à-vis the social learning theory. Social learning theory asserts that individuals learn deviant behavior from significant groups. This learning specifically operates through the four main concepts of differential association, definitions, differential reinforcement, and imitation. This chapter examines the manner in which mechanisms of social learning theory is used by terrorist groups on the Internet. These methods are then examined to determine how they might be used for better purposes by antiterrorism groups.

Chapter 9 examines the links between low self-control, rational choice, value, and digital piracy. Several researchers have shown that attitudes, low self-control, social learning theory, and deterrence theory explain digital piracy. No study has examined whether the rational choice theory mediated the link between low self-control and digital piracy. In addition, no research in digital piracy or criminological literature has considered the role of value in such an examination. This study, built on the mediating model presented by Piquero and Tibbetts (1996), reasons how the rational choice theory establishes the link between low self-control and digital piracy. It is a significant addition to the cyber criminological literature.

Chapter 10 discusses the Recording Industry Association of America, which filed a lawsuit to prevent the illegal sharing of music files. Despite these legal efforts, results show that most music downloaders show little awareness of wrongdoing, and in turn the popularity of pay-to-play networks has been steadily increasing. The implications for the music and video industry as well as future research are discussed. Future studies should examine the effectiveness of efforts employed by the Motion Picture Association of America and the role that increasingly popular legal download alternatives have for the pirating of copyright-protected material.

Chapter 11 addresses the issue of Internet piracy among college students. This study investigates the empirical validity of differential association and deterrence as applied to multiple forms of digital piracy. Data used in this research were collected through student surveys from two mid-Atlantic higher-education institutions, one of which is a small, private, liberal arts college, whereas the other is a moderately sized public university. This chapter concentrates on the fact that social interaction theories can help in radically bringing down the levels of piracy. The author concludes that college students with peers engaging in piracy and parents supportive of piracy are more likely to engage in piracy themselves.

The authors of Chapter 12 discuss the issue of digital piracy. Digital piracy has two sides. First, it is governed by laws of developed nations to encourage prevention; second, less developed nations do not see this as a big issue, and laws to prevent digital piracy do not exist in an ideal manner. There are reasons for this. Less developed nations cannot afford to buy software or music that are expensive, and they feel that capitalistic nations alone should not own this software. Many sites on the Internet are found, and they give free access (hacked!) to copyrighted version of software or music. There are no laws to govern this. The study presented in Chapter 12 was conducted in a developed nation such as the United States. However, there is a need to analyze this issue in less developed nations. More than likely the results will be quite different.

Chapter 13 tries to analyze digital piracy with neutralization theory. There are some earlier studies of this nature by Higgins et al., and the study presented in Chapter 13 adds to that literature. The authors found that some neutralization techniques had been adopted by their respondent during the usage of pirated software or music. As pointed out earlier, digital piracy is still an issue of debate, and not many may accept it as a crime.

Chapter 14 emphasizes the causes of computer-crime victimization by examining an individual's lifestyle patterns. The central argument revolves around creating a distinction between an individual's actual personality vis-à-vis a virtual presence. It presents an overview of lifestyle-exposure theory and routine activities theory, how routine activities theory is merely an expansion of lifestyle-exposure theory, and an overview of computer crime and victimization. The author has substantiated his point by conducting empirical research on college students and analyzing their behavior patterns, specifically by looking at where they are on the Internet, what their behaviors are on the Internet, and what they are doing to protect themselves while they are on the Internet. The purpose is to create a link between the elements of an online lifestyle and the level of computer-security protection, with the resultant levels of computer-crime victimization experienced by the students.

Today, the benefits of the Internet are being reaped in both a positive and negative manner. The global community has become a tight-knit space for communications through the Internet. However, the Internet has also provided an easy platform for online victimization. Chapter 15 aims to create awareness on adolescent victimization online by conducting a full-fledged study on college freshmen and their experiences with online victimization. The three constructs of the routine activities theory have been utilized to create the methodology and study the data. The population for the research included all freshmen enrolled in 100-level course at a midsized university in the Northeast during the spring 2008 academic term. Surveys were administered to enrolled freshmen in the spring of 2008, with a focus on their frequency and types of Internet use and experiences with different types of Internet victimization. The findings of this study indicated that respondents who spent an increased amount of time using the Internet were more likely to be victimized. The purpose of this study is to bring about awareness on the dangers present online. Adolescents need to be educated about these dangers rather than being prevented from using them. The knowledge gained from this study should be utilized to create effective policies and programs that educate youth and families on how to protect themselves while online.

Chapter 16 is an introduction to online harassment and intimidation, which is termed *cyber stalking*. In this chapter, the author discusses how the Internet has facilitated criminal activities. He states that cyber stalking is an extension of traditional stalking but is not as predictable as traditional stalking. The author gives some cases of cyber stalking and how things have become very easy for the criminal looking to harass a victim. The crime of cyber stalking is linked with mental abnormality and gives a clear picture as to why such incidents happen. The author states ways to avoid being a victim in such cases (which are suggested by the law enforcement officials) and concludes by saying that although the problem is in its infancy, it is growing rapidly.

Web 2.01 has redefined the virtual life of ordinary individuals and has given ample opportunities to Internet users, including women, to exchange ideas, interact with like-minded people, and participate in the development of virtual societies per one's own choices. Social networking websites (SNWs), a segment of Web 2.0, are very popular among Internet users. However, there is a dark side to these SNWs too. They have become havens for offenders looking to victimize women, the most vulnerable targets on the Internet after children. The authors of Chapter 17 examine the victimization of women in social networking websites, analyze the trends of such victimization from a sociological, legal, and victimological angle, and ascertain the reasons for the growth of such victimization.

The authors of Chapter 18 on malware victimization have tried to analyze it with Cohen and Felson's (1979) routine activities theory (RAT). RAT is often considered a victimological theory, and many have used this theory in victimological studies. Although the authors' application of RAT is not novel in cyber crime studies, it does bring in a new empirical approach to this theory. The authors with the college student samples have tried to bring in both victimization and perpetration patterns. Cyber crime studies from victimological perspectives are now developing, and Chapter 18 has significantly added to this growing literature.

Chapter 19 explores the Islamic world in cyberspace and how the propagation of Islamic ideology via the Internet has become a popular medium. In the Islamic world, the issue of hacktivism has hardly ever bothered religious consciences. Indeed, religious leaders refrained from condemning hacktivism and even made it appear as if it were perpetrated to defend Islam. Therefore, Islamic extremism, fanaticism, and violence have sprung up on the Internet. To tackle this problem, the author takes a look at the Shariah legal system, which is the ultimate criminal justice system in the Muslim world. In an attempt to understand this system, contemporary Muslim thought (both traditionalist and reformist) and its role in shaping a modern criminal law is studied in depth. The constructs of the Shariah legal system are studied in the chapter in reference to the above views to understand the inflexibility of the law and its inability to respond to the problem of cyber crime. This chapter urges Muslim scholars to bring about amendments in the traditional legal system to accommodate the seriousness of cyber crime and make it punishable by law.

Cyber bullying is a psychologically devastating form of social cruelty among adolescents. Chapter 20 reviews the current policy vacuum of the legal obligations and expectations of schools to monitor and supervise online discourse, while balancing student safety, education, and interaction in virtual space, which also encompasses a discussion of the institutional responses to cyber bullying. An emerging and established law is highlighted to provide guidelines to help schools reduce cyber bullying through educational means that protect students and avoid litigation.

The final chapter, Chapter 21, looks at how advances in information and communications technologies have created a range of new crime problems while conversely facilitating prevention, detection, investigation, prosecution, and punishment of crime. This chapter identifies the principal areas of human rights concerns that the digital age has created. The chapter concludes with the ways by which the infringement of human rights in the digital age could be prevented. They suggest that rigorous evaluative research needs to be conducted once new technologies have been introduced to monitor their potential for denigration of human rights and infringements of international and national laws.

The book closes with a conclusion that discusses the future of cyber criminology.

References

Jaishankar, K. (2007). Cyber criminology: Evolving a novel discipline with a new journal. *International Journal of Cyber Criminology, 1*(1), 1–6.

Jaishankar, K. (2008). Space transition theory of cyber crimes. In F. Schmalleger & M. Pittaro (Eds.), *Crimes of the Internet* (pp. 283–301). Upper Saddle River, NJ: Prentice Hall.

Jewkes, Y. (2006). Comment on the book *Cyber Crime and Society* by Majid Yar, Sage Publications. Retrieved from http://www.sagepub.co.uk/booksProdDesc. nav?prodId=Book227351

Jewkes, Y. (2007). *Crime online*. Cullompton, United Kingdom: Willan.

Jewkes, Y., & Yar, M. (2009). *Handbook of Internet crime*. Cullompton, United Kingdom: Willan

Littlewood, A. (2003). Cyberporn and moral panic: An evaluation of press reactions to pornography on the internet. *Library and Information Research*, 27(86), 8–18.

Mann, D., & Sutton, M. (1999). NetCrime. More change in the organisation of thieving. *British Journal of Criminology*, 38(2), 201–229.

McKenzie, S. (2000). *Child safety on the Internet: An analysis of Victorian schools and households using the routine activity approach* (Master's thesis). Retrieved from http://www.criminology.unimelb.edu.au/research/internet/childsafety/index.html

McQuade, S. C. (2005). *Understanding and managing cyber crime*. Upper Saddle River, NJ: Allyn & Bacon.

Nhan, J., & Bachmann, M. (2010). Developments in cyber criminology. In M. Maguire & D. Okada (Eds.), *Critical issues in crime and justice: Thought, policy, and* practice (pp. 164–183). Thousand Oaks, CA: Sage Publications.

Schmalleger, F., & Pittaro, M. (Eds.). (2008). *Crimes of the Internet*. Upper Saddle River, NJ: Prentice Hall.

Smith, R., Grabosky, P., & Urbas, G. (2004). *Cyber criminals on trial*. Cambridge, United Kingdom: Cambridge University Press.

Thomas, D., & Loader, B. (2000) Introduction—cyber crime: Law enforcement, security and surveillance in the information age. In D. Thomas & B. Loader (Eds.), *Cyber crime: Law enforcement, security and surveillance in the information age*. London, United Kingdom: Routledge.

Wall, D. S. (2007). *Cybercrime: The transformation of crime in the information age*. Cambridge, United Kingdom: Polity.

Wall, D. S. (Ed.). (2001). *Crime and the Internet*. London, United Kingdom: Routledge.

Wall, D. S. (Ed.). (2003). *Cyberspace crime*. Aldershot, United Kingdom: Dartmouth/Ashgate (Dartmouth International Library of Criminology and Penology).

Wall, D. S. (Ed.). (2009). *Crime and deviance in cyberspace*. Aldershot, United Kingdom: Dartmouth/Ashgate (Dartmouth International Library of Criminology and Penology).

Yar, M. (2005). The novelty of 'cyber crime': An assessment in light of routine activity theory. *European Journal of Criminology*, 2(4), 407–427.

Yar, M. (2006). *Cybercrime and society*. London, United Kingdom: Sage Publications.

Deviance and Criminal Subculture in Cyberspace

I

Café Culture and Heresy of Yahooboyism[1] in Nigeria

1

ADEBUSUYI I. ADENIRAN

Contents

Introduction

The advent of Internet technology has significantly improved the state of human existence. In fields as far-reaching as educational research, public administration, commercial and business transactions, industrial production and biotechnological development, and global networking, the Internet offers limitless opportunities. Indeed, affirming that global society can no longer function adequately in the absence of the Internet is an affirmation of the obvious. In spite of all of its benefits, however, the Internet is also used in a destructive, antisocial manner by individuals often referred to by such names as *hackers*, *cyber fraudsters*, *web criminals*, and so forth. In Nigeria—a notable haven for such criminal disposition—they are known as *yahooboys*.

---

[1] *Yahooboyism* is a coinage by the author to represent the activity of online youth fraudsters in Nigeria.

3

The Internet has altered the patterns of cultural cleavages, the process of socialization, and identifiable social institutions across varying human societies. However, unlike traditional criminal groups, both males and females are involved in what has been termed *yahooboyism* in Nigeria, albeit with differing degrees of specialized functions. The culture of fraud and corruption prevalent within larger Nigerian society is believed to have facilitated the institutionalization of yahooboyism as a subset. But such a level of "modernization of criminality" among Nigerian youths has been enabled solely by the Internet—an intrinsically insecure space in which "nobody knows you are a dog" (Steiner, 1993). The yahooboys use the Internet as a platform for engaging in online fraud. Examples of the yahooboys' objectionable engagements include selling fictitious goods/services and buying what they will not pay for (or paying in no real value); money laundering; hacking; and engaging in credit card scams, pornography, and unconventional sexuality.

Ironically, the yahooboys' criminal applications of the Internet in Nigeria can be directly linked to the failure of a political leadership (Adeniran, 2006). Out-of-school students (who are not in school because of distortions in the school calendar) and unemployed youths constitute a considerable percentage of the yahooboys in Nigeria. Indeed, they ignorantly but proudly claim that their involvement in cybercrime is a way of getting back at such an unjust social system in a "nonviolent" way. Therefore, I center the focus of this study on investigating the roles of the failing national leadership and the insecure Internet platform in the emergence of the yahooboys phenomenon in Nigeria.

What Is a Café Culture?

It has been observed that a *café culture* is prevalent among contemporary Nigerian youths, especially those living in the cities or in semiurban settlements that offer easy access to modern technologies such as the Internet. Café culture is indicative of an emergent way of life in which involved youths conceive of the Internet as their "everything," from a school (where they can practice and polish their acts of deceit) to a money-making venture (where they can fraudulently eke out a living, thereby escaping the poverty doldrums prevalent in the country and, ultimately, government and society). In their café culture, these individuals live practically a virtual life and are more familiar with the developments via the Internet than those unfolding within their immediate "real" society.

Despite being one of the most endowed countries (in terms of human and natural resources) on earth, Nigeria remains one of the poorest nations in the world, where the state of the human condition has continued to deteriorate over the years (United Nations Development Programme, 2009). Unemployment, lack of social support, and the deteriorating condition of the country overall has made the country's youths a ready tool for the conduct of cogent nefarious activities such as those easily attainable through the Internet. Meanwhile, technological advances such as the Internet have brought astonishing alterations to Nigeria's institutional and cultural cleavages. Nigerian youths have accepted the Internet as a way of life with unusual speed. Specifically, the Internet has not just imprinted a potent amendment on the Nigerian culture, but it has irredeemably affected the behavioral patterns of Nigerian youths. Ostensibly, yahooboyism has emerged as a result.

The phenomenon of yahooboyism could be said to represent a state of "cultural lag" within Nigerian society—that is, inferring from the conceptualized two aspects of a culture: the technological (i.e., the material aspects such as the Internet) and the sociological (i.e., usually theoretical or ideological aspects such as norms and beliefs). The period of maladjustment when the nonmaterial culture is still struggling to adapt to new material conditions is deemed a *cultural lag* (Ogborn, 1922). With regard to Nigeria, the cultural lag created by the introduction of the Internet to Nigerian society has provided a platform for the emergence of the infamous café culture, which is set to unproductively alter the developmental process of the country's youths.

Within the larger social superstructure in Nigeria—especially among the political class—wealth, often ill gotten, is worshipped. In assuming political positions, leaders overemphasize the place of money. Upon assumption of office, individuals flagrantly embezzle public money. As such, the provision of services to the citizenry, such as the training of youths, is neglected. On the other hand, among most Nigerians, money from any source typically is the most potent yardstick for determining the level of existential attainment. Money—rather than a good education, scientific discovery, or solid career development—is the yardstick against which people are measured. Hence, society is exposed to youths who have been disillusioned and have not been taught the good virtue of genuine hard work. Such youth have had no trouble immersing themselves in the Internet phenomenon of yahooboyism.

If, as outcomes of cogent observations suggest, the Internet continues to spread and becomes essentially ubiquitous in socioeconomic relations, then Nigerian society will indisputably become increasingly dependent on a fragile and insecure information structure. As such, our youths' future is in avoidable jeopardy: The cultural patterns of yahooboyism are bound to be transmitted across generations if nothing concrete is done to regulate its spread and usage in Nigerian society.

Of course, the Nigerian nation has been described as a largely unordered society in which rules are sacrificed and shame no longer exists for despiteful acts. Conspicuously, shameful acts are celebrated and success is redefined as wealth becomes more significant than the means of attaining it. Instant wealth, regardless of its source, is usually celebrated among the Nigerian populace. In fact, it is usually equated with smartness and is rarely rebuked. In Nigeria, corrupt practices are characteristic not only of the political leadership but also of other types and levels of leadership. As such, values of integrity and honesty are despised, as there is total disregard for rules and regulations across all strata of society. For instance, at both the household and community levels, respective agents of socialization often tend to inculcate in the children and young adults the value of hard work and integrity, but most often, it is at odds with what they observe the elders themselves doing.

The EFCC and the Struggle Against Yahooboyism in Nigeria

The Economic and Financial Crimes Commission (EFCC) is an agency created by the Nigerian government in 2002 to champion the fight against antidevelopment behavior such as that being perpetrated through yahooboyism. Unfortunately, the same system that created this antigraft body has become its own greatest undoing. The EFCC began on a promising note, with the onerous assignment of ridding the country of fraudulent financial activities such as cyberfraud. This was even reflective in the vibrancy and seriousness with which the chairman of the agency at the time, Nuhu Ribadu, pursued the EFCC's objectives.

With the approach of the 2007 general elections in Nigeria, Ribadu compromised and made himself a ready tool in the hands of then-President Segun Obasanjo. Identifiable and imagined political enemies, such as Vice President Atiku Abubakar, were witch hunted through the platform of the EFCC. Thus, the vision, dignity, and goals of the EFCC became soiled in the muddy water of Nigerian politicking. Most of the cases instituted against the EFCC were convincingly won. The former head of the EFCC is now a wanted person in Nigeria, consequent upon his unceremonious removal from that position.

Although the new EFCC leadership has been trying to stem the tide of yahooboys syndrome in Nigeria, they are spending a considerable amount of time on image repositioning (the entity's image had been seriously battered by years of institutional misplacement of priorities). The unfortunate implication of this is that the prevalent café culture has been allowed to continue, facilitating the potentiality of yahooboyism syndrome among Nigerian youths.

Another major constraint in the struggle against yahooboyism in Nigeria is the lack of official control over the operations of cyber cafés in terms of monitoring and the EFCC's lack of necessary operational equipment. Even the laws guiding the EFCC's operations are needlessly protective of the political elite and, as such, are defective in realizing the entity's conceptual objectives. Essentially, however, the fight against the menace of yahooboyism in Nigeria seems far from being won yet.

The Study's Conceptual Framework

Robert Merton (1936) emphasized the "causal-cum-intentional terminology of intended and unintended consequences" (p. 894) view (hereafter referred to as, simply, the *Mertonian view*) that is popularly associated with social sciences analysis. He identifies useful mechanisms through which the actual effects of intentions/inventions could deviate from the intended ones. Although this theory offers limited explanation vis-à-vis the possibility of how others will act in a specific situation, it is generally unambiguous in context. If this view is used to analyze the diversion created by yahooboyism in Nigeria (in terms of deviating from the original purposes and uses for the Internet platform), the claim of both intended and unintended actions is particularly relevant. Therefore, in this study, this Mertonian view will help analyze why a certain segment of Nigerians have deviated from the intended (manifest) functions of the Internet, instead using it in unintended (latent) ways (such as its integral role in yahooboyism in Nigeria).

Essentially, an understanding of the relationship between acquired Internet behavior and increasing incidence of yahooboyism in Nigeria will require potently situating the related details of this development within a concise definitional framework that sufficiently links the vagaries of both concepts together. Relationship 1 reveals a conceptual framework that is useful in understanding such linkage. The conceptual framework has one superdeterminant component (i.e., Internet technology [café culture]) and three distinct factors (i.e., political, economic, and social) contributing to the growth of yahooboyism in Nigeria.

> Relationship 1: Conceptualization of the existing association
> The café culture (superdeterminant) – political factors
> The café culture (superdeterminant) – economic factors
> The café culture (superdeterminant) – social factors

The solitary superdeterminant component is defined by vagaries of the Internet platform—that is, an array of applications that it has provided for use. These applications include *webonomics* (Internet trading), uncontrolled access, pornography, and gender switching. The distinct factors are defined by broader political, economic, and social contexts (e.g., visionless leadership, corrupt elite, unemployment, dysfunctional development policy, defective educational system), within which the youths (yahooboys) pursue their

interests and their ability to take purposeful action. Although the superdeterminant component serves as the means, the distinct factors functionally
affect one another—and together, they have implications for the menace of
yahooboyism in Nigeria.

Implications of the Conceptual Framework

Sustained interaction between vagaries of Internet technology (i.e., the
super determinant component and relevant distinct factors—political, economic, and social) will often lead to the growth of yahooboyism in Nigeria.
The distinct factors do not just rest on the superdeterminant: Rather, both
elements affect each other equally. That is, the prevalence of one necessarily
facilitates the prevalence of the other. If the politics, economy, or social system continues to be distorted, the tendency is high for youths to continue
engaging in the café culture. Equally, involvement in the café culture—as
exemplified by nefarious Internet applications—is seen as a way of making
a living.

The Study Location

The Lagos metropolis is made up of two parts: the Island and the Mainland
(further subdivided into 20 local government areas [LGAs]). Lagos, Nigeria's
commercial capital and former seat of the federal government, was chosen as
the study location because it serves as home to a large majority of Nigerians.
The Lagos metropolis has nearly 20 million inhabitants and is the most pop-
ulous urban center in Nigeria. It is estimated that rural-to-urban migration
makes up 78% of the metropolitan population growth (Africa Atlases, 2002).
As such, 12 urban blights in which housing conditions—including refuse
disposal, health facilities, and access to public utilities—are very low have
been identified in the metropolis. Transportation disorganization is usually a
common feature because of the absence of an integrated metropolitan trans-
port system.

The Lagos metropolis has the single largest concentration of Nigeria's
commerce. The Lagos seaports handle more than 80% of Nigeria's maritime
trade, and the Lagos airport is the busiest in the country. Lagos has two public universities and many notable five-star hotels. With an annual population expansion of 5%, it is projected to become a megacity with an estimated
35 million inhabitants by 2020 (UN-HABITAT, 2006). Because of its cosmo-
politan status, the city has the highest concentration of yahooboys in Nigeria.
As such, the Lagos metropolis was deemed suitable for generating useful data
for the study.

Method

The research design combined two research methods: (a) survey research and (b) participant observation. For the purposes of this household survey, a sample size of 400 youths (ages 15–35 years) was considered appropriate, considering timeframe and financial constraints. I conducted the survey based on the existing National Population Commission (NPC) enumeration areas (EAs) within the Lagos metropolis. In this study, a *household* is defined as a dwelling unit in which one or more persons live and share living expenses.

The respondents were systematically drawn from four randomly selected LGAs (i.e., Ikeja, Amuwo-Odifin, Island, and Ibeju-Lekki) of the 20 LGAs in Lagos. This assisted me in obtaining needed information on online activities of youths with varying degrees of access to the Internet (i.e., from occasional Internet users to frequent Internet users). The sample was drawn bearing in mind the variables of gender, age, education, residence, and occupation within the study population. The stratified random sampling technique that combined both randomization and stratification was used to make the sample sufficiently representative of the study population. The applied research instrument was the structured interview schedule.

The second method incorporated into the design was the observation of information accessible to youths on the Internet. Thus, I explored the possible outcomes of contacts that are made online by youths in Nigeria. This research strategy complemented as well as assisted in cross-checking interviewed users of the Internet.

Explanation of the Research Data

Four hypotheses were tested in the study, and their outcomes are presented in the paragraphs that follow.

Hypothesis 1: The Nigerian political system facilitates the prevalence of yahooboys syndrome in the country. A total of 381 responses were cross-tabulated. Although the χ^2-calculated equals 23.5, at a .05 level of significance, χ^2-tabulated equals 3.84. Because χ^2-calculated is greater than χ^2-tabulated— that is, 23.5 > 3.84—Hypothesis I is deemed valid and accepted. A corrupt and visionless political leadership was used as a measure of persistence of café culture among the youths—that is, yahooboyism being a subset of corruption in an elite group of the society. The finding equally revalidated aspects of the notion of Mertonian perspective on the "unintended consequences of purposive social action" (p. 894).

Hypothesis 2: Poor economic condition in Nigeria enhances youths' involvement in a café culture. Here, 346 responses were cross-tabulated. χ^2-calculated equals 7.84, whereas χ^2-tabulated equals 3.84, at a .05 level of significance. Therefore, Hypothesis 2 is validly accepted, considering χ^2-calculated is greater than χ^2-tabulated. This discovery indicates that unfavorable economic conditions indeed have a negative impact on youths' development. In fact, it encouraged the youths to attempt illicit activities such as yahooboyism for socioeconomic survival. This scenario further supported the assertion of the theoretical platform—that is, the use of the Internet as a medium for unwholesome "unintended" economic gains.

Hypothesis 3: Decayed value system causes evolution of yahooboys syndrome in Nigeria. A total of 317 respondents were cross-tabulated. At a .05 level of significance, χ^2-tabulated equals 3.84 and χ^2-calculated equals 40.0. Because χ^2-calculated is greater than χ^2-tabulated, Hypothesis 3 is deemed relevant and, thus, is validly accepted. Ostensibly, the prevalent value system in Nigeria places a heavy emphasis on the accumulation of riches, regardless of their source. This ultimately encourages sustenance of yahooboys syndrome in the country.

Hypothesis 4: The EFCC has been effective in eradicating yahooboyism in Nigeria. To test this hypothesis, 312 respondents were cross-tabulated. Although χ^2-tabulated equals 3.84, at a .05 level of significance, χ^2-calculated equals 40.0. Therefore, Hypothesis 4 was validly accepted, considering χ^2-calculated is greater than χ^2-tabulated. That is, there was an existing relationship between the activities of the EFCC and the uncovering of yahooboys' nefarious activities in Nigeria. A considerable percentage of total respondents (i.e., 22%) deliberately skipped responses to the EFCC's inquiry because, ostensibly, they feared possible involvement of the "dreaded agency" in this study or because they were disgruntled with the organization as a result of its recent involvement in Nigerian political maneuverings. However, the majority of those who responded (i.e., 57%) affirmed that the agency saddled with the task of eradicating yahooboyism from the country has been functional despite obvious deviation from its primary objectives.

Discussion

From this study, it can be deduced that the menace of yahooboyism in Nigeria has been prominent among the youths, especially those residing in the urban centers such as Lagos. Considering the results of the study's hypotheses, inactivity on the part of the political leadership—which has failed in giving needed direction and opportunities to the youths in Nigeria—has been the major factor facilitating the unwholesome use of the Internet (café culture) in defrauding unsuspecting individuals around the world. Equally, the extent of anonymity provided by the Internet has been serving as a potent impetus for enhanced nefarious application by Nigerian youths.

Specific Findings of the Study

The following findings were revealed from this study:

- The advent of Internet technology in Nigeria has facilitated the modernization of fraudulent practices among the youths and subsequent evolution of the café culture.
- Online fraud has been observed as a popularly accepted means of economic sustenance among Nigerian youths, especially those of college age.
- The corruption of the political leadership has successfully enhanced the growth of yahooboys phenomenon among youths.
- The value that society has placed on wealth accumulation has been a potent determinant of youths' involvement in online fraudulent practices in Nigeria.
- Unemployment was also seen as a crucial factor luring youths to yahooboyism in Nigeria.
- And, more important, many Nigerian youths are aware of the existence of the EFCC and, indeed, applaud some of its activities. However, recent use of the EFCC as a political tool by the political class has substantially damaged the agency's image and, by extension, its effectiveness.

Recommendations and Conclusion

On the basis of the study's findings—which emanated from the study's reviewed text, utilized established theoretical framework, and the outcomes of the data analyses—the following suggestions should be considered for policy planners, in particular, and the entire society, in general, to tackle the menace of yahooboyism that is now common among youths in Nigeria.

- The Nigerian government should improve and strengthen official regulations regarding the use and applications of Internet technology to limit the propensity of unwholesome use by the country's youth.
- The Nigerian government should establish intervening socioeconomic measures, such as social benefits for the youths (especially the unemployed).
- Adequate checks should be engendered to make official corruption unattractive and, ultimately, eliminated from Nigerian society.
- Meaningful societal value reorientation should take place, whereby virtues of honesty, selflessness, and hard work—attributes formerly

associated with Nigerian traditional society—should be made relevant in contemporary Nigeria.
- Proactive economic policies that could engender employment opportunities for the youths should be encouraged.
- Agencies such as the EFCC that were established to eradicate the menace of fraudulent practices should be made truly independent of various political maneuverings in the country in order to enhance their effectiveness.

This chapter draws a definitive link between (a) the acceptance and prevalence of the menace of *yahooboyism* among youths in Nigeria and (b) the advent and acceptance of the highly unregulated Internet in the country. Ending such social incongruence in Nigeria will require a top-down and bottom-up institutional reappraisal of basic societal structures (i.e., social system, economy, and politics). Also, a functional autonomy needs to be granted to established antifraud outfits such as the EFCC in order to make them more productive and effective.

References

Adeniran, A. (2006, August 23). A non-dependent framework for development. Retrieved from http://www.thisdayonline.com

Africa Atlases (Nigeria). (2002). Paris, France: Les Editions J.A.

Merton, R. (1936). The unintended consequences of purposive social action. *American Sociological Review, 1*, 894–904.

Ogburn, W. F. (1922). *Social change with respect to culture and original nature.* New York, NY: B.W. Huebsch.

Steiner, P. (1993). On the internet nobody knows you are a dog [Cartoon]. *New Yorker, 69*(20), 61.

UN-HABITAT. (2006). *State of the world's cities report 2006/7.* London, UK: Earthscan Publications, Ltd.

United Nations Development Programme. (2009). *Overcoming barriers: Human mobility and development* [Human Development Report 2009]. New York, NY: Author.

Internet Gambling

2

HENRY N. PONTELL
GILBERT GEIS
GREGORY C. BROWN

Contents

Introduction

Now one of the fastest growing industries, legal gambling already attracts more customers than the movies. Most people see Internet gambling as a recreational and leisure activity. However, for some people, Internet gambling can be a trap. All of an individual's resources and interests become focused on the next chance to gamble on the Internet. Studies indicate that approximately 5% of the U.S. population is currently experiencing problems with gambling (Kossman, 2006). Internet gambling has both positive and negative aspects. For some people, gambling at home on the computer avoids feelings of discomfort about the wagering procedures at places such as blackjack tables, where many eyes—most especially, those of the dealer—are focused on gamblers' movements. However, this "advantage" of at-home gambling also can be regarded as a disadvantage for several reasons: (a) Gambling in one's own home can be a lonesome enterprise, (b) the travel and the glitz of the casino world can be exhilarating, and (c) the multitude of other customers at the betting venues can provide an assurance that one is participating in an exciting and respectable enterprise. These assets and debits of Internet gambling vis-à-vis brick-and-mortar gambling sites cannot readily be assayed in order to claim which of the two arrangements is truly "better."

Internet gambling contains many ingredients that characterize the outsourcing of manufacturing from a rich country, where wages and other costs tend to be high, to a poorer nation, where the skill of workers is equivalent to that of the domestic labor force but where such workers command lower wages—in part, because their cost of living is less than that of the country exporting the services. Outsourcing makes sense in a capitalist economy. In regard to Internet gambling, it introduces moral and criminal elements that provide leverage for the exporting country to seek an interdict for the activity and to retain, domestically, whatever sums might otherwise move overseas.

The status of Internet gambling on the world scene has been notably addressed in the David and Goliath dispute between the United States and the small Caribbean islands of Antigua and Barbuda, which constitute a single nation. The dispute represented the first attempt by the World Trade Organization (WTO) to examine cross-border electronic services, with the added ingredient that the behavior itself under review has, at certain times and in certain places, been regarded as criminal. In this chapter, we trace the development of the WTO case and attempts at its resolution. We also offer a view of what we regard as the most sensible—and, probably, the inevitable—path that the trajectory of Internet gambling will take.

Antigua

Antigua, which gained its independence from Great Britain in 1981 (Sanders, 1982), is the largest of the English-speaking Caribbean countries. It is an island of 108 square miles and is 14 miles long and 11 miles wide, with a population of 70,000. It was sighted by Columbus on his second voyage to the Americas in 1493, and legend has it that he named it for a Spanish church in Seville, Saint Maria Antigua.

Until the 1960s, Antigua's economy relied on sugar cane exports, but a devastating decline in the price of the product on the world market in the 1990s led it to turn to tourism for revenue. That venture suffered a severe blow on September 5, 1995, when Hurricane Lulu sent winds of 145 miles an hour through the island, knocking four hotels into the sea. Some other revenue-generating program was necessary, and Antigua chose telecommunications and Internet gambling. It edged out competitors with the development of an undersea fiber-optic link with the United States that guarantees Americans continuous telecommunications contact, even in the event of a hurricane (D. Schwartz, 2005, p. 9). Antigua also created a free trade zone in which gambling operations were excused from paying import duties and local taxes. Antigua's economy benefited from the $100,000 annual fee for a casino license and $75,000 for a sports betting license.

The Jay Cohen Case (2001)

The international dispute between Antigua and the United States has its roots in the criminal prosecution of Jay Cohen, one of the founders of the World Sports Enterprise (WSE) that was licensed in Antigua in 1997 and became the second largest employer on the island. Customers were required to transmit $300 before they were permitted to gamble, and the WSE exacted 10% off the top of each wager. In its first 15 months of operation, the company took in $3.5 million. To establish a criminal case, Federal Bureau of Investigation (FBI) agents in America placed bets at WSE by means of telephone calls from jurisdictions where Internet betting was illegal. Thereafter, Cohen was charged in a New York court with violation of the Interstate Wire Act of 1961 (more commonly known as the Wire Act), a statute that was enacted well before the dawn of Internet gambling, in an effort to keep organized crime syndicates from using communication networks to facilitate gambling, particularly on horse races.

Cohen was the victim of a federal policy that, as one writer observes, has been marked by "fierceness" and has been "unpredictably inhospitable to online gambling" despite an earlier bow to the prerogative of state governments to make what arrangements they desire about gambling and the endorsement of Native American tribal gambling (Hurt, 2006, p. 375). Similarly, another writer emphasizes what she believes is the U.S. Congress' "obsession with sinful activities," which moved it "to take aggressive (and aberrational) approaches to Internet gambling" (Crawford, 2005, p. 697). In *United States v. Cohen* (2001), the judge's instructions to the jury after a 10-day trial left it no room to exonerate the defendant, had it been so inclined. The judge declared that if Cohen's company had accepted bets over the telephone, the jury was obligated to find him guilty. Cohen was sentenced to a 21-month prison term and incarcerated in a minimum-security institution located outside of Las Vegas, Nevada (*United States v. Cohen, 2001*). He later explained why he had returned home to defend himself while many of his colleagues remained in their Antigua haven:

> I came back to the United States because I wanted to clear my name .... Here I sit in the shadow of the [Las Vegas] Strip while billion-dollar corporations engage in the same activity every day for which I am serving a sentence. And for what? For running a legal business in another country. (Massoud, 2004, p. 996)

Cohen maintained that his Internet gambling business was no different than the stock market transactions he had conducted in an earlier job that he held in San Francisco. "I came from the stock market," he asserted, "and if that isn't gambling, I don't know what is, except that the folks I work with now are less sleazy" (Lubben, 2003, pp. 321–322).

The World Trade Organization

The idea of an organization to deal with matters of international trade was fostered at the Bretton Woods, New Hampshire, meeting of the Allied leaders during World War II (Eichengreen, 2007). It ultimately led to the General Agreement on Tariffs and Trade (GATT), which from 1947 until 1974 was the primary agency addressing cross-border trade issues. Subsequently, it became evident that an updated treaty was required to cure the initial problems of GATT (Jackson, 2000). The result was the World Trade Organization (WTO), which became operational in 1995. The WTO then put in place a General Agreement of Trade in Services (GATS) that was based on an agenda agreed upon by WTO delegates at a meeting in September 1984 at the resort site of Punta del Este in Uruguay. In a series of conferences over the next seven and a half years, delegates hammered out a treaty that sought to lower custom tariffs and other barriers to trade and to keep service markets open. The delegates also reached the agreement that special concessions were to be accorded to developing countries. The treaty covers 26,000 pages, which even the WTO itself admits makes for "daunting" reading. It was ratified at Marrakesh, Morocco, on April 15, 1994. Today, the WTO has a membership of 148 countries that, taken together, are responsible for 95% of the world's trade.

Among the four modes of supply specified by Article I.2(a) in the treaty was "the supply of a series of products from the territory of one member into the territory of any other member." An exception was provided in Article XIV(a), which indicated that trade could be restricted if the product constituted a danger to public morals or public order. *Public order* was defined as "the preservation of the fundamental interests of a society, as reflected in public policy and law" (WTO, 2004, p. 236). The rule specified that "the public order exception may be invoked only where a genuine and sufficiently serious threat is posed to one of the fundamental interests of society" (WTO, 2004, p. 238). Other exceptions include the protection of human, animal, and plant life and health as well as the protection of exhaustible natural resources. An instance of the legitimacy of a public morals claim would be the banning of the importation of alcoholic beverages into Muslim countries. But for that point to prevail, the Muslim countries must not permit the production of intoxicating beverages domestically, a situation far from the reality of gambling in the United States. The ambiguous wording eventually would produce a good deal of semantic jousting in the dispute between Antigua and the United States, although it would appear that the terms "sufficiently serious threat" and "fundamental interests" erect a high barrier against readily granted exceptions.

Antigua Challenges the United States

Antigua's Internet gambling business—*remote access gambling,* as it was called—fell off dramatically in the wake of the *United States v. Cohen* (2001) decision, with a reported decline in sites from a high of 119 licensed operators employing approximately 3,000 people and accounting for 10% of the country's gross national product in 1999 to 29 sites employing fewer than 500 people in 2003. Prodded by the *United States v. Cohen* decision (Blustein, 2006), Antigua filed a charge on March 13, 2003, with the WTO claiming that the country of Antigua was being denied access to a legitimate outlet in violation of the GATS provision that mandated open transnational markets for "recreational, cultural and sporting services." The Antigua filing—which was the first charge made before the WTO by a country with a population under 100,000—asked that the WTO "find that the United States' prohibition on the cross-border supply of gambling and betting services and its measures restricting international money transfers and payments relating to gambling and betting services are inconsistent with its specific commitments to GATS" (WTO, 2004, p. 2). The United States pointed out that when it had signed the treaty in 1994, it had exempted itself from its open market obligation regarding "sporting services," but this was interpreted to represent a desire to control overseas athletic teams from entering the American market, not wagering (Newnham, 2007). As I. Nelson Rose, a leading expert on gambling law, notes: "The funny thing is that if the U.S. did want to keep out gambling, all it had to do was to say so" (Rose, 2005, p. 437). Senegal, for instance, had specifically ruled out its agreement to cross-border betting (WTO, 2005, p. 63). But the United States did not do so, and now it had been hauled before an international adjudicatory body to try to defend its position.

Antigua sought to override objections raised by the United States about possible irregularities in its arrangements for Internet betting. Typically, such criticisms focus on the prospect of underage gamblers participating in Internet gambling, fraud, money laundering, and the creation of compulsive pathological gamblers. The most prominent covert issue in this case, obviously, was the loss of revenue faced by the United States if its gamblers placed their bets offshore, but this matter was not addressed because it was contrary to the essence of the trade agreement.

Antigua pointed out that each of its Internet gambling operations maintained an "'anti-fraud' department with the objective of preventing ... collusion among players, financial fraud and credit card abuse, underage playing, and other [undesirable] occurrences" (WTO, 2004, p. 4). It said that underage gambling was explicitly prohibited by Antiguan law, monitored by a sophisticated age-identification program, and inhibited by the need to fund an account before wagering, which would require access to instruments such as checks or bank accounts and would involve a wire transfer. "This is a significant barrier which most minors are unable to overcome, particularly given the practice in the industry to either send winnings and deposits directly back to the account from which deposits were received or crediting winnings directly back to the applicable credit card" (WTO, 2004, p. 4). Antiguan officials also looked at gamblers' ties to websites such as Cybersitter and Net Nanny as a way of screening minors. The government of Antigua also noted that the United States was hardly in a position to assume a superior air in regard to underage persons, citing the report of the National Gambling Impact Study Commission, which found that although selling lottery tickets to individuals below the age of 18 years was illegal throughout the United States, such sales occurred with "disturbing frequency." A study in Minnesota found that 27% of 15- to 18-year olds had purchased lottery tickets, and in several states, the tickets were sold by vending machines that were readily accessible to youths (Gearey, 1997). In Massachusetts, an experiment by the Attorney General's office had determined that 80% of underage persons, some as young as 9 years old, had been allowed to purchase lottery tickets (National Gambling Impact Study Commission, 1999, pp. 3–4).

The Antigua filing further noted that, by law, operators there are required to display warnings on their sites about the addiction possibilities of gambling and information about contacting organizations such as Gamblers Anonymous. The filing claimed that "most operators appear to be able to detect patterns of problem gamblers either at the sign-up stage ... or later during the course of the relationship with the player, in which event the player's account often will be closed and the balance returned to the player" (WTO, 2004, p. 4).

The Antigua filing stated that money laundering and other organized crime involvement was not a serious consideration in the Antiguan Internet gambling realm, in large part because operators were not allowed to accept cash and were required to authenticate the bettor's identity. However, the Antiguan brief did not resist a jab here and there at its competing litigant. "This is in stark contrast," it observed, "to land-based casinos and other gaming outlets in the United States, where not only can players wager with complete anonymity, but gamble almost exclusively with cash" (WTO, 2004, p. 5).

The Dispute Settlement Body Panel

After initial negotiations between Antigua and the United States had reached an impasse, Antigua requested the formation of a Dispute Settlement Body Panel. The U.S. representative to the WTO, Linnet Deily, a former investment banker, sought to block the move, declaring that "the United States has grave concerns over the financial and social risks posed by such activities to its citizens, particularly but not exclusively children" (Bissett, 2004, p. 371). He added, "We are surprised that another WTO member has chosen to challenge measures to address these concerns—particularly in an area in which the United States made no market access commitment" (Bissett, 2004, p. 371). Before long, the United States would learn that it could not high-handedly use these rather weak defenses against what it likely saw, initially, as a gnat that required a quick, decisive swat. The Dispute Settlement Body Panel ultimately determined that the United States had indeed made an access commitment and that its express concern for children had constitutional free speech problems and other difficulties.

Unimpressed by the United States' filing, WTO Director-General Supachai Panitchpakdi, from Thailand, formed a three-person group that was led by B. K. Zushi, vice chairman of the Telecom Regulatory Agency of India (TRAI) and former Indian ambassador to the WTO who had co-authored a well-regarded article on negotiations (Self & Zushi, 2003). The other two members of the panel were Virachai Plaasai, director-general of the Department of Internal Affairs in Thailand, and Richard Plender, a Queen's Counsel from the United Kingdom. Besides the contesting nations, Canada, the European Union, Japan, Mexico, and Taiwan joined the litigation as third parties, indicating the considerable international significance of the issue. In theory, third parties have a "significant interest" in the proceedings; in practice, they are any country that desires to contribute its views on the subject under consideration (Guohua, Mercurio, & Yongjie, 2005, pp. 99–108).

The United States claimed before the Panel that gambling was illegal in various American jurisdictions. It further argued that Internet gambling offended the "public morals" of the country and, therefore, could legitimately be excluded from the embrace of the trade treaty (see Chanovitz, 1998). The United States' response contained both condescension and a sizeable portion of obfuscation. At one point, it scolded Antigua for inaccuracies in its summary of American gambling law and its tardiness in submitting corrections. It scored occasional debating points—arguing, for instance, that "children have ready access to payment instruments, and no technology has yet been developed to enable constraints on Internet gambling approaching those that are possible in other settings where gambling can be confined and access to it strictly limited" (WTO, 2004, pp. 14–15). Some of the dispute over legal matters focused on the entertainment and recreational services heading in the United Nations' classification of products that included a subsection specifically listing "gambling and betting" (United Nations, 1991, Code 904). The United States argued that the roster was not binding and that its federal ban on interstate gambling in the Wire Act automatically exempted it from adherence to the United Nations schedule.

Antigua, for its part, adopted a somewhat feisty and combative tone in debating the American claims. "The U.S. should not be allowed to in essence 'hide behind' the complexity and opacity of its own legal structure to deflect attention from the fundamental simplicity of this complaint" (WTO, 2004, p, 31). The Antiguan pleaders also put on record a biting criticism of the American presentation to the WTO of a television documentary presented by the Canadian Broadcasting System in October 2001:

> Antigua submits that the video is offensive and totally irrelevant to the legal questions that arise in this proceeding: [T]he fact that the United States seeks to adduce it as evidence at all … makes the ruse all the more obvious. The program portrays Antigua as a backwater; the Antiguan Solicitor General, who is African and whose mother tongue is not English, finds himself depicted as incompetent …. If the United States is struggling so much in this case that it needs to resort to a media hatchet job of a small developing country that does not have the clout to get a retraction, then the United States is really clutching at straws. The most offensive fact of all, however, is that by submitting this video as evidence, the United States implicitly adopts the view expressed in its own formal view vis-à-vis Antigua. If put in the context of the rest of the U.S. argument, the United States is essentially saying that Antigua is backward, irredeemably incapable of operating a respectable gaming, or any other industry. This is an astonishing statement [and] outright prejudice. (WTO, 2004, pp. 86–87)

This protest may not have been altogether impelled by bruised national feelings but could have been an attempt to call attention to the mandate of the WTO to pay special attention to the needs of Third World countries. It might also have been an effort to counteract what writers have interpreted as a bias in WTO decisions. Khor and Khor (2005) claimed, "The global economy is not managed impartially [by the WTO], but favors rich countries and multinational corporations" (p. 42).

The Panel's report, issued on November 10, 2004, contained three major findings:

1. The GATS was applicable to betting and gambling.
2. The United States was in violation of the treaty when it relied on the Wire Act and other laws to interdict Internet gambling with Antigua. Its actions violated the intent of fair trade and access to markets in Antigua by persons living in America.

3. The United States had failed to demonstrate that its action was necessary to protect "public morals," defined as "standards of right and
wrong conduct maintained on behalf of a country or a community"
(WTO, 2004, *passim*).

The Panel granted that the Wire Act and its two complementary statutes
clearly were designed to protect public morals and public order in the United
States. But the Panel was well aware that some form of gambling is legal in
all American states except Hawaii and Utah, and that Antigua had undertaken programs to deal with the risks enunciated by the United States. The
Panel thought that the United States had failed to diligently explore alternative approaches that might permit it to meet its trade treaty obligations to
its own satisfaction, and it labeled the United States' position as "a disguised
restraint on trade" that "amounts to arbitrary and unjustifiable discrimination between countries" (Weiler, 2006, p. 816) and insisted that countries
cannot unilaterally define what constitutes "public morals" (Maxwell, 2006;
Witt, 2008).

The Appellate Body Ruling

Both the United States and Antigua appealed aspects of the Panel findings
to the Appellate Body. Fundamentally, the Appellate Body's decision upheld
the original finding (although, in some instances, for different reasons) that
the United States had acted in a manner inconsistent with its treaty obligations, but it disagreed with the earlier conclusion that federal antigambling
laws in America were not fashioned to protect public morals and maintain
public order. The Appellate Body also disagreed with the Panel's consideration of many of the American state laws as relevant to its ruling. It focused
considerable attention on the legislative tools upon which the United States
was relying to try to end cross-border Internet gambling: the Wire Act (1961),
the Interstate and Foreign Travel or Transportation in Aid of Racketeering
Enterprises Act (1961; more commonly known as the Travel Act), and the
Illegal Gambling Business Act (1970).
     Violation of the Wire Act (1961), as noted earlier, had been successfully
invoked to convict Jay Cohen of illegal gambling practices on the Internet.
The Travel Act was, like the Wire Act, a 1961 enactment directed against
organized crime, outlawing interstate or foreign commerce with the intent
to distribute the proceeds of an unlawful activity, such as gambling. The
Illegal Gambling Business Act, passed in 1970, also was put in place as a
weapon against organized crime, making it a federal offense to operate a
gambling business that violates state law, providing other conditions are
met, such as the involvement of at least five people and an operation that

has existed for more than 30 days and that has taken in $2,000 or more on any given day.

The core conclusion of the Appellate Body was that the three acts—the Wire Act, the Travel Act, and the Illegal Gambling Business Act—were measures necessary to protect public morals or maintain public order, although as one writer noted, the Body employed "a very lax test" to reach this conclusion (Broude, 2005, p. 684). Nonetheless, the Body ruled that the United States had not shown—particularly in regard to the Interstate Horseracing Act—that its enforcement actions were carried out against both foreign and domestic service suppliers of remote betting services. Therefore, as Antigua had alleged, the United States was in violation of GATS as alleged by Antigua. The Interstate Horseracing Act (IHRA) had been passed in 1978 with a crucial amendment in 2000 that was put in place over the strong objections of the U.S. Department of Justice. The IHRA permits interstate wagering on racetrack events that is transmitted by means of telephone or other electronic means, presumably including the Internet, provided that the wagering is legal in both states. The United States had tried to finesse the inconsistency between the permissive IHRA and its claims of a legitimate exemption from the trade requirements by maintaining, rather awkwardly, that the horse racing stipulation did not replace the interdictions of measures such as the Wire Act. That claim was, of course, accurate but beside the point because the Wire Act could not be used against interstate wagering on hose races in a state that had legalized such betting. Simply put, the conclusion of the WTO Appellate Body was that the United States was using its laws relating to gambling selectively to punish Internet offshore gambling and gamblers while exempting some domestic operations from equal enforcement of the law interdicting Internet betting. At the same time, it should be noted that, as one commentator has said, the vast and dense verbiage of the Panel and the Appellate Body reports and the language and diction employed at times render its precise views "less than clear" (Hurt, 2006, pp. 437–438).

In conclusion, the report stated the following:

> The Appellate Body *recommends* that the Dispute Settlement Body request the United States to bring its measures, found in this Report and in the Panel Report as modified by this Report to be inconsistent with the *General Agreement on Trade in Services*, into conformity with its obligations under this Agreement (WTO, 2005, p. 126; italics in original).

The U.S. trade representative deemed this judgment to be "deeply flawed," insisting that it contradicted the evidence and that the amendment to the horse racing law did not contravene existing American criminal statutes. He said he hoped that Antigua and the WTO would disabuse themselves of this "misperception." Negotiations again were inaugurated between the two countries; these negotiations lasted 4 months but proved fruitless. An arbitrator turned down a request by the United States that it be granted an additional 15 months to respond to the Appellate Body recommendations. Thereafter, Antigua announced that it would request the formation of another review body to decide what action the United States was required to take and, if it failed to adopt such remedies, what penalties should be imposed on it. Possibilities included an extra tariff on export products from America. For its part, Antigua was asking permission to copy and export American-made CDs, DVDs, and similar products.

A comprehensive examination of WTO law and practice, however, points to a significant shortcoming in its adjudication process. "A problem with the implementation of WTO dispute settlement recommendations and rulings are a lack of guidance over what exactly a losing party must do to comply," Matsushita and colleagues wrote. Then, they added wryly, "The tendency has been for the losing party to take minimal steps and declare itself in full compliance." The winning party often disagrees (Matsushita, Schoenbaum, & Mavroidis, 2003, p. 30).

The European Union's Third-Party Submission

Among the submissions of various third parties to the dispute between Antigua and the United States regarding offshore Internet gambling was that of the European Community, which cut to the heart of what was at stake. The submission was by Carlo Trojan, Italian born but a Dutch citizen, who had been a European Union (EU) secretary-general and now was the EU ambassador to the WTO.

The EU's third-party stance reflected a case involving England and Italy. In that case, Piergiorgio Gambelli and 137 other persons had appealed a charge of illegally taking bets in Italy for an English bookmaker in violation of the monopoly on betting enjoyed by the Italian government. The EU court noted that "if a Member state incites and encourages customers to participate in lotteries and betting to the financial benefit of the state, the state may not use the pretext of protecting public order in order to justify restrictions" (*Gambelli v. Italy*, 2003; Del Nemo, 2004). The European Community's submission on the Antigua–United States dispute was the only one to discuss what truly was at stake:

> All other conditions being equal, such prohibition [as sought by the United States] provides an incentive to consumers to turn to service providers within the U.S. territory over like services supplied from the territory of other Members, thereby modifying the conditions of competition. The incentive

obviously is a particularly powerful one, since consumers who continue to gamble through websites operated e.g. from Antigua and Barbuda are doing so in breach of law (WTO, 2004, p. 125).

In the Wake of the Appellate Ruling

On the basis of the favorable ruling by the WTO Dispute Settlement Body Panel and the appellate bodies, Antigua sought compensation for damages of $3.1 billion from the United States and asked permission to violate property laws by allowing free distribution of copies of American music, movies, software, and other items. Two comments on this development indicate its significant implications. Harvard Law School Professor Charles Nesson, founder of the Berkman Center for Internet & Society, focused on the dilemma and difficulty of the WTO taking on its most powerful members:

> There is this fledgling organization dominated by a huge monster .... People there must be scared out of their wits with the prospects of enforcing a ruling that would instantly galvanize public opinion in the United States against the World Trade Organization. (Riflin, 2007, p. C2)

This appears to be only a partial truth. What little evidence is available suggests that it would not be public opinion but government indignation that would force the issue, and perhaps only in the conservative Bush administration and not in that of his successor. The seeming hypocrisy of the Bush officials was expressed in a statement on the WTO dispute by Lode Van Den Hende, an international trade lawyer headquarted in Brussels:

> One day they [the United States] are saying how scandalous it is that China doesn't respect WTO decisions. But the next day, there's a dispute that doesn't go their way, and their attitude is that the decision is completely wrong, judges don't know what they're doing, and why should we comply? (Rivlin, 2007, p. C1)

By 2009, the United States still had not complied with the WTO decision that awarded $2.1 million annually to Antigua as compensation for the loss of its Internet gambling rights in the American market. In 2008, the United States asked for a delay in invoking the sanction and thereafter enacted the Unlawful Internet Gambling Enforcement Act of 2006—a law that, the United States now claimed (during an early 2009 unsuccessful settlement negotiation with Antiguan representatives), allowed it to ban offshore gambling operations from the American marketplace. So, rather than responding to the WTO decision, the United States somewhat strengthened its legislation against online gambling. In essence, the United States was again turning its back on its international treaty obligations (Reysen, 2009).

Conclusion

Both Antigua and the United States had sparred at great length—often in niggling terms—about whether organized crime would infiltrate the Antiguan gambling endeavor or whether such gambling would allow underage participants and thus create additional compulsive, pathological gamblers. These arguments, in the nature of debating tactics, would hopefully persuade those judging the case to favor one party or the other. A back-and-forth duel also took place concerning the precise nature of the United States' obligations under treaty provisions. Fundamentally, the United States was seeking to criminalize enterprises that outsourced gambling services. Outsourcing is a new and legitimate aspect of international trade, as market considerations move businesses from Bangor, Maine, to Bangalore, Karnataka. The practice initially aroused strong public and political indignation in the United States regarding the export of jobs. But later research indicated that the concern was greatly overrated. For example, a 2006 study found that more domestic jobs are created in a few months than are lost to external sites in a year (Gross, 2006). Many factors work against outsourcing—most notably, in the retail and health care sectors, where face-to-face interactions are required (Gross, 2006, p. B5). An influential essay by an economist in the highly prestigious journal, *Foreign Affairs,* claimed that "outsourcing actually brings more benefits; both now and in the long run" (Drezner, 2004, p. 23).

For some, the continued truculence in regard to offshore Internet gambling by the United States was seen as "an ineffective and futile stance on a crucial social issues" (J. Schwartz, 2005, p. 138) in the nature of a Luddite resistance to an emergent and vitalizing trend toward freer international commercial interaction. Most particularly, it was regarded as a self-serving camouflage staged to divert attention from its real purpose, which was "a marked attempt to channel American dollars away from offshore gambling into American casinos" (Bissett, 2004, p. 403). Another move on the part of the United States in that direction took place in the closing moments of the 2006 Congressional session, when the leader of the Senate attached a rider to a port security measure that mandates that banks and credit card companies halt the use of credit cards for the transmission of Internet gambling stakes to overseas sites (Unlawful Internet Gambling Enforcement Act of 2006). The bill was passed without being presented for committee consideration or floor debate. Commentators saw it primarily as a symbolic political gesture to appeal to conservative voters and predicted that it would merely force bettors to locate other routes for transferring funds.

In a prescient appraisal of the likely developments that would ensue from, or perhaps despite, the Antigua–United States conflict in the realm of Internet gambling, I. Nelson Rose offers the following prediction—a view that we, too, support:

Eventually, those states that wish to license operators and allow citizens to wager online will be allowed to do so. As more developing countries turn to legalization, taxation, and regulation, and as more states pass enabling statutes, the U.S. federal government will be forced to shift away from a complete prohibitionist position to one of reluctant tolerance. Federal permission will, at first, be limited to state licensed operations, if for no other reason than foreign and non-licensed operations have no lobbying power in Washington. (Rose, 2000, p. 40)

References

Bissett, C. (2004). All bets are off (line): Antigua's trouble in virtual paradise. *University of Miami Inter-American Law Review, 36*, 367–403.

Blustein, P. (2006, August 4). Against all odds. *Washington Post*, p. D1.

Broude, T. (2005). Taking "trade and culture" seriously: Geographical indications and cultural protection in WTO law. *University of Pennsylvania Journal of International Economic Law, 9336*, 621–692.

Chanovitz, S. (1998). The moral exception in trade policy. *Virginia Journal of International Law, 38*, 689–745.

Crawford, S. P. (2005). Responsibility on the Internet: Shortness of vision: Regulatory ambition in the digital age. *Fordham Law Review, 74*, 695–745.

Del Nemo, A. (2004). Italy responds to the *Gambelli* case. *Gaming Law Review, 8*, 308–309.

Drezner, D. W. (2004, May–June). The outsourcing bogeyman. *Foreign Affairs, 83*(3), 22–34.

Eichengreen, B. J. (2007). *Global imbalances and the lesson of Bretton Woods.* Cambridge, MA: MIT Press.

Gambelli v. Italy, No. C-243/01 (European Community, Ct of Justice, November 6, 2003).

Gasper, D. B. (1993). Sugar cultivation and slave life in Antigua before 1800. In I. Berlin & P. D. Moran (Eds.), *Cultivation and culture* (pp. 101–123). Charlottesville, VA: University of Virginia Press.

Gearey, R. (1997, May 19). The numbers game. *The New Republic*, p. 19.

Gross, D. (2006, August 13). Why "outsourcing" may lose its power as a scare word. *The New York Times*, p. B5.

Guohua, Y., Mercurio, B., & Yongjie, L. (2005). *WTO dispute settlement understandings: A detailed interpretation.* The Hague, the Netherlands: Kluwer Law International.

Hurt, C. (2006). Regulating public morals and private markets: Online securities trading, Internet gambling, and the speculation paradox. *Boston University Law Review, 86*, 371–441.

Illegal Gambling Business Act of 1970, 18 U.S.C. § 1955 (1970).

Interstate and Foreign Travel or Transportation in Aid of Racketeering Enterprises Act, 18 U.S.C. §1952 (1961).

Interstate Horseracing Act of 1978, 15 U.S.C. § 3001 (1978).

Interstate Wire Act of 1961, 18 U.S.C. § 1604 (1961).

Jackson, J. H. (2000). *The jurisprudence of GATT and the WTO: Insights on treaty law and economic relations.* Cambridge, United Kingdom: Cambridge University Press.

Khor, K. P., & Khor, M. (2005). *WTO and the global trading system: Developmental impacts and reform proposals*. London, United Kingdom: Zed Books.

Kossman, M. (2006). *Internet gambling.* Retrieved from http://www.uwec.edu/Counsel/pubs/internetGambling.htm

Lubben, T. A. (2003). The federal government and the regulation of Internet sports gambling. *Sports Lawyers Journal, 10,* 317–334.

Massoud, S. (2004). The offshore quandary: The impact of domestic regulation on licensing offshore gambling companies. *Whittier Law Review, 25,* 989–1009.

Matsushita, M., Schoenbaum, T. J., & Mavroidis, P. C. (2003). *The World Trade Organization: Law, practice, and policy.* New York, NY: Oxford University Press.

Maxwell, J. C. (2006). Trade and morality: The WTO public morals exception after gambling. *New York University Law Review, 81,* 802–830.

National Gambling Impact Study Commission. (1999, June 8). *National Gambling Impact Study Commission final report.* Washington, DC: Government Printing Office.

Newnham, T. (2007). WTO case study: United States—Measures affecting its cross-border supply of gaming and betting services. *Aspen Review of International Business and Trade Law, 7,* 77–100.

Reysen, Y. (2009). Taking chances: The United States' policy on Internet gambling and its international complications. *Cardozo Arts and Entertainment Law Journal, 26,* 873–897.

Rivlin, G. (2007, August 23). Online gambling case pits Antigua against U.S. and challenges WTO. *The New York Times,* p. C1.

Rose, I. N. (2000). Gambling and the law. The future of Internet gambling. *Villanova Sports and Entertainment Law Journal, 71,* 9–53.

Rose, I. N. (2005). Internet gambling: United States beats Antigua in World Trade Organization. *Gaming Law Review, 9,* 437–438.

Sanders, R. (Ed.). (1982). *Antigua and Barbuda independence.* St. John's, Antigua: Ministry of Economic Development, Tourism, and Energy.

Schwartz, D. B. (2005). *Cutting the wire: Gaming prohibition and the Internet.* Reno, NV: University of Nevada Press.

Schwartz, J. (2005). Click the mouse and bet the house: The United States' gambling restriction before the World Trade Organization. *University of Illinois Journal of Law, Technology and Policy, 2005,* 125–140.

Self, R. J., & Zushi, B. K. (2003). Mode 4: Negotiating challenges and opportunities. In A. Mattoo & A. Carzaniga (Eds.), *Moving people to deliver services* (pp. 27–58). Washington, DC: World Bank and Oxford University Press.

Unlawful Internet Gambling Enforcement Act of 2006, 31 U.S.C. § 5361–5367 (2006).

United Nations. (1991). *Provisional central product classification* [Situational Paper, Series M, No. 77]. New York, NY: Author.

United States v. Cohen, 260 F. 3d 68 (2d Cir., 2001), *denied* 536 U.S. 926 (2002).

Weiler, P. C. (2006). Renovating our recreational crimes. *New England Law Review, 40,* 809–830.

Witt, M. (2008). Free trade and the protection of public morals: An analysis of the newly emerging public morals clause doctrine. *Yale Journal of International Law, 33,* 215–250.

World Trade Organization. (2001, January 10). *Korea—Measures affecting imports of fresh, chilled and frozen beef.* [Appellate Body Report WT/DS161/R]. Geneva, Switzerland: Author.

World Trade Organization. (2004, November 10). *United States—Measure affecting the cross-border supply of gambling and betting services: Report of the panel* [Appellate Body Report WT/D285/R (No. 04-2687)]. Geneva, Switzerland: Author.

World Trade Organization. (2005, April 7). *United States—Measures affecting the cross-border supply of gambling and betting services* [Appellate Body Report WT/DS528/AB/R (No. 05-1426)]. Geneva, Switzerland: Author.

Perpetrators' Perspectives and Offender Use of the Internet

II

Identity Construction Among Hackers

3

ORLY TURGEMAN-GOLDSCHMIDT

Contents

Introduction

The present study analyzes the ways in which hackers interpret their lives, behavior, and beliefs, as well as their perceptions of how society treats them. The study examines hackers' life stories that explain who they are and what they do, which provides a deeper, sharper picture on the complexity of the phenomenon than a survey could (Lieblich, Tuval-Mashiach, & Zilber, 1998). The focus is on the social construction of deviant identity among hackers and on the meanings that they assign to their reality (Charmaz, 2000).

Computer-related deviance has not been sufficiently studied, especially from the perspective of the perpetrators themselves (Yar, 2005). The computer underground forms a worldwide subculture (Holt, 2007; Meyer & Thomas, 1990). The symbolic identity of the computer underground generates a rich and diverse culture consisting of justifications, highly specialized skills, information-sharing networks, norms, status hierarchies, language, and unifying symbolic meanings (Meyer & Thomas, 1990). The *hacker* label is often used to refer to the computer underground as a whole. Hackers have a distinct image—an imagined identity that binds them, even if they never meet each other (Jordan & Taylor, 1998).

There are also differences between subgroups, which are classified depending on their expertise, areas of interest, and behavior patterns (Voiskounsky & Smyslova, 2003). The perplexity surrounding the label *hacker* has to do with the fuzzy definition of the term and the vague boundaries between computer experts and hackers (Jordan & Taylor, 1998) as well as those characteristics that differentiate between various types of hackers. Hackers themselves have suggested different terms and meanings to define hackers and hacking (Coleman & Golub, 2008; Holt, 2007). The best known members of the computer underground are *hackers/crackers* (usually referring to those who break into computer systems), *phreaks* (those who use technology or telephone credit card numbers to avoid long distance charges), and *pirates* (those who distribute copyrighted software illegally). As there are differences in the meaning and practice of being a hacker, it is essential to examine if and how it is represented by differences in the hackers' self-presentation. This research outlines the differences between deviant and less deviant computer hackers.

Hacker as a Socially Constructed Label

The term *hacker* has evolved through the years (Jordan & Taylor, 2004). From the beginning, hacking has raised serious concerns about the misuse of powerful, new electronic technology (Hannemyr, 1999). Yet, initially, the term had connotations of honorable motives of virtuoso programmers overcoming obstacles. Sterling (1992) says, "Hacking can signify the free-wheeling intellectual exploration of the highest and deepest potential of computer systems. Hacking can describe the determination to make access to computers and information as free and open as possible" (p. 53). This is *hacking* as defined in Levy's (1984) history of the computer milieu.

Hackers: Heroes of the Computer Revolution

Hacking has evolved into unauthorized access to computer networks (Jordan & Taylor, 1998). The label *hacker* has acquired the negative connotation of computer criminal and electronic vandal (Chandler, 1996), a national security threat, and a threat to intellectual property (Halbert, 1997). However, Skibell (2002) calls the computer hacker a myth and states that few computer hackers possess sufficient skills or desire to commit more than nuisance crimes.

Hackers developed the Internet and personal computers (Wall, 2001), and "it might, in fact, even be suggested that the personal computer would never have existed without the computer hacker" (Chandler, 1996, p. 229). The earliest generations of hackers (Jordan & Taylor, 2004; Levy, 1984) passionately wanted computers and computer systems designed to be useful and accessible to individuals and, in the process, pioneered public access. Hannemyr (1999) concludes that the hackers have successfully created several usable and unique software programs, ranging from text editors to the Internet. Furthermore, the *open source movement,* an alternative and successful way of developing and distributing software (Ljungberg, 2000), has been rooted in the hacker culture since the early 1960s (Levy, 1984). And it seems that in recent years, the positive connotation of hacking has been partially returned in connection with the involvement of hackers in the open source movement and their influence on it.

In its short history, the *hacker* label has changed from a positive to a negative one. Most sociological knowledge on the stigma focuses on what Goffman called "information management" rather than on the contested nature of stigma (Kusow, 2004). The focus here is on the contested nature of stigma and shows that hackers not only reject the stigma attached to them but go farther and empower themselves as "positive deviants," regardless of their specific practices as hackers. Therefore, the theoretical framework that seems productive for understanding these behaviors is *labeling theory* (Becker, 1963; Lemert, 1951).

Davies and Tanner (2003) contend that labeling theory has three different concerns. The first concern is *secondary deviance*—that is, deviant behavior that goes unnoticed, undetected, or hidden and is said to be less generative of further deviant behavior than publicly sanctioned behavior. The second concern pertains to the social–psychological effect of labeling, with labels changing the individual's self-conception for the worse. The third concern examines the effect of labeling on life opportunities, specifically in the area of employment. These concerns are addressed in the present chapter.

According to Becker (1963), individuals labeled as *deviant* identify themselves first and foremost as deviant. Any other status vanishes before that of deviant, which becomes the "master status," yet this also depends on the type of deviance (Becker, 1963). Becker argues that violating criminal law is one reason for being labeled as *deviant,* but whether this takes place and the extent to which it does depends on key contingencies such as race, age, and socioeconomic status.

Positive deviance is a controversial term (Goode, 1991) but seems useful for the construction of deviant identity among hackers. Dodge (1985) defines *positive deviance* as "those acts, roles/careers, attributes and appearances … singled out for special treatment and recognition, those persons and acts that are evaluated as superior because they surpass conventional expectations" (p. 18). Heckert (1989), who applies the relationships of labeling theory to positive deviance by examining the labeling of the French Impressionists, claims that the genius or an exceptional athlete should be examined in a manner similar to that for negative deviants. Becker (1978) has also used labeling theory to show how geniuses were once defined as "mad." Ben-Yehuda (1990) argues that the label of *deviant* can be negative or positive, a position that is implicit in the labeling approach and becomes more explicit once one accepts the relative view of deviance, the negotiated nature, its emergent quality, and its fluidity.

Hackers are a good example of Becker's (1963) approach whereby labeling an activity as *deviant* is based on the creation of social groups and not on the quality of the activity itself. Becker (1963) uses the term *outsider* to describe labeled rule breakers or deviants who accept the label attached to them and view themselves as different from "mainstream."

Method

This study is based on interviews with individuals who constitute a subculture by virtue of their membership in a self-defined subculture. On the basis of the phenomenological–interpretive approach (Geertz, 1973), the objective of this research was not to reveal the actual reality but to describe how self-defined hackers experience, explain, and interpret reality.

The starting point for this study was the *grounded theory* (Strauss, 1987; Strauss & Corbin, 1990, 2000), a data-driven method that produces theoretical propositions and concepts and systematically processes them. The outcome of grounded theory is "a social construction of the social constructions found and explicated in the data" (Charmaz, 1990, p. 1165). In this respect, the researcher's text is itself an interpretive structuring of reality. The hackers' narratives are reconstructions of experience; they are not the original experience itself (Charmaz, 2000).

Participants

Finding interviewees required intensive efforts to establish connections and make the acquaintance of various informants and of suitable potential interviewees (see Table 3.1). The interviews were conducted in 1998 and 1999, yet it seems that they are still meaningful, as the practices and perceptions that were reported by the interviewees coincide with reports on hackers today. The interviews were conducted in the hackers' homes or in public places such as coffee shops, according to the interviewee preference. I took notes during the interviews, recording the words of the interviewees almost verbatim. Each interviewee was assigned an identification number that contained no identifying details.

Table 3.1   Locating Interviewees

Media reports (one was interviewed on a television show, and the rest were interviewed for magazine reports)	7
Israeli hacker conferences (one was called "Movement," a demo scene party, and the other was called "Y2Hack")	5
Israeli conference about information security	1
Through the Internet (arranging a face-to-face interview in ICQ)	2
Other informants (journalists, a radio broadcaster, and the owner of a computer company)	6
Interviewees approached me when I was lecturing on computer crime (each at a different lecture)	2
Acquaintances and family members and friends	6
Snowball or chain referrals; I asked interviewees to refer me to others	25

Fifty-one of the 54 Israeli self-defined hackers were men, and three were women (see Table 3.2). Only six participants reported having criminal records, five of which were computer related. The interviews provided an opportunity to study successful lawbreakers outside an institutional context (i.e., uncaught deviants). The interviewees tended to be young, single, educated, earning an above-average income, of European or American origin, and secular. This profile is consistent with the literature, which reports that hackers are mostly nonviolent, White, young, middle- or upper-class men with no criminal record (e.g., Hollinger, 1991).

Data Analysis

Fifty-four unstructured, in-depth, face-to-face interviews were conducted using the narrative interview technique (Rosenthal & Bar-On, 1992). The first part contains the main narrative—usually the life story—told without any interruptions. I started all interviews with a generative question ("Tell me the story of your life") to guarantee an extensive narration. I used nonverbal means and paralinguistic expressions of interest and attention to encourage

Table 3.2   Sociodemographic Characteristics of Interviewees

Variable	Frequency
Gender	F = 5.5%; M = 94.5%
Age	Range = 14–49 years; average age = 24; common age group = 20–30 years
Marital status	Single = 78%; married = 13%
Education	12 years or more = 74%
Income	Above average = 74%
Origin	European or American = 74%
Religion	Secular = 83%

F, female; M, male.

interviewees to open up: body language (an attentive listening posture and a degree of eye contact) and nonverbal sounds such as "hmm," indicating that I was listening. The second part was the "asking questions" stage. I collected information based on the narrative, elaborating on the biographical events mentioned earlier by the interviewees.

The interviews lasted an average of 3 hours (the shortest was 2 hours; the longest was 8 hours). At the end of the interview, I asked whether there was anything they wanted to add or felt that they had missed, and then I thanked them and ended the session. Later, usually the following day, I sent them a thank you note (by e-mail). Many of the interviewees responded positively. For example, Eran (all names are fictitious) said, "One of the reasons for sitting here and talking to you today was the opportunity to recall, think, and understand. Each of these conversations is an introspection, which eventually helps me understand myself."

The data were analyzed based on the grounded theory (Strauss & Corbin, 1990). The generation of categories of data, known as *coding,* is an ongoing process that Strauss (1987) calls the *concept-indicator model.* After a close reading of the interviews, I assigned names to classes of actions or events based on a series of indicators. Comparing indicators and comparing and contrasting similarities, differences, and inconsistencies helped generate the coded categories. I continued this process until the categories were verified and saturated—when, despite new data and additional detail, they remained stable.

Having established a robust set of categories that covered the hackers' self-perceptions and behaviors and uncovered their life stories, I generated a series of theoretical propositions (Strauss & Corbin, 1990). These propositions started from a conjecture or an idea (jotted down as memos), based on relationships between categories and subcategories—for example, between general behavior patterns and hacking activities. I tested these theoretical propositions by constantly referring back to the data for impressions.

Different Identity Construction Among Hackers

The *self-defined hacker* in this study is someone who commits any of the 12 computer offenses in one or more of the following three areas:

1. *Software piracy:* Unauthorized duplication of pirated software; unauthorized distribution of pirated software, cracking software, or games; selling cracked–pirated software.
2. *Hacking:* Unauthorized accessing of computer systems, using illegal Internet accounts, development and/or distribution of viruses, browsing or reading other users' files, stealing computer-stored

information, causing computer systems to crash, and using stolen credit cards from the Internet.

3. *Phreaking:* Cracking the phone network mainly to make free long-distance calls. These offenses are similar to those identified by Hollinger (1988), who differentiated among pirates, browsers, and crackers in terms of who had the most technical ability and who were the most serious abusers. These offenses are also similar to those studied by Rogers, Smoak, and Liu (2006). These offenses match the attacks detected by the *2006 CSI/FBI Survey* (Gordon, Loeb, Lucyshyn, & Richardson, 2006; e.g., unauthorized access to information, system penetration, theft of information, and sabotage).

Hackers typically assign different meanings and interpretations to operating as a hacker. These participants showed different self-presentation according to differences in the variety and extent of their hacking activities. The reported differences are manifest from early childhood through adulthood. Those who reported mischievous behavior since childhood (not related to computers) and presented themselves as talented and gifted since childhood committed statistically significantly more numerous and diverse computer offenses (practicing piracy, hacking, and phreaking) than those who reported normative good behavior and who did not report themselves as being diagnosed with high intellect (for the full analysis, see Turgeman-Goldschmidt, 2002). In other words, the "bad" hackers (also referred to as *crackers*) were much more likely to present themselves as having a wild and gifted persona than the "good" hackers, who reported good behavior since childhood.

The hackers' report of computer-related or hacking activities fits their basic self-image. Kevin Mitnick, perhaps the most famous hacker, also describes his desire and ability to learn and discover going back to his childhood (Mitnick & Simon, 2002). The actor fits "his/her self into the dominant character of the situation or structure: adjusting to an obdurate reality" (Fine, 1993, p. 78). These moral constructions are precarious social constructions rather than essences. Gad, for instance, portrayed himself as the eternal iconoclast—mentioning having quit his bachelor of arts (BA) studies and an advertisement course—and frequently changed jobs. He stated, "I don't like to do things that I have to." However, a careful look into his life story reveals that he successfully completed several serious undertakings such as schooling, a scriptwriter course, and military service as an officer. Gad, as others, chooses to construct his life story around a certain theme—as a nonconformist and eternal iconoclast. As Stryker (1968) contends, individuals with highly salient identities enact these identities over others that are less salient, even when both may be appropriate in a given situation.

"Good" Hackers

The term *hacker* was originally defined in the following ways:

1. A person who enjoys learning the details of computer systems and how to stretch their capabilities, as opposed to most users of computers, who prefer to learn only the minimum amount necessary.
2. One who programs enthusiastically or who enjoys programming rather than just theorizing about programming (Raymond, 1991).

Ami, a 19-year-old, third-year student of computer science who works at the computer help desk of a university, describes what it is like to be a hacker:

> I define myself as a hacker. A hacker can cope with technical details. Last year, when my dad was abroad, every time I drove his car, I'd hear a boom whenever I made a turn. There were two bottles of water and a bottle of radiator fluid [in the trunk], so I had to slow down every time I turned. This is what it means to be a hacker: I went home, I took some wire, and I built a cage for the bottles, and since then, they've stayed in place. A hacker is someone with (1) a knack for the technical, usually having something in connection with computers and (2) someone who has the ability to improvise and [be] resourceful .... It's not a matter of breaking the law. It's a fact that there's this system, and you can manipulate it. The presence of a crack in the system means that it's possible.

Although Ami clearly sees himself as a hacker, he does not perceive hacking to necessarily include unauthorized penetration of computer systems (break-in) or viewing others' files without permission but, rather, as having technical capabilities. He says, "It is not just the end result—the maximal change in improving software—but how you got there." By referring to programmers who demonstrate virtuosity in their ability to overcome obstacles, his usage of the term *hacker* differs from the prevailing definition and matches the previous usage (Levy, 1984).

As computer hobbyists, the good hackers described their development and progress in computers as the natural outgrowth of their basic good identities. Ami suggests a positive connotation of the term hacker: a computer technology expert who "does the impossible," proves his or her ability and superior expertise, and belongs to an elite subculture of experts in the field who are leading society toward a better technological future. According to the metaphor used by Na'ama, who practices only authorized hacking, hackers see themselves as deviants who ultimately became leaders:

> I like the image of ants; there are those that join a trail and those that leave the trail. That's always been my image of the marginal types, who are actually

those who discover alternative paths, and thanks to them the rest of society discovers alternative paths.

Good hackers have been involved primarily in copyright violations such as copying and distributing software. Although they negotiate their label by using a moral construct, they are usually involved in software piracy to a higher extent and with a greater commitment than individuals who are nonhackers. As Ami said, "I feel a moral commitment to screw Microsoft." In Idan's words, "It's the way to a better world, not letting companies like Microsoft control the market."

Furthermore, as the participants' narratives reveal, they have usually tried both hacking and phreaking but were not interested in a long-term career of break-in activity. "Technically, I know how [to] and could actually penetrate a remote computer belonging to someone else, but I have no reason to do so. I'm not interested," says Ami. Yoni tells of a break-in he committed once just to see what it was like. "Before I knew what it was like, like lots of kids, I thought it was cool." This sheds light on the process of becoming a hacker, which is not only a matter of learning the technical aspects but also learning to enjoy it. As Becker (1953) said about marijuana users, "the motivation or disposition to engage in the activity is built up in the course of learning to engage in it and does not antedate this learning process" (p. 235). Yoni, who also reported having written viruses to learn a new skill, says: "What made me stop [break-in] was not because I cared what people think; I simply lost interest in it. I can laugh afterwards at someone who wasted his time, when I didn't." In Becker's (1953) words, during the sequence of Yoni's social experiences, he has not acquired a conception of the meaning of "break-in activity," which makes it desirable.

The stories sometimes touched upon morality. Udi, who talked about the fun in doing the impossible with computer systems, was raised as an orthodox Jew. "Much of my religious life still remains in me with respect to values. The fact that I've never committed a crime may be related to this. I'm a good boy, in whom the good side survived." Udi did not acquire the perceptions and judgments of unauthorized hacking that make the activity desirable. Rogers, Smoak, and Liu (2006) found that self-reported computer deviants scored lower on social moral choice than non-computer deviants, yet when Rogers, Seigfried, and Tidke (2006) replicated Rogers, Smoak, and Liu's (2006) study, they failed to find any significant effect for moral choice.

The good hackers remain open to finding alternatives to penetrating computer systems to achieve their desire for recognition (Taylor, 1999). Good hackers do not feel the desire to engage in computer break-in because they are usually engaged in other activities that yield the same results, recognition, and esteem for their abilities. They are engaged as gamers or as demo sceners. *Demo* is a short, computer-generated multimedia production that demonstrates its creator's talent and creativity in computer music, graphics, and animation. For example, Yoav, an 18-year-old who is about to be drafted into the army's Intelligence Corps, achieved recognition for his activities as a gamer when he invented and produced a network game that gained inspired admiration: "We eventually turned it into a film with a plot and an ending, we released it, and people liked it. It made us very popular."

"Bad" Hackers

The bad hackers in this study described themselves as having a wild and gifted persona. They described their computer-related activities as a natural out-growth of their childhood behavior. Their mischievous image followed them through childhood, school, military service, work, and so forth. Hackers, like others, seek to have their identities verified by others, whether the identity is positive or negative (Swann, Wenzlaff, & Tafarodi, 1992). Whereas good hackers are involved as gamers or demo sceners, the bad hackers are members of hacking or cracking groups.

Meir, a 24-year-old founder of a high-tech start-up, reported committing eight types of computer offenses in the areas of software piracy, hacking, and phreaking. He mentioned testing into the genius range as a child and his effortless science-related capabilities, and he said that his ability to "rapidly assimilate information is a gift from God if there is one, or maybe from my parents." Meir portrayed himself as mischievous in various contexts. At school, "they were always sending notes home to my parents. I was considered as one of the troublemakers. Not disturbed but misbehaved. I wouldn't do my homework; I would cut classes or make a mess in the computer lab or hack into the school's computers." In the army, too, "I was a terrible conscript. I blew off my commanders, and there was nothing they could do." He attributed his being different and special both to original thinking ("Lots of people think I'm strange") and to original actions, such as having a tattoo in an unusual place on his body. In the interview, he wanted to convey that he was not an ordinary person. "I like the fact that I'm different; I'm more in love with myself for having done the impossible."

Neli, a 16-year-old, describes the process of becoming a hacker as part of the progress he made in computer knowledge, describing achieving a university degree and hacking into a website in analogous terms:

> My approach has always been that if someone else can do it, so can I. That's been my motivation ever since I can remember. If others can finish university in 3 years, so can I. If others can hack into websites and sabotage them, so can I. After a while, the excitement fades, and you go on to something else.

Neli moved on to cracking computer systems as a "sneaky thrill" (Katz, 1988, p. 53). Katz views young property criminals as committing sneaky crimes for the thrill; hackers take on hacking as a social entertainment that usually excites them (Turgeman-Goldschmidt, 2005). Hacking becomes just another skill to acquire—if not the most exciting one, as far as they are concerned. Neli first expressed his excitement by building websites, then by studying programming, and, eventually, hacking. He describes his experience as follows:

Hacking was the thing that's taken me the longest to learn. The nicest thing was simply finding the answer. That's the thing that excited me the most, and for one reason: HTML. You create and change things that are yours; you recreate yourself. You control something outside yourself. It creates a feeling. It's incredible. You have access, and the door's wide open. The possibility to change and destroy others—you, yes, you! It's a turn-on. It is the exact opposite of being in a mall where you want a certain store to open and another one to close. You can [control it], and it's soooo nice."

Like others, Neli disavows the label of *deviant* and negotiates his identity by portraying hacking as just another realm to conquer—that is, demonstrating mastery and knowledge. Neli chooses to portray himself as a troublemaker ("the bad boy, the wild child, whatever you want to call it") who is academically successful without even trying. But beyond disavowing the label of *deviant,* Neli negotiated his identity as morally "better" by choosing the target, which is penetrating the computer systems of Israel's enemies, such as the Hamas and neo-Nazis. He portrays himself as a guardian of the state. He says, "I see myself the state's guardian. If the government isn't doing anything, I feel I should, and I do something." His story was in the papers and received a lot of attention:

First of all, I didn't go to school on the first day because I was all over the papers. When I went to school, everyone asked, "How's it going?" even though they knew all about my whereabouts and what I had been up to. Students pointed at me, stating, "I saw you on television." It was like a party. The whole school was really nice to me. I had to turn the kids away; they were all over me. Their admiration was deserved because I did something unique; I learned something specific; so why not? I know it probably sounds like I'm full of myself, but according to the Walla [an Israeli portal] poll, they admired me for it. Except for a scathing article against me in *Ma'ariv l'Noar* [a teen magazine], most of the coverage was supportive. I like to make a scrapbook of all of the articles. After the publicity I got, it gained momentum.

Neli's story is an excellent example of the experienced fame and recognition that go with hacking in the hackers' eyes, even when it crosses the publicity line from being news among hackers to the general public domain. Neli, who regularly committed computer offenses, won fame for his hacking activities. He also succeeded in translating fame and recognition into a different type of prestige by accepting an after-school job at a leading computer company.

Arik, a 22-year-old student who learns how to write viruses "only as a technical part of understanding," says, "Another common denominator of this underground is that what motivates us is not money. We despise commercialism. What motivates us is the fame and prestige that one receives." It seems that this motivation distinction enables hackers to feel superior to traditional criminals.

Indeed, the manner in which hackers' activities should be treated has become blurred and uncertain. Sometimes, society functions as a reinforcing spawn factor of deviance for which at least the informal sanctions are more positive than negative (as in Neli's example). Occasionally, even formal reactions are positive. Yaron, the 30-year-old owner of a successful information security company, says, "The judge saw things the right way, unlike the police. A successful, talented kid who committed a prank, not for profitable gain," letting Yaron off with no punishment and with a "recommendation from the judge." Yaron explains, "Compared to the other less sophisticated criminals, computer criminals get more sympathy. There's a certain favor for sophistication." It seems that Yaron's experience with labeling enabled him to succeed later in life and to avoid secondary deviance, although he was initially labeled a deviant.

In March 1998, Ehud Tenenbaum—the Israeli "Analyzer"—penetrated the Pentagon's computer system (among other computer-related crimes). One U.S. Defense Department official called this the most organized and systematic attack the Pentagon had seen to date (Zetter, 2008). In Israel, the headlines labeled him "The Israeli Computer Genius," and a degree of admiration and awe was discernible even among journalists and Israeli leaders. The following quote, by a leading Hebrew daily (*Ha'aretz*), is representative of other reports:

> Israeli leaders also viewed Tenenbaum as a hero. Prime Minister Benyamin Netanyahu called him "superb;" Industry and Trade Minister Dalia Itzik said: "He's a wizard who should not stand trial because his knowledge could aid the state." Tenenbaum's attorney, Amnon Zichroni, known for his ties to the security establishment, was quoted as saying that in a meeting with former Chief of Staff Amnon Lipkin-Shahak, he had suggested drafting Tenenbaum to penetrate Syrian intelligence systems. "A young person like him could serve our society," said Zichroni. Tenenbaum was invited to appear before the Knesset Science and Technology Committee, whose website he is said to have also hacked. A few weeks later, Tenenbaum starred in a computer company's advertisement. The papers called his actions "youthfully mischievous," and commentators claimed that Tenenbaum, who had sabotaged the websites of Hamas and of neo-Nazi groups, was actually a patriot. (Dror, 2001, p. 6)

Tenenbaum and three Canadians were arrested for allegedly hacking the computer system of a Calgary-based financial services company and inflating the value on several prepaid debit card accounts before withdrawing about CDN $1.8 million (about U.S. $1.7 million) from ATMs in Canada and other countries (Zetter, 2008).

Exit (or Semi-Exit) From the "Bad" Hacker Role

In most situations of loss, such as a change that is related to a loss of personal ability, individuals look for means to preserve their former identities or to establish new ones to regain a sense of continuity (Charmaz, 1994). Studies conducted on individuals who were "exiting the deviant career" focus on identifying the process whereby deviant individuals abandon certain behaviors, ideologies, and identities by replacing them with occupations in professional counseling (Brown, 1991). Brown claims that "ex-deviants" do not "leave it all behind" (p. 227) to replace their lifestyles with more conventional lifestyles, values, beliefs, and identities but, rather, use remnants of their deviant background as explicit strategies for their occupations. In this regard, ex-hackers also suggest that ex-deviants tend not to shed or forget their pasts but reinvent them by transforming them into social capital, proclaiming membership in a group that provides each of its members with the backing of the collectivity-owned capital—a "credential" that entitles them to credit in the various senses of the word (Bourdieu, 1986, p. 248). Meir, an ex-hacker, certainly does not "leave it all behind" (Brown, 1991), as seen from the following excerpt:

> Once you know that everything's possible, it takes your desire away. The fact is that it no longer excites me .... Hacking grew out of a high degree of expertise, from an attitude of "as hard as you try, you'll never be able to do it." It's truly a war. A lot of respect is at stake. It's competitive—the most competitive of people competing against each other. It's like two opposing countries' armies. Once I worked for an antivirus company. It was for my own interests, since I liked being the bad guy and engaging in [viruses]. At one point in time, it was for fun. Now, I just crack stuff that I need. I hack, but lawfully. I try to find the loopholes. The law places obstacles in my path, so I go around them. There are levels of risk that I used to take, but I don't today, and there are principles that you don't violate. Occasionally I'm tempted to hack into the Interior Ministry to see if the owner of my friend's apartment is the real one because certain things there look suspicious. But it's not out of evil intent; I do it only when there's no other recourse. Today, it's a profession. I do it because I need to—not for the same reasons I used to.

Meir explains this change in motivation as a moral responsibility that he did not feel previously, but it is also the result of a lack of interest that follows from the status definition of his role and from the burnout that now charac-terizes hacking. To this day, he perceives various hacking activities as legiti-mate; therefore, he has not undergone a serious transformation. Ex-hackers occupying professional positions carefully consider the risks involved in hack-ing activities. There are, says Meir, "levels of risk that I once took but don't anymore." Moreover, the pleasure that accompanied committing computer offenses diminishes with time, particularly as hackers feel that they have reached the apex of their technical abilities. As Meir says, "There's no longer the fun of 'I can do it.'" At the same time, their computer expertise remains. Hackers treasure this expertise and sometimes check that it is still up to date. Ex-hackers still use their hacking skills when the need arises, albeit for differ-ent purposes, such as obtaining information that others cannot or gaining an advantage over a competitor.

Ex-hackers are hackers who grew up, joined the establishment, and hold respected, lawful positions—in most cases, owing precisely to their hacking abilities. Their crossing over to lawfulness is external and structural. They perceive themselves as especially gifted people whose acts, branded by the law as "computer crimes," do not cause damage and fall under the category of "pranks" or "mischief." They have no moral problem with hacking itself or with their status as ex-hackers. Consequently, their life stories are not those of reformed criminals but of heroes who gained the type of social recognition that places them at center stage. Fine (1986) maintained that as children grow older, they view their former "dirty play" (such as aggressive pranks, sex-ual talk, and racist remarks) as morally offensive rather than fun. Contrary to claims by Arluke (2002) and Fine (1986), none of the ex-hackers present themselves as feeling guilty about their former hacking activities.

As Hollinger (1993) assumed, outsider hackers eventually become inside workers. The distinction between criminal hackers and hired ones is based on the perception that hired hackers are employed "to conduct hacking attacks to test security, while criminal hackers literally violate the law" (Jordan & Taylor, 1998, p. 771). The computer security industry benefits from the hack-ers' technological knowledge, which motivates hackers to act. They had pur-sued and found social recognition and status in the hacker subculture (see also Holt, 2007), which had won them a coveted place in its hierarchy. Now, they seek and obtain recognition in society, which offers them a profession with a high socioeconomic status as ex-hackers. Says Omer, "You still look for and receive recognition, but in a different way."

Shared Identity Construction Among Hackers

In my interviews, I found that regardless of the number and severity of the computer offenses they had committed, both good and bad hackers explain their practices in terms of "breaking boundaries," "shattering conventions," and "doing the impossible." It is known that hackers do not view themselves as criminals but as adventurers (cf., Jordan & Taylor, 1998, 2004; Taylor, 1999). Yet, they all portray themselves in the same manner—as technological wizards who break boundaries, adding new contributions to society's knowledge regarding the differences between the two types of hackers. Both good and bad hackers perceived themselves positively, capable of insight into what "regular people" cannot grasp about that mysterious box called a computer.

Many interviewees talk about the positive reaction that their computer hobby has produced. Some even aspire to be hackers, mainly to gain the aura of prestige and mystery that surrounds hackers. Individuals learn how to distinguish the objects with which they come in contact from their interactions with others. In this process, they also learn how they are expected to behave in reference to those objects (Stryker, 1980). Dan says, "Maybe the drive [to learn computers] came from the environment. It contains a dimension of uniqueness. Also, within the milieu, they treated those who dealt with computers as geniuses."

Hackers view hacking or penetrating computer systems as "pushing outside the envelope" or "breaking boundaries." Yif'at, a 19-year-old female soldier, perceives hackers as ambassadors of intelligence, with the ability to oppose the establishment in a proactive manner. She can teach us about the desire to become a hacker, as she believes the following:

> The thing about hacking is the excitement, the adrenaline, the fun of doing something illegal, unlawful. Like when we were kids, a group of us friends would wait together outside a mini-market and steal hot buns and cartons of chocolate milk. The fun is in the subversive act, in rebellion for its own sake. I don't think that governments and institutions should keep secrets and information from the public. Information should be free. So it's also a matter of principle.
>
> It's showing that I'm smarter, I'm in control, and I'll triumph over you. Learning hacking is the cutting edge. It's where the world is going; it's important. It counts as … a good job, and a great living. It's knowledge. Today, women are learning computers because it's good money. The information is all there. It's for real. For example, the Analyzer, look what a good job he has. Hacking is doing the impossible, the unexpected, and the fun stuff. It's also a matter of proving that you can. In every area of my life, I like to test the limits, to go as far out on the edge as I can, and not bend to external restrictions.

Yif'at's words exemplify three of the general characteristics of symbolic interactionism (Blumer, 1969). Yif'at interacts with friends who feel and behave alike. Her response to this behavior is based on meaning and interpretation, in this case, attributing positive meaning and interpretation to hacking activities. Hacking is perceived as a way not to bend to external restrictions—it is viewed as "the cutting edge," "a good job," and "also a matter of principle" (i.e., information should be free). Ami, a good hacker, explains why hackers perceive themselves as capable of doing the impossible. It is "[b]ecause of the breaking of boundaries. It's almost mystical, like a secret society with a certain aura. Security captures the imagination of the public. It is all about being smarter than the next guy."

Their ability to hack is the key to a secure career path that promises status and respect. Indeed, the Analyzer is a founding partner in a high-tech company that specializes in computer security. Although labeling may restrict access to legitimate job networks (Davies & Tanner, 2003), hacking may be a rare instance in which a criminal record serves as a "resume" for gaining entry into legitimate, profitable, and respected occupations. This "occupational retrofitting" seems to support the idea that the line between hero and criminal is thin (Ben-Yehuda, 1992, p. 80).

Discussion

This study focused on the entire life story of the participants in a holistic way rather than on the object matter alone (hacking). The study is a tool for learning the way in which hackers perceive themselves and how they think that others have perceived them since childhood. The bad hackers (also referred to as *crackers*) presented themselves as having a wild and gifted persona, whereas the good hackers reported having good behavior since childhood. The present study advances understanding by showing that hackers base their current hacking practices (good or bad, authorized or not) on the way in which they perceive themselves and on their notion of how others have perceived them since childhood (good vs. wild and gifted).

This analysis advances knowledge on the differences between those hackers who practiced unauthorized penetration to computer networks and those who do not. As a social identity, the process of becoming a hacker could, therefore, be seen as a socially negotiated passage from primary to secondary deviance (Lemert, 1951). Cooley (1902) said that individuals' feelings about themselves are products of their relationships with others that have affected them since early childhood. This study has shown the importance of the informal early labeling of deviant individuals in addition to the formal labeling process.

Yet a process of social learning must take place in a context of social interaction to commit a computer illegal act (Skinner & Fream, 1997). The social construction of reality among hackers results from a process in which "the person develops a new conception of the nature of the object" (Becker, 1953, p. 242). Generally, the process of becoming a hacker is reminiscent of the process that individuals undergo to become capable of using marijuana for pleasure (see, e.g., the process described in Becker's [1953] article titled

"Becoming a Marihuana User"). Becker's research challenged the theories that attribute past behavior or early personality traits to the smoking of marijuana. The Analyzer said on a talk show, "Hacking is not something in your personality; it's a hobby." Not all those who possess the technical knowledge to hack have learned the "fun" of break-in; therefore, they refrain from doing it.

Although shame is a key element in the labeling process (Hayes, 2000), the present study shows that hackers feel no shame, and this applies both for good and bad hackers. Even their crossing over to lawfulness is external and structural. They hold respectable positions, in most cases owing precisely to their hacking abilities, and none of them profess any guilty feelings about their former hacking activities. Indeed, the "possible relevance of labeling theory to behaviors that are not highly visible or easily stigmatized challenges social scientists to discover how, if at all, labeling theory evokes social definitions of deviance and illuminates self-definition and feelings of potentially stigmatized individuals" (Hayes, 2000, p. 29).

Hackers construct themselves as positive deviants. They do so by portraying themselves as "extraordinary people" who are smarter than others, display unusual or superior behavior or a trait that is rewarded as such (Heckert, 1989), or see themselves as agents of social change (Ben-Yehuda, 1990). The manner in which hackers construct themselves as positive deviants likely is based partly on the historical change in the connotation of the hacker label but also on the hackers' backgrounds. Hackers come from the established stratum of society, and social status mediates stigma differentially (Riessman, 2000). Furthermore, hackers contend that deviance constitutes a challenge to social conventions, leading to a legitimate debate about moral boundaries. As Bar says, "If there is a software that can make someone in the world do something good, why should he be deprived of it?" Perhaps this is why it is difficult to view them as criminals in the negative sense (Weisburd, Waring, & Chayat, 2001).

This finding—that all the respondents portray themselves as technological wizards and breakers of boundaries, regardless of the number and severity of the computer offenses they had committed—is very intriguing and shows that hackers view the "computer expert" label as that of "master status" (Becker, 1963) rather than "deviant." Gil says, "In my eyes, everything adds up, I mean between playing computer games, and being a Linux hacker, and being a cracker. Actually, all of these acts stem from the same place—the will to learn, to know, and the good feeling and satisfaction that this knowledge gives me." Future research could benefit from following quantity examination of the sociological differences between computer deviants and nondeviants.

Some of the limitations of the present study can be addressed in the future. The study was carried out in Israel years ago. Voiskounsky and Smyslova (2003, p. 173) claimed that hacking is a universal activity, showing few (if any) differences. The Israeli hackers' characteristics seem to be similar to those of hackers in other Western societies. For example, Kevin Mitnick, perhaps the most famous hacker, also describes his desire and ability to learn and discover going back to his childhood (Mitnick & Simon, 2002). Holt (2007) found that a hacker's identity is built on knowledge and the devotion to learn. Although the nature of cybercrime is constantly changing, the basic characteristics of the hacker, such as the not-for-profit motivation, persist and are similar to those described in the present chapter. Woo, Kim, and Dominick (2004) found that 70% of the web defacements by hackers were pranks, whereas the rest had more political motives. We frequently hear cover stories of hackers who attack computer sites for ideological reasons. Recently, for example, Russian hackers have been attacking Georgian websites, and another hacker used a Trojan horse to hack into the computers of Bloomsbury Publishing to discover text of the latest *Harry Potter* book before its publication.

Conclusion

The present study shows that hackers, who are not easily stigmatized, succeed in avoiding the effects of labeling and manage to avoid secondary deviance. Contrary to labeling theory, their self-conception does not change for the worse (if anything, it changes for the better), and their life chances in the domain of employment do not decrease (if anything, they increase). This particular kind of deviance illustrates that the labeling process is more complex than its portrayal in labeling theory and requires further inquiry. Of special interest are the conditions under which the process takes place and the directions that it can take. Hacking, for example, seems to be a type of deviance in which the labeling process works in the reverse direction.

References

Arluke, A. (2002). Animal abuse as dirty play. *Symbolic Interaction, 25,* 405–430.

Becker, G. (1978). *The mad genius controversy.* London, England: Sage.

Becker, H. (1953). Becoming a marihuana user. *American Journal of Sociology, 59,* 235–242.

Becker, H. (1963). *Outsiders.* Glencoe, IL: Free Press.

Ben-Yehuda, N. (1990). Positive and negative deviance: More fuel for a controversy. *Deviant Behavior, 11,* 221–243.

Ben-Yehuda, N. (1992). Criminalization and deviantization as properties of the social order. *Sociological Review, 40,* 73–108.

Blumer, H. (1969). *Symbolic interactionism.* Englewood Cliffs, NJ: Prentice-Hall.

Bourdieu, P. (1986). The forms of capital. In J. G. Richardson (Ed.), *Handbook of theory and research in the sociology of education* (pp. 241–258). New York, NY: Greenwald Press.

Brown, J. D. (1991). The professional ex-: An alternative for exiting the deviant career. *Sociological Quarterly, 32,* 219–230.

Chandler, A. (1996). The changing definition and image of hackers in popular discourse. *International Journal of the Sociology of Law, 24,* 229–251.

Charmaz, K. (1990). Discovering chronic illness: Using grounded theory. *Social Science and Medicine, 30,* 1161–1172.

Charmaz, K. (1994). Identity dilemmas of chronically ill men. *Sociological Quarterly, 35,* 269–288.

Charmaz, K. (2000). Grounded theory: Objectivist and constructivist methods. In N. K. Denzin & Y. S. Lincoln (Eds.), *Handbook of qualitative research* (pp. 509–536). Thousand Oaks, CA: Sage.

Coleman, E. G., & Golub, A. (2008). Hacker practice: Moral genres and the cultural articulation of liberalism. *Anthropological Theory, 8,* 255–277.

Cooley, C. H. (1902). *Human nature and the social order.* New York, NY: Scribner.

Davies, S., & Tanner, J. (2003). The long arm of the law: Effects of labeling on employment. *The Sociological Quarterly, 44,* 385–404.

Dodge, D. L. (1985). The over-negativized conceptualization of deviance: A programmatic exploration. *Deviant Behavior, 6,* 17–37.

Dror, Y. (2001, April 24). Is it an expression of opinion or slander? *Ha'aretz,* p. 6.

Fine, G. A. (1986). The dirty play of little boys. *Society, 24,* 63–67.

Fine, G. A. (1993). The sad demise, mysterious disappearance, and glorious triumph of symbolic interactions. *Annual Review of Sociology, 19,* 61–87.

Geertz, C. (1973). *The interpretation of cultures.* New York, NY: Basic Books.

Goode, E. (1991). Positive deviance: A viable concept? *Deviant Behavior, 12,* 289–309.

Gordon, L. A., Loeb, M. P., Lucyshyn, W., & Richardson, R. (2006). *CSI/FBI computer crime and security survey.* Retrieved from http://i.cmpnet.com/gocsi/db_area/pdfs/fbi/FBI2006.pdf

Halbert, D. (1997). Discourses of danger and the computer hacker. *The Information Society, 13,* 361–374.

Hannemyr, G. (1999). Technology and pleasure: Considering hacking constructive. *FirstMonday, 4*(2). Retrieved from http://firstmonday.org/htbin/cgiwrap/bin/ojs/index.php/fm/issue/view/102

Hayes, T. A. (2000). Stigmatizing indebtedness: Implications for labeling theory. *Symbolic Interaction, 23,* 29–46.

Heckert, D. M. (1989). The relativity of positive deviance: The case of the French impressionists. *Deviant Behavior, 10,* 131–144.

Hollinger, R. C. (1988). Computer hackers follow a Guttman-like progression. *Sociology and Social Research, 72,* 199–200.

Hollinger, R. C. (1991). Hackers: Computer heroes or electronic highwaymen? *Computers and Society, 21,* 6–17.

Hollinger, R. C. (1993). Crime by computer: Correlates of software piracy and unauthorized account access. *Security Journal, 4,* 2–12.

Holt, T. J. (2007). Subcultural evolution? Examining the influence of on- and off-line experiences on deviant subcultures. *Deviant Behavior, 28,* 171–198.

Jordan, T., & Taylor, P. (1998). A sociology of hackers. *Sociological Review, 46,* 757–780.

Jordan, T., & Taylor, P. (2004). *Hacktivism and cyberwars: Rebels with a cause?* London, England: Routledge.

Katz, J. (1988). *Seductions of crime.* New York, NY: Basic Books.

Kusow, A. M. (2004). Contesting stigma: On Goffman's assumptions of normative order. *Symbolic Interaction, 27,* 179–197.

Lemert, E. W. (1951). *Social pathology.* New York, NY: McGraw-Hill.

Levy, S. (1984). *Hackers.* Harmondsworth, England: Penguin.

Ljungberg, J. (2000). Open source movements as a model for organising. *European Journal of Information Systems, 9,* 208–216.

Lieblich, A., Tuval-Mashiach, R., & Zilber, T. (1998). *Narrative research: Reading, analysis, and interpretation.* Thousand Oaks, CA: Sage.

Meyer, G., & Thomas, J. (1990). The baudy world of the byte bandit: A postmodernist interpretation of the computer underground. In F. Schmalleger (Ed.), *Computers in criminal justice* (pp. 31–67). Bristol, IN: Wyndham Hall.

Mitnick, K., & Simon, W. L. (2002). *The art of deception.* Hoboken, NJ: Wiley.

Raymond, E. S. (Ed.). (1991). *The new hacker's dictionary.* Cambridge, MA: MIT Press.

Riessman, C. (2000). Stigma and everyday resistance practices: Childless women in south India. *Gender and Society, 14,* 111–135.

Rogers, M. K., Seigfried, K., & Tidke, K. (2006). Self-reported computer criminal behavior: A psychological analysis. *Digital Investigation, 3,* 116–120.

Rogers, M., Smoak, N. D., & Liu, J., (2006). Self-reported deviant computer behavior: A big-5, moral choice, and manipulative exploitive behavior. *Deviant Behavior, 27,* 245–268.

Rosenthal, G., & Bar-On, D. (1992). A biographical case study of a victimizer's daughter's strategy: Pseudo-identification with the victims of the holocaust. *Journal of Narrative and Life History, 2,* 105–127.

Skibell, R. (2002). The myth of the computer hacker. *Information, Security and Society, 5,* 336–356.

Skinner, W. F., & Fream, A. M. (1997). A social learning theory analysis of computer crime among college students. *Journal of Research in Crime and Delinquency, 34,* 495–518.

Sterling, B. (1992). *The hacker crackdown: Law and disorder on the electronic frontier.* London, England: Viking.

Strauss, A. L. (1987). *Qualitative analysis for social scientists.* New York, NY: Cambridge University Press.

Strauss, A. L., & Corbin, J. (1990). *Basics of qualitative research: Grounded theory procedures and techniques.* London, England: Sage.

Strauss, A. L., & Corbin, J. (2000). Grounded theory methodology: An overview. In N. K. Denzin & Y. S. Lincoln (Eds.), *Handbook of qualitative research* (pp. 273–285). Thousand Oaks, CA: Sage.

Stryker, S. (1968). Identity salience and role performance. *Journal of Marriage and the Family, 4,* 558–564.

Stryker, S. (1980). *Symbolic interactionism: A social structural version.* Menlo Park, CA: Benjamin Cummings.

Swann, W. B., Jr., Wenzlaff, R. A., & Tafarodi, R. W. (1992). Depression and the search for negative evaluations: More evidence of the role of self-verification strivings. *Journal of Abnormal Psychology, 101,* 314–317.

Taylor, P. A. (1999). *Hackers: Crime and the digital sublime.* New York, NY: Routledge.

Turgeman-Goldschmidt, O. (2002). *Becoming deviant: The social construction of computer deviants (hackers, crackers, and others).* Unpublished doctoral dissertation, Hebrew University of Jerusalem, Jerusalem, Israel.

Turgeman-Goldschmidt, O. (2005). Hackers' accounts: Hacking as a social entertainment. *Social Science Computer Review, 23,* 8–23.

Voiskounsky, A. E., & Smyslova, O. V. (2003). Flow-based model of computer hackers' motivation. *CyberPsychology & Behavior, 6,* 171–180.

Wall, D. S. (Ed.). (2001). *Crime and the Internet.* London, England: Routledge.

Weisburd, D., Waring, E., & Chayat, E. (2001). *White-collar crime and criminal careers.* Cambridge, England: Cambridge University Press.

Woo, H.-J., Kim, Y., & Dominick, J. (2004). Hackers: Militants or merry pranksters? A content analysis of defaced web pages. *Media Psychology, 6*(1), 63–82.

Yar, M. (2005). Computer hacking: Just another case of juvenile delinquency? *Howard Journal of Criminal Justice, 44,* 387–399.

Zetter, K. (2008). Israeli hacker "The Analyzer" suspected of hacking again. *Wired.* Retreived from http://www.wired.com/threatlevel/2008/09/the-analyzer-su

Virtual Sex Offenders
A Clinical Perspective

4

KIMBERLY YOUNG

Contents

Introduction

Statistics show a sharp rise in the number of sexual predators who prowl the Internet looking for vulnerable children, then make arrangements to meet the child for sex (Andrews, 2000). The Federal Bureau of Investigation (FBI) calls these criminals *travelers*. The numbers are hard to document, but travelers are clearly part of the Internet-era crime wave. According to a CBS News report, the FBI alone opens up six new traveler investigations every week (Andrews, 2000). This same report indicated that the Center for Missing and Exploited Children receives about 15 new leads about online enticements each week, and a traveler is arrested somewhere in the United States almost every day. A disturbing number of recent traveler cases involve men who are first-time offenders with no criminal history of sexual activity toward minors. Some high-profile cases include Patrick Naughton, a top executive at Infoseek/Go.com; Terry Spontarelli, a Los Alamos research chemist; and George DeBier, a former Belgian diplomat (Andrews, 2000). Their profiles were similar: men who held upper-income jobs and were otherwise law-abiding citizens but who were arrested for traveling to meet an undercover agent posing as a minor on the Internet.

Chat rooms exist in cyberspace with names such as "Daddy4daughter," "Men for Barely Legal Girls," and "Family Fun." Although these are branded as "fantasy only" chat rooms and require participants to be over the age of 18, it is difficult to decipher what is fact and what is fantasy, based on the chat dialogues in such pedophilic virtual communities (Treibcock, 1997). It is unclear from the discussion whether users are describing fictional stories, sexual fantasies, stories about past activities, or plans for the future (Lanning, 1998). Given the lack of restrictions in cyberspace and its sexual subculture, predators have a new medium in which to not only pursue potential contacts with children but also unite and unionize with fellow users in a way that allows them to validate and normalize their sexual proclivities (Lanning, 1998).

Psychologists have begun to question how the anonymous availability of child-oriented sexual material not only creates an ideal breeding ground for pedophiles but also opens up a Pandora's box for unsuspecting users (Farella, 2002). Unlike in the physical world, conventional messages about sexual behavior are ignored in cyberspace. Users are free to explore pedophilic themes within the sexually uninhibited environment of the Internet. In this way, cyberspace becomes an enabler, allowing users to create personalized content without any limitations and thus providing them with an outlet to explore sexually deviant online behavior.

Internet Sexuality

Early studies of Internet sexuality, or *cyber sex*, emphasized the fantasy nature of online sexuality and focused on use of the Internet for criminal and deviant behavior (Durkin & Bryant, 1995). They distinguished various motivations for erotic computer communication, from mild flirtations to seeking and sharing information about sexual services to frank discussions of specific deviant sexual behavior. They posited that cyber sex allows a person to operationalize sexual fantasies that would otherwise have self-extinguished if it were not for the reinforcement of immediate feedback provided by online interactions. As the Internet gained in popularity, researchers began to identify similar patterns in the addictive aspects of online communication.

Internet addiction, as it is often called, is a pathological preoccupation with Internet use (Young, 1998). Studies estimate that nearly 6 percent of online users suffer from Internet addiction (Greenfield, 1999), and this addiction can lead to significant occupational, social, familial, and psychological problems (Morahan-Martin, 1997; Scherer, 1997; Young, 1998). In one of the largest studies of online sexuality, Cooper, Scherer, Soies, and Gordon (1999) posted an online survey on the MSNBC website, netting a sample of 9,177 respondents, 86 percent of whom were men. The study found that 8 percent of users showed signs of sexually compulsive online behavior and that among both men and women, "the most powerful and potentially problematic" interactions happened in online chat rooms.

According to the study, this "seems to corroborate an association of sexually compulsive or addictive behavior with social isolation" (p. 35). Young (2004) consistently found that online sexual compulsives became increasingly socially isolated as they retreated into a sexual fantasy world inside the computer. The majority of these cases involved previously law-abiding men who had no history of sexual addiction and no history of renting adult movies, visiting strip clubs, or collecting pornography, but their sole problem with sex stemmed from using the Internet.

A user can explore darker parts of their sexuality using the anonymous and limitless context of the Internet, changing his or her name, age, occupation, or physical description. A woman can pretend to be lesbian online, or a middle-aged man can pretend to be a hot young stud when talking to women in an online chat room. Young (2001) referred to these individuals as *fantasy users*—that is, individuals who use online chat rooms and instant messaging for the express purpose of role playing in online fantasy sex chat. Fantasy users often progressed into dialogue that was sexually more explicit—a novelty created through cyberspace—and within the anonymous context of these virtual environments, these fantasy users gradually experimented with more obscene types of chat. Fantasy users hid their online interactions from others and, despite feelings of guilt or shame, continued to engage in such acts. Most important, fantasy users dissociated from what they did or said online and often expressed that their online fantasies did not represent what they wanted in real life.

In one noted example, Donald Marks, the attorney for Patrick Naughton, won a hung jury in the case, arguing that Naughton was only playing out a fantasy and that he never would have acted upon that fantasy had it not been for the Internet (Andrews, 2000). The *fantasy defense*, as it is often called, directly questions the addictive nature of online adult fantasy sex chat rooms and their ability to enable users to develop an unhealthy obsession with the Internet.

Despite its success, the fantasy defense has sparked a heated debate in both the legal and psychiatric communities, and little has been discussed in the literature to explain how "fantasy" online users develop a sexual interest in children using the Internet. On the basis of a case study analysis, this chapter examines the psychological perspective of online sex offenders and the role of cyberspace in the development of deviant behavior. Specifically, this chapter profiles how these "fantasy" online users can be assessed from an addiction perspective and—using Young's (2001) five-stage model to explain the development of online sexually compulsivity—examines how fantasy users progress to sexually deviant behavior online involving adult–child fantasies.

A Case Study Methodology

The cases involved 22 clients seen through the Center for Online Addiction, which was established in 1995 and provides education, support, and treatment to those concerned about Internet addiction. The Center for Online Addiction also provides diagnostic and forensic evaluations of Internet addiction; these evaluations are conducted by me. In all 22 cases, the clients were men arrested for engaging in sexual misconduct with a minor using the Internet. In each case, this was a first offense, and the client had no previous criminal record or sexual history involving children.

Clients ranged in age from 34 to 48 ($M = 38$). Fifty-eight percent were employed in white-collar professional work (often engineers, doctors, or lawyers), 17 percent were blue-collar workers (often working in factories or in manufacturing), 15 percent were unemployed, and 10 percent were on disability. In 10 cases, extensive collections of pornographic images downloaded from the Internet were found; in three cases, the images contained child pornography; and, in one case, the client had a longstanding history of meeting women on the Internet for sex. At the time of arrest, 47 percent of the clients suffered from depression or anxiety, 39 percent had a history of alcoholism or drug dependence, 19 percent had a history of sex addiction, and 10 percent had a history of sexual abuse.

In all cases, clients engaged in pedophilic-themed adult chat rooms, unknowingly chatting with a federal agent or police officer posing online as a minor. The undercover agent established an online persona of a prepubescent girl or boy, and online conversations led to an arranged meeting in person. In 10 of the cases, clients arrived at the designated meeting place but, when spotting the police decoy (someone posing as a minor), made no attempt to approach the minor and were arrested at the scene. In nine cases, clients were arrested immediately upon arrival at the designated meeting place. In two cases, the client never showed up at the arranged meeting time and was arrested at home for attempting to engage in sexual misconduct with a minor over the Internet. In one case, the client sat down with the police decoy and was then arrested.

Online behavior patterns were analyzed in each case through the use of clinical interview and available discovery materials such as psychological reports, progress notes from therapists who were currently treating the individual, presentencing reports, warrants or affidavits by investigators, and transcripts of chat room dialogues. Clients were also administered the *Internet Addiction Scale* developed by Young (1998), an eight-item questionnaire that examines the symptoms of Internet addiction—such as a user's preoccupation with Internet use, ability to control online use, extent of fantasizing when online, and continued online use despite its potential consequences. This screening instrument modified the *Diagnostic and Statistical Manual of*

Mental Disorders–Fourth Edition (DSM-IV) criteria for Pathological Gambling and evaluated a client's nonessential computer or Internet usage (i.e., non-business or academically related use). Clients were considered addicted users when answering "yes" to five (or more) of the questions over a 6-month period, when not better accounted for by a manic episode (Young, 1998).

Results

In all 22 cases, clients met the basic criteria of Internet addiction. Similar to an alcoholic who consumes greater levels of alcohol in order to achieve satisfaction, clients routinely spent increasingly significant amounts of time online. Clients went to great lengths to mask the nature of their online activities, primarily to conceal the extent and nature of the behavior. In most cases of impulse-control disorder, an individual's compulsion is often associated with increasingly painful states of tension and agitation, which are relieved through completion of the act. For example, an alcoholic is often driven to drink at moments of excessive stress, or an overeater is often driven to binge on food during moments of tension. The compulsive behavior serves to reduce underlying emotional tension and serves as a reward for future behavior. Similarly, clients reported finding that they turned to the computer to find relief from moments of mental tension and agitation present in their lives. That is, their computer use was less about using it as an informational tool and more about finding a psychological escape to cope with life's problems.

The Addiction Perspective

Unlike classic child sex offenders who exhibit chronic and persistent patterns of sexualized behavior toward children that typically begins in early adolescence (Salter, 2003), each of the 22 cases involved first-time offenders with no previous history of sexual activity toward children. Their offenses seemed entirely related to online sexual fantasy role-play rooms. Based on Young's (2001) addiction model, fantasy users follow five stages of development: discovery, exploration, escalation, compulsion, and hopelessness or regret. The stages are interdependent and highlight how users utilize the Internet as a progressive means of escape as part of an addiction cycle. Through the use of Young's model to analyze the case studies, each stage is described in more detail to discuss user behavior from an addiction perspective.

Discovery

In the discovery stage, users come to the initial realization that adult websites and sexually explicit chat rooms exist and are available on the Internet. A man doing research online may accidentally bump into a pornographic website, or a woman enters a social chat room and meets a man who entices her to "talk dirty" with him. In either case, the person discovers the sexual thrill of the act, which opens the door for further exploration.

Many Internet Service Providers (ISPs) permit sexually oriented chat rooms to exist with names that clearly indicate the types of sexual practices that will be discussed by the participants. Those practices range from the most ordinary to the most deviant. In all 22 cases, clients began as fantasy users, engaging in erotic dialogue in sexually oriented chat rooms often known as *cyber sex*, in which two online users privately exchange discourse about sexual fantasies, and the act may be accompanied by sexual self-stimulation. Online chat sex or cyber sex allows two users to co-create an online erotic fantasy typically tailored to each one's desires—and, in many cases, the assumptions for what is desired are made based on the nature of the other person's handle and the chat room description. It is not uncommon to find pedophilic chat room themes such as "Want F Under 15," "Daddy4daughter," "Family Fun" and "Barely Legal" that freely allow users to exchange fantasies related to sexual themes that involve adult-child interactions.

For clients, the fantasy theme began and progressed as a novelty created through cyberspace chat rooms and their anonymous availability. Jack was a 48-year-old senior executive at an engineering firm near Palo Alto, California. He was highly educated and spent long hours with his team researching new product designs. Late at night, in his office alone while doing research on the web for work, he discovered Naughty Chat, an adult site. "I was instantly curious," he said. "I didn't think it would lead to anything serious until the police arrived at my office." Jack had been arrested for sexual misconduct with a minor.

Exploration

In the exploration stage, the user may begin to experiment, exploring new websites such as pornography or gambling sites, or they may enter a chat room for the very first time. Whatever the behavior, for the person who becomes addicted, it is usually something new and tempting—and it is usually not something that they would have tried if they thought someone was watching.

In Jack's case, once he discovered Naughty Chat, he started to use the Internet to search for other adult websites.

> I did it a couple of hours a week at first, then it escalated to more. I started to stay late at work and coming in on the weekends just to look at porn. I hated myself. I became bored [with] pornography and started chatting with other women. We had phone sex, some showed me their webcams, and they would be naked and some even masturbated for me.

Many individuals secretly begin to experiment online without the fear of being caught (Young & Klausing, 2007). They feel encouraged by the acceptance of the cyberspace culture, especially when cloaked behind the anonymity of the computer screen, and many feel less accountable for their actions over the Internet. Within the anonymous context of cyberspace, conventional messages about sex are eliminated, allowing users to play out hidden or repressed sexual fantasies in a private lab. Furthermore, online experiences often occur in the privacy of one's home, office, or bedroom, facilitating the perception of anonymity and that Internet use is personal and untraceable. For anyone who has ever been curious about a particular hidden or deviant fantasy, cyberspace offers an anonymous way to explore and indulge in those fantasies.

Escalation

In the escalation stage, the behavior escalates as users feel that they have to look for new pornography every time they are online, they have to make another bet at a virtual casino, or they have to enter the chat room and see who else is online. They cross a line from using the Internet as a productive tool to developing a recurrent habit. The user feels compelled to go online, feeling more obsessed with being online, and the behavior becomes more ingrained and ritualistic. They enjoy particular sites, and they establish online relationships with a regular set of fellow users with whom they have cyber sex, have phone sex, or meet for in-person sex.

Jack started surfing chat sites looking for women. He describes his experience:

> It was so erotic, hearing about their wildest fantasies, things I never thought of. I told myself it was harmless. I rationalized lying to my wife about needing to work late, and I started missing deadlines at work, but after 20 years of marriage, it [was] exciting to rekindle something about my own sexuality. I played off what these women said. It was all just a fantasy. They were all ages and backgrounds. I felt like a virtual playboy, but it all seemed okay—as long as it was only online, it didn't seem wrong.

The risk of experimenting in sexually deviant online fantasies is that the virtual sex offender begins to distort what "normal sex" is. One participant described it as follows:

> I masturbate nightly to nasty and kinky online pornography. What turns me on the most is the "devious" aspects of viewing otherwise inaccessible photos, such as naked teens, water sports, and scat pictures. Now, sex with my wife seems so dull in comparison. When I do have sex with my wife, I am always fantasizing about the pictures I recently saw from the web. This is destroying

my marriage. We are now sleeping in separate beds, and I am alone all night with my computer instead of her. I know this is sick. I want to quit doing this, but I just feel too weak to stop.

Similar to how the alcoholic requires larger and larger doses of the drug to achieve the same sensation and pleasure from the experience, the virtual sex offender becomes bored with routine fantasies and starts looking for the next big virtual thrill. In the escalation stage, the behavior becomes more chronic and pronounced such that fantasy users become saturated with a continuous stream of sexual content that can take on riskier and riskier forms. In cases of virtual sex offenders, they begin to engage in pedophilic sexual fantasies and use more graphic online handles such that "John Engineer" becomes "M4Teen," or "Pamela" changes to "Teen Slut."

In order to deal with the double life that occurs, the fantasy user often rationalizes the behavior and disowns what he or she says or does online with self-statements such as, "It's just a computer fantasy" or "This isn't who I really am." They detach from the online sexual experience and perceive their secret fantasy world as a parallel life that is completely separate from whom they are in real life. However, these rationalizations are temporary and eventually break down as the user becomes more and more disgusted by his or her online actions and experiences episodes of despair as promises to stop are broken and attempts to quit fail. Users may also progress into more sexually deviant topics that they normally would find reprehensible, yet over time, these topics become acceptable as the user becomes increasingly desensitized to the experience.

Compulsivity

The habitual behavior becomes more ingrained and develops into a compulsive obsession. In this stage, life becomes unmanageable, as relationships or careers are jeopardized because of the compulsive behavior. In his pioneer book, *Out of the Shadows*, Patrick Carnes (1992) best explains sexual compulsivity:

> The sexual experience is the source of nurturing, focus of energy, and origin of excitement. The experience turns into a relief from pain and anxiety, the reward for success, and a way to avoid addressing other emotional issues in the person's life. The addiction is truly an altered state of consciousness in which "normal" sexual behavior pales by comparison in terms of excitement and relief from troubles that is associated with sex. (p. 142)

Jack often described his online sessions as a "drug high." He felt an altered reality, as if the person who he was online did not overlap with the person he was in real life. It is a common theme among all 22 subjects. They each described their Internet use, whether it involved sex chat rooms or Internet pornography, as a rush or a high that they experienced while online. They felt as though their Internet usage was less about using it as an information tool and more as a form of psychological escape.

In the same way, the fantasy online user's online sexual experience produces an altered state of consciousness that becomes associated with tension reduction, and he or she displays a progressive retreat into the use of the computer as a means to avoid life's complications and responsibilities. In this stage, the fantasy user is driven largely by increasingly painful states of tension and agitation, as an alcoholic is driven to drink at moments of excessive stress or an overeater is driven to binge on food during moments of tension. The fantasy user exhibits addictive patterns as he or she becomes preoccupied with the computer, attempts to conceal the nature of his or her online activities, and continues to engage in the activity despite its known potential risks, including arrest and incarceration. After his arrest, Jack explained:

> [A]fter a while I knew it was wrong; I knew I was bordering on big trouble and for what? My life became a lonely, isolated mess. I realized that I could lose my job, my marriage, and the respect of everyone I love if I was caught. I have two daughters and would never think about doing anything inappropriate with them, but I could not bring myself to stop, despite knowing all the consequences for my actions.

Hopelessness

In the hopelessness stage, the addict hits that metaphorical "rock bottom" only to realize the extent of damage done because of this addiction. Feelings of helplessness develop, especially as the addict becomes fully aware of how out of control life has become. In this stage, the addict realizes the unhealthy excess of the behavior and attempts total abstinence. He or she will often cancel their Internet service, disconnect the modems, or install filtering software in an attempt to stop the compulsive behavior. The addict struggles with staying clean and sober and feels desperate to put his or her life back on track. Considering relapse is only a mouse click away, the addict slips back into his or her old patterns, thus beginning the cycle once again.

Given that the addict lacks proper impulse control, he or she may be more likely to dabble in sexually inappropriate or deviant material, which is easily accessible through the Internet. This is especially troublesome when the addict experiments in pedophilic- and incest-themed chat rooms with names such as "Daddy for Daughter," "Barely Legal Females Wanted," and "Horny Teens for Sex," which abound in cyberspace. Although these sites are branded as "fantasy only" chat rooms, it is difficult to decipher what is fact and what is fantasy, based on the chat dialogues. For instance, when one user entered a pedophilic fantasy role-play room, another user instantly typed, "So what is your pleasure? Do you want me to be your mom, sister, daughter, or aunt?"

For addicts, going into these rooms created feelings of despair—they felt unable to pull away. In these 22 cases, each client described feelings of low self-worth, making statements such as "I hate myself," "I am weak," "I am defective," or "I am disgusting because of my dirty habit." They made repeated attempts at abstinence and experienced repeated incidences of relapse. They cycled in this way for months or years prior to their arrests; in this case, often they are actually hoping to get caught. They see it as a way of relieving themselves from their secret online lives and as way to ultimately stop.

Conclusion

With its proliferation of sexually explicit chat rooms, newsgroups, and websites, the Internet provides an outlet for a curious person's initial exploration, and cyberspace—with its lack of restrictions—creates immediate access to sexually explicit chat rooms considered offensive, including adult–child interests. Most people do not yet realize that there is any risk involved in engaging in online sexual pursuits. Although, in some ways, it may seem like a journey into "foreign territory," online sexual behaviors occur in the familiar and comfortable environment of home or office, thus reducing the feeling of risk and allowing even more adventurous behaviors.

The variety and scope of these computer-enabled fantasies are limitless and still evolving. In the post-Internet era, new chat rooms, new technology, and new online users all help to build new sexual fantasy experiences. From the legal perspective, given the proliferation of sexually explicit content on the Internet, forensic psychologists, law enforcement, and the court system, in general, should consider the role of the Internet and its potential for addiction in the development of inappropriate or deviant online sexual behavior, especially as it relates to pedophilic interests.

Clinical research suggests that deviant sexual fantasies carried out online do not always originate from individuals with a preexisting disposition for deviancy, but cases document how once prosocial citizens will engage in this same behavior. In several legal cases against certain ISPs (e.g., AOL), it has been noted that the ISPs have neglected to monitor chat room activity and failed to respond to public complaints. In cases of child pornography, ISPs often neglect to provide warnings informing subscribers that looking at or downloading these images is a crime in the prevention of these events. It has been argued that in this manner, those ISPs act as "enablers"—similar to those who provide alcohol to an alcoholic—by allowing virtual environments that serve to encourage and validate potentially criminal behavior.

Given the sexual permissiveness of the cyberspace subculture, forensic evaluations should examine conduct that differentiates classic sex offenders from virtual sex offenders, or addicted fantasy users who engage in pedo-philic themes, in the context of how they use the Internet. Specifically, three key variables should be assessed: (a) the chat room theme, (b) handles used, and (c) the level of intimacy and engagement between the alleged predator and the child.

From a clinical perspective, forensic evaluations of virtual sex offenders should also evaluate if the user exhibits symptoms of compulsive Internet use. Does the client demonstrate a significant and regular loss of impulse control? Does the client exhibit a preoccupation with the Internet? Does the client continue to engage in the activity, knowing its potential consequences?

If compulsivity is present, the examination should further evaluate the presence of psychological stress such as marital discord, job dissatisfaction, or health concerns. The more extreme and extensive the stress, the more users will utilize the online world as a means of coping with problems or escaping one's real-life roles and responsibilities. It is also important to assess if the client reports failed attempts at self-regulation and an inability to con-trol online behavior.

Internet addiction and the involvement of otherwise prosocial and law-abiding persons in illegal online sexual behavior with children have distress-ingly been on the rise, as the availability of the Internet has grown. Research has hypothesized that traditional notions about the type of person involved in these illegal online acts frequently do not apply to such Internet use. The goal of this chapter is to document this recently evolving phenomena and to pro-vide insight in relation to it for use by treating professionals, academia, and the general public. New and continued research in the area of online sex offenders will also assist the courts in achieving learned, accurate, and just evaluation of such matters as they become presented with increasing frequency.

References

American Psychiatric Association. (1994). *Diagnostic and statistical manual of mental disorders* (4th ed.). Washington, DC: Author.

Andrews, W. (2000). *How to fight off online predators.* Retrieved from http://www.cbsnews.com/stories/2000/05/19/national/main197288.shtml

Carnes, P. (1992). *Out of the shadows: Understanding sexual addiction.* Hazelden, MN: Hazelden Publishing.

Cooper, A., Scherer, C., Boies, S. C., & Gordon, B. L. (1999). Sexuality on the Internet from sexual exploration to pathological expression. *Professional Psychology: Research and Practice, 30,* 33–52.

Durkin, K. F., & Bryant, C. D. (1995). Log on to sex: Notes on the carnal computer and erotic cyberspace as an emerging research frontier. *Psychological Reports, 16,* 179–200.

Farella, C. (2002). The unthinkable problem of pedophilia. *Nursing Spectrum.* Retrieved from http://community.nursingspectrum.com/magazine/articles. cfm?AID=8291

Greenfield, D. (1999, August). *Internet addiction: Disinhibition, accelerated intimacy, and other theoretical considerations.* Paper presented at the 107th annual meeting of the American Psychological Association, Boston, MA.

Lanning, K. (1998). Cyber pedophiles: A behavioral perspective. *The APSAC Advisor, 11*(1), 2–8.

Morahan-Martin, J. (1997, August). *Incidence and correlates of pathological Internet use.* Paper presented at the 105th annual meeting of the American Psychological Association, Chicago, IL.

Salter, A. (2003). *Pedophiles, rapists, and other sex offenders: Who they are, how they operate, and how we can protect ourselves and our children.* New York, NY: Basic Books.

Scherer, K. (1997). College life online: Healthy and unhealthy Internet use. *Journal of College Development, 38,* 655–665.

Treibcock, B. (1997, April 1). Child molesters on the Internet: Are they in your home? *Redbook,* p. 19.

Young, K. S. (1998). Internet addiction: The emergence of a new clinical disorder. *CyberPsychology and Behavior, 1*(3), 237–244.

Young, K. S. (2001). *Tangled in the web: Understanding cybersex from fantasy to addiction.* Bloomington, IN: Authorhouse.

Young, K. S. (2004). Profiling online sex offenders: A preliminary analysis of 22 cases. *The Journal of Behavioral Profiling, 5,* 1–19.

Young, K., Cooper, A., Griffin-Shelley, E., Buchanan, J., & O'Mara, J. (2000). Cybersex and infidelity online: Implications for evaluation and treatment. *Sexual Addiction and Compulsivity, 7,* 59–74.

Young, K., & Klausing, P. (2007). *Breaking free of the web: Catholics and Internet addiction.* Cincinnati, OH: St. Anthony's Messenger Press.

Self-Reported Internet Child Pornography Consumers

5

A Personality Assessment Using Bandura's Theory of Reciprocal Determinism

KATHRYN C. SEIGFRIED-SPELLAR
RICHARD W. LOVELY
MARCUS K. ROGERS

Contents

Introduction

The Internet is the largest computer network, which allows people from all over the world to communicate and share information on anything and everything. From this description alone, one could expect the exponential impact that the Internet would have on the child pornography tradecraft. With this latest technological advancement in communication, and despite legislative efforts, the underground child pornography industry grew more rapidly than previously experienced after the invention of the printing press or camera (Adler, 2001). In 2006, research suggested that the child pornography industry generated $3 billion annually, with approximately 100,000 websites offering sexualized images of children (Ropelato, 2006). In addition, the number of children involved as participants in pornography has increased from 15% in 1997 to 26% in 2000 (Finkelhor & Ormrod, 2004). Nonetheless, statistics on the actual number of Internet child pornography consumers remain unknown (Taylor & Quayle, 2003).

There is a clear relationship between the Internet and increased consumption of child pornography. According to Morahan-Martin and Schumacher (2000), the Internet may be providing a playground for risky behaviors and lowered inhibitions because of the perceived anonymity and lack of direct, face-to-face interaction in cyberspace. It is easier to engage in controversial behaviors when one feels anonymous and separated from the other parties involved, which in this case includes child victims of sexual abuse. These feelings of deindividuation may weaken a person's "ability to regulate behavior, ... engage in rational, long-term planning, ... and he/she will be less likely to care what others think of his or her behavior" (McKenna & Bargh, 2000, p. 61). Overall, with the Internet creating a cyberspace of deindividuation, it is clear why the number of child pornography consumers has substantially increased as a result of this technological advancement.

In addition, from a sociocultural perspective, the increase in child pornography consumption may be a direct result of the delicate relationship among legislature, the Internet, and the Internet users' personality. According to Bandura (1977), the *theory of reciprocal determinism* states that behavioral, psychological and cognitive, and environmental factors all intermingle and exert bidirectional influences on human nature (see Figure 5.1). In other words, the factors are constantly interacting and affecting one another in multiple directions, and the strength or direction of the influence of each factor depends on the context of each situation (Bandura, 1977, 1994).

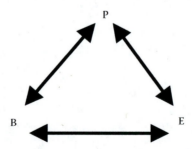

Figure 5.1 The three factors for reciprocal determinism (i.e., P = psychological, B = behavioral, and E = environmental) may interact in different directions with varying degrees of power (Bandura, 1977, 1994).

According to Bandura (1994), people with certain personality traits are attracted to certain types of media content. Research conducted by Williams, Howell, Cooper, Yuille, and Paulhus (2004) applied Bandura's tripartite model to explain why some of their sample of college students used pornography when others did not. The results suggested that those individuals with the subclinical psychopathy personality trait (i.e., the individual meets some but not all diagnostic criteria for psychopathy) were more likely to actively seek out pornographic materials than were those students who did not exhibit the same personality trait (Williams et al., 2004). Overall, the Williams et al. (2004) study successfully applied Bandura's model to non-Internet pornographic materials, for those individuals who chose to engage in pornography use exhibited a different personality characteristic than those individuals who chose not to engage in the same behavior.

In addition, Bandura's theory suggests that "when situational constraints are weak, personal factors serve as the predominant influence in the regulatory system" (1986, p. 24). Currently, there is a significant disconnect between the social and environmental constraints for Internet child pornography. Despite intense legislative efforts at regulating and criminalizing various child pornography behaviors (i.e., high social constraints), the Internet has reached globalization, which has increased the accessibility of child pornography (i.e., weak environmental constraints). As suggested by Bandura's theory, when environmental constraints are weak (e.g., Internet access), the psychological factors of the individual will become extremely important when trying to explain his or her behavior.

Despite the increased availability and accessibility of child pornography, little empirical research has been conducted on those individuals who engage in Internet child pornography consumption. Currently, descriptive analyses tend to focus on the criminal or forensic population of child pornography users (e.g., Alexy, Burgess, & Baker, 2005; Frei, Erenay, Dittmann, & Graf, 2005), which may or may not be a representative sample. In addition, a significant gap exists in the literature regarding the personality and psychological differences between Internet child pornography consumers and nonconsumers (Taylor & Quayle, 2003). Therefore, the purpose of the current study was to investigate the personality and psychological differences between self-reported Internet child pornography consumers and nonconsumers using Bandura's theory of reciprocal determinism.

Current Study

Demographic, personality characteristics, and Internet child pornography use were measured via an anonymous, online survey. In the online survey, we included several questionnaires to operationalize the three factors in

Bandura's tripartite model (i.e., psychological, environmental, and behavioral). However, due to brevity, only the psychological and behavioral factors are discussed in this chapter, for the environmental factor alone would be greater served in a separate but related piece. The psychological factor was measured using the following three self-report questionnaires, which were used previously in studies related to deviant computer behavior (cf. Rogers, Seigfried, & Tidke, 2006; Rogers, Smoak, & Liu, 2006): (1) Goldberg's (1992) modified Five-Factor model, (2) the Moral Decision-Making Scale (MDKS; Rogers, Smoak, & Liu, 2006), and (3) Altemeyer's (1998) Exploitive–Manipulative Amoral Dishonesty (EMAD) scale.

To measure Bandura's behavioral factor, we categorized the respondents as either Internet child pornography consumers or nonconsumers on the basis of their responses to the Online Pornography Survey (OPS). The respondents were identified as Internet child pornography consumers if they self-reported any of the following behaviors involving or featuring individuals under the age of 18 years:

- Knowingly searched for pornographic materials
- Knowingly accessed a website to view pornographic materials
- Knowingly downloaded pornographic materials
- Knowingly exchanged or shared pornographic materials with someone else over the Internet

Those individuals who did not report any of the previous behaviors were labeled as nonconsumers of Internet child pornography.

To develop a possible framework for understanding the personality characteristics of child pornography consumers, research focusing on other deviant computer behaviors was reviewed (cf. Rogers, Smoak, & Liu, 2006). By measuring the psychological and behavioral relationship in Bandura's (1977) theory of reciprocal determinism, the current study theorized that individuals who consume Internet child pornography (i.e., behavioral) differed in their personality characteristics (i.e., psychological) from those individuals who did not use Internet child pornography. On the basis of findings from research studies concerning other forms of deviant online behaviors, the following expectations were based on the relationship between the psychological factor and behavioral aspect (P→B) of Bandura's (1977) model:

- Neurotic individuals are more likely to use child pornography.
- Introverted individuals are more likely to use child pornography.
- Individuals open to experience are more likely to use child pornography.
- Agreeable individuals are less likely to use child pornography.
- Conscientious individuals are less likely to use child pornography.

- Exploitive and manipulative individuals are more likely to use child pornography.
- Individuals with lower moral decision-making scores are more likely to use child pornography.

Method

Participants

Respondents were voluntarily recruited via the Internet by publicizing or advertising the survey using various online resources, such as chat rooms, bulletin boards, and e-mail discussion forums. To take the online survey, the respondents had to indicate that they were 18 years of age or older. Because of missing data for unknown reasons, the number of respondents who completed the individual scales varied for each questionnaire. Four-hundred eighty-two participants completed the demographics questionnaire; 426 participants completed the modified Five-Factor model; 375 participants completed the OPS; 357 participants completed the MDKS (Rogers, Smoak, & Liu, 2006); and 346 respondents completed the EMAD (Altemeyer, 1998). After removing the respondents who did not complete the survey, along with those individuals who left sections uncompleted, we had 307 respondents who completed the online survey.

Of the 307 respondents, 126 were male (41%) and 181 were female (59%), and the majority (79.8%) of respondents self-reported a White racial identity (see Table 5.1). The mean age of the respondents was 34.6 years, with 79.2% of the same under the age of 45 years. Of the respondents, 49.5% were single and never married, whereas 42% were married or in a common-law relationship. Almost half (48.9%) of the respondents were Christian, and 31.9% self-reported that they were agnostic or had no religion. Finally, 80.2% of the respondents had completed some form of college education (i.e., associate, bachelor's, master's, PhD); however, the majority (77.7%) of respondents reported an annual income of $60,000 or less.

Materials

The questionnaires appeared in the following order for all respondents: demographics survey, Big 5 Personality Inventory, OPS, MDKS (Rogers, Smoak, & Liu, 2006), and the EMAD scale (Altemeyer, 1998). The OPS was a modified version of Rogers' (2001) Computer Crime Index (CCI), which measures the frequency and prevalence of self-reported deviant computer behavior. Instead, the OPS identified whether the individual intentionally searched, accessed, downloaded, or exchanged adult, animal, or child pornography images. For the purposes of the current study, only the

Table 5.1 Respondents' Demographics by Group Membership of Child Pornography Use

Variable	Demographic	Frequency (%) CP User	Frequency (%) Non-CP User	Frequency (%) Total
Gender[a]	Female	10 (33.3)	171 (61.7)	181 (59.0)
	Male	20 (66.7)	106 (38.3)	126 (41)
	Total	30 (100)	277 (100)	307 (100)
Age (yrs)	18–25	12 (40.0)	85 (30.7)	97 (31.6)
	26–35	12 (40.0)	85 (30.7)	97 (31.6)
	36–45	3 (10.0)	46 (16.6)	49 (16.0)
	46–55	2 (6.7)	33 (11.9)	35 (11.4)
	56 or older	1 (3.3)	28 (10.1)	29 (9.4)
	Total	30 (100)	277 (100)	307 (100)
Race[b]	White	16 (57.1)	229 (83.9)	245 (81.4)
	Other	12 (42.9)	44 (16.1)	56 (18.6)
	Total	28 (100)	273 (100)	301 (100)
Religion[c]	Either "no religion" or "agnostic"	7 (23.3)	91 (33.2)	98 (32.2)
	Christian	10 (33.3)	140 (51.1)	150 (49.3)
	Other	13 (43.3)	43 (15.7)	56 (18.4)
	Total	30 (100)	274 (100)	304 (100)
Marital status	Single, never married	19 (63.3)	133 (48.2)	152 (49.7)
	Married or common law	9 (30)	120 (43.5)	129 (42.2)
	Separated, divorced, or widowed	2 (6.7)	23 (8.3)	25 (8.2)
	Total	30 (100)	276 (100)	306 (100)
Highest degree of completed education	<HS diploma	1 (3.6)	2 (.7)	3 (1.0)
	GED or HS diploma	4 (14.3)	50 (18.2)	54 (17.8)
	Associate or bachelor's	17 (60.7)	137 (49.3)	154 (50.8)
	Master's or PhD	6 (21.4)	86 (31.3)	92 (30.4)
	Total	28 (100)	275 (100)	303 (100)
Annual income	$0–$20,000	12 (40)	76 (27.6)	88 (28.9)
	$20,001–$40,000	7 (23.3)	74 (26.9)	81 (26.6)
	$40,001–$60,000	3 (10)	65 (23.6)	68 (22.3)
	$60,001–$80,000	3 (10)	22 (8)	25 (8.2)
	$80,001–$100,001	2 (6.7)	18 (6.5)	20 (6.6)
	>$100,001	3 (10)	20 (7.3)	23 (7.5)
	Total	30 (100)	275 (100)	305 (100)

CP, child pornography; yrs, years; HS, high school; GED, General Educational Development; PhD, doctor of philosophy degree.

[a] $X^2(1, N = 307) = 9.02, p < .01.$
[b] $X^2(1, N = 301) = 11.99, p < .01.$
[c] $X^2(2, N = 304) = 13.76, p < .01.$

individuals' use of child pornography images was analyzed. We used the modified version of Goldberg's (1992) Five-Factor model to measure the following traits: extraversion, neuroticism, openness to experience, conscientiousness, and agreeableness. The MDKS (Rogers, Smoak, & Liu, 2006) measured the respondents' moral choice and decision-making tendencies, specifically on the dimensions of social, internal, and hedonistic decisions. Finally, the EMAD scale (Altemeyer, 1998) identified the respondents' level of social dominance in the areas of exploitation, manipulation, and dishonest behavior.

We calculated the Cronbach's alpha to measure the reliability of each scale. The following are the reported Cronbach's alphas for the Big 5 subscales: Extraversion, $\alpha = .86$; Agreeableness, $\alpha = .86$; Conscientiousness, $\alpha = .86$; Neuroticism, $\alpha = .79$; and Openness to Experience (Intellect), $\alpha = .86$. For the EMAD (Altemeyer, 1998) total score, the Cronbach's alpha was .86. The MDKS (Rogers, Smoak, & Liu, 2006) subscales had the following reported Cronbach's alphas: Social, $\alpha = .73$, Internal, $\alpha = .76$, and Hedonistic, $\alpha = .72$. Finally, the OPS yielded a Cronbach's alpha of .91.

Design and Procedure

The study was conducted electronically using an Internet-based survey, which was advertised using various electronic mediums such as chat rooms, bulletin boards, and discussion forums. Once the respondents accessed the website, the home page explained the study while also acting as a consent form to which the respondents had to agree or decline to participate. If the prospective respondents agreed, they were asked to fill out five questionnaires, which took a total of approximately 20 to 30 min to complete.

At no time were the respondents asked for any identifying information (e.g., name). In order to protect their anonymity and confidentiality, we provided the respondents with an ID number, which the database randomly assigned to the their responses. Thus, the responses to the questionnaires could not be linked or matched to any particular participant; it was extremely important to uphold the respondents' anonymity, considering some of the questions involved the admission of criminal activity via the Internet (e.g., exchanging child pornography). The survey items were not forced-choice; instead, the respondents were capable of skipping any question at any time.

Throughout the survey, the word *pornography* was defined by the participant's age in the sexualized images. Specifically, *child pornography* was defined in the OPS as "pornographic materials featuring individuals under the age of 18 years." By defining *child pornography* without the word *child* in the definition, it was thought this would be less inhibiting for the respondents when admitting to criminally sanctioned behaviors. Thus, the word *child* was never mentioned throughout the OPS. After data collection, we conducted statistical analyses to determine whether there were psychological differences between child pornography users and nonusers.

Results

Descriptive Statistics

Of the 307 respondents, 277 (90.2%) were classified as nonusers of child pornography, and 30 (9.8%) were classified as users of child pornography. In other words, nearly 1 out of 10 people are consuming child pornography in this study. As shown in Table 5.1, of the 30 child pornography users, 20 were male and 10 were female. Interestingly, this indicates that there was a 2:1 ratio of men to women who were using child pornography, which amounted to 15.9% of the males and 5.5% of the females.

The descriptive statistics in Table 5.1 indicate that the respondent's gender, religion, and race were correlated with the respondent being classified as either a child pornography user or nonchild pornography user. Of those, the differences in gender and race are notable; however, the religion breakdown is less interpretable given that the "other" category comprised numerous religions. Finally, non-White males were more likely to report the use of Internet child pornography.

Psychological and Behavioral (P→B) Relationship

We conducted independent *t* tests to determine if there was a relationship between any of the psychological factors (the Big 5, MDKS, and the EMAD [Altemeyer, 1998] personality traits) and the behavioral factor (child pornography use). As shown in Table 5.2, the analysis revealed that child pornography users showed significantly higher scores on the EMAD total compared with nonchild pornography users ($M = 80.73$ vs. $M = 63.14$, respectively; $t (305) = -4.15, p < .001$). In addition, child pornography users had lower scores on the Moral Choice Internal Values (IV) total than the nonchild pornography users ($M = 25.73$ vs. $M = 28.90$, respectively; $t(31.56) = 2.54, p < .01$; see Table 5.2).

The remaining psychological traits (moral choice hedonistic values, moral choice social values, extraversion, neuroticism, openness to experience, agreeableness, and conscientiousness) were not significantly related to child pornography use (see Table 5.2). Overall, the analysis suggested that there is a relationship between people's psychological factors (EMAD and Moral Choice IV) and their behavior (child pornography use). Specifically, individuals with higher scores on the exploitive–manipulative amoral dishonesty trait

Table 5.2 *t* Test Results for Psychological Traits and Child Pornography Use

| | M | | | SD | | | |
| | Score | | | SD | | | |
	Non-CP User	CP User	Difference	Non-CP User	CP User	*t*	*p*
EMAD total	63.14	80.73	−17.593	1.323	4.067	−4.152	.00***
Moral Choice							
HED	25.62	25.50	0.121	4.779	6.786	0.095	.92
SV	22.86	20.43	2.426	5.854	7.389	1.740	.09
IV	28.90	25.73	3.169	4.240	6.700	2.536	.01**
Big 5							
Extravert	43.20	43.20	0.002	9.107	13.066	0.001	.99
Neurot	49.03	47.73	0.900	8.078	12.447	0.387	.70
O to E	50.47	50.60	−0.131	7.360	13.158	−0.053	.95
Agree	49.03	47.73	1.292	8.420	13.212	0.524	.60
Conscien	48.29	45.67	2.622	8.396	13.850	1.017	.31

CP, child pornography; EMAD, Exploitive Manipulative Amoral Dishonesty; Moral Choice, Moral Choice Decision Making; HED, Hedonistic Values; SV, Social Values; IV, Internal Values; Big 5, Big 5 Personality Inventory; Extravert, Extraversion; Neurot, Neuroticism; O to E, Openness to Experience; Agree, Agreeableness; Conscien, Conscientiousness.
$t(31.56) = 2.54$, $p < .01$; *$t(305) = -4.15$, $p < .001$

and lower scores on the Moral Choice IV trait were more likely to engage in child pornography use.

Discussion

The purpose of the current study was to answer the following question, "Who are these consumers of Internet child pornography?" The analysis provides valuable information regarding the types of individuals who consume sexualized images of children. The consumption of Internet child pornography is related to whether the individual expressed an exploitive–manipulative personality trait and lower moral choice internal values, which supported our expectations. However, the remaining psychological traits (moral choice hedonistic values, moral choice social values, extraversion, neuroticism, openness to experience, agreeableness, and conscientiousness) are not significantly related to Internet child pornography use. An exploitive–manipulative trait and lower moral choice internal values may be expected because the individuals involved in Internet child pornography are engaging in an illegal activity, and their success depends on their ability to manipulate and exploit various facets within the Internet in order to gain access to the deviant pornographic materials. In addition, the exploitive–manipulative trait is related to other individuals engaging in deviant computer crimes such as hacking (Rogers, Smoak, & Liu, 2006).

Lower moral choice internal values suggest that the consumers of Internet child pornography may not have the same personal and moral compass that nonusers refer to when determining what is "right and wrong." A person's internal values are not determined by society's laws or regulations but are instead a private, moral choice. For instance, drinking alcohol is illegal for individuals that are under an age set by law. Despite the fact that society says it is illegal for people who are younger than the drinking age to consume alcohol, some people make the moral choice that drinking is, nonetheless, "right for me." This moral decision is an example of an individual's internal choice rather than it resulting from society or hedonistic (pleasure-seeking) factors. Thus, Internet child pornography consumers may understand that engaging in this behavior is socially illegal, but they may not believe that it is "wrong" for them personally, compared with non–child pornography users who believe it is morally wrong both at the social and the individual level. Further exploration is needed in order to understand the differences in moral decision-making choices for Internet child pornography users and nonusers.

The survey results also suggest that women may be engaging in Internet child pornography consumption more than was originally suspected in previous literature. Among this sample, 5.5% ($n = 10$) of the women were child pornography users. This is a surprising statistic, as the crime of child pornography has clearly been considered to be a male phenomenon. This finding alone implores the need for future research to gather samples that are not gender biased. Differences between male and female Internet child pornography users should be analyzed to determine if there are any interactions between gender and other psychological, behavioral, and environmental factors.

In addition to gender, both the racial and age characteristics of the study sample vary from previous demographic profiles of Internet child pornography consumers. In particular, the racial background was surprising—only 57.1% of the child pornography consumers were White, whereas 83.9% of the non–child pornography users were White. For instance, the National Center for Missing and Exploited Children's National Juvenile Online Victimization (N-JOV) study noted that 91% of the offenders in their sample were White (Wolak, Finkelhor, & Mitchell, 2005). However, the current study suggests that the use of Internet child pornography for the current study's sampled population may be more racially diverse. In addition, the respondents' ages varied greatly in the current study compared with the N-JOV's study, with 80% of individuals using Internet child pornography being under the age of 35 years compared with only 58% of the N-JOV offenders being under the age of 39 years (Wolak et al., 2005).

Overall, the demographic information gathered in the current study suggests that more research is needed in order to determine if there are any background characteristics common amongs child pornography users. As technology continues to develop and expand, it is likely that the typical consumer of Internet child pornography will continue to change as well. Thus, previous research may have suggested that Internet child pornography was the crime of a "dirty old man." In addition, previous research suggesting that women have a "complete lack of susceptibility to visual 'erotica' or ordinary pornography seems to be the expression of a fundamental difference between the two sexes" (Frei et al., 2005, p. 492). However, this current study suggests otherwise; thus, there is an obvious need for future research to further investigate the modern consumer of child pornography.

Conclusion

Technological advancements clearly have an impact on society; however, one can never be sure of its impact from a global perspective. For instance, the Internet clearly has the ability to facilitate a better, more connected world and yet at the same time produce massive isolation and deindividuation. Although it was never intended, the Internet has become the modern-day playground for creating and collecting sexualized images of children because of the perceived anonymity and "cloak of safety" offered to each Internet user. As the environmental constraints of child pornography remain weak, a thorough understanding of the personality and psychological differences between users and nonusers of child pornography has never been more important. However, empirical research must continue if a statement is to be made about the relationship between personality characteristics and Internet child pornography use. It is important to understand the individuals who consume Internet child pornography, as this knowledge will assist therapeutic treatment strategies while aiding law enforcement in serious criminal investigations. Child pornography consumption over the Internet is likely to continue increasing—and unless researchers decide to make this area of study a priority, society's knowledge and ability to understand the relationship between this crime and technology will remain stagnant and lost in the web of cyberspace.

Limitations

The current study is not without limitations. First, the sample was not randomly chosen from an Internet population; thus, there is no claim that it is representative of the population of Internet users at large. In addition, there may be individual differences between those individuals who chose to answer the survey completely or at all versus those who did not. The respondents obviously were willing to take the time to answer the questionnaires, so there may be a "volunteer bias." In addition, it was impossible to validate any of the demographic information. Essentially, some respondents could have misrepresented themselves by incorrectly responding to the items in a way that distorted their true characteristics or behavior. Of course, the same problem presents itself in any anonymous, hard-copy survey of deviant behavior. However, one of the clear advantages to conducting research via the Internet for this population is the fact that the behavior in question is criminally sanctioned; thus, it is extremely important to provide anonymity and confidentiality to these respondents if honesty is what the researcher desires. The method used for this study provided an effective cloak of safety, privacy, and anonymity for respondents, which allowed them to be open and honest about their experiences in engaging in deviant and/or illegal behavior.

Despite these limitations, conducting research via the Internet provides researchers with the opportunity to investigate active users of child pornography within their own environment. Rather than a forensic or therapeutic setting, this sample is the first to provide extensive information about those individuals who use the Internet in a deviant manner for child pornography while the person remains in his or her cyberspace atmosphere. Future psychological research conducted over the Internet in the area of child pornography is possible and should continue, as there are an unlimited number of respondents in the realm of cyberspace, all having the ability to provide psychological, environmental, and behavioral information.

References

Adler, A. (2001). The perverse law of child pornography. *Columbia Law Review, 101*, 209–273.

Alexy, E., Burgess, A., & Baker, T. (2005). Internet offenders: Traders, travelers, and combination trader–travelers. *Journal of Interpersonal Violence, 20*, 804–812.

Altemeyer, B. (1998). The other 'authoritarian personality.' In M. Zanna (Ed.), *Advances in experimental social psychology* (Vol. 30, pp. 47–92). San Diego, CA: Academic Press.

Bandura, A. (1977). *Social learning theory*. Englewood Cliffs, NJ: Prentice-Hall.

Bandura, A. (1986). *Social foundations of thought and action: A social cognitive*. Englewood Cliffs, NJ: Prentice-Hall.

Bandura, A. (1994). Social cognitive theory of mass communication. In J. Bryant & D. Zillmann (Eds.), *Media effects: Advances in theory and research* (pp. 61–90). Hillsdale, NJ: Erlbaum.

Finkelhor, D., & Ormrod, R. (2004, December). Child pornography: Patterns from NIBRS. *Juvenile Justice Bulletin*. Washington, DC: U.S. Department of Justice.

Frei, A., Erenay, N., Dittmann, V., & Graf, M. (2005). Paedophilia on the Internet—A study of 33 convicted offenders in the Canton of Lucerne. *Swiss Medical Weekly*, *135*, 488–494.

Goldberg, L. (1992). The development of markers for the big-five factor structure. *Psychology Assessment*, *4*, 26–42.

McKenna, K., & Bargh, J. (2000). Plan 9 from cyberspace: The implications of the Internet for personality and social psychology. *Personality and Social Psychology Review*, *4*, 57–75.

Morahan-Martin, J., & Schumacher, P. (2000). Incidence and correlates of pathological Internet use among college students. *Computers in Human Behaviour*, *16*, 13–29.

Rogers, M. (2001). *A social learning theory and moral disengagement analysis of criminal computer behavior: An exploratory study* (Unpublished doctoral dissertation). University of Manitoba, Winnipeg, Manitoba, Canada.

Rogers, M., Seigfried, K., & Tidke, K. (2006). Self-reported computer criminal behavior: A psychological analysis. *Digital Investigation*, *3*, 116–120.

Rogers, M., Smoak, N., & Liu, J. (2006). Self-reported computer criminal behavior: A big-5, moral choice and manipulative exploitive behavior analysis. *Deviant Behavior*, *27*, 1–24.

Ropelato, J. (2006). *Internet pornography statistics*. Retrieved from http://internet-filter-review.toptenreviews.com/internet-pornography-statistics.html

Taylor, M., & Quayle, E. (2003). *Child pornography: An Internet crime*. New York, NY: Brunner-Routledge.

Williams, K., Howell, T., Cooper, B., Yuille, J., & Paulhus, D. (2004, May). *Deviant sexual thoughts and behaviors: The roles of personality and pornography use*. Poster sessions presented at the 16th Annual Meeting of the American Psychology Society, Chicago, IL.

Wolak, J., Finkelhor, D., & Mitchell, K. J. (2005). *Child pornography possessors arrested in Internet-related crimes: Findings from the National Juvenile Online Victimization Study*. Alexandria: VA: National Center for Missing & Exploited Children. Retrieved from http://www.missingkids.com/en_US/publications/NC144.pdf

Online Social Networking and Pedophilia
An Experimental Research "Sting"

6

RODERIC BROADHURST
KASUN JAYAWARDENA

Contents

Introduction

The online exploitation of children is no longer a novelty or a risk that can be addressed by exposé alone. This form of exploitation is also not confined to sexual abuse, although such cases have attracted the most alarm. It is predicted that various forms of commercial exploitation will become so ubiquitous that measures such as the Australian government's $189 million NetAlert (Australian Government, 2007; Salek, 2007) National Filtering Scheme for libraries and households and other screening or monitoring systems will be essential, even though they may offer less protection than hoped (Minow, 2004). Although child pornography is now more or less universally outlawed,[1] it may be still be viewed by thousands via the Internet (Grabosky, 2007) and will continue to generate demand for young victims. This chapter provides an initial exploration of the role that Web 2.0 network technology may play in providing access to underage victims who may be vulnerable to online sexual predators.

Fears about the potential risks of the Internet, especially for children, have been long held within society. However, the advent and rapid uptake of websites such as MySpace (http://www.myspace.com) and Facebook (http://www.facebook.com) have added to these fears (Pascu, Osimo, Ulbrich, Turlea, & Burgelman, 2007). The fact that the Internet is lawless is now widely acknowledged (Broadhurst, 2006, p. 11).

Without a seamless web of mutual legal assistance and comity between nations, and without public/private partnerships, policing the information superhighway will be impossible and the "frontier" of cyberspace will be as lawless as any wild west.

For example, MySpace administrators found that from among the approximately 180 million profiles on their popular social networking website, more than 29,000 registered U.S. sex offenders had profiles on the site ("MySpace sex offenders," 2007). This presumably excludes those who may have sought to hide their real identities. Facebook.com recently gained attention because personal information about the newly appointed director of the United MI6 was inadvertently disclosed by his wife on her Facebook page ("MI6 boss," 2009). In these circumstances, how can the risks for children be minimized, and what can governments, schools, parents, and the Internet industry do about increasing safety on the information superhighway?

Many studies have been undertaken from the criminological, psychological, and sociological perspective on child abuse and pedophilia. Considerable work has been done to psychologically profile pedophiles, to categorize their behavior, and to characterize both victims and predators (see Goldstein, 1999). A recent focus has been identifying risk factors and responding to media-induced—especially, Internet-driven—moral panics about "stranger danger." Researchers addressing the role of web search engines and logs in promoting sexual crimes found that although sex and pornography were major topics for search engine users, these topics had declined in frequency from about 16.8% of web inquiries in 1997 to less than 4% by 2004 (Spink, Partridge, & Jansen, 2006). However, this reduction may be a result of the evolution of more secure file transfer protocols (FTPs) such as Bittorrent

---

[1] However, not all jurisdictions share the same age definitions, and variations occur in the age of sexual consent (e.g., in Japan, the age of consent for sexual activity is 13 years). It remains legal to possess child pornography, although Article 7 of the 1999 Laws for Punishing Acts Related to Child Prostitution and Child Pornography, and for Protecting Children prohibits distribution, sale, rental, or display (see http://www.interpol.int/Public/Children/SexualAbuse/NationalLaws/csaJapan.asp).

(www.bittorrent.com). These FTPs enable users to search for legal or illegal content files and download these files from decentralized networks of users. The present state of research, however, does not allow certainty as to whether the abrupt decline noted previously was due to such FTPs or, rather, to other causes such as the rapid uptake of Internet use by a broader and older demographic. Willingness to visit such sites also may be exaggerated. Spink et al. (2006) cite Bogaert (2001), who reports a number of studies exploring what sort of sexually explicitly material male students (undergraduates) choose to see. When given the opportunity, half did not want to see any sexually explicit material, whereas only 4% chose violent pornography and 3% chose child sexual activity.

In many ways, the implications of the Internet for child sexual abuse—both in a real-world context and an online context—have yet to be comprehensively and systematically studied. The increasing commercialization and privatization of the Internet also pose complex regulatory questions, as earlier versions of the "free" Internet are colonized by identity and information miners of all stripes (Sarikakis, 2004). Thus far, researchers have tended to concentrate on identifying various technologies and Internet areas that pedophiles use. Although now dated, Forde and Patterson's (1998) article, *Paedophile Internet Activity*, is a good example. In the article, the authors identified and explored dimensions of online child sexual abuse and exploitation from a technical, law-enforcement viewpoint. They examined pedophile activity online (using websites, newsgroups[2], Internet Relay Chat [IRC] rooms, etc.) to document and analyze ways in which pedophiles use these services to target victims, to publish child pornography, and to network with one another. Although this research was thorough, Forde and Patterson (1998) nevertheless acknowledged that "There is a need for reliable information and competent investigation because a sophisticated level of technological competency was demonstrated by many paedophiles" (p. 1).

Existing research concentrates on the extent and nature of online pedophilia and child abuse, focusing overwhelmingly on the use of certain Internet technologies. An example is Bilstad's (1996) study, which explores the use of newsgroup/bulletin board technologies as a way of publishing obscene material. The study also includes written forms of child pornography. Similarly, a study by Stanley (2002) covers the psychological profiles of at-risk victim groups and pedophiles and explores the methods and technologies used in the solicitation of children. Both studies are useful as guides about the nature

---

[2] *Newsgroups* are discussion groups that utilize Usenet, a worldwide, noncentralized group of services that stores messages and files and forwards their content to other servers on demand. Alt.Sex.Stories is one of many discussion groups within Usenet. Newsgroups are accessed through Newsgroup Readers software, which is designed to access Usenet (see Feather, 1999).

of the problem, but they do not provide direct evidence of how these behaviors are manifested, and they offer no tests (experiments) for theories that explore grooming strategies with "at-risk" children.

Choo's (2009a) policy-oriented literature review of online child grooming aimed to gather "evidence of the extent and nature of the criminal threat and the measures being undertaken by Australia and other countries to deal with this problem" (p. 4). He described the nature of the victims and offenders as well as the technologies and environment of the offenses, and he detailed the response and likely means of prevention. The review noted the importance of social networking sites and the potential role of safety rating systems, website filtering, and education, and it concluded by emphasizing the need for a multidimensional response:

> This should focus on effective coordination and collaborative activities among governments, law enforcement agencies, professionals such as teachers and health workers, and other private organisations. Partnerships between public sector law enforcement and regulators and private sector agencies will continue to be a guiding principle of online child exploitation crime policing in the future. (Choo, 2009a, p. xix)

Choo (2009a) used case studies and other primary sources of information in creating an overall picture of the nature of grooming on social networking platforms but did not apply "real-time" observational methods used here.

Mitchel, Finkelhor, and Wolak's (2001) study goes some way toward bridging this gap. The work is based on a telephone survey of 1,501 American youths ages 10–17 years and explores the "demographic and behavioural characteristics associated with solicitation risk and distress due to solicitation" (p. 3011). The study found that "Nineteen percent of youth who used the Internet regularly were the targets of unwanted sexual solicitation in the last year. Girls, older teens, troubled youth, frequent Internet users, chat room participants, and those who communicated online with strangers were at greater risk" (Mitchel et. al., 2001, p. 3011).

The higher risk for "troubled" youths than "nontroubled" youths has been a focal point for various studies of online child abuse. *Troubled youths* are defined by Mitchel et al. (2001) as follows:

> [A] composite variable that includes items from a negative life events scale (death in the family, moving to a new home, parents divorced or separated, and/or a parent losing a job); from the physical and sexual assault items on a victimisation scale; and a depression scale (≥5 depression symptoms in the past month). (p. 3012)

The authors stress that these risk factors should not be overstated, as 75% of youths who were sexually solicited online were not classified as "troubled."

But one of the inherent flaws in such research is that the respondents may not respond truthfully—especially given the subject matter—and considering that parental consent has to be given for an interview to proceed, children may not admit to having been solicited online due to the sensitivity of the subject. They also may fear that their Internet privileges will be withheld if their parents are alarmed by what their children are disclosing.

Nevertheless, a real risk of victim selection via the routine scanning of social network sites and chat rooms does exist. Dissemination about victims also can occur via private bulletin boards with password control or via highly secure and anonymous content publishing protocols such as Freenet (http://freenetproject.org) and by using cryptography software or steganography techniques (Choo, 2009a, p. 11; Choo, 2009b, p. 2). These technologies of anonymity enable a person to create a false identity, and "it is possible that participants in such bulletin boards or on such websites have never met face to face, and do not know one another" (Grabosky, 2007, p. 6). For example, a recent case involved three men who had never met in person and knew one another only online. All three were convicted in a London court of conspiracy to rape a girl under 16 years of age, based on a discussion in an Internet chat room (Choo & Smith, 2007, p. 4).

Such closed networks are also ideal vectors for both dissemination and sale of child-related sexual exploitation. For example, Operation Cathedral was one of the first major international investigations of child pornography that targeted the Wonderland Club, a network operating in at least 14 nations from Europe to North America to Australia and involving more than 100 offenders. The club periodically rotated servers in order to avoid detection, and access to the system was password protected. The commercialization of child pornography has also led to the involvement of credit card payment processing companies to manage the revenue that is being generated. In 2004, a major investigation called Operation Falcon led to indictments against two companies as well as against a number of individuals (Ashcroft, 2004, as cited in Grabosky, 2007).

The Research Problem

The answer to the difficulties of obtaining useful data about potential risks on the Internet can be partly overcome through application of methods similar to those used by O'Connell (2003) and Demetriou and Silke (2003). In the latter's experimental research, they used a purpose-built website, with real legal and fake illegal/pornographic content, to record and track which areas visitors accessed in order to "determine whether people who visited for the purpose of gaining access to legal material would also attempt to access illegal and/or pornographic material" (Demetriou & Silke, 2003, p. 213). The authors found that about 7% (58) of the 803 persons who had visited the site over an 88-day period attempted to access illegal pornography (although no actual materials were provided). This "sting" is similar to the activities of law enforcement officers in detecting and apprehending pedophiles online.

The necessity of such methods has been upheld by the Australian High Court. The court found in 2002 that the effective investigation of certain crimes such as drug importation needed to use "subterfuge, deceit and the intentional creation of opportunity to commit an offence" (*Ridgeway v. R*, 2002, as cited in Dixon, 2002, p. 6). This decision was reflected in amendments to the Queensland *Criminal Code* in 2003 that criminalized the use of electronic means to solicit or expose a child under 16 years of age to pornographic material. Examples of these "undercover" investigations and the research opportunities inherent in them can be found in Krone's (2005) innovative observation of police sting operations that involved the use of fictitious underage identities within online chat rooms. This strategy enabled him to better understand the strategies and behaviors of Internet pedophiles who attempted to entice children into meeting for sex. Krone's (2005) observational approach provided a method that allowed closer examination of the behavior than is typical in such studies; however, there remains a distance between the researcher and the environment/population being studied as well as restrictions imposed by the demands of a police operation.

O'Connell (2003) also used a sting to explore the methods and strategies used by online pedophiles in grooming and exploiting vulnerable children on the Internet. In a number of chat rooms, she posed as a vulnerable 8-, 10-, or 12-year-old female child (e.g., with characteristics such as social isolation and negative family life). This strategy showed the style of communication between pedophiles and the partial online profiles (whether on social networking platforms, personal websites, or chat room profiles) played an important role in the grooming process. O'Connell's (2003) research demonstrated the complexity of the grooming process, often underplayed in the relevant literature. The transcripts of the chats, for example, effectively illustrate the actual methods, language, and fantasies used by online pedophiles in grooming children. Understanding the grooming process enables practical advice to be given to caregivers, children, and law enforcement organizations regarding prevention and identification of pedophiles' suspicious online approaches. However, O'Connell's (2003) study focused only on the vulnerable child personality profile; in this study, we compare both a vulnerable and nonvulnerable online presence. Pedophiles may use different grooming strategies for nonvulnerable children or may utilize different grooming processes when engaged with different forms of online communication and social networking.

Approaching the problem from another direction was the investigative journalism of *The New York Times'* Kurt Eichenwald (2005). Here, the reporter makes contact with a former underage amateur "porn star": an 18-year-old man who started doing live strip shows through his webcam at the age of 13 years. The subject then progressed to more and more obscene material until he ended up recording sessions with prostitutes. The reporter engages in an explorative study with the subject, helping him move away from his lifestyle while documenting the process by which he was first solicited for sexual content by online pedophiles and consequently was drawn into the world of webcam child pornography. Eichenwald's (2005) work is one of the most compelling investigations of online solicitation, child sexual grooming, and exploitation. The methods used by pedophiles, the responses of victims, and their interactions are explored in a direct way.

Such explorative and evidence-based research into the use of the Internet by pedophiles may be the direction in which future research must venture, perhaps in close cooperation with law enforcement agencies carrying out online sting operations. Monitoring past Internet activity of pedophiles—as with the Forde and Patterson study (1998)—is not enough. Observing crimes as they unfold—from initial contact to solicitation and sexual grooming and then to victim manipulation, which ultimately leads to a potential in-person meeting—is vital, as with the O'Connell (2003) study. Only this form of research will help identify and understand the methods, thought processes, and characteristics of victims that make them particularly attractive to pedophiles.

Future research also needs to be practical and aimed at law enforcement and crime prevention, especially now that the world is beginning to look beyond issues of jurisdiction and national boundaries in fighting online child abuse. With the growing Web 2.0 phenomenon and the corresponding growth of social networking platforms (see O'Reilly, 2005, Appendix A), it is vital that sting-oriented experimental research be used to discover the risk factors and dangerous behavioral patterns that lead to online solicitation. The study presented in this chapter explores the online environment by conducting such research and assessing the feasibility of such an approach.

We performed a simple sting experiment, in which we set up four profiles of 12-year-old girls on various social networking platforms. Three variables were tested: (a) vulnerability; (b) the effect of *avatars*, or personal photos; and (c) the presence of a direct method of contact—in this case, an e-mail address (note that the second and third variables are related). These profiles were advertised on various IRC[3] rooms that young girls would likely frequent.

The aim of this research was threefold: (a) to explore the feasibility and dimensions of research using a criminological sting design; (b) to gain knowledge of the dynamics and security performance of social networking

---

[3] *Internet Relay Chat* (IRC) is a protocol using TCP communications between computers and servers, facilitating chat rooms (called *channels*) that are used for group communication (see Feather, 1999).

platforms present at the current stage of the Web 2.0 phenomenon; and (c) to gain an understanding of which personal characteristics tested are more likely to be attractive to pedophiles.

Using this approach, we built upon the work of Demetriou and Silke (2003), Krone (2005), and O'Connell (2003). We further developed their approach by broadening the characteristics of the children likely to be targeted and concentrating on the methods and strategies used by online pedophiles on social networking platforms. The social networking platforms differ because they provide not only real-time communication with the child but also a ready means to screen for desirable targets through the personal information contained within the profiles, blogs, and other features of these platforms.

For the purposes of this study, it should be noted that the scope was intentionally limited to a pilot exploratory research design. Such an approach raises the ethical issue of deception in the design and the unavoidable absence of consent by the "participants" who contacted the fictitious children. On balance, it can be argued that no person was harmed or exposed to unnecessary risk through this study, and, indeed, the research model that we used mimics what is now common practice among police units that are tasked with monitoring the Internet for such activities. Also, for reasons of anonymity, the names of the social networking platforms involved have been deidentified, and respondents' e-mail addresses and other identifying details have been removed.

Methodology

Four fictitious identities, or *profiles,* were set up on three social networking platforms: In this article, we refer to them as Adulescentia.com (*Adulescentia*), Osirus.com (*Osirus*), and Horizon.com (*Horizon*). The objective was to discover how best to conduct a direct, experimental research sting. The secondary objectives, although necessarily constrained because of the nature of this pilot study, were to discover which sets of variables are most attractive to pedophiles and whether the security of social networking platforms makes it easier or harder for underage users to set up profiles and for pedophiles to find and solicit them. These fictitious profiles are described in Table 6.1 and were named as follows: *Alicia* (Profile 1), *Michaela* (Profile 2), *Kate* (Profile 3),

Table 6.1 Summary of Variables in Each Fictitious Identity

Profile 1: Alicia	Profile 2: Michaela	Profile 3: Kate	Profile 4: Kelsey
Vulnerable	Vulnerable	Not vulnerable	Not vulnerable
Avatar/photo	No avatar/photo	Avatar/photo	No avatar/photo
Contact (e-mail)	No contact (e-mail)	Contact (e-mail)	No contact (e-mail)

and *Kelsey* (Profile 4). The control groups in this experiment were Michaela and Kelsey, created without an avatar or photo and without an openly displayed e-mail address. These profiles represent underage users, both vulnerable and nonvulnerable, whose identities do not have the two risk factors (contact address and photograph) under examination.

Variables Applied to the Profiles

The profiles chosen displayed the three main variables for the research, as noted: vulnerability (referred to in the Mitchel et al., 2001, study as the characteristic of being "troubled"), the presence or lack of an avatar or photo, and the ease of direct contact, measured by the presence or lack of an openly displayed e-mail address. Table 6.1 summarizes the variables and how they are used in each profile. Tables 6.2 and 6.3 describe the profiles as displayed

Table 6.2 Fictitious Profiles of Two Vulnerable Children

Profile 1: Alicia	Picture: Avatar/Photo	E-Mail: star.struck_95@ hotmail.com	Female Age 12

Headline: Quiet and plotting.
About Me: Well not much to know really … I'm actually 12 years old (hush, I just wanted a public profile), I'm kinda quiet, I like reading, writing and listening to music. I'm also addicted to the Sims. I live with my mum, who thinks I should be just like her (perfect) and my older sis (kill me now, please), but I try not to pay too much attention to them. I spend most of my time on the net, and probably the rest of my time at school, which sucks most of the time … star.struck_95@hotmail.com
I'd Like to Meet: People who'd actually listen to what I say instead of what's in their heads.
Interests: Reading and writing bad fanfics, listening to music, avoiding mum and sis
Music: Guy Sebastian, Good Charlotte, Powderfinger … all kinds of stuff.
Films: Loved Spiderman but shh, I wasn't suppose to see it.
Television: Don't get to watch much, mum and sis watch boring crap. I prefer the net.
Books: Harry Potter (yum yum), Diary of Anne Frank (saddest book ever)
Heroes: Spiderman … wish I could get an upside down kiss.

Profile 2: Michaela	Picture: None	E-Mail: None	Female Age 12

Headline: Lonely girl on a lonely planet
About Me: I'm really 12 years old (shh), I'm a bit of a loner, I like books and music and watching cool movies, I'm fairly quiet and I don't make friends easily (who needs 'em, right?). I'm an only child who lives with my parents who I don't get on with much, I live on the world wide interweb and I like chatting and annoying people.
I'd Like to Meet: New people to chat to.
Interests: Listening to awesome music, brooding, reading and writing. And chatting.
Music: I have a lot of music but mostly like Wolfmother, Avril Lavigne and Coldplay.
Films: Too many to count.
Television: I like House (yummy!) and Supernatural (two yummies?).
Books: So many books and not enough time. Currently reading The Queen of the Damned by Anne Rice.
Heroes: House! :p

Table 6.3   Fictitious Profiles of Two Nonvulnerable Children

		E-Mail: powered_by_cheese@	
Profile 3: Kate	Picture: To Be Supplied	hotmail.com	Female Age 12

Headline: Look at me, I'm awesome, cool and sooo modest!

About Me: Hey all :) I'm really 12 (whisper whisper), female, and decidedly awesome (of course!). I'm part of a wonderful and large family (one older brother, one younger sister, two parents (not three, and four is right out), one really cool grandmother and two Doberman Pinschers) and I like going places and doing things. Apparently to an annoying extent. I like abseiling, netball, skiing (in Australia, which is mostly desert … typical, huh?) and swimming. I also like chatting to new and interesting and weird people! … powered_by_ cheese@hotmail.com

I'd Like to Meet: Outgoing, awesome strange beings of the Internets.

Interests: Repeating myself :p abseiling, swimming, skiing, netball, going on runs with two huge doggies, family get-togethers (seriously awesome fun when I have such a huuuuuuge family!) and hanging out with friends.

Music: I like all kinds of music, from classical stuff to R&B

Films: Latest one I watched and liked was 'Lady in the Water'. So touching!

Television: Not too into TV, and I think Big Brother is silly. I don't mind admitting that I watch Home and Away with my family during dinner, kind of a tradition here, but its too soapy sometimes.

Books: I do like reading, but never seem to have enough time to finish books!

Heroes: My mum and dad and grandmother (yeah, I know, I'm a sap) and I guess my friends!

Profile 4: Kelsey	Picture: None	E-Mail: None	Female Age 12

Headline: Average girl seeks tin can. Will open for food.

About Me: Let's see … I'm only 12 years old (my profile is such a liar), an only child, I'm into drama (as in acting, not melodrama!) and music (I play the saxamaphooone) and I'm pretty much your basic high-flying girl … yeah sure :p I live with my mother who's annoying but really awesome and our dog Wuff (called that because when you ask "what's your name?" he makes a "Wuff!" sound!). I also like doing art and plan to go on being me for the rest of my life! Challenging, hey?

I'd Like to Meet: Other cool and creative people.

Interests: Music, learning how to play the piano as well as the sax, drama, reading, filling out silly profiles on here.

Music: Evanescence, Bach, John Coltrane

Films: Hot Fuzz. Too awesome.

Television: I'm a big fan of Doctor Who (David Tennant is hot!!), and it's so unfair that the Brits get it first! I also like Lost and Big Brother.

Books: Currently reading The Good Soldiers.

Heroes: My dog Wuff!

on the Internet sites. The constants in all four profiles are the age (12 years), location, and gender (all female subjects, for the purposes of this pilot study). Although pedophiles target boys as well as girls, the majority of child sexual abuse is perpetrated by adult males against underage females (see Finkelhor, 1994). Further research should use both male and female profiles, as variation based on the gender of the target is likely. All cases were stated to be located in Brisbane, Australia. We gave each profile different personal content to reduce the risk that they may have been detected as fakes. Instead, we kept them broadly true to the variables and constants, while the situation of each profile was different. A small focus group of female undergraduate and high school students assisted in developing "authentic" profiles.

Vulnerability included factors such as the relationship with immediate family, a quiet disposition, lack of friends, self-esteem problems, reliance on an Internet-oriented lifestyle, and an identification with the "Emo," "Goth," and other alternative subcultures that are stereotypically regarded as having depressive or antisocial tendencies (demonstrated within the profiles through the act of listening to music associated with these subcultures).

Profiles on social networking platforms such as Adulescentia and Osirus enable a user to select an image, which is then associated with the profile's public presentation. This image could be a photograph of the user, which is common in social networking platforms, or an avatar, which is more common in forums[4] and other such websites. An avatar can be a picture, graphic, or other image that represents the person using it. The effect of a profile with a graphical avatar to draw attention, as opposed to one without, would be of interest to law enforcement stings especially, as well as Internet users in the at-risk category. Two avatars were created from an online "doll-maker" program, which allows the user to customize a human figure with clothes and other items. The figures that were created represented the personalities of the two profiles involved. These avatars were used initially and then were replaced with photographs digitally manipulated to disguise their true identity.

The setup of social networking platforms such as Adulescentia, Osirus, and Horizon enables communication by members via a private messaging system, which is akin to an e-mail service, that is exclusively for website members' use. Members are generally discouraged from revealing their actual e-mail addresses on their profile. Some do, however, thus providing sexual predators with easier access to inexperienced Internet users, especially children who may consider it exciting to be e-mailed. Openly displayed e-mail addresses may create a more attractive target for solicitation.

Social Networking Platforms

We chose three different social networking services on which to place the fictitious profiles. These platforms varied in terms of their scale and community orientation. As previously noted, these platforms have been given the following *nom de plumes*: Adulescentia, Osirus, and Horizon. At the time

---

[4] *Forums* are discussion groups that use Internet protocol (IP)–based communication and present a graphic interface for messages and discussions to be read. Information is usually stored in a single location within a database. Forums can be accessed through a browser's normal hypertext transfer protocol (HTTP) and are presented as a website, albeit one with dynamic content.

of research, Adulescentia had two layers of membership: one for the 14- to 18-year-old age group and the other for the 18+ age group. The 14- to 18-year age group membership did not have publicly viewable profiles. Instead, the user had to allow a request from another member to be part of his or her "friends list" for access to the full profile or be a part of that age-group membership. There was a member search function on Adulescentia similar to that contained in personals websites. This function enabled a user to search by gender, age, and relationship/marital status as well as to ascertain what a member was searching for on Adulescentia (dating, relationships, networking, or friendships), plus a host of other descriptive factors such as height and physical build. The 14- to 18-year-olds were able to search for members who were 16 to 68 years of age, whereas the 18+ age group could search various chat rooms for those users over 18 to 68 years of age.

To test the integrity of the security that protects underage users on Adulescentia, Michaela and Kelsey were placed in the 14- to 18-year age group. Both profiles stated that the user was actually 12 years old from the outset. Alicia and Kate were placed in the 18+ age group, and their profiles also stated openly that the user was actually 12 years old.

The Osirus platform was originally designed for use by university students for networking purposes. It has been expanded, however, to include other interest groups and regional groups while retaining a focus on educational establishments. Profiles only become available to the groups in which the user chooses to partake: the general Australian regional group was selected, which exposed the four profiles to approximately 52,000 members. Thus, the Osirus platform, because of the nonpublic nature of their profiles, was an ideal control for the experiment. The same profile information, including the specified "real" ages of the users, was supplied.

Horizon is a Canadian-based social networking platform with a worldwide membership and is unique in that it has no layered memberships and has completely public profiles. The lowest age permitted is 14 years, which is also Canada's age of consent (with certain exceptions). Horizon is much more community oriented and is designed with an ethos more akin to Internet forums and moderated chat rooms than to merely social networking platforms. This design is reflected in the site's strong administrator and moderator presence. It has more than 1 million members, with approximately 300,000 of them active. A large number of its users are under the age of 18 years, and, as such, the service caters to a younger membership.

Response Types in Social Network Platforms

Within the experiment and the structure of these social networking platforms, three broad response types are available. The first is the *friends list* feature, in which members can send a request to be added to another member's list of friends. In Adulescentia's 14- to 18-year age group, acceptance of such a request gives the requester access to the member's complete profile. It is similar to the contact list available in e-mail and instant messenger software[5] and, as such, provides a means of tracking and bookmarking the profiles of people who are of interest to a member.

The second response type is the *private message* feature, which is similar to an e-mail that can only be accessed through the social networking platform and is limited to members. Private messages can be sent without members having accepted any friend requests, with the exception of the 14- to 18-year age group in Adulescentia, where only those individuals on a user's friends list can exchange messages. The third response type is the *direct e-mail* feature, which uses addresses supplied with Alicia's and Kate's profiles.

Suspicious responses within these three response types were defined as those from accounts that are not spam (advertising for musical groups or musicians, products, or services) and those from members over the age of 18 years. The primary indicator of a suspicious response was sexual content in the first instance or after a reply. Once sexual content was established, all contact with the responder ceased. The limited scope of this study, of course, excluded the possibility of an experienced pedophile initiating a long-term sexual grooming process or establishing one by posing as another child. Research about such responses would necessitate more in-depth and correspondingly long-term studies.

Results

The findings are reported over the three stages of the experiment—each stage leading to more extensive exposure of the profiles. In Stage 1, profiles were initially set up on Adulescentia and Osirus and were left untouched for 14 days in order to ascertain the "unencouraged lure" of underage girls. Within this period, no photographs were used for Alicia and Kate. Instead, two avatars were created using an online "doll-maker." A *doll* is a cartoon representation of a person, and the software allows the user to change the doll's clothing, hair, and expression. To match personality characteristics, Alicia was given paler skin, a blank expression, and darker clothes as well as a set of black wings, whereas Kate received tanned skin, a happier expression, and trendier clothes in bright colors. There were no results for this initial experiment from the Osirus platform at all, although there were limited results from Adulescentia, as can be seen in Table 6.4.

---

[5] *Instant messenger* programs are software that can be used to communicate with people who are also signed up to use the same software and are added onto a private friends list (Gross, Juvonen, & Gable, 2002).

Table 6.4 Responses to Profiles at 14 Days

Response	Alicia	Michaela	Kate	Kelsey
Total friend requests	13	0	24	0
Legitimate requests	1	0	4	0
Spam requests	12	0	20	0
Total private messages	2	0	3	0
Legitimate private messages	1	0	2	0
Spam messages	1	0	1	0
Direct e-mails	0	NA	0	NA

NA, not applicable.

There were no responses for Michaela and Kelsey, which were the profiles without avatars. In fact, an examination of the count of individual visits to these profiles, listed in the profile page, showed no visits by any other member of Adulescentia at this stage, even by other members within the 14- to 18-year age group. In searching for other members within Adulescentia, users could choose whether to search for members without avatars, and most did not. In fact, the default option was to search only for members with avatars.

Stage 2 of the experiment involved answering all legitimate responses from Adulescentia (see Table 6.4) to discern which responses were innocent or suspicious. Alicia's lone legitimate friend request proved to be innocent, with the member deleting Alicia from her friends list after realizing her "true" age. However, Alicia's lone legitimate private message was suspicious. After the requester established contact, the conversation rapidly turned sexual, with the member asking about masturbation and boyfriends. Three of Kate's four legitimate friend requests were innocent, with one proving to be a member randomly adding profiles and the other two not fully reading Kate's profile and true age. However, one friend request appeared suspicious after three replies, with the requester asking for personal details about intimate clothing and requesting personal photographs despite having again been reminded of Kate's age. Similarly, both of Kate's legitimate private messages were suspicious, with the members becoming sexual soon after the reply. This process of answering legitimate responses was carried on throughout the remainder of the experiment.

The modest response to Stage 1 of the experiment was indicative of the presence of pedophiles willing to track and solicit young girls; however, the experiment required the presence of these girls on the Internet to be "known"—or, in other words, "advertised." In a normal situation, these girls would have been heavily active in forums, chat rooms, other networking platforms, instant messenger programs, and so forth. All of these activities would feature links back to the profiles. In the experiment, we had to advertise the profiles in order to achieve this degree of realism. Thus, Stage 3 involved three expansions of the experiment: (a) the addition of profiles to another social networking platform, Horizon; (b) the use of photographs as opposed to graphical avatars; and (c) the participation in IRC rooms for advertising purposes. Note that in expanded experiments, researchers should take care to use more than chat rooms for advertising. A complete online presence must be maintained for each girl, including the activities listed previously. For this explorative study, however, it is sufficient that such advertising be tested to gain an understanding of the effect on the number of suspicious responses.

Horizon provides human security in the form of moderators who accept or reject each profile as it is created. For this reason, Alicia's and Kate's profiles were created 1 day before Michaela's and Kelsey's, and their "true" ages were omitted until after they had been accepted. When all four profiles were accepted into the system, Alicia's and Kate's profiles were updated with childhood photographs.[6] The childhood photographs were, in turn, slightly digitally manipulated to ensure the safety of the women who had provided them and to make them appear as though they were photographs taken from a digital camera. After the photographs were uploaded, all four profiles were changed to reflect their "true" ages. Although receiving plenty of attention (mostly spam messages and requests), within 3 days, all four profiles were suspended by Horizon staff. Although the real impetus for this action is impossible to ascertain, a reasonable assumption is that a member reported it as a potential "illegal profile" to the moderators.

Expanding on this, the photographs replaced the avatars on Alicia's and Kate's profiles within the Adulescentia and Osirus platforms. Both platforms were used in the advertising, with 1 week's advertising used for each platform. The Undernet network of IRC—arguably the largest—was chosen for the advertising because of the unmoderated nature of the medium and the presence of tens of thousands of users at any given time. We used an IRC client known as *mIRC software* (http://www.mirc.com/mirc.html) to access the Undernet network (http://www.undernet.org), as it was the mainstream software for IRC. The two chat rooms chosen from Undernet's list were #Teens and #Teenchat. Other, more obviously sexual, chat rooms for all age groups were available but were rejected for the purposes of this study because the solicitations should occur within an "innocent" medium. Because of the practical considerations involved in advertising two sets of four profiles within a short exposure period of 2 weeks, we decided to sacrifice a realistic schedule (particularly due to the international nature of IRC) and to partition each day into four slots, advertising each of the four profiles 6 hours apart and rotating them each day into different time slots, as shown in Table 6.5.

---

[6] These images were provided with the informed consent of two adult female associates who agreed to be involved in the experiment.

Table 6.5 Timetable for Adulescentia and Osirus Profiles Advertised in IRC

Day of Week	12:00 AM	6:00 AM	12:00 PM	6:00 PM
Monday	Alicia	Michaela	Kate	Kelsey
Tuesday	Kelsey	Alicia	Michaela	Kate
Wednesday	Kate	Kelsey	Alicia	Michaela
Thursday	Michaela	Kate	Kelsey	Alicia
Friday	Alicia	Michaela	Kate	Kelsey
Saturday	Kelsey	Alicia	Michaela	Kate
Sunday	Kate	Kelsey	Alicia	Michaela

IRC, Internet Relay Chat.

Profiles were advertised both in the main chat room and in private chat to any person who initiated a conversation. An example of an advertisement in the main chat room would be, "Hi I'm Alicia, 12/f/Australia, bored n' lonely, anyone wanna talk or whatever add me on Adulescentia!" followed by the appropriate URL. If there was conversation going on in the chat room, the characters would participate with the appropriate knowledge of Internet abbreviations and speech patterns. The roles of Kate and Kelsey, as the nonvulnerable profiles, were appropriately more spirited and socially aware in discussions, whereas Alicia and Michaela were shy and withdrawn. Interestingly, Kate and Kelsey received more attention from real or supposed younger people, whereas Alicia and Michaela attracted attention from those who did not identify directly as young and who were more dominant in conversation.

There were also many requests for photographs, with Alicia and Kate responding with links to their profiles, whereas Michaela and Kelsey denied having access to digital cameras. Although plenty of suspicious attention was directed at the girls within the chat room, it was beyond the scope of this study to explore these interactions—but it is an area that needs further research, especially considering IRC is particularly involved with content crimes such as the trading of child pornography (Choo, 2009a; Forde & Paterson, 1998; Hellard, 2001).

The results of this final stage in the experiment were mixed. The Osirus profiles attracted some attention but mostly from other young members (actual or posing), some of whom became sexual as well. Alicia and Kate received all of the responses, with Alicia receiving three friend requests, one of which turned sexual after three replies, and Kate receiving five friend requests, with three becoming sexual after a few replies. Note that the chat rooms—although primarily intended for what #Teens called "clean chat"— were also used by these younger people to initiate sexual discussion with the opposite sex. This has been argued by some sources—for example, social worker Patrick O'Leary (cited in Munro, 2006, p. 23)—to be a part of normal

Table 6.6   Stage 3 Results for Adulescentia

Response	Alicia	Michaela	Kate	Kelsey
Total friend requests	16	6	13	3
Legitimate requests	7	1	5	0
Spam requests	0	0	0	0
Total private messages	9	4	11	3
Legitimate private messages	4	2	5	1
Spam messages	0	0	0	0
Direct e-mails	3	NA	2	NA

NA, not applicable.

sexual exploration. Of course, as Taylor (2002) points out, these younger people could be victims of child abuse who copy the abuse they have suffered and inflict it on other children—thus, the result of learned behavior (see White & Haines, 2004, pp. 60–62). The results of the Adulescentia profiles were more pronounced and are reported in Table 6.6.

Discussion and Analysis

The main objective of this explorative study was to discern how best to conduct direct criminological research through experimentation using a sting-oriented approach. Stage 1 showed that even a passive approach netted results. However, the results gained are relevant only for a specific category of pedophile that actively sorts through profiles. But such results were still surprising in a number of ways. The objective was to determine which profile (and which set of variable characteristics, the major one being vulnerability) attracted the most suspicious contacts. Or, in other words, which profile was the most attractive to online pedophiles? The research of Mitchel and colleagues (2001) reiterated the common belief—reflected in official government literature—that one of the most at-risk groups is "troubled" children (NetAlert, 2005; Stanley, 2002). By Stage 2, the profile with the most suspicious contacts was Kate's; it was nonvulnerable, with an avatar and a contact e-mail, which is similar to Mitchel and colleagues' (2001) finding that 75% of those contacted were not "troubled" teenagers. However, these results were limited because of the lack of advertising in the other sites of interest—chat rooms.

By Stage 3, these results had evened out further. Alicia and Kate received the most attention and, ignoring direct e-mails, received 44% and 42% (respectively) of suspicious responses out of the total they attracted. Although a lengthier study may yield more results that may show a more significant percentage increase for one or the other, the presence of public profiles and photographs seems to indicate that vulnerability may not be the key issue, as has been previously thought. But a vulnerable child would be psychologically easier to control and manipulate than a nonvulnerable child. More interestingly, the difference between Michaela and Kelsey was more pronounced, with the more outgoing Kelsey receiving 17% suspicious responses of her total, as opposed to Michaela's 30%.

It may be misleading to focus on the view that vulnerable children are more likely to be targeted than nonvulnerable children—as comforting as it may be to think that nonvulnerable children are at low risk. Thus, pedophiles who have the patience, intelligence, and understanding of the psychology (or pathology) of children may succeed by undertaking the complex child sexual grooming process so succinctly summed up in NetAlert's "Paedophiles and online grooming" article (NetAlert, 2005, p. 2) and explored so thoroughly in Choo's (2009a) review and O'Connell's (2003) study. Nevertheless, even outgoing and family-oriented children such as Kate and Kelsey were at possible risk. Therefore, it is important to avoid perceiving pedophiles, especially those encountered online, as the type of sex offender who selects and strikes only a vulnerable target—a woman walking alone, drugged or drunk, for example—then disappears. It is equally important to bear in mind that children are essentially vulnerable in the sense that they are naïve and inexperienced and are generally eager to please an adult and to make new friends.

The results for Michaela and Kelsey seem to indicate that without the presence of public profiles and photographs, the risk of suspicious contacts may be low. The results tend to support Mitchel and colleagues' (2001) concerns about the greater risk of more suspicious contacts for "troubled" or vulnerable children than others on the Internet. The presence of an e-mail address does not seem to affect the risks to the extent anticipated, with Alicia receiving a 5% increase and Kate receiving a 4% increase. This observation seems to indicate that ease of access and a photograph may spur on pedophiles either because of the ease of action and knowledge of the victim or because the presence of a photograph sparks an attraction that overrides security and safety concerns. This would be closer to a psychologically positivistic explanation of pedophilia as a form of pathology (Goldstein, 1999, pp. 27–29). The use of photographs in Stage 3 was revealing from the outset. For example, one of the initial private messages received by Alicia via Adulescentia shows the opportunity that this offers for manipulation through flattery: "Nice pic good angle on your face. You are very cute and I would like to chat with you. Australia is one of my favorite places, have not visited yet. Hope to chat with you soon" [sic] (personal communication, June 12, 2007). This supports O'Connell's (2003) findings that describe how pedophiles in chat rooms commonly seek more information via online profiles and requests for photographs (pp. 7–8). Unlike IRC, social networking platforms provide an easier and more subtle way of gaining this personal information before contact has even been established.

Although the avatars made a difference, the photographs for Alicia and Kate seemed to heighten interest, as seen in the results from the Osirus platform in particular, with Michaela and Kelsey not receiving any responses at all. From a security standpoint, the best solution seems to be to design social networking sites around forum communities rather than as an abstract service governed by rigid staff member hierarchies. Horizon provided the best security, with profiles being suspended as soon as the "true" ages of the fictitious girls were revealed. This seems to have resulted from the integration (empowerment) of users as staff: The platform is further moderated by the users themselves. Thus, the more intense the sense of community, the more likely that individuals will intervene as responsible members of that community. Additionally, the relatively small size of Horizon as compared with Adulescentia and Osirus is probably a major factor—although Horizon is sufficiently large for a purely "elitist" staff to be unable to handle all the services alone.

Had there been no media attention on child abuse within social networking platforms such as Adulescentia and Horizon (Mah, 2007; Rawstorne, 2007) during the conduct of this research, and had Adulescentia, in particular, not upgraded the security and structure of its service as a result, it is not inconceivable that there would have been even more suspicious responses than those observed. The Adulescentia upgrades resulted in a safer environment for the 14- to 18-year age group. Internet service providers have pressured to complement and cooperate with the efforts of law enforcement, and this has resulted in partnerships among social networking platforms, software designers, academia, and others to design Internet safety into the core processes of Web 2.0 technologies (Choo, 2009a). For example, MySpace interfaces with law enforcement at local, state, and federal levels to share information and streamline subpoena processes and investigations and provides instruction to law enforcement officials on how to directly access MySpace staff. However, where there is online communication (and the anonymity it often provides), there will always remain the risk of predatory behavior, which designers cannot always foresee.

However, it is difficult for any social networking platform to take into account the deindividuation theory that Demetriou and Silke (2003) explore in their study. In the world of the Internet, responsibility is low. It is tempting for underage users to have an 18+ profile because it is publicly viewable and has certain advantages that being in the 14- to 18-year age group does not. It is also tempting for pedophiles to create accounts under the guise of young children to gain the trust of their chosen victims (O'Connell, Price, & Barrow, 2004) or to view the Internet as a safe and anonymous environment in which to freely interact with children. Further, it is tempting for both predator and prey to feel completely safe within their homes while allowing the world to visit via their computers.

Conclusion

An effective way to conduct direct research on online child sexual solicitation and the activities of Internet pedophiles can occur by establishing several complete Internet identities. Focusing on one medium alone—for example, chat rooms without social networking platforms or forums—leaves an incomplete picture of underage users' Internet activities. Social networking platforms can provide a major arena for pedophile activities and, when expanded with advertising, constitute an almost unexplored domain for study. Although this study provided limited exposure and advertising, it did demonstrate that such techniques can yield useful data.

With the cooperation of social networking platforms, this study has shown that action-oriented research could be undertaken by using many different profiles and characteristics to discover how Internet pedophiles operate and what factors—such as avatars, photographs, publicly accessible profiles, e-mail addresses, and personality characteristics—affect their behavior. In this case, the initial experimental design proved too passive and short lived to be a method for attracting enough responses from Internet pedophiles.

In this small pilot study, the strongest variables involved were the presence of photographs and e-mail addresses. With these in use, suspicious responses for both vulnerable and nonvulnerable profiles were roughly equal, thus showing, perhaps, that these factors encouraged pedophiles to ignore caution and security in favor of gratification. Profiles without these variables had a more predictable outcome, with vulnerable profiles receiving more attention than nonvulnerable profiles. From these initial results, it is recommended that all underage users of social networking platforms be very cautious about placing photographs of themselves in their profiles and to avoid publication of e-mail addresses. In general, education of parents and children about the importance of privacy and the power of the databases underpinning much of the Internet is essential (Barnes, 2006).

In terms of security, Horizon was by far the best of the three platforms tested, thus suggesting that a community-based social networking platform seems to be the safest. This platform enabled self-policing to occur. Paradoxically, Horizon allows 14-year-old members to create completely public profiles. Both Adulescentia and Osirus appeared to have insufficient security in place to detect and suspend the accounts of underage members. However, Osirus' completely nonpublic profiles did provide a measure of security as compared with Adulescentia's layered membership feature.

Partly owing to these findings, further research is being undertaken with the cooperation of the Queensland Police Service and the Australian Federal Police. In this research, we seek to observe the environments in which Internet pedophiles network, discuss child abuse, and attempt to groom potential victims. Preliminary findings indicate that suspected Internet pedophiles are using a "suite" of new Web 2.0 technologies as well as enhanced anonymity and security to carry out their illicit activities. An Internet pedophile can use software such as Tor (http://www.torproject.org/overview.html.en), which routes Internet traffic through anonymous proxy servers, to ensure anonymity on IRC. This enables pedophiles to share and discuss digital images of child abuse that are, in turn, stored on international image-hosting servers. These secret exchanges help normalize the conduct within such groups because these child abuse images appear on untraceable, anonymous websites, forums, and newsgroups using Freenet. Step-by-step guides to using each product or service can be found within all of these products and services. In this follow-up research, we seek to further the goals of the study presented in this chapter: to provide practical criminological data and intelligence to respond to and prevent child sexual abuse in an ever-evolving online sphere.

In the end, however, the best security must come from within the user's home and habits. Underage users such as the one in Eichenwald's (2005) investigation are at greater risk by having computers in their bedrooms coupled with unsupervised, unlimited Internet access (O'Reilly, 2005). The Australian government's concept of the distribution of free filtering software cannot keep pace with children's ever-increasing knowledge of Internet technology and the increasing role of online friendships or "friending" among teens that will undermine these forms of control (Boyd, 2006). This was proven when a 16-year-old male user "cracked" the NetAlert filter in 30 min and cracked an upgraded filter within 40 min (Higginbottom & Packham, 2007, pp. 1–23). The alternative, an Internet service provider–level filter, has been dismissed as ineffective in blocking all pornography (a problem with the filtering software, as well) and may also limit access to legitimate sites (e.g., health; see Minow, 2004). It is likely that the impact of the associated slower Internet speeds (LeMay, 2006) will also be resisted by e-commerce, and it is unlikely that the speed of Internet connections may be sacrificed for the safety of vulnerable users. Ultimately, the best form of Internet security is parental monitoring in the form of human supervision as well as the education of children about the dangers posed by the Internet and the importance of privacy self-protection (Barnes, 2006). Frequent users are also most at risk; yet, if Hutchings and Hayes' (2009) example of "phishing" is a guide, then users—once alerted—are also capable of rapidly adopting protective measures that reduce the risk of attack. It may be better to empower children to police the Internet and to recognize their rapid absorption of the changes released by Web 2.0—as well as the relentless privatization and commercialization that is now increasingly apparent.

Acknowledgments

We gratefully acknowledge the assistance of Nick Chantler, Peter Grabosky, and Warren Reed for helpful comments on an earlier draft of this chapter.

References

Australian Government. (2007). *NetAlert: Protecting Australian families online.* Canberra, Australia: Department of Communications, Information Technology and the Arts. Retrieved from http://www.netalert.gov.au

Barnes, S. B. (2006). A privacy paradox: Social networking in the United States. *First Monday, 11*(9). Retrieved from http://firstmonday.org

Bilstad, B. T. (1996). Obscenity and indecency on the Usenet: The legal and political future of Alt.Sex.Stories. *Journal of Computer-Mediated Communication, 2*(2), 1.

Boyd, D. (2006). Friends, friendsters, and top 8: Writing community into being on social network sites. *First Monday, 11*(12). Retrieved from http://firstmonday.org

Broadhurst, R.G. (2006). Content cybercrimes: Criminality and censorship in Asia. *Indian Journal of Criminology, 34*(1–2), 11–30.

Choo, K.-K. R. (2009a). *Online child grooming: A literature review on the misuse of social networking sites for grooming children for sexual offences* [Research and Public Policy Series, Vol. 103, pp. 1–108]. Retrieved from http://www.aic.gov.au/documents/3/C/1/%7B3C162CF7-94B1-4203-8C57-79F827168DD8%7Drpp103.pdf

Choo, K.-K. R. (2009b). *Responding to online child sexual grooming: An industry perspective* [Trends and Issues in Crime and Criminal Justice Report No. 379]. Retrieved from http://www.aic.gov.au/publications/current%20series/tandi/361-380/tandi379.aspx

Choo, K.-K. R., & Smith, R. G. (2007, June). Criminal exploitation of online systems by organised crime groups [Special Topic Part II: Organised Crime in Asia]. *Asian Journal of Criminology, 3*, 37–59.

Demetriou, C., & Silke, A. (2003). A criminological Internet sting: Experimental evidence of illegal and deviant visits to a website trap. *British Journal of Criminology, 43*, 213–222.

Dixon, N. (2002, November). *Catching 'cyber predators': The Sexual Offences (Protection of Children) Amendment Bill 2002 (Qld)* [Research Brief No. 2002/35]. Brisbane, Australia: Queensland Parliamentary Library. Retrieved from http://www.parliament.qld.gov.au/view/publications/documents/research/ResearchBriefs/2002/2002035.pdf

Eichenwald, K. (2005, December 19). Through his webcam, a boy joins a sordid online world. *The New York Times.* Retrieved from http://www.nytimes.com

Feather, M. (1999, June). Internet and child victimisation. *Proceedings of Children and Crime: Victims and Offenders Conference* (pp. 1–22). Brisbane, Australia: Australian Institute of Criminology.

Finkelhor, D. (1994). Current information on the scope and nature of child sexual abuse. *The Future of Children, 4*(2), 31–53. Retrieved from http://www.futureofchildren.org

Forde, P., & Patterson, A. (1998). Paedophile Internet activity. *Trends and Issues in Crime and Criminal Justice, 97*(1), 1–6.

Goldstein, S. L. (1999). *The sexual exploitation of children: A practical guide to assessment, investigation, and intervention* (2nd ed.). New York, NY: CRC Press.

Grabosky, P. (2007, June). *The Internet, technology, and organised crime.* Paper presented at Organised Crime in Asia conference, National University of Singapore.

Gross, E. F., Juvonen, J., & Gable, S. L. (2002). Internet use and well-being in adolescence. *Journal of Social Issues, 58*(1), 75–90.

Hellard, P. (2001, March 23). Schoolgirl deluged with porn. *Herald Sun.* Retrieved June 4, 2007 from http://www.heraldsun.com.au

Higginbottom, N., & Packham, B. (2007, August 26). Student cracks government's $84M porn filter. *Herald Sun.* Retrieved from http://www.heraldsun.com.au

Krone, T. (2005). Queensland police stings in online chat rooms. *Trends and Issues in Crime and Criminal Justice, 301,* 1–6.

LeMay, R. (2006, June 14). ISP-level porn filters a bad idea. *ZDNet Australia News.* Retrieved from http://www.zdnet.com.au/news/communications/soa/ISP-level-porn-filters-a-bad-idea/0,130061791,139259795,00.htm

Mah, B. (2007, May 31). Man guilty of luring teens over Internet. *Edmonton Journal.* Retrieved from http://www.canada.com/edmontonjournal/news/story.html?id=cdc5a315-6b17-41a7-b361-c9817ffae455

MI6 boss in Facebook entry row. (2009, July 5). *British Broadcasting Corporation.* Retrieved from http://news.bbc.co.uk/2/hi/uk_news/8134807.stm

Mitchel, K. J., Finkelhor, D., & Wolak, J. (2001). Risk factors for and impact of online sexual solicitation of youth. *JAMA: The Journal of the American Medical Association, 285,* 3011–3014.

Minow, M. (2004). Lawfully surfing the net: Disabling public library internet filters to avoid more lawsuits in the United States. *First Monday, 9*(4). Retrieved from http://firstmonday.org

Munro, I. (2006, March 18). The harm when women prey on boys. *The Age.* Retrieved from http://www.theage.com.au/news/national/the-harm-when-women-prey-on-boys/2006/03/17/1142582526948.html?page=fullpage

MySpace sex offenders increase fourfold. (2007, July 25). *Sydney Morning Herald.* Retrieved from http://www.smh.com.au/news/technology/alarming-increase-in-myspace-sex-offenders/2007/07/25/1185043145104.html

NetAlert. (2005). *Paedophiles and online grooming.* Retrieved from http://www.netalert.net.au/02333-Paedophiles-and-Online-Grooming.pdf

O'Connell, R. (2003, July). *A typology of cybersexploitation and online* grooming practices. Paper presented at Netsafe conference, Auckland, New Zealand. Retrieved from http://image.guardian.co.uk/sys-files/Society/documents/2003/07/17/Groomingreport.pdf

O'Connell, R., Price., J., & Barrow, C. (2004). *Cyber stalking, abusive cyber sex and online grooming: A programme of education for teenagers.* Retrieved from http://www.meldpunt-kinderporno.nl/files/Biblio/NewCyberStalking.pdf

O'Grady, R. (2001). Eradicating pedophilia: Toward the humanisation of society. *Journal of International Affairs, 55,* 123–141.

O'Reilly, T. (2005). *What is Web 2.0: Design patterns and business models for the next generation of software.* Retrieved from http://www.oreillynet.com/lpt/a/6228

Pascu, C., Osimo, D., Ulbrich, M., Turlea, J. C., & Burgelman, J. C. (2007). The potential disruptive impact of Internet 2 based technologies. *First Monday, 12*(3). Retrieved from http://firstmonday.org

Pilon, M. (2001). *Canada's legal age of consent to sexual activity*. Retrieved from http://www2.parl.gc.ca/content/lop/researchpublications/prb993-e.htm

Rawstorne, T. (2007, May 27). Who is your child talking to on MySpace? *Daily Mail*. Retrieved from http://www.dailymail.co.uk/pages/live/femail/article.html?in_article_id=457752&in_page_id=1879

Ridgeway v. R. 184 CLR 19 (1995).

Rind, B. (2002). Moral panic: Changing concepts of the child molester in modern America. *Archives of Sexual Behaviour, 31*, 543–546.

Salek, N. (2007, 10 August). NetAlert helps public libraries. *ITNEWS*. Retrieved from http://www.itnews.com.au

Sarikakis, K. (2004). Ideology and policy: Notes on the shaping of the Internet. *First Monday, 9*(8). Retrieved from http://firstmonday.org

Smith, M. C. (1997). The recovered memory/false memory debate. *Canadian Journal of Experimental Psychology, 51*, 258–261.

Spink, A., Partridge, H., & Jansen, B. J. (2006). Sexual and pornographic Web searching: Trends analysis. *First Monday, 11*(9). Retrieved from http://firstmonday.org

Stanley, J. (2002). Child abuse and the Internet. *Journal of the Home Economics Institute of Australia, 9*, 5–27.

Taylor, M. (2002, July 18). Teenage paedophiles are victims too. *The Society Guardian*. Retrieved from http://society.guardian.co.uk/children/comment/0,,756822,00.html

White, R., & Haines, F. (2004). *Crime and criminology*. Melbourne: Oxford University Press.

Adult–Child Sex Advocacy Websites as Learning Environments for Crime

7

ROB D'OVIDIO
TYSON MITMAN
IMAANI JAMILLAH EL-BURKI
WESLEY SHUMAR

Contents

Introduction

E-mail, instant messengers, chat rooms, and websites are just a few of the many tools available to facilitate communication over computer networks. E-mail provides users with an alternative to postal mail and the fax machine and can be used to send a myriad of communiqués—including business contracts, office memos, and love letters—across the globe in seconds. Instant messenger programs enable real-time text communication and provide an alternative to the telephone. They can be used to send a quick greeting to an overseas friend or to keep parents in touch with children who are away at school. Like the local pub, the computer chat room can bring together prospective lovers or provide a meeting place for people to debate politics, sports, the arts, or any conceivable topic. Websites facilitate commerce by bringing together merchants with distant customers and allow for the easy distribution of information, such as the latest headlines or a novel on *The New York Times* bestseller list. Social networking websites remove psychological and geographic barriers to social relationships and link like-minded people from around the world.

To date, however, the effects of computers on society have not been entirely positive. Just like past innovations in communication, computers and related networking technologies have created new opportunities for crime—especially for those looking to sexually exploit children (D'Ovidio & O'Leary, 2006; Durkin, 1997; Taylor & Quayle, 2003). Digital cameras, personal computers, digital editing software, the Internet, and remote storage drives have, for example, simplified the creation, distribution, and collection of child pornography (Jenkins, 2001; McAuliffe, 2001; Wolak, Finkelhor, & Mitchell, 2005). The virtual spaces where children congregate online have created alternatives to the playground and ball field for adults looking to sexually solicit children. The World Wide Web offers adults a means in which to promote and search for sexual liaisons involving children (Brunker, 1999; Hall, 2003; McKim, 2006). Encryption, steganography, remailers, and other anonymizing tools have further aided criminals looking to sexually exploit children by providing a means by which to conceal their identity and criminal activity from law enforcement officials and significant others (Denning & Baugh, 1997; Jossi, 2001).

In this chapter, we report on a content analysis of websites that promote, advocate, and convey information in support of sexual relationships between adults and children and the elimination of age-of-consent laws. Specifically, we examine how adult–child sex advocacy websites are structured to foster social relationships and interaction among adults interested in sexual relationships with children. These interactions are, according to differential association theory, an integral part of the process by which criminal behavior is learned (Sutherland, 1947/1974). This research also looks at adult–child sex advocacy websites as environments in which interested parties can learn criminal behavior. We were particularly interested in examining these websites for content that exposes users to rationalizations for crimes involving the sexual exploitation of children and content that, if modeled, would result in the sexual assault of children. In the next section, we explore criminogenic considerations concerning online communities. We then describe the research methodology. Next, we report the results and discuss the findings and implications for the criminal justice system. Last, we discuss the limitations of the current research and recommend future directions for research in this area.

Criminogenic Considerations Concerning Online Communities

Computer networks, including the Internet, reduce the impact of space and time on social interactions and provide opportunities to form relationships that were previously cost prohibitive. The disembodiment of humans and ensuing interactions through online communities have challenged the traditional notion that communities are composed of people and entities linked by geographic proximity. Computer networks, according to Kollock and Smith (2003), "renew community by strengthening the bonds that connect us to the wider social world while simultaneously increasing our power in that world" (p. 4). It is through this connectivity to the wider social world that the Internet and online communities offer new opportunities for commerce (Bressler & Grantham, 2000; Gonyer, 2007; Jeon, Crutsinger, & Kim, 2008), education (Hofer, 2004; McIntosh, 2005; Renninger & Shumar, 2002), entertainment (Fisher, 2004; Kline, Dyer-Witheford, & DePueter, 2003; Lastowka & Hunter, 2006), romance (Mahfouz, Philaretou, & Theocharous, 2008; Reid, 2005; Turkle, 1997), and political activism (Denning, 2001; Jordan & Taylor, 2004; Kahn & Kellner, 2004).

The same features of the Internet that enable humans to easily traverse time and space to offer new opportunities for education, commerce, entertainment, love, and activism also provide new opportunities for crime and can influence the proclivity to commit crime. Namely, the Internet and the spaces of community that it comprises provide access to victims who might otherwise not be viable targets for crime were it not for their presence in cyberspace (Cox, Johnson, & Richards, 2009; D'Ovidio & O'Leary, 2006). Social networking websites, chat rooms, and instant messaging (IM) services, for example, place children in environments devoid of traditional guardians (e.g., parents and teachers) and, thus, leave them vulnerable to sexual advances by adults (Mitchell, Wolak, & Finkelhor, 2005; Wolak, Mitchell, & Finkelhor, 2006).

Online communities also bring together like-mind people from throughout the world and create an environment in which crime can be learned. Past research has made the connection between social learning theory and crime involving computers and the Internet (Higgins & Makin, 2004a, 2004b; Higgins, Wolfe, & Ricketts, 2009; Hollinger, 1993; Skinner & Fream, 1997). *Social learning theory* explains crime in terms of four processes: differential association, definitions, imitation, and differential reinforcement (Akers, 1998). Learning crime begins, according to Sutherland (1947/1974), with the process of *differential association,* which involves interactions with people who favor criminal behavior. These interactions can be direct or indirect exchanges and can include verbal and nonverbal communication (Akers, 1998; Akers,

Krohn, Lanza-Kaduce, & Radosevich, 1979). They include exchanges with individuals, primary groups, secondary groups, and reference groups.

Internet tools and services have evolved to offer online communities a plethora of options for site administrators to communicate with users and for users to communicate with one another either directly or indirectly. Chat rooms and instant messengers, for example, enable synchronous two-way exchanges and offer online community members instant feedback from those members with whom they are communicating. Message boards, on the other hand, are asynchronous but provide an archive of the exchange between community members that is searchable and available for all community members to read and, subsequently, learn from. E-mail, listservs, and blogs can be integrated into the structure of an online community to also support two-way interactions among members. Content published by community administrators to a web page or to an online calendar of community events limits the communication to a one-way interaction but, nevertheless, exposes members to ideas that may advocate crime and fosters community participation.

It is through these interactions, or through the process of differential association, that people learn the techniques to carry out a criminal act and the motives, attitudes, and rationalizations that favor committing a specific criminal act (Akers, 1998; Sutherland, 1947/1974). Rationalizations for committing crime serve to neutralize psychological restraints (i.e., guilt) against criminal behavior. Sykes and Matza (1957) offer five *rationalizations*, or *techniques of neutralization,* that are used by offenders to explain their involvement with crime. Offenders can deny responsibility for engaging in crime and place the blame on forces outside their control, such as bad friends or unloving parents. Offenders can trivialize the criminal act by denying or discounting any resulting injury. Offenders also seek rationalization by seeing the victim as a rightful recipient of any harm resulting from the crime or when the resulting harm to the victim is not obvious because the victim is not physically present when the crime occurs. Offenders can also find a release for their criminal activities by shifting the focus away from their behavior and toward the motives and actions of the people who condemn the crime. Last, offenders can prioritize and rank norms in such a way that societal norms that promote law-abiding behavior are superseded by the norms of a smaller reference group that support violations of the law. These rationalizations create, according to Sykes and Matza (1957), definitions that favor criminal violations. It is through an "excess in definitions favorable to violations of the law over definitions unfavorable to violations of the law" that a person becomes delinquent (Sutherland, 1947/1974, p. 75).

Interactions in cyberspace serve a purpose other than establishing definitions favorable to violations of the law when it comes to the learning process associated with crime. Direct interactions through synchronous and asynchronous communication tools and indirect interactions where users happen upon archived content left on a message board, posted on a blog, or displayed on a website provide users, at times, with the methods by which to carry out specific criminal acts and convey stories of criminal exploits that can later be imitated or modeled. For example, Skinner and Fream (1997) found a positive relationship between the use of computer bulletin boards and illegal access to networks, given the frequent posting of passwords and access credentials in these online forums. Adult–child sex advocacy websites can be a source of imitation, with respect to the process of learning crime, to the extent that they contain stories of sexual liaisons with children, suggest security techniques that offenders can use to elude the detection of law enforcement when such offenders are using the Internet to lure children or exchange child pornography, or provide links to resources containing sexually explicit materials involving children.

Additionally, interactions in cyberspace can provide insight into the possible consequences of criminal behavior. This insight can be derived from the experiences of others who have committed similar acts and from third-party accounts (e.g., media reports) referenced in an online forum. The consequences, expressed in the form of the anticipated and potential rewards or punishments, serve to reinforce the decision of whether to engage in a criminal act. It is the differential between the contingent rewards and the punishments that, according to Akers (1998), guides our actions.

Adult–child sex advocacy websites and the resulting associations that they create in cyberspace can, thus, be criminogenic in that they expose people to various techniques for committing crime, definitions that present crime in a favorable light, potential punishments and rewards, and stories of criminal behaviors that can be imitated. In the following section, we provide a methodological roadmap for assessing the criminogenic structure of adult–child sex advocacy communities on the Internet to the extent that they support the learning of crime. We discuss the process by which the adult–child sex advocacy websites were selected, operationalize our measures, and describe the data collection process.

Method

For inclusion in the present study, a website needed to satisfy four criteria. First, the website needed to encourage sexual relationships between adults and children and support the elimination of age-of-consent laws. Second, the website needed to provide information to users beyond the content contributed by those who visited the website. Third, the website needed to be interactive; it must have allowed for user participation, inquiry, contribution, or interaction with other users or the website administrators. Last, the website needed to be published in English or have an English-language translation.

Sampling

The Internet is a dynamic network with content that is constantly changing. The lack of a search engine that catalogs and indexes all web content in real time makes identifying the population of adult–child sex advocacy websites problematic. For example, an Internet search on the phrase "pedophilia activism" using the Google (http://www.google.com), Yahoo! (http://www.yahoo.com), and Windows Live (http://www.live.com) search engines returned different results in terms of content and ordering.[1] Without a known population, the use of probability sampling techniques to identify a representative sample of adult–child sex advocacy websites was not possible. As a result, we used purposive and snowball sampling techniques to identify the websites used in this study. The use of nonprobability sampling techniques to identify websites for content analysis is consistent with the approaches used by Schafer (2002) and Gerstenfeld, Grant, and Chiang (2003) in their examination of hate groups and extremist websites.

Sixty-four adult–child sex advocacy websites meeting the four selection criteria previously described were identified. Table 7.1 lists the name of each identified website. We began our search for adult–child sex advocacy websites using purposive sampling techniques. We first examined websites listed in the "sexuality organizations" directory of the Yahoo! search engine and under the Wikipedia (http://www.wikipedia.com) entries for "pedophilia activism" and the "history of pedophilia activism" to identify those sites that satisfied the four selection criteria described above.

We then used snowball sampling techniques to find additional adult–child sex advocacy websites that met our selection criteria. Specifically, we used Google[2] to search for adult–child sex advocacy websites that were categorized as being similar to the adult–child sex advocacy websites identified through the purposive techniques described above. Then, we examined external links off the websites identified through Yahoo!, Wikipedia, and Google to search for additional sites that met our selection criteria.

Measures

The variables collected on each website were organized into three constructs: communication and participation, neutralization content, and imitation content.

[1] The search was performed on May 10, 2007, at 9:00 a.m. Microsoft replaced its Windows Live search service with its Bing search service (http://www.bing.com) in June 2009.
[2] Google has a built-in function that returns a listing of websites that are similar in nature to a specified site.

Table 7.1   Adult–Child Sex Advocacy Websites

Name of Website	
About Boylove	Girl Chat
Age Taboo	Glorious Girls
Alice Pix	Haven 4 Boys
Americans for a Society Free From Age Restrictions (ASFAR)[a]	The Human Face of Pedophilia
	A Hundred Years of Pedophilia
Angels Boylove Forum	International Boylove Magazine
Backwoodsman's Bits	International Boylovers United
Boy Bliss	IPCE
Boy Chat	JON
Boyland Online	Kid Shady
Boylove Channel	Koinos Magazine
The Boylove Online Community	LifeLine
Boy Lover	Magic Boy Angels
Boy Moment	Martijn
Boy Sky	Mhamic
Boy Tales	North American Man/Boy Love
BoyWiki	Association (NAMBLA)
Boyz World	Open Hands
Boyz World Photo Gallery	Paedo UK
Butterfly Kisses	Paiderastia
Cerius Love	Pedofilie
The Childlove News	Pedologues
Christian Boylove Forum	Pedophiles Against Child Molestation
The Church of Zeus and Ganymede	Pedophilia: Truth vs. Myth
CLogo	Perspectives
Common Ground	Philia
Critical Estoppel	Proud to Love
Crossroads Debate	Puellula
Danish Pedophile Association	RoboFrosh
Debate Guide	SafeTnet
DreamScape	Somersault's Lounge
Elijah's Forum	Starry Twilight
Free Spirits	Teen Boys World

[a] Debate does exist as to whether ASFAR constitutes an adult–child sex advocacy group. We include ASFAR because it meets the selection criteria for the present study. In its call for the elimination of laws that establish age of consent for sexual relationships, ASFAR believes that children have the capacity to make the determination as to whether they want to have a sexual relationship with an adult and if such relationships are consensual, then they should not be prohibited. Early in its history, ASFAR became fractured as a group due to the active participation of pedophiles in its activities.

Communication and Participation Construct

This first construct refers to the structure of the website in terms of enabling participation and interaction among users and between site administrators and users. It reflects the capacity to build, on these websites, associations with other people who are interested in sexual relationships with minors. Communication and participation capabilities were assessed through the use of 11 variables. The two variables presented below were gathered on each website.

- *Country of registration*: The country in which the registrant of the adult–child sex advocacy community is located. Registrant information was gathered on each website using the publicly accessible online directory known as WhoIs (http://www.networksolutions. com/whois/index.jsp). This directory catalogs information on the registrant of a particular domain name, including name, e-mail address, and postal address. It also includes technical information on the domain name, including the host Internet Protocol (IP) address and location.
- *Language*: Language in which website content was published. Indicates a capability for interaction and participation among users with diverse linguistic backgrounds.

The remaining communication and participation variables were defined as dichotomous variables, with two response options (0 = *No*; 1 = *Yes*). Nine variables were gathered for each website:

- *Synchronous chat/IM*: The presence of a chat room or IM within the website structure.
- *Asynchronous forum*: The presence of a forum or message board within the website structure that allows users to post content and replies to previous posts. The postings must be archived and accessible by those who use the website.
- *Listserv*: The presence of a listserv, or mailing list, that is operated by the website to which users can subscribe.
- *Calendar of events*: The presence of a calendar on the website that displays group events or website functions (e.g., guest chats).
- *Donations*: Whether users can make a donation to the advocacy group through the website.
- *Children's section*: The presence of content on the website that was specifically marketed or directed at children to encourage their participation in the online community.
- *Official website membership*: The presence of a registration process for membership to the website or advocacy group.

- *Members-only section*: Pertains only to those websites or advocacy groups that have an official membership and whose content or resources can be accessed only by members.
- *Membership fee*: Pertains only to those websites or advocacy groups that have an official membership. It refers to whether there is a fee charged to gain membership to the website or advocacy group.

Techniques of Neutralization Construct

This second construct focuses on content that justifies sexual relationships between adults and children. These justifications serve to neutralize feelings of self-blame for transgressions that are deemed deviant by society at large and give rise to definitions that favor violations of the law. With respect to the techniques of neutralization put forth by Sykes and Matza (1957), we were particularly interested in looking for the presence of website content that offered the following justifications:

- *Condemnation of the condemners*: The presence of content on the website that attacks and discredits those who view sexual relationships between adults and children as wrong.
- *Denial of injury*: The presence of content that rejects the notion that harm falls upon children when they are involved in a sexual relationship with an adult.
- *Appeal to high loyalties*: The presence of content that associates the adult–child sex advocacy community with social movements that are not tied to pedophilia activism and that garner acceptance by segments of society (e.g., gay and lesbian rights groups and civil rights groups).

Each neutralization variable was defined as a dichotomous variable, with two response options (0 = *No*; 1 = *Yes*).

Imitation Content Construct

This third construct refers to the presence of stories that describe sexual relationships between adults and children. These stories convey a healthy sexual relationship. The positive portrayal of the relationship idealizes the behavior and, thus, increases its attractiveness for imitation. The following variables were gathered on each website:

- *Stories by adults*: The presence of stories that describe sexual relationships between adults and children as told through the eyes of an adult.
- *Child testimonial*: The presence of stories that describe sexual relationships between adults and children as told through the eyes of a child.

Both variables in the imitation content construct were defined as dichotomous variables, with two response options (0 = *No*; 1 = *Yes*).

Data Collection

All websites used in this study were identified and examined between December 18, 2006, and June 5, 2007. The boundaries of a particular website were limited to the publicly accessible pages included under the domain name used by the adult–child sex advocacy group. Our analysis for the present research was limited to content created by website administrators. Therefore, content created by website users that appeared in site forums, on bulletin boards, in chat rooms, or on listservs was not used in this study. At no point during the data collection process did members of the research team find, access, view, or download child pornography.

All measures were coded for each website by two independent raters. Prior to beginning the coding process, both raters were trained on the technical concepts associated with each measure. The raters were shown examples of chat rooms, IM interfaces, and listservs so that they understood the difference among these communication tools. The raters sat through a tutorial on using the WhoIs directory, in which they learned how to search for the country in which a website was registered. Definitions of the *condemnation of the condemners*, *denial of injury*, and *appeal to higher loyalties* variables were given to each rater; these definitions guided them in their searches for the presence of neutralization techniques in the content of the targeted websites. Training on the neutralization construct also involved the raters reviewing Sykes and Matza's (1957) seminal article on techniques of neutralization and previously published research by De Young (1988) and Durkin and Bryant (1999) involving rationalizations used by adults with sexual predilections toward children.

Individual websites were coded on the same day by both raters to minimize coding errors resulting from content changes on the target websites. Scheduling conflicts did, however, prevent the raters from coding some individual sites on the same day. In these instances, raters coded each individual website within 5 days of one another. The Cohen's kappa coefficient was used to assess interrater reliability on all measures. Kappa coefficients exceeding .75 are considered very good and indicative of high coding reliability, or agreement, among raters (Bryman, 2004). The kappa coefficients for all measures in the present study exceeded .81. A third rater was used when raters disagreed on a particular measure. The third rater coded only those measures that were in question for a particular website. The values coded by the third rater were then matched to the similar values coded by one of the original raters and were selected for inclusion in the final analysis.

Findings

Table 7.2 is a descriptive summary of the countries in which the adult–child sex advocacy websites were registered. Over 60% (62.5%) of the websites were registered in the United States. The Netherlands, Canada, and the United Kingdom rounded out the top four countries, with 14.1%, 7.8%, and 6.3% of the websites being registered in these places, respectively. The countries of Brazil, the Czech Republic, Finland, France, Liechtenstein, and Slovakia were home to the registrant of one website.

Table 7.3 is a descriptive summary of the languages in which the websites were published. As part of the selection criteria for this study, websites needed to be published in English or have an English-language translation available. Therefore, all 64 adult–child sex advocacy websites used in this study contained English-language content. Almost 19% of the websites were available in French and Spanish. Approximately 17% of the sites were available in German. Dutch-language translations were available on 15.6% of the websites. Czech, Danish, Farsi, Finnish, Hungarian, Italian, Polish, Portuguese, Russian, and Slovak translations were all available in less than 10% of the adult–child sex advocacy websites used in this study.

Table 7.4 is a descriptive summary of the website tools that enable interaction among users and between site administrators and users. Only 20.3% of adult–child sex advocacy websites hosted a chat room or supported IM for site users. Asynchronous forums were more popular than synchronous communication tools. Approximately 58% of the adult–child sex advocacy websites had online forums or bulletin boards for users to post topical messages and replies to earlier postings. For example, a post to the forum section of the Girl Chat website on January 9, 2007, by a user named *paper-doll* extolled the benefits of sexual relationships between children and adults and elicited six other community members to post a message about their relationship

Table 7.2 Country Where Website Is Registered

Country of Registration	Number of Sites	Percentage of Total Sites ($N = 64$)
United States	40	62.5
The Netherlands	9	14.1
Canada	5	7.8
United Kingdom	4	6.3
Brazil	1	1.6
Czech Republic	1	1.6
Finland	1	1.6
France	1	1.6
Liechtenstein	1	1.6
Slovakia	1	1.6

Table 7.3 Content Languages Appearing on Websites

Language	Number of Sites	Percentage of Total Sites (N = 64)
English	64	100
French	12	18.8
Spanish	12	18.8
German	11	17.2
Dutch	10	15.6
Italian	5	7.8
Portuguese	4	6.3
Czech	3	4.7
Hungarian	2	3.1
Polish	2	3.1
Danish	1	1.6
Farsi	1	1.6
Finnish	1	1.6
Russian	1	1.6
Slovak	1	1.6

experiences with children. Later that same day, a *Girl Chat* community member named *Lateralus* began a dialogue in the forum about the child actors in the movies *MirrorMask*, *Silent Hill*, and *Little Miss Sunshine*.

Listservs were not popular among adult–child sex advocacy websites. Only one site operated a listserv. Slightly more than 14% of the advocacy groups included a calendar on their website to display dates for upcoming events such as a group meeting or an online chat organized by the site administrators. Almost one quarter of the advocacy groups accepted donations online through their website. Only 6.3% of the adult–child sex advocacy websites contain content specifically directed at children who visit the site. Lastly, a majority (51.6%) of the websites had an official membership.

Table 7.4 Website Communication and Participation Tools

Communication/Participation Tools	Number of Sites	Percentage of Total Sites (N = 64)
Synchronous chat/IM	13	20.3
Asynchronous forum	37	57.8
Listserv	1	1.6
Calendar of events	9	14.1
Donations accepted on website	15	23.4
Children's section	4	6.3
Official site membership	33	51.6

IM, instant messaging.

Table 7.5 Membership Participation

Membership Participation Variable	Number of Sites	Percentage of Websites With Official Membership ($N = 33$)
Members-only section on site	25	75.8
Membership fees	2	6.1

Table 7.5 is a descriptive summary of measures concerning websites or advocacy groups that have an official membership. More than three-quarters (75.8%) of the websites with an official membership had content on the site that was restricted to members. Far fewer websites charged a membership fee. Only 6.1% of the websites with an official membership required users to pay a fee as part of the registration process.

Table 7.6 is a descriptive summary of the techniques of neutralization measures. Approximately 63% of the websites contained content that advocated at least one of the three neutralization measures gathered in this study. With respect to specific justifications or techniques to neutralize deviant behavior, 42.2% of the adult–child sex websites appealed to higher loyalties to gain acceptance of their actions by linking to websites of social movements that are not tied to pedophilia activism or causes supporting sexual relationships between adults and children. For example, the Age Taboo website (http://www.agetaboo.org) framed the issue of sexual relationships between adults and children in terms of the rights of sexual minorities by linking to the website of the American Civil Liberties Union's Lesbian Gay Bisexual & Transgender Project (http://www.aclu.org/lgbt-rights). Another example is the Boy Moment website (http://www.boymoment.com), which provided a link to the website of The Volunteer Institute (http://members.tripod.com/~Volunteer_Institute/index.html) to draw a connection between the care that adults show to children in whom they have a sexual interest and the concern that society shows to children who are homeless or runaways.

Twenty-three of the websites (35.9%) contained content condemning those people who speak out against sexual relationships between adults and children. For example, the following excerpt from the Free Spirits ("Participants are also," n.d.) website labels the police as the real abusers of children and

Table 7.6 Neutralization Content

Variable	Number of Sites	Percentage of Total Sites ($N = 64$)
Techniques of neutralization	40	62.5
Appeal to higher loyalties	27	42.2
Condemnation of the condemners	23	35.9
Denial of injury	23	35.9

chastises them for unscrupulous police procedures and inciting vigilantism against adults who engage in sexual relations with minors:

> Participants are also very aware of the legal issues. They understand the extreme penalties for even the slightest physical contact or suspicion of sexual contact between adult and minor. They know about the knock on the door in the middle of the night, the removal of and destruction of property, the planting of evidence and the extraordinary mental and sometimes physical torture of possible victims. They know that boys, even if not already victims, will become so at the hands of the police in the name of child protection. Readers are aware of the bashings and rapes in prison; the informing of neighbors and employers and the sign in the yard, the modern Scarlet Letter. ("Participants are also," n.d.)

Another attempt to neutralize one's own deviance by condemning the actions of those who speak out against adults who engage in sexual relationships with children was found on the Pedologues ("To those who do not like," n.d.) website. The following excerpt demonizes those people who do not understand the lure of sexual relations between adults and children and labels them as bigots and hypocrites:

> To those who do not like me and who purport to understand "what I'm about" yet are blind and deaf to your [sic] own ignorance, intolerance, and bigotry—those who have wished for my imprisonment for merely practicing my 1st Amendment rights, and would wish me dead or publicly humiliated simply for being attracted to minors—I pity you. Time will show just how hypocritical and lost you are. ("To those who do not like," n.d.)

Twenty-three of the websites (35.9%) contained content denying the notion that harm falls upon children when they are involved in a sexual relationship with an adult. For example, the following excerpt from the About Boylove ("Many, many prominent psychiatrists," n.d.) website uses alleged testimony from therapists, medical professionals, and university professors as the basis for stating that no harm comes to children who engage in sexual relationships with adult men:

> Many, many prominent psychiatrists, psychologists and other physicians, university professors and well-educated persons around the globe agree that the effects of boylove on pre-adolescent and adolescent boys cause no harm to the child at all! In fact, most of the time, the contact is seen as a very positive experience. ("Many, many prominent psychiatrists, n.d.)

A similar theme was found on the SafeTnet ("Boylovers," n.d.) website. The following excerpt from SafeTnet shows (a) a concern for the well-being of boys who capture the sexual interest of adult men, and (b) a denial that harm falls upon these boys from any subsequent physical relationship.

Boylovers ... are people whom you know. Men who deeply love and are concerned about the boys with whom they come in contact, men who would not harm a boy in any way. Men who are just like every other man except that they have been born with a sexual attraction to boys. ("Boylovers," n.d.)

Table 7.7 is a descriptive summary of the imitation measures. Approximately one quarter (23.4%) of the websites contained a specific section of stories describing sexual encounters between adults and children. Ten of these sites (15.6%) included stories of sex between adults and children as told through the eyes of the adult. For example, the following excerpt appeared on the Cerius Love website ("I am not sure," n.d.) as part of a story describing the internal dialogue that the adult author had with himself leading to his decision to have sex with a 14-year-old boy.

I am not sure that I ought to have sex with Gary. Physically, I find him attractive. I admire his maturity. I am flattered by the way he seems to like me. But I have reservations about going to bed with him. First of all, I have no idea how interested he is in going to bed with me. He has said he is gay, but I wonder how reliable such a pronouncement can be from a fourteen-year-old boy.

The second truth is that I will not turn him down. No matter what the origin of his desire is, whether his sexual orientation is stable or uncertain, I will not reject his sensuality. I am not a machine, and my responses are only governed by logic when significant desires are not at hand. If this boy comes to me, if he touches me, if he looks into my eyes and kisses me, my groin will respond with my approval. Whatever the purpose of my reservations about sleeping with Gary may be, their effect will not be to stop me from doing so. ("I am not sure," n.d.)

Nine of the sites (14.1%) included stories of consensual sex between an adult and a child as purportedly told through the eyes of the child. The following excerpt from the Boy Chat ("It was two years," n.d.) website is, for example, part of a larger story written by a 16-year-old boy who describes his sexual relationship with a 37-year-old man. The author claims that he was 13 years old when the sexual relationship began. He wrote, "It was two years before I went to bed with him. We'd never talked about it before; it was just friendship between us. But I'd known all along that he was a pedophile; he'd told me that in the first week I'd known him" ("It was two years," n.d.).

Table 7.7 Imitation Content

Variable	Number of Sites	Percentage of Total Sites ($N = 64$)
Stories of sexual interactions between adults and children	15	23.4
Stories by adults	10	15.6
Testimonials/stories by children	9	14.1

Discussion and Conclusion

In the present study, we report on a content analysis of websites that promote, advocate, and convey information in support of sexual relationships between adults and children. We examined criminogenic factors of adult–child sex advocacy websites to determine whether they were structured as learning environments for crimes involving the sexual exploitation of children. Specifically, we analyzed these sites to determine their capacity for fostering social ties and associations among people who favor sexual relationships between children and adults. We also analyzed these websites for the presence of content that can neutralize psychological restraints against crimes involving the sexual exploitation of children and, in turn, promote definitions favorable to violating the law. Last, we looked to see if these websites contained content that, if imitated, would result in children being sexually assaulted.

The adult–child sex advocacy community, or the collective of adult–child sex advocacy websites examined in this study, was multinational and offered the ability to participate in 15 different languages. The websites were registered across 10 countries, with a majority of the sites being registered in the United States. All sites were registered in countries that hold freedom of expression in high regard, scoring at least 15 out of 16 in 2007 on the Freedom of Expression Index calculated annually by Freedom House (2007). With the global reach of the Internet, advocates of sexual relationships between adults and children have sought countries in which to register their sites where speech supporting sexual relationships between adults and children is legally tolerated. The ability to use and contribute to the online communities of these adult–child sex advocacy groups in multiple languages reduces the barriers that language places on fostering social ties.

The multinational dimension of the online adult–child sex advocacy community is consistent with the global penetration of online communities that exist for trading child pornography images and video (Johnston, 2004; Ryan & Cook, 2008). The Wonderland Club, for example, amassed more than 750,000 child pornography images and required prospective members to contribute 20,000 images to gain entrance into the club (Wakefield, 1999; Wearden, 2001). At the time that this online child pornography ring was taken down by the international law enforcement community, the Wonderland Club had more than 200 members across 12 countries. The Teenboys online child pornography community dwarfed the Wonderland Club in its size and reach, with 1,800 members from around the world.

The adult–child sex advocacy websites examined in this study offered their users a number of options to foster relationships with like-minded people. More than half (57.8%) of the websites had *forums*, or *bulletin boards*, where users could post comments or request information from other users.

Real-time interaction was also available on some of the websites through chat rooms or IM services. The sites were also structured to promote a sense of community. For example, more than half (51.6%) of the websites had an official membership. On most sites, membership was free and gave users access to exclusive members-only content. Free membership is an important way of enticing users to forums supporting adult–child sexual relationships in that it eliminates the need to provide site administrators with credentials that divulge one's true identity (e.g., legal name, mailing address, and credit card number). Requiring users to provide identifying information to access online services catering to adult–child sexual relationships is considered a security risk by child pornographers and pedophiles that could result in their arrest (Jenkins, 2001; Sheldon & Howitt, 2007). In their attempt to build a community, some websites even posted a calendar to keep users informed of upcoming events related to the group and its mission.

In our analysis, we also found content that exposes users to rationalizations for crimes involving the sexual exploitation of children. Approximately 63% of the advocacy websites contained content that was meant to neutralize feelings of self-blame for sexual actions against children. The *appeal to higher loyalties*, or the attempt to gain legitimacy by drawing connections to more socially desirable causes than causes advocating sex between adults and children, was the most common technique used by adult–child sex advocacy websites to neutralize feelings of self-blame. Advocacy websites also sought to neutralize self-blame by denying that their members' actions cause harm to children and by condemning the actions of people or groups who are outspoken against adults who engage in sex with minors. In their analysis of postings by self-proclaimed pedophiles to Internet newsgroups pertaining to sex between adults and children, Durkin and Bryant (1999) found the use of the same exculpatory accounts as those found on the websites examined for this study. However, the use of neutralization techniques by advocacy groups to justify sexual relationships between children and adults is not new to the age of the Internet. De Young's (1988) analysis of hard copy publications by three adult–child sex advocacy groups in the United States (i.e., the Rene Guyon Society, the North America Man/Boy Love Association, and the Childhood Sensuality Circle) found content consistent with Sykes and Matza's (1957) four neutralization techniques (i.e., denial of injury, denial of victim, condemnation of the condemners, and appeal to higher loyalties).

Portrayals of criminal behavior have produced imitative effects through indirect forms of communication such as media reports (Akers, 2000; Donnerstein & Linz, 1986), television (Phillips, 1983), and online forums (Skinner & Fream, 1997). The effect size increases as a person shares characteristics with the model and views the outcome of the behavior favorably. Approximately one quarter of the websites studied contained personal stories that described a sexual relationship between an adult and child in a positive light. Alarming was the inclusion of stories as told from the perspective of the child who purportedly consented to the sexual relationship. The positive spin on these stories helps idealize sexual encounters with minors and, in turn, makes the behavior attractive to imitate for website users with predilections toward sex with children.

In terms of the impact on practice within the criminal justice system, our findings can guide the courts and community corrections officials when setting release conditions on Internet use for offenders being released on parole and defendants being released on probation for sex crimes involving children. Restrictions on computer and Internet use for sex offenders who act against minors are regularly imposed by the courts and have been upheld on appeal on many occasions (e.g., *United States v. Boston*, 2007; *United States v. Johnson*, 2005; *United States v. Paul*, 2001; *United States v. Thielemann*, 2009). A total ban on computer use and Internet access for people on probation or parole for a sex crime against a minor is not recommended and can be seen as a hardship by the courts, given the increasing reliance on these technologies for everyday tasks, including work and education (Smith, Grabosky, & Urbas, 2004). Instead, computer and Internet restrictions for those under the supervision of a community corrections agency for sex crimes against minors have traditionally included a ban against access to child and adult pornography and online interactions with minors, whether these interactions occurred in chat rooms, via IM, through e-mail, or on social networking sites (Hyne, 2002; Smith et al., 2004).

A number of technology solutions have recently become available to assist community corrections agencies in enforcing computer use restrictions imposed on sex offenders released into their jurisdiction by the courts. For example, Image Scan is a tool created by the U.S. Federal Bureau of Investigation that searches a computer for child pornography by cataloging image files stored on a hard drive or external storage media. Probation and parole officers can use Image Scan on site during supervision visits in the field. Impulse Control, by Internet Probation & Parole Control, Inc. (IPPC), is another tool that helps probation and parole officers manage sex offenders who have computer and Internet restrictions placed upon them by the courts. With Impulse Control, probation and parole officers can remotely set and manage the computer and Internet restrictions of the offenders they supervise. The software also allows officers to monitor offenders' online activities and automatically notifies them if restrictions are violated so that they may respond expeditiously.

Given the present findings, the courts should consider banning people who are under the supervision of a community corrections agency for sex crimes against minors from using adult–child sex advocacy websites. These bans would reduce the criminogenic concerns of exposing patrons of adult–child sex advocacy websites to like-minded people who can provide supporting definitions, or rationalizations, for criminal behavior. Community corrections agencies can adopt Internet management and monitoring tools, such as Impulse Control, to help enforce these restrictions.

Forced removal of adult–child sex websites from the Internet by government authorities is unlikely, given a general prohibition of criminal content on the sites by site administrators and the protections afforded to speech and expression in countries in which the sites are registered and hosted. Companies providing website hosting services can, however, be selective with the customers they decide to take on. For example, in its terms-of-service agreement for hosting online content, Web Site Source ("Company restrictions policy," n.d.) states that it has the right to refuse service to anyone. Thus, hosting companies with terms similar to the terms used by Web Site Source should make it a practice not to host sites advocating adult–child sexual relationships. Although not as broad as the hosting policy put forth by Web Site Source, the policies of companies such as MidPhase ("Terms of service," n.d.b) and WebHostingWorld ("Acceptable use policies," n.d.) restrict website content that contains, for example, satanic themes, hate speech, and pornography. These restrictions could easily be expanded to include content that advocates sexual relationships between adults and children. Some hosting companies, such as Yahoo! ("Yahoo! Small business consolidated terms of service," n.d.) and Infusion Hosting ("Terms of service," n.d.a), have policies that forbid content that is harmful to minors. These companies would be justified in banning adult–child sex advocacy websites from their servers, given that these sex advocacy websites foster communication among adults who have a sexual interest in children and contain content that advances rationalizations for sexually exploiting children.

Researchers examining adult–child sex advocacy websites in the future should consider the methodological limitations of the present study. The Internet—as a collection of computers, services, websites, and content—is constantly changing. The population of adult–child sex advocacy websites used for this study and the content on these sites have, most certainly, changed since the data were collected. Some websites, such as the website of International Boylovers United, are, for example, no longer available.[3] Likewise, new adult–child sex advocacy websites may have emerged. New online tools and services have materialized since the data were collected that may have changed the structure of existing adult–child sex advocacy websites, the methods by which website patrons communicate, and the places in which adult–child sex advocates congregate. One example is the emergence of the virtual community Second Life (http://secondlife.com/?v=1.1), which

---

[3] Our research team accessed the International Boylovers United website at http://www.iblu.net during the data collection phase of this study. This URL was no longer active when checked on January 26, 2010.

offers patrons of adult–child sex advocacy websites an alternative place to congregate—a physical space in which they can meet and interact with like-minded people ("Pedophile playground discovered," 2007).

Our analysis was limited to content created by website administrators; thus, we have not taken into consideration content created by visitors who use the asynchronous forums, listservs, and chat rooms affiliated with a website. This content may contain rationalizations and stories of sexual interactions with minors—which, in turn, may affect the social learning process as it pertains to the proclivity of adults to sexually assault children. The interplay between the physical and virtual worlds as it pertains to adult–child sex advocacy groups was also not considered in the present study. Future research should recognize that "social groups in cyberspace spill out in to [sic] the real world and vise [sic] versa" and should look to see how adult–child sex advocacy communities online affect how these groups organize in the physical world and, in turn, affect the victimization of children (Kollock & Smith, 2003, p. 18).

In the present study, we found that adult–child sex advocacy websites are criminogenic in that they contain myriad communication tools (e.g., chat rooms, instant messengers, and message boards) to foster interaction among site users. The bringing together of people who favor criminal behavior (i.e., sexual relationships between adults and children) is how—according to Akers (1998) and Sutherland (1947/1974)—the process of learning crime begins. Additionally, the adult–child sex advocacy websites exposed users to rationalizations for offending and, in turn, definitions favorable to sexual violations against minors. The personal accounts of sexual encounters offered by adults and minors on these websites play a vital role in the social learning process because they advance behaviors that, if imitated, would result in harm to children. Repeated exposure to these websites, the people who use these websites, the testimonials by adults and children about their sexual relationships, and the accompanying rationalizations for crime can set a normative reference for users. This repeated exposure can, thus, result in an excess of definitions favorable to sexual violations against minors over definitions unfavorable to sexual violations against minors. We, thus, recommend that courts ban the use of adult–child sex advocacy websites when setting community release conditions for sex offenders who have acted against minors. We also recommend that companies hosting websites modify their content restrictions to include content that is harmful to minors, including adult–child sex advocacy websites.

Acknowledgments

This project was supported by Grant No. 2006-DD-BX-0471 awarded by the Bureau of Justice Assistance. The Bureau of Justice Assistance is a component of the office of Justice Programs, which also includes the Bureau of Justice Statistics, the National Institute of Justice, the Office of Juvenile Justice and Delinquency Prevention, and the Office of Victims of Crime. Points of view or opinions in this document are those of the author and do not represent the official position or policies of the United States Department of Justice.

References

Acceptable use policies. (n.d.). On *WebHostingWorld* website. Retrieved from http://webhostingworld.net/aup.html

Akers, R. (1998). *Social learning and social structure: A general theory of crime and deviance.* Boston, MA: Northeastern University Press.

Akers, R. (2000). *Criminological theories: Introduction, evaluation, and application.* Los Angeles, CA: Roxbury Publishing Company.

Akers, R., Krohn, M. D., Lanza-Kaduce, L., & Radosevich, M. (1979). Social learning and deviant behavior. *American Sociological Review, 44,* 636–655.

Boylovers … are people whom. (n.d.). On *SafeTnet* website. Retrieved from http://safet.net

Bressler, S. E., & Grantham, C. E. (2000). *Communities of commerce: Building Internet business communities to accelerate growth, minimize risk, and increase customer loyalty.* New York, NY: McGraw-Hill.

Brunker, M. (1999, June 2). Streetwalkers in cyberspace: Oldest profession dons high-tech cloak. *MSNBC.* Retrieved from http://www.msnbc.msn.com/id/3078778

Bryman, A. (2004). *Social research methods.* New York, NY: Oxford University Press.

Company restrictions policy. (n.d.). On Web Site Source website. Retrieved from http://www. websitesource.com/company/restrictions.php#5

Cox, R. W., Johnson, T. A., & Richards, G. E. (2009). Routine activity theory and Internet crime. In F. Schmalleger & M. Pittaro (Eds.), *Crimes of the Internet* (pp. 302–316). Upper Saddle River, NJ: Pearson-Prentice Hall.

Denning, D. E. (2001). Activism, hacktivism, and cyberterrorism: The Internet as a tool for influencing foreign policy. In J. Arquilla & D. Ronfeldt (Eds.), *Networks and netwars: The future of terror, crime, and militancy* (pp. 239–288). Santa Monica, CA: RAND.

Denning, D. E., & Baugh, W. E. (1997). *Encryption and evolving technologies: Tools of organized crime and terrorism.* Washington, DC: U.S. Working Group on Organized Crime.

De Young, M. (1988). The indignant page: Techniques of neutralization in the publications of pedophile organizations. *Child Abuse and Neglect, 12,* 583–591.

Donnerstein, E., & Linz, D. (1986). Mass media sexual violence and male viewers. *American Behavioral Scientist, 29,* 601–618.

D'Ovidio, R., & O'Leary, B. (2006). *Online sexual exploitation of children.* Washington, DC: National Governors Association.

Durkin, K. F. (1997). Misuse of the Internet by pedophiles: Implications for law enforcement and probation practice. *Federal Probation, 61,* 14–18.

Durkin, K. F., & Bryant, C. D. (1999). Propagandizing pederasty: A thematic analysis of the on-line exculpatory accounts of unrepentant pedophiles. *Deviant Behavior, 20,* 103–127.

Fisher, W. W. (2004). *Promises to keep: Technology, law, and the future of entertainment*. Stanford, CA: Stanford University Press.

Freedom House. (2007). *Freedom in the world 2007 subscores*. Washington, DC: Freedom House. Retrieved from http://www.freedomhouse.org/template.cfm?page=372&year=2007

Gerstenfeld, P. B., Grant, D. R., & Chiang, C. (2003). Hate online: A content analysis of extremist Internet sites. *Analyses of Social Issues and Public Policy, 3*(1), 29–44.

Gonyer, J. (2007). The future of computing in business: How the Internet will change business. *Futurics, 31*(1–2), 37–39.

Hall, M. (2003, September 13). The darker side of travel. *U.K. Telegraph*. Retrieved from http://www.telegraph. co.uk

Higgins, G. E., & Makin, D. A. (2004a). Does social learning theory condition the effects of low self-control on college students' software piracy? *Journal of Economic Crime Management, 2*(2), 1–22.

Higgins, G. E., & Makin, D. A. (2004b). Self control, deviant peers, and software piracy. *Psychological Reports, 95*, 921–931.

Higgins, G. E., Wolfe, S. E., & Ricketts, M. L. (2009). Digital piracy: A latent class analysis. *Social Science Computer Review, 27*, 24–40.

Hofer, M. (2004). Online digital archives: Technology that supports rich, student-centered learning experiences. *Learning & Leading With Technology, 32*(2), 6–11.

Hollinger, R. C. (1993). Crime by computer: Correlates of software piracy and unauthorized account access. *Security Journal, 4*, 2–12.

Hyne, D. (2002). Examining the legal challenges to the restriction of computer access as a term of probation or supervised release. *New England Journal on Criminal and Civil Confinement, 28*, 215–246.

I am not sure. (n.d.). On *Cerius Love* website. Retrieved from http://www.cerius.org

It was two years. (n.d.). On *Boy Chat* website. Retrieved from http://www.boychat.org

Jenkins, P. (2001). *Beyond tolerance: Child pornography on the Internet*. New York, NY: New York University Press.

Jeon, S., Crutsinger, C., & Kim, H. (2008). Exploring online auction behaviors and motivations. *Journal of Family and Consumer Sciences, 100*, 31–40.

Johnston, L. (2004, January 15). Global kiddie porn ring busted. *CBS News*. Retrieved from http://www.cbsnews.com

Jordan, T., & Taylor, P. (2004). *Hacktivism and cyberwars: Rebels with a cause?* London, England: Routledge.

Jossi, F. (2001). Hiding in plain sight. *Wired*. Retrieved from http://www.wired.com

Kahn, R., & Kellner, D. (2004). New media and Internet activism: From the "battle of Seattle" to blogging. *New Media & Society, 6*(1), 87–95.

Kline, S., Dyer-Witheford, N., & DePueter, G. (2003). *Digital games: The interaction of technology, culture, and marketing*. Montreal, Quebec, Canada: McGill-Queen's University Press.

Kollock, P., & Smith, M. A. (2003). Communities in cyberspace. In M. A. Smith & P. Kollock (Eds.), *Communities in cyberspace* (pp. 3–25). New York, NY: Routledge.

Lastowka, F. G., & Hunter, D. (2006). Virtual worlds: A primer. In J. M. Balkin & B. S. Noveck (Eds.), *The state of play: Law, games, and virtual worlds* (pp. 13–28). New York, NY: New York University Press.

Mahfouz, A. Y., Philaretou, A. G., & Theocharous, A. (2008). Virtual social inter-
actions: Evolutionary, social psychological and technological perspectives. *Computers in Human Behavior, 24,* 3014–3026.

Many, many prominent psychiatrists. (n.d.). On *Boy Love* website. Retrieved from http://tperkins.com/bl.html

McAuliffe, W. (2001, February 13). Wonderland paedophiles are sentenced. Retrieved from http://news.zdnet.co.uk/itmanagement/0,1000000308,2084402,00.htm

McIntosh, S. (2005). Expanding the classroom: Using online discussion forums in college and professional development courses. In K. St. Amant & P. Zemliansky (Eds.), *Internet-based workplace communications: Industry and academic applications* (pp. 68–86). Hershey, PA: Information Science Publishing.

McKim, J. (2006, July 12). Pimp pleads guilty to prostituting minor. *Orange County Register.* Retrieved from http://www.ocregister.com/ocregister/news/atoz/article_1209170.php

Mitchell, K. J., Wolak, J., & Finkelhor, D. (2005). Police posing as juveniles online to catch sex offenders: Is it working? *Sexual Abuse: A Journal of Research and Treatment, 17,* 241–267.

Participants are also very. (n.d.). On *Free Spirits* website. Retrieved from http://www.freespirits.org

Pedophile playground discovered in 'second life' virtual world. (2007, November 7). Fox News. Retrieved from http://www.foxnews.com/story/0,2933,306937,00.html

Phillips, D. P. (1983). The impact of mass media violence on U.S. homicides. *American Sociological Review, 48,* 560–568.

Reid, E. (2005). Hierarchy and power: Social control in cyberspace. In M. A. Smith & P. Kollock (Eds.), *Communities in cyberspace* (pp. 107–133). New York, NY: Routledge.

Renninger, K. A., & Shumar, W. (2002). Community building with and for teachers at the Math Forum. In K. A. Renninger & W. Shumar (Eds.), *Building virtual communities: Learning and change in cyberspace* (pp. 60–95). New York, NY: Cambridge University Press.

Ryan, J., & Cook, T. (2008, December 12). Global child porn ring taken down. *ABC News.* Retrieved from http://abcnews.go.com

Schafer, J. A. (2002). Spinning the web of hate: Web-based hate propagation by extremist organizations. *Journal of Criminal Justice and Popular Culture, 9,* 69–88.

Sheldon, K., & Howitt, D. (2007.) *Sex offenders and the Internet.* Chichester, West Sussex, England: Wiley.

Skinner, W., & Fream, A. M. (1997). A social learning theory analysis of computer crime among college students. *Journal of Research in Crime and Delinquency, 34,* 495–518.

Smith, R. G., Grabosky, P., & Urbas, G. (2004). *Cyber criminals on trial.* Cambridge, England: Cambridge University Press.

Sutherland, E. H. (1947/1974). *Criminology* (4th ed.). Philadelphia, PA: J. B. Lippincott.

Sykes, G. M., & Matza, D. (1957). Techniques of neutralization: A theory of delinquency. *American Sociological Review, 22,* 664–670.

Taylor, M., & Quayle, E. (2003). *Child pornography: An Internet crime.* New York, NY: Brunner-Routledge.

Terms of service. (n.d.a). On *Infusion Hosting* website. Retrieved from http://
    infusionhosting.com/engb/index. php?page=terms
Terms of service. (n.d.b). On *MidPhase* website. Retrieved from http://www.midphase.
    com/terms/terms-of-service.php
To those who do not. (n.d.). On *Pedologues* website. Retrieved from http://pedologues.
    libsyn.org
Turkle, S. (1997). *Life on the screen: Identity in the age of the Internet*. New York, NY:
    Simon & Schuster.
United States v. Boston, 494 F.3d 660 (8th Cir. 2007).
United States v. Johnson, 446 F.3d 272 (2nd Cir. 2006).
United States v. Paul, 274 F.3d 155 (5th Cir. 2001).
United States v. Thielemann, 575 F.3d 265 (3rd Cir. 2009).
Wakefield, J. (1999, March 2). The net: Home to paedophile rings. March 22, 1999.
    http://news.zdnet. co.uk/security/0,1000000189,2071258,00.htm
Wearden, G. (2001, June 11). Police probe 1,800 strong Internet paedophile ring.
    Retrieved from http://news.zdnet.co.uk/communications/0,1000000085,20886
    57,00.htm
Wolak, J., Finkelhor, D., & Mitchell, K. J. (2005). *Child pornography possessors
    arrested in Internet-related crimes: Findings from the National Juvenile Online
    Victimization Study*. Alexandria: VA: National Center for Missing and Exploited
    Children.
Wolak, J., Mitchell, K. J., & Finkelhor, D. (2006). *Online victimization of youth:
    Five years later*. Alexandria, VA: National Center for Missing and Exploited
    Children.
Yahoo! Small business consolidated terms of service. (n.d.). On *Yahoo!* website.
    Retrieved from http://smallbusiness.yahoo.com/tos/tos.php

The Internet as a Terrorist's Tool
A Social Learning Perspective

8

TINA FREIBURGER
JEFFREY S. CRANE

Contents

Introduction

In the last 10 to 15 years, terrorists' use of the Internet has become of great concern to policymakers and academics. The fact that practically all terrorist groups are using the Internet and have established their own websites (Weimann, 2004b) has given rise to research examining the consequences of terrorist use of this resource. This research has found that the Internet allows terrorist groups to more effectively run their operations, reach out to supporters across larger geographic areas, and reduce their likelihood of being detected and apprehended (Weimann, 2004b; Whine, 1999). Many of these accomplishments have been possible because of the unique benefits that the Internet offers its users. It is host to a worldwide audience, requires a low level of skill to use, is able to immediately transfer information at a low cost, and allows the user to remain anonymous (Lachow & Richardson, 2007; Weimann, 2004b; Whine 1999). Given these functions and the lack of regulation imposed upon users, it is not surprising that the Internet has changed the many functions and effectiveness of terrorist organizations.

Although prior research has examined the prevalence of terrorist groups' usage of the Internet (e.g., Conway, 2006; Crilley, 2001; Gerstenfeld, Grant, & Chiang, 2003; Hoffman, 2006; Hosenball, Hirsh, Soloway, & Flynn, 2002; Kohlmann, 2006; Lachow & Richardson, 2007; Rosenau, 2005; Thomas, 2002, 2003; Weimann, 2004a, 2004b, 2006; Whine, 1999; Zanini & Edwards, 2005), the abundance of these inquiries have only offered descriptive accounts of the Internet as a safe place for terrorist groups to engage in recruitment, training, and propoganda distribution. This research has failed to apply criminological theory to the issue. Application of criminological theory enables a better understanding of how Internet use has increased terrorist groups' abilities to build operations, recruit new members from other geographical locations, and distribute information to further their cause. With this understanding, more effective policy responses can be formulated.

Social Learning and Terrorist Internet Activity

Social learning theory, developed by Akers (1985, 1998), has become a prominent theory in the study of criminal behavior. This perspective has been successfully applied to explain a variety of criminal behaviors across a variety of criminal populations, such as adolescent substance abuse (Akers & Cochran, 1985; Akers, Krohn, Lanza-Kaduce, & Radosevich, 1979; Akers & Lee, 1999), elderly drinking (Akers, La Greca, Cochran, & Sellers, 1989), and male college student–perpetrated sexual assault (Boeringer, 1992; Boeringer, Shehan, & Akers, 1993). Given the findings of the prior research conducted on terrorists' use of the Internet and the prior success of applying this theory to various types of criminal behavior, it appears that a better understanding of this issue can be generated by formulating the issue around social learning theory. *Social learning theory* operates through the four mechanisms of differential association, definition, differential reinforcement, and imitation (Akers, 1985, 1998; Akers & Sellers, 1994). Social learning theory argues that it is through these four mechanisms that deviant behavior is learned. By applying these four constructs to terrorists' uses of the Internet, researchers can better understand how the Internet is being used to enhance terrorist operations.

Differential Association

Differential association refers to the groups with which individuals associate. These groups supply the definitions that are both favorable and unfavorable to criminal behavior. All individuals are exposed to both types of definitions. Whether a person engages in criminal behavior depends on the types of definitions (favorable or unfavorable to criminal behavior) to which a person is exposed the most. In addition to the number of each type of definition to which an individual is exposed, the impact of the differential associations providing the definitions varies by the priority, frequency, and intensity of the differential associations (Akers, 1985; Akers & Sellers, 1994). Therefore, groups that are close to an individual, that have frequent contact with the individual, and that have been involved with the individual for a long period of time will have a greater impact on the individual's behavior (Akers, 1985, 1998).

Terrorist groups have successfully used the Internet to increase their memberships (Coll & Glasser, 2005; Crilley, 2001; Thomas, 2003). It appears that differential associations have been an important aspect in this success. Thanks to the Internet, terrorist groups have been able to successfully establish relationships with youths from various geographical areas and have transferred those group definitions that favor terrorist activities. Therefore, it appears that the terrorist group has become an important differential association for certain individuals, thus making it easy for groups to recruit these individuals as members. These groups have been so successful with Internet recruitment that they have even successfully recruited European-born youths who were living in Europe. For example, while living in France, Peter Cherif (a French citizen) was recruited by Al Qaeda via the Internet (Powell et al., 2005). Individuals like Peter Cherif, who are second-generation Islamic youths living in other countries, are especially susceptible to terrorists' recruitment via the Internet. These youths are unfamiliar with their country of origin and at the same time feel very different from others in their new country. Thus, they are unable to identify with either country. This feeling of not belonging is often confounded by economic hardships. Many of these individuals are unemployed and feel discriminated against because they do not physically look like citizens in their current country of residence. Therefore, they lack the relationships and differential associations that are present in the lives of other youths their age. However, instead of dealing with their feelings of isolation alone, they turn to the Internet to find a support system with other individuals in similar situations who share the same beliefs and frustrations (Powell et al., 2005). Through the Internet, they find a group with whom they can associate.

Although the same differential association can be developed in the physical world, it seems that the Internet has been able to more effectively build these relationships. To understand the Internet's full capacity to recruit terrorist members and allow individuals to form these associations, researchers must examine prior research showing the effects of the Internet on stigmatized groups. Although the ultimate message is vastly different across different stigmatized groups, it is reasonable to assume that feelings of isolation, loneliness, and disconnectedness felt by members of other groups are similar to those experienced by the youths who are enticed into terrorist groups through the Internet. Therefore, it may be assumed that Internet communication will change terrorists' operations in many of the same ways in which it has changed the activities of other groups and their members.

As mentioned earlier, the power of differential associations to affect individuals depends on duration, priority, and frequency (Akers, 1998). Because the Internet is accessible at all times, there is no limit on the frequency to which an isolated youth can access these web pages and associate with other members. Although they are unable to find solace and camaraderie in their physical environment, they find a virtual community available to them at all times where they are accepted and become a member. Due to the natural tendency to want to belong to a group and the boosting effect that support from others has on one one's self-esteem (Duaux, 1996; Ethier & Deaux, 1994), these youths are especially enticed by the existence and availability of other youths sharing the same feelings.

Because of the lack of prior attachment to other groups and feelings of isolation, it is possible that the terrorist group is the first differential association that these youths experience. Although this relationship is not created until later, the lack of earlier associations causes this association to quickly achieve higher priority. Research by McKenna and Bargh (1998) offers support for this argument. Their research suggests that the influence of virtual communities is especially influential for certain groups. When studying marginalized groups with concealable identities,[1] they found that individuals with stigmatized sexual identities and stigmatized ideological beliefs were more likely to share their beliefs and identities with friends and family in real life if they were part of online support groups. McKenna and Bargh's (1998) finding suggests that support garnered over the Internet affects individuals' real-world activities, causing them to act more quickly in their real lives. This finding also suggests that the differential associations developed via the Internet may be especially strong and influential for stigmatized groups. This is likely due to the higher priority given to this association—as it is possibly the first association to whom members are able to fully express themselves— and to the high frequency of use that websites (which are accessible 24 hours a day, 7 days a week) allow.

As discussed earlier, youths who are recruited via the Internet often experience feelings of isolation and a lack of belonging. Because these are many of the same feelings experienced by other stigmatized groups, it is likely that the Internet will have a similar influence on youths finding support from terrorist groups, and these youths will also be more likely to act out in the real world. Given the power of the Internet to elicit action from individuals,

---

[1] Concealed marginalized identities were defined by Frable (1993) as those who are able to hide their marginalized identities and keep them a secret from larger society.

it is reasonable, therefore, to predict that terrorist group members who are recruited and groomed through the Internet will be more willing to resort to violent action more quickly than terrorists of the past. Once these youths begin to share their beliefs and frustrations and participate more in discussions, their association with the group intensifies. Their increased identification with the group further internalizes their identity as members of the terrorist group. At this point, youths will start to accept definitions favorable to terrorism and incorporate these definitions into their belief system.

Definitions

The term *definitions* refers to the meanings that individuals assign to given behaviors and situations. Specifically, definitions determine whether certain behavior is considered to be right or wrong. These assignments are typically associated with individuals' attitudes and beliefs (Akers, 1998). Once an individual accepts more definitions that are favorable to deviant behavior than definitions that are unfavorable to deviant behavior, the individual is free to engage in the given deviant behavior. As shown in prior research, the Internet serves as a very useful tool that groups can use to allocate those definitions that are favorable to terrorist activities. This allocation is especially easy for online groups: The Internet lacks any type of regulation, thus allowing groups to present themselves in a positive light. This can be very helpful in attracting potential recruits and converting them into supporters, especially those who are "fence sitters" (Thomas, 2003). The ability to connect individuals across large geographical areas also can give the illusion that the group is larger than it really is, thus making the groups' deviant beliefs appear less extreme and more widely held.

It appears that groups also take great care to direct focus away from their negative actions and to justify their violent behavior by arguing that violence was the last option after all other avenues had been exhausted (Tsfati & Weimann, 2002). These authors also found that groups portrayed their target as the aggressor and the terrorist group as the passive recipient of that aggression. In fact, many groups showed the target actively engaging in violence against group members who were seeking a peaceful resolution. This leaves the viewer with the impression that violence by the terrorist group is necessary and is the only option available to fight the injustice inflicted upon the group by the target.

Terrorist group web pages also work to sensationalize the violent acts that are committed by showing well-designed websites that contain digital content. This can be especially appealing to computer-savvy, video-playing, media-consuming youths (Zanini & Edwards, 2005). Such actions also make violent activities appear less real and more like a video game, working to dehumanize the targets of the attack and to make the justification of violence easier.

All of these strategies can work to make definitions that are favorable to terrorist behavior easier for youths to accept. Violence that is applied only when it is justifiable and righteous fits more easily into these individuals' existing belief structures. Further, the presentation of the target as "evil" and "artificial" makes the use of violence seem like an acceptable response. This more easily allows the youths to incorporate definitions favorable to violent terrorist activities.

Differential Reinforcement

The term *differential reinforcement* refers to the perceived and actual consequences of an individual's behavior. If an individual engages in a behavior and is later rewarded, it is likely that they will continue to engage in that behavior. However, if the person suffers negative consequences, it is unlikely that the behavior will continue. Differential reinforcement can occur (a) before the initial behavior is engaged, through perceived consequences, and (b) after the initial behavior is engaged, through actual consequences. Differential reinforcement also can occur vicariously through the positive or negative consequences given to others. In other words, individuals currently engaging in or considering engaging in a behavior will be influenced by the consequences that they witness others around them experiencing (Akers, 1985, 1998).

The element of differential enforcement is easily created via the Internet. Here, members of terrorist groups can become instant celebrities: Terrorist groups can create their own image of a member, exaggerating the positive consequences and downplaying the negative consequences of engaging in a certain behavior. This is evident in research examining the content of terrorists' websites, such as that conducted by Tsfati and Weimann (2002). In their content analysis, the authors found that terrorist groups tend to glorify members who had engaged in terrorist activities (e.g., suicide bombers), presenting them as heroes who will reap the benefits of their actions in the afterlife. For youths, whose identity to the group is being strengthened, this glorification gives the impression that the negative consequences of their actions will be greatly outweighed by the vast positive consequences. For example, a member who is convinced to engage in suicide bombing will suffer the negative consequence of death, but this consequence is greatly minimized by the rewards granted in the afterlife.

In addition to the promise of reward in the afterlife, youths who engage in actual terrorist activities may be rewarded with a boost of self-esteem and an increased feeling of belonging. Researchers have found that participation in activities related to identification with one's group increases the amount of self-esteem garnered from being a member of that particular group (Duaux, 1996; Ethier & Deaux, 1994). For example, Ethier and Deaux (1994) conducted a study of Hispanic college students and found that actively participating in Hispanic cultural groups and activities led to an increase in self-esteem and an increase in members' identification with their group.

Imitation

Imitation refers to the modeling of behaviors that can be copied by those learning the behavior (Akers, 1985). Although Internet recruitment (especially across vast geographic regions) reduces the possibility for imitation in the physical world, terrorist groups have used the Internet to provide the information and directions necessary online for recruits to imitate terrorist activities (Gips, 2005). Often, groups will openly post this information on the Internet, which any member (or potential member) can access. For example, Forest (2006) found an Al Qaeda website encouraging supporters to attack the Alaska pipeline. The website provided a great deal of information (e.g., maps) about the pipelines. Several online books on bomb making and suicide bombings also were available for viewing online (Forest, 2006). Other sites provided instructions on kidnapping hostages and on the treatment of those hostages (Faye, 2004). With these online resources available, groups are therefore able to reduce the need for physical imitation and training.

Sequence of Events

Prior research has found that many youths who are recruited via the Internet are social outcasts and have difficulty fitting into mainstream society. These youths are turning to the Internet to establish differential associations where they find belonging and acceptance. Terrorist websites are especially attractive to these youths, as such sites offer a very sensational message that is illustrated with graphic media images (Gips, 2005). These images offer entertainment and are always available. The more frequently that youths access these websites, the more likely they are to accept definitions favorable to the groups' activities.

After becoming a member of the group and accepting the definitions favorable to group activities, differential reinforcement becomes an important component for eliciting action. To account for this, it appears that terrorist websites emphasize the positive consequences of engaging in group activities. Not only are positive consequences of engaging in operations emphasized, but engagement also offers certain immediate benefits. The more time that youths spend consuming the terrorists message, the more committed they become to the issue online, thus increasing their desire to make terrorist activities part of their "real" life. In fact, the actual act may be the only way to really feel like they "belong" and may act as a tool to increase self-esteem. In addition, with many viewers and "members" on the

Internet, it might be more difficult to feel as if one really truly belongs and is truly committed to the cause. Therefore, it may take this physical act to feel special, unique, different, and fully committed. Once the decision is made to engage in a terrorist activity, numerous websites are available to give directional information on how to perform the action train, thereby reducing the need for real-life imitation.

Policy Response

Use of the Internet by terrorist groups has increased the ability of these groups to enlist new recruits and persuade members to take actions on a particular terrorist group's behalf. Therefore, counterterrorist efforts must consider the Internet's unique influence on terrorist efforts and adopt similar strategies to counter terrorist groups' messages. The Internet should be seriously considered as a social learning tool that the government can use to counter terrorists' accomplishments.

Given the importance of differential associations and definitions reflected in current research on terrorists' Internet recruiting operations, counterterrorists' efforts should strongly focus on offering equivalent alternatives. Counterstrategies should offer some of the same things that the terrorist organizations offer—such as companionship and belonging. To properly facilitate this, the individuals offering support must understand the circumstances and feelings that these "potential recruits" are experiencing. To increase the priority, frequency, and intensity at which these individuals access the counterterrorist websites, the websites should offer sensational and entertaining images to attract youths.

It is important that antiterrorist groups offer definitions that are unfavorable to terrorist activities and beliefs—but not in an overly aggressive manner. Instead, the focus should be on supporting the group's members and helping them work through their frustrations. These sites can provide an emotional outlet that is an alternative to what is offered on the terrorist websites. However, information should also be provided that supports an antiterrorism viewpoint, which youths can use to formulate a balanced opinion. Offering this type of alternative support group with an antiterrorism viewpoint could reduce the likelihood that these youths will begin or continue engaging in extremist activity.

In addition to providing information that counters the views of terrorist groups and offering support systems to those who are in need of companionship, antiterrorist groups and countries must be cautious of the information that is put forth on their behalf. Even information that is distributed by private citizens that expresses negative views of minority groups can be harmful to antiterrorist efforts. For example, Rosenau (2005) argues that anger and ignorance toward Muslims has contributed to hatred of the United States by giving the appearance that U.S. citizens dislike Muslims. If potential recruits view citizens as an enemy, terrorist groups' efforts to recruit these individuals will likely be much more successful. Additionally, antiterrorist information distributed by governments will likely be rejected and viewed as untrustworthy. Therefore, antiterrorist groups should also send the message that traditional Muslim beliefs are accepted and respected. As suggested by Rosenau (2005), the U.S. government should highlight the traditional beliefs of Muslims to illustrate the inconsistencies between them and the extreme beliefs of Al Qaeda. Further education should also be provided on basic U.S. ideology. However, up to now, the United States' efforts to educate Muslims on U.S. ideology have been weak and ineffective (Lachow & Richardson, 2007; Rosenau, 2005). By also focusing on more universal values and goals (e.g., basic human rights) and by not pushing democracy, countries combating terrorism can more readily garner support. Successfully introducing even a small amount of doubt in the minds of groomed recruits may be enough to prevent them from accepting definitions favorable to terrorist activity into their belief system.

To counter terrorist groups' abilities to differentially reinforce the positive value of engaging in their activities, antiterrorist efforts should offer information on the negative consequences associated with these activities. These efforts can educate youths on the harm and suffering that has been produced by these terrorist acts. It may be especially important to publicize incidents in which Muslims were the victims of the terrorist activities.

Because of the free flow and accessibility of information allowable on the Internet, it is unlikely that counterterrorist actions will be able to stop websites from posting materials for training and imitation (see discussions in Nemes, 2002; Talbot, 2005). A common response to this problem has been to regulate Internet use. This argument suggests that the government should force private Internet companies to regulate who uses the Internet and to keep a record listing their reasons for using it (Lewis, 2005; Valeri, 2000). Terrorist groups using the Internet would then be identifiable, and governments would be able to ban these groups' Internet use. Such efforts have been implemented in China and Vietman (Gomez, 2004).

Opponents of this strategy, however, argue that an absolute ban is impossible. Kohlmann (2006) argues that this task would be too laborious to be effective; instead, the government needs to monitor the websites. Terrorists will simply access the Internet from another country where restrictions are less strict or will access the Internet fraudulently and hide their messages on other web pages (Kohlmann, 2006; Weimann, 2004a). The prospect of shutting down terrorists' websites also creates questions regarding the constitutionality of such efforts. Given the rights set forth by the First Amendment, U.S. courts have ruled that propaganda distributed on the Internet is protected (Nemes, 2002; Talbot, 2005). Therefore, it appears that terrorists will continue to be able to house websites inside the United States. Because of the questions surrounding the effectiveness and plausibility of obtaining an international consensus for shutting down websites, this does not seem to be a viable response option.

Given these concerns, counterterrorist efforts should instead concentrate on the monitoring of these websites. This strategy can be especially beneficial, as many of the terrorists' Internet postings can be viewed by anyone, including antiterrorist agencies. In the past, law enforcement officials have used technological traces to intercept terrorists' activities (Zanini & Edwards, 2005). Kohlmann (2006) argues that governmental monitoring of these websites can produce knowledge regarding terrorists' plans and motives. If terrorists' web pages are removed, terrorist affiliates will no longer be able to gather information; however, counterterrorist agencies also will be shut off from gathering information on terrorists' activities. By remaining aware of the content on these websites, counterterrorist efforts can encrypt terrorists' messages and infiltrate the planning strategies conducted online.

Conclusion

In this chapter, we have examined the issue of terrorists' use of the Internet. As discussed, use of the Internet has greatly benefited terrorist groups by allowing them to more effectively perform operations with a reduced risk of apprehension. Up to now, research on terrorists' use of the Internet has been largely descriptive. There have been few attempts to apply theoretical understanding to the issue. By combining the fields of description and theoretical knowledge, researchers and counterterrorist agencies can develop a deeper understanding of the consequences of terrorists' use of the Internet.

Therefore, as a way of better understanding this issue, the four elements of social learning theory were applied to offer insight into this issue and to provide a policy response. First, differential association offers support and identity to youths who suffer from feelings of isolation, disconnectedness, and loneliness. Next, an individual begins to adopt the group's definitions being presented as favorable to terrorist action. At the same time, differential reinforcement is given through messages being displayed to the individual that focus on the positive consequences of engaging in terrorist activities. Websites also are available that provide the information and direction needed for the new recruit to imitate terrorist behavior.

When developing an antiterrorist strategy, these same concepts should be explored. First, alternative groups that oppose terrorist ideology should be available as an alternative to isolated youths seeking companionship. These groups can offer many of the same benefits that the terrorist groups offer to youths, such as companionship and a sense of belonging. When youths access these groups, they can also communicate definitions unfavorable to terrorist ideology and activity, pointing out contradictions in the beliefs set forth in terrorist ideology and the negative aspects of terrorist groups.

References

Akers, R. (1985). *Deviant behavior: A social learning approach*. Belmont, CA: Wadsworth.

Akers, R. (1998). *Social learning and social structure: A general theory of crime and deviance*. Boston, MA: Northwestern University Press.

Akers, R. L., & Cochran, J. K. (1985). Adolescent marijuana use: A test of three theories of deviant behavior. *Deviant Behavior, 6*, 323–346.

Akers, R. L., Krohn, M. D., Lanza-Kaduce, L., & Radosevich, M. (1979). Social learning and deviant behavior: A specific test of a general theory. *American Sociological Review, 44*, 636–655.

Akers, R. L., La Greca, A. J., Cochran, J., & Sellers, C. (1989). Social learning theory and alcohol behavior among the elderly. *The Sociological Quarterly, 30*, 625–638.

Akers, R. L., & Lee, G. (1999). Age, social learning, and social bonding in adolescent substance use. *Deviant Behavior, 19*, 1–25.

Akers, R., & Sellers, C. (1994). *Criminological theories* (4th ed.). Los Angeles, CA: Roxbury.

Boeringer, S. (1992). *Sexual coercion among college males: Assessing three theoretical models of coercive sexual behavior* (Unpublished doctoral dissertation). University of Florida, Gainesville, FL.

Boeringer, S., Shehan, C. L., & Akers, R. L. (1993). Social contexts and social learning in sexual coercion and aggression: Assessing the contribution of fraternity membership. *Family Relations, 40*, 558–564.

Coll, S., & Glasser, S. G. (2005, Aukgust 7). Terrorist turn in the web as base of operations. *The Washington Post*. Retrieved from http://www.washingtonpost.com/wp-dyn/content/article/2005/08/05/AR2005080501138_pf.html

Crilley, K. (2001). Information warfare: New battlefields terrorist, propaganda and the Internet. *Aslib Proceedings, 53*, 250–264.

Duaux, K. (1996). Social identification. In E. T. Higgins & A. W. Kruglanski (Eds.), *Social psychology: Handbook of basic principles* (pp. 777–798). New York, NY: Guilford Press.

Ethier, K. A., & Deaux, K. (1994). Negotiating social identity when contexts change: Maintaining identification and responding to threat. *Journal of Personality and Social Psychology, 67*, 243–251.

Faye, B. (2004, July 28). Terrorists spread their messages online. *Christian Science Monitor, 96*(170), 3–4.

Forest, J. J. F. (2006). The Democratic disadvantage in the strategic communications battlespace. *Democracy & Security, 2*(1), 73–101.

Gerstenfeld, P. B., Grant, D. R., & Chiang, C. (2003). Hate online: A content analysis of extremist Internet sites. *Analyses of Social Issues and Public Policy, 3*(1), 29–44.

Gips, M. A. (2005). Global jihad, one hit at a time. *Security Management, 49*(7), 16–17.

Gomez, J. (2004). Dumbing down democracy: Trends in Internet regulation, surveillance and control in Asia. *Pacific Journalism Review, 10*(2), 130–150.

Hoffman, B. (2006). *The use of the Internet by Islamic extremists.* Retrieved from http://www.rand.org/pubs/testimonies/2006/RAND_CT262-1.pdf

Hosenball, M., Hirsh, M., Soloway, C., & Flynn, E. (2002, December 30). Al Qaeda's new life. *Newsweek, 141*(1), 47. Retrieved from http://www.newsweek.com/2002/12/29/al-qaeda-s-new-life.html

Kohlmann, E. (2006). The real online terrorist threat. *Foreign Affairs, 85*(5), 115–124.

Lachow, I., & Richardson, C. (2007). Terrorist use of the Internet: The real story. *JFQ: Joint Force Quarterly, 45,* 100–103.

Lewis, J. A. (2005). Aux armes, citoyens: Cyber security and regulation in the United States. *Telecommunications Policy, 29,* 821–803.

McKenna, K. Y. A., & Bargh, J. A. (1998). Coming out in the age of the Internet: Identity "demarginalization" through virtual group participation. *Journal of Personality and Social Pyschology, 75,* 681–694.

Nemes, I. (2002). Regulating hate speech in cyberspace: Issues of desirability and efficacy. *Information & Communications Technology Law, 11*(3), 193–220.

Powell, B., Carsen, J., Crumley, B., Walt, V., Gibson, H., & Gerlin, A. (2005, September 26). Generation Jihad. *Time, 166,* 56–59. Retrieved from http://www.time.com/time/magazine/article/0,9171,1109334-1,00.html

Rosenau, W. (2005). Waging the "war of ideas." In D. Kamien (Ed.), *Homeland security handbook* (pp. 1131–1148). New York, NY: McGraw-Hill.

Talbot, D. (2005). Terror's server. *Technology Review, 108*(2), 46–52.

Thomas, T. L. (2002). Information-age 'de-terror-ence.' *Military Review, 82*(1), 32–38.

Thomas, T. L. (2003). Al Qaeda and the Internet: The danger of "cyberplanning." *Parameters, 23*(1), 112–123.

Tsfati, Y., & Weimann, G. (2002). www.terrorism.com: Terror on the Internet. *Studies in Conflict & Terrorism, 25,* 317–332.

Valeri, L. (2000). Securing Internet society: Toward an international regime for information assurance. *Studies in Conflict & Terrorism, 23,* 128–146.

Weimann, G. (2004a). The theater of terror: The psychology of terrorism and the mass media. *Journal of Aggression, Maltreatment, & Trauma, 9,* 379–390.

Weimann, G. (2004b). *www.terror.net How modern terrorism uses the Internet.* Washington DC: United States Institute of Peace.

Weimann, G. (2006). *Terror on the Internet: The new arena, the new challenges.* Washington DC: United States Institute of Peace.

Whine, M. (1999). Cyberspace—A new medium for communication, command, and control by extremists. *Studies in Conflict & Terrorism, 22,* 231–246.

Zanini, M., & Edwards, S. J. A. (2005.) *The networking of terror in the information age.* In J. Arquilla & D. Ronfeldt (Eds.), *Networks and netwars: The future of terror, crime, and militancy* (pp. 29–60). New York, NY: Rand Corporation.

Digital Piracy III

Value and Choice
Examining Their Roles in Digital Piracy

9

GEORGE E. HIGGINS

Contents

As the Internet has grown, so have the opportunities to carry out different forms of criminal behavior. One such form is digital piracy. *Digital piracy* is defined as the illegal copying of digital goods, software, digital documents, and digital audio (including music and voice) for any reason other than to back up without the explicit permission from and compensation to the copyright holder (Gopal, Sanders, Bahattacharjee, Agrawal, & Wagner, 2004). Digital piracy has been illegal since the 1974 Copyright Act that was expanded in the No Electronic Theft Act (Koen & Im, 1997). From these laws emerged several court cases related to pirating software, music, and movies from the Internet (Motivans, 2004).

These laws pertain to the United States, but the World Intellectual Property Organization (WIPO) has developed several treaties to assist in the protection of copyrights. These treaties include *The Copyright Treaty, The Performers and Produces of Phonograms Treaty,* and *The Databases Treaty.* The development of these treaties has not reduced the veracity of piracy. In fact, Rao (2003) showed that the international piracy rates increased between 2000 and 2001, providing evidence that piracy is a worldwide endeavor.

The worldwide nature of piracy comes as no surprise, considering the attributes of the Internet. The Internet provides *pirates* (i.e., individuals who participate in digital piracy) with a haven in which to perform this behavior. In fact, the perceived anonymity of the Internet provides pirates with a sense of security as they perform their criminal acts. Pirates' criminal activity has cost the software industry billions of dollars in lost revenue, along with a substantial number of lost jobs and government revenue (Business Software Alliance, 2003).

Given that digital piracy is illegal but still performed, it is important to understand the individual who is likely to carry out such criminal behavior. Some researchers have shown that software piracy takes place at a rampant pace among college students (Hinduja, 2001, 2003; Hollinger, 1988), which is not surprising given the cost of software and the necessity of having it in order to survive college life (Higgins, 2005). Other researchers have shown that positive attitudes (Rahim, Seyal, & Rahman, 2001), low self-control (Higgins, 2005; Higgins, Wilson, & Fell, 2005), and pieces of social learning theory (Higgins et al., 2005) are important correlates to software piracy. Gopal et al. (2004) showed that parts of deterrence theory were relevant in reducing software piracy. With these advances, no study has examined the mediational role of rational choice between self-control and digital piracy. To that end, the role of value has gone understudied in rational choice research.

The purpose of this study is to contribute to the literature by examining the links among low self-control, rational choice, value, and digital piracy. This study builds on the groundbreaking work from Piquero and Tibbetts (1996) by assuming that rational choice mediates the link between low self-control and digital piracy. This assumption enables this study to contribute to the literature in two ways: (a) validate the Piquero and Tibbetts (1996) model of rational choice, and (b) advance the literatures of rational choice, self-control theory, and digital piracy by including a measure of value in the model as a form of motivation. To make these contributions, this study presents self-control theory and rational choice theory. The role of value in self-control and rational choice theories is discussed, followed by a discussion of the methods, results, and discussion.

Self-Control Theory

Gottfredson and Hirschi's (1990) *self-control theory* is the latest advance in a long line of self-control theories in criminology (Agnew, 1995; Tibbetts & Gibson, 2002). In this version of the theory, low self-control is the single individual-level cause of crime and deviance. *Low self-control* is a time-stable individual propensity for crime and deviance that is the probable result of poor or ineffective parenting practices that occur before the age of 8 years. To develop proper levels of self-control, parents need to have established an emotional bond with their child. Once this bond is established, the parents are able to gather behavioral information about their child. Then, the parents can analyze the behavioral information to determine if it is deviant and can noncorporally discipline deviant behavior. When parents poorly or ineffectively perform these tasks, the child is likely to develop low self-control. Individuals with low self-control tend to prefer simple and easy tasks; choose physical over mental activities; engage in risky behaviors; be self-centered; and be unable to control their tempers. Given these characteristics, individuals with low self-control are more likely to disregard the long-term effects of their decisions for themselves and others (Gottfredson & Hirschi, 1990).

With this disregard, low self-control may show itself in a number of ways. One way is through criminal and deviant acts. Gottfredson and Hirschi (1990) argued that a crime is an act of force or fraud that an individual pursues to satisfy their own interests. Crimes and deviant acts are attractive to individuals who have low self-control because they prefer tasks that are risky, immediately gratifying, and easy and simple to perform (Gottfredson & Hirschi, 1990).

Given that digital piracy is a criminal act, in many ways, its characteristics are similar to those of individuals with low self-control. For instance, the individual with low self-control is not likely to honor the trust in the licensing agreement between the creator of the digital media and the copyright holder. To some people, digital piracy provides a thrill. The Internet is a simple device to manipulate, so digital piracy—in many instances—is simple and easy to perform.

Researchers have consistently supported Gottfredson and Hirschi's (1990) theory. The majority of the research has focused on the connection between low self-control and crime. Pratt and Cullen's (2000) meta-analysis shows that low self-control has at least a moderate link with crime. Some researchers have shown that low self-control remains relatively stable over time (Arneklev, Cochran, & Gainey, 1999; Turner & Piquero, 2002). Other researchers have shown that low self-control is linked to digital piracy (Higgins, 2005; Higgins & Makin, 2004a,b; Higgins et al., 2005). Based on these results, it is expected that low self-control has a direct effect on digital piracy. Next, we explore the roles of rational choice theory and value in the digital piracy literature.

Rational Choice Theory

Rational choice theory contains three components. First, the individual is likely to perform criminal acts that he or she believes are beneficial. This behavior implies that the individual makes a distinction between the perceived costs and the perceived benefits. To do so, the individual needs to have all available information. This is not likely, so a decision needs to be made using *bounded rationality*.

Second, to understand the decision-making process, researchers must make the focus crime specific; this type of focus enables researchers to capture the idiosyncrasies of different needs that are attached to a criminal act. This enables the focus to be on the criminal situation or context rather than the individual perpetrator. Without this type of focus, an important context for intervention is lost.

Third, an important distinction is made between criminal involvement and the criminal event. *Criminal involvement* is the process of acting upon information to become involved in a particular crime (Cornish & Clarke, 1986). The *criminal event* is what perpetrators use to participate in a specific crime. The information that emanates from the criminal event is short term.

Rational choice theory has a substantial amount of support in the empirical literature (Bachman, Paternoster, & Ward, 1992; Nagin & Paternoster, 1993; Piquero & Tibbetts, 1996; Tibbetts, 1997; Tibbetts & Myers, 1999). Three streams of research were available that concerned the integration of self-control theory and rational choice theory: theory, moderating effects, and mediating effects. Theoretically, self-control theory is built on a base of rational choice (Gottfredson & Hirschi, 1990). Specifically, Gottfredson and Hirschi (1990) argued that an individual's level of self-control influences the ability to see the consequences (i.e., potential costs) of his or her actions. Researchers have shown that rational choice measures moderate the link between self-control and crime (Wright, Caspi, Moffitt, & Paternoster, 2004). Other researchers have shown that rational choice mediates the link between self-control and crime (Higgins & Marcum, 2005; Nagin & Paternoster, 1993; Tibbetts, 1997; Tibbetts & Myers, 1999). Only one study has provided an examination of this type with digital piracy. Higgins and colleagues (2005) showed that severity of punishment reduced the likelihood for digital piracy. Thus, it is expected that external beliefs, shame, morality, and prior behavior have a link with digital piracy.

Piquero and Tibbetts (1996) used responses to a factorial survey from college students and structural equation modeling (SEM) to examine the mediating role of situational characteristics between low self-control and crime (i.e., drinking and driving, shoplifting). Their results indicated that a large portion of the effects on crime were indirect through the situational characteristics. In the end, the results indicated that situational characteristics were influenced by individual propensities, thus supporting the view that individual propensities would supersede situational characteristics (Cornish & Clarke, 1986).

Although these studies provided advances to understanding digital piracy, the studies do not take into account the role of value. Given that rational choice measures may not always account for all the variation or changes in behavior, additional research is necessary in the context of digital piracy.

The Role of Value in Rational Choice and Self-Control Theories

The central tenant of rational choice theory is subjective expected utility. *Utility* is defined as follows:

> The concept of utility respects the variety of human goals. It represents whatever people want to achieve. Some people do not want pleasure as much as they want other things (such as virtue, productive work, enlightenment, respect, or love—even when these are painful things to have). The utility of an outcome is also different from the amount of money we would pay to achieve it. (Baron, 1988, p. 493)

This definition comes from the utilitarian moral philosophy. The behaviors that provide happiness are usually deemed correct, whereas the behaviors that are not correct usually evoke an emotion that is the opposite of happiness. With this in mind, the *subjective expected utility (SEU) theory* assumes that rational beings will seek to maximize the utility and subjective probability of happiness. Under this supposition, researchers and theorists asserted that value is the equivalent of happiness (Deci & Ryan, 1991).

The Present Study

The present study addresses a gap in the literature by examining the roles of value, rational choice, and self-control in the context of digital piracy. This study contributes to these respective literatures by going beyond previous research (Nagin & Paternoster, 1993; Piquero & Tibbetts, 1996; Tibbetts & Myers, 1999).

Method

After Institutional Review Board and Human Subject Protection review, the data for this study were collected during the fall 2004 semester. College students from a university in the southeastern United States responded to self-report questionnaires after being informed of the voluntary nature of the study and their rights as respondents. The students were enrolled in courses that were open to all majors. This set of procedures yielded 382 completed surveys. Although some researchers say that college student samples are problematic (Wright et al., 2004), for this study, the sample resembles the characteristics of other digital piracy studies (Hinduja, 2001, 2003; Hollinger, 1988; Husted, 2000).

Measures

Dependent Measure

Similar to previous deterrence research (Pogarsky, 2002), the dependent measure for this study was the students' response to a single item, "What is the likelihood that you would take the software under these circumstances?" This item followed a scenario that had undergone a substantial amount of pilot testing (see Higgins, 2007, for complete details). The students marked their responses on an 11-point scale (0 = *not likely*; 10 = *100% likely*). Higher scores reflected a greater likelihood that the student would perform an act of digital piracy.

Low Self-Control

To measure self-control, we used the 24-item scale developed by Grasmick, Tittle, Bursik, and Arneklev (1993). The response categories for this scale were 1 (*strongly disagree*) and 4 (*strongly agree*). Higher scores on the scale indicated lower levels of self-control. The internal consistency for the measure was .83, suggesting adequate levels of reliability. Similar to previous research (Nagin & Paternoster, 1993; Piquero & Tibbetts, 1996), factor analysis indicated that the scale was unidimensional.

Extra-Legal Sanctions

A number of measures were used to capture extra-legal sanctions. From Piquero and Tibbetts (1996), social and self-disapproval measures were "How likely is it that your family would find out that you used a copy of the program under the circumstances described in the scenario?" and "How likely is it that your friends would find out that you used a copy of the program under the circumstances described in the scenario?" The students addressed these questions using an 11-point scale (0 = *not likely*; 10 = *likely*). To measure the expected influence of self-disapproval, the students were asked (similar to Paternoster and Piquero [1995]), "How likely would you [be to] feel shame if you were to use the copy of the program in the circumstances described in the scenario?" The students addressed these questions using an 11-point scale (0 = *not likely*; 10 = *100% likely*). In addition, as in Bachman et al. (1992), the students addressed the following question: "How morally wrong would it be if you were to use the copy of the program in the circumstances described in the scenario?" The students answered this question using an 11-point scale anchored by "not wrong" and "100% wrong."

Additional Control Measures

The students also responded to a number of control measures. They marked the number of times that they had pirated software, and they marked their gender (0 = *male*; 1 = *female*) and their race (1 = *White*; 0 = *non-White*); age was an open-ended item. Further, the students were asked how much they would value the software in the scenario. They marked their responses on an 11-point scale (0 = *not at all*; 10 = *100% value*).

From the control measures, the median age was 20 years. More than half the sample was female (56% female; 44% male), and more than 80% of respondents were White (83%). The sample closely approximates the population from which it was drawn.

Analysis

The analysis for this study took place in steps. The first step was a presentation of the bivariate correlations of the measures. This presentation allowed for an inspection of whether the measures shared variance. The second step was a presentation of an SEM analysis. This analysis was important because SEM uses maximum likelihood estimates that are much more robust than regression coefficients. In addition, SEM allows for estimation of the links without the influence of measurement error.

In interpreting the structural equation models, two pieces of information are important. First, the researchers should make sure that they understand the fit between the model and their data. They should use a number of fit statistics to gain the best understanding. Several researchers have shown that the chi-square statistic, confirmatory fit index (CFI), root-mean-square error of approximation (RMSEA), and standardized root-mean of the residual (SRMR) should be consulted during examination of the model-to-data fit (Gibbs, Giever, & Higgins, 2003; Hu & Bentler, 1999; Kline, 2005).

Second, SEM enables examination of the direct and indirect effects among the measures—that is, an understanding of the direct effect of the measures. Therefore, this type of analysis is consistent with the analysis from Piquero and Tibbetts (1996).

Results

Table 9.1 presents the correlation results that we used to develop the structural equation model. In particular, shame (−.53), value (.50), external sanctions (−.41), moral behaviors (−.37), prior behaviors (.20), and low self-control

Table 9.1   Correlations Among Independent Measures

Measure	1	2	3	4	5	6	7
1. Intentions	1.00						
2. Shame	−.53	1.00					
3. Value	.50	−.49	1.00				
4. External controls	−.46	.70	−.45	1.00			
5. Moral	−.44	.66	−.37	.57	1.00		
6. Prior piracy	.23	−.22	.35	−.28	−.24	1.00	
7. Low self-control	.21	−.11	.19	−.09	−.11	.06	1.00

(.21) correlated with digital piracy. Further, the cost measures of rational choice theory (i.e., moral beliefs [.66] and external sanctions [.70]) positively correlated with shame. Further, value (−.49), prior behavior (−.22), and low self-control (−.11) negatively correlated with shame. Low self-control (.19) and prior behavior (.35) positively correlated with value, but external sanctions (−.45) and moral beliefs (−.37) negatively correlated with value. Thus, correlations exist among low self-control, rational choice theory, value, and digital piracy. These results are consistent with the literature in these areas (Deci, Eghari, Patrick, & Leone, 1994; Gottfredson & Hirschi, 1990; Higgins, 2005; Nagin & Paternoster, 1993; Piquero & Tibbetts, 1996; Tibbetts & Myers, 1999).

Figure 9.1 shows the structural equation model that empirically examined the links among low self-control, rational choice theory, value, and digital piracy. The chi-square analysis, $\chi^2(6) = 13.88$, $p = .03$, indicated that the model did not fit the data very well. As stated previously, the sample size forced the chi-square statistic to be statistically significant; however, after consulting the CFI (.99), RMSEA (.05), and SRMR (.02), we decided that the model did fit the data very well.

Figure 9.1 shows the results of examining the direct effect of low self-control on intentions to digital pirate and the indirect effects on intentions to digital pirate through situational factors. Low self-control had a direct link with digital piracy ($\beta = .11$) and a direct positive effect on value ($\beta = .14$). This result indicates that the lower an individual's level of self-control, the more likely they are to perform digital piracy and to highly value digital media. Unlike Piquero and Tibbetts (1996), low self-control did not have links with shame or external sanctions. Further, low self-control had not only direct links but an indirect link with digital piracy through value ($\beta = .04$). This is consistent with Gottfredson and Hirschi's (1990) view that individuals with low self-control are unlikely to see the consequences of their digital piracy and is consistent with previous research (Piquero & Tibbetts, 1996).

In addition, Figure 9.1 shows whether situational factors would have a direct effect on intentions to digital pirate and indirect effects on intentions

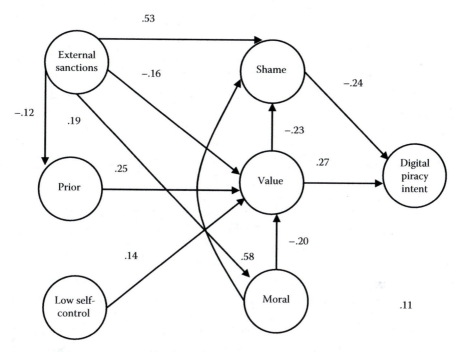

Figure 9.1 Integrated model of low self-control, rational choice, value, and digital piracy.

to digital pirate through other situational factors. Value (β = .28), moral beliefs (β = −.12), and shame (β = −.29) have links with intentions to digital pirate in the expected directions. These findings mean that as the value of digital media increases for the individual, the likelihood of pirating also increases. Further, these results indicate that moral beliefs and shame are important measures in reducing the instances of digital piracy. The results of this study did not show that prior behavior or external sanctions would be relevant in digital piracy. These results were expected, given that some researchers (Hirschi & Gottfredson, 1993) argued that prior behavior may be an indication of low self-control—that is, this measure was conflicting with the attitude-based measure of self-control. Further, external sanctions were not significant in reducing the likelihood of digital piracy (M = 3.94). This result suggests that respondents were not very certain that external sanctions would be prominent in reducing their digital piracy.

For other effects, moral beliefs (β = .58) had a link with shame. This link indicated that as the individual's belief that digital piracy was morally wrong increased, so did situational shame that accompanied digital piracy. Moral beliefs had an indirect effect (β = −.17) on digital piracy through shame. Value (β = −.23) had an interesting link with shame—that is, when the value of digital media increased for the individual, the situational shame for intending to pirate the digital media also decreased. Value had an indirect effect ($\beta = -.07$) on digital piracy through shame, suggesting that shame may reduce the motivation or want for digital piracy.

Other effects included a direct effect between moral beliefs ($\beta = -.20$), low self-control ($\beta = .14$), prior behavior ($\beta = .25$), and external sanctions ($\beta = -.16$) and value ($\beta = .27$). The links between moral beliefs and external sanctions indicated that as they increase, the value of the digital media is likely to decrease for the individual. Conversely, as low self-control and prior behavior increase, the perceived value of the digital media increases. Indirectly, moral beliefs had a link with intentions to pirate software ($\beta = -.06$) through value, indicating that as an individual's moral beliefs increase, his or her perceived value of the digital media decreased, and this reduced the likelihood of digital piracy. Others also had indirect links with intentions to pirate software through value: low self-control ($\beta = .04$), prior behavior ($\beta = .07$), and external sanctions ($\beta = -.05$). With the exception of external sanctions, as low self-control increased and prior behavior increased, the value of the digital media increased—which increased the likelihood of digital piracy. However, when external sanctions increased, the individual was less likely to value the digital media, thus reducing the likelihood of digital piracy. Overall, these findings indicated that the situational factors were important in the increase and decrease in how an individual valued the digital media that had an effect on their likelihood for piracy. Three measures had effects on the perceptions of external sanctions.

In particular, when moral beliefs ($\beta = .19$) and shame ($\beta = .53$) increased, the perceptions of external sanctions for digital piracy increased. However, when prior behavior increased, the perceptions of external sanctions for digital piracy decreased ($\beta = -.12$). These measures did not have indirect links with intentions for digital piracy.

Discussion and Conclusion

The purpose of this study was to address the gap in the literature by presenting the first systematic examination of self-control, rational choice, and value in the context of digital piracy. This research contributes to the literature on self-control theory, rational choice theory, and digital piracy. The results of this study show that low self-control has direct and indirect effects on intentions to commit digital piracy (Higgins, 2005; Higgins & Makin, 2004a,b; Pratt & Cullen, 2000). Further, this study shows that low self-control has indirect links with a modified version of situational factors (i.e., value; Deci et al., 1994; Nagin & Paternoster, 1993; Piquero & Tibbetts, 1996; Tibbetts & Herz, 1996; Tibbetts & Myers, 1999). In addition to these results, this study shows that situational factors have both direct and indirect effects on digital piracy (Piquero & Tibbetts, 1996; Tibbetts & Herz, 1996; Tibbetts & Myers, 1999). These results indicate that the theories of low self-control and rational choice may be compatible theories that can explain digital piracy.

This study helps criminologists understand more about the decision-making mechanisms for digital piracy. The results indicate that low self-control and rational choice theory can be applied and integrated to understand the intentions to digital pirate. These findings go beyond previous research in the digital piracy literature (i.e., Higgins, 2005; Higgins & Makin, 2004a,b; Higgins et al., 2005). Thus, this study contributes to the literature by outlining some of the motivational components (i.e., prior behavior, low self-control, and value) and the deterrent components (i.e., shame and moral beliefs).

Understanding the motivational and deterrent components of digital piracy from the integrated low self-control and rational choice theory model provides important information for college administrators and other policymakers that may reduce instances of digital piracy—that is, to reduce instances of digital piracy, college administrators can develop policies and programs on campus that reiterate the immorality of digital piracy as well as the shame that may come from it. Security specialists can use this information to develop specific technological innovations that remind students of the unethical nature of, and potential shame involved in, digital piracy.

Although this study informs the literature about the links among low self-control, rational choice theory, value, and digital piracy, this study has some noteworthy limits. In particular, we used responses to a scenario as the dependent measure rather than an actual measure of behavior; however, this technique has become rather typical in rational choice theory studies because it enables proper temporal ordering. But in doing so, this limits the trash talking. In this study, we used data from only one university in the United States, and it may have limited the international generalization. However, this is the first study to examine this type of model, and the results should be considered preliminary and in need of large-scale replication. The data for this study are cross-sectional. Longitudinal data may provide very interesting insights into the development of the decision-making process. This is an area for future research.

Despite the limitations of this study, low self-control, rational choice theory, value, and digital piracy do have connections. Specifically, the link between low self-control and digital piracy is partially mediated by an individual's perceived value of the digital media. Further, the effects of situational factors (i.e., moral beliefs and shame) on digital piracy are mediated by value. Therefore, the value that an individual places on digital media is an important piece of the decision-making process. However, future studies that use actual measures of piracy, that are from multiple universities, and that are longitudinal will inform our understanding about the links among low self-control, rational choice, value, and digital piracy. For now, the results of this study show that the value an individual places on digital media is important, regardless of his or her low self-control, moral beliefs, or perceptions of situational shame.

References

Agnew, R. (1995). Testing the leading crime theories: An alternative strategy focusing on motivational processes. *Journal of Research in Crime and Delinquency, 32*, 363–398.

Arneklev, B. J., Cochran, J. K., & Gainey, R. R. (1998). Testing Gottfredson and Hirschi's "low self-control" stability hypothesis: An exploratory study. *American Journal of Criminal Justice, 23*, 107–127.

Bachman, R., Paternoster, R., & Ward, S. (1992). The rationality of sexual offending: Testing a deterrence/rational choice conception of sexual assault. *Law and Society Review, 26*, 343–372.

Baron, J. N. (1988). The employment relation as a social relation. *Journal of the Japanese and International Economies, 2*, 492–525.

Business Software Alliance. (2003). *Software piracy fact sheet*. Washington, DC: Author. Retrieved from http://www.bsa.org

Cornish, D., & Clarke, R. V. (1986). *The reasoning criminal: Rational choice perspectives in offending*. New York, NY: Springer-Verlag.

Deci, E. L., Eghari, H., Patrick, B. C., & Leone, D. R. (1994). Facilitating internalization: The self-determination theory. *Journal of Personality, 62*, 119–142.

Deci, E. L., & Ryan, R. M. (1991). A motivational approach to self: Integration in personality. In R. Dienstbier (Ed.), *Nebraska symposium on motivation* (Vol. 38, pp. 237–288). Lincoln, NE: University of Nebraska Press.

Gibbs, J. J., Giever, D., & Higgins, G. E. (2003). A test of Gottfredson and Hirschi's general theory using structural equation modeling. *Criminal Justice and Behavior, 30*, 441–458.

Gopal, R., Sanders, G. L., Bahattacharjee, S., Agrawal, M., & Wagner, S. (2004). A behavioral model of digital music piracy. *Journal of Organizational Computing and Electronic Commerce, 14*, 89–105.

Gottfredson, M. R., & Hirschi, T. (1990). *A general theory of crime*. Palo Alto, CA: Stanford University Press.

Grasmick, H. G., Tittle, C. R., Bursik, R. J., & Arneklev, B. J. (1993). Testing the core empirical implications of Gottfredson and Hirschi's general theory of crime. *Journal of Research in Crime & Delinquency, 30*, 5–29.

Higgins, G. E. (2005). Can self-control theory help understand the software piracy problem? *Deviant Behavior, 26*, 1–24.

Higgins, G. E. (2007). Digital piracy: An examination of low self-control and motivation using short-term longitudinal data. *CyberPsychology & Behavior, 10*, 523–529.

Higgins, G. E., & Makin, D. A. (2004a). Does social learning theory condition the effects of low self-control on college students' software piracy? *Journal of Economic Crime Management, 2*, 1–22.

Higgins, G. E., & Makin, D. A. (2004b). Self-control, deviant peers, and software piracy. *Psychological Reports, 95,* 921–931.

Higgins, G. E., & Marcum, C. D. (2005). Can the theory of planned behavior mediate the effects of low self-control on alcohol use? *College Student Journal, 39,* 90–103.

Higgins, G. E., Wilson, A. L., & Fell, B. D. (2005). An application of deterrence theory to software piracy. *Journal of Criminal Justice and Popular Culture, 12,* 166–184.

Hinduja, S. (2001). Correlates of Internet software piracy. *Journal of Contemporary Criminal Justice, 17,* 369–382.

Hinduja, S. (2003). Trends and patterns among online software pirates. *Ethics and Information Technology, 5,* 49–61.

Hirschi, T., & Gottfredson, M. R. (1993). Commentary: Testing the general theory of crime. *Journal of Research in Crime and Delinquency, 30,* 47–54.

Hollinger, R. C. (1988). Computer hackers follow a Guttman-like progression. *Sociology and Social Research, 72,* 199–200.

Hu, L., & Bentler, P. M. (1999). Cutoff criteria for fit indexes in covariance structure analysis: Conventional criteria versus new alternatives. *Structural Equation Modeling, 6,* 1–55.

Husted, B. W. (2000). The impact of national culture on software piracy. *Journal of Business Ethics, 13,* 431–438.

Koen, C. M., & Im, J. H. (1997). Software piracy and its legal implications. *Security Journal, 31,* 265–272.

Kline, R. B. (2005). *Principles and practices of structural equation modeling* (2nd ed.). New York, NY: Guilford Press.

Motivans, M. (2004, October). Intellectual property theft, 2002. *Bureau of Justice Statistics Special Report* [Report No. NCJ 205800]. Washington, DC: U. S. Department of Justice.

Nagin, D. S. (1998). Deterrence and incapacitation. In M. H. Tonry (Ed.), *Handbook of crime and punishment* (pp. 345–368). New York, NY: Oxford University Press.

Nagin, D. S., & Paternoster, R. (1993). Enduring individual differences and rational choice theories of crime. *Law & Society Review, 27,* 467–496.

Paternoster, R., & Piquero, A. (1995). Reconceptualizing deterrence: An empirical test of personal and vicarious experiences. *Journal of Research in Crime & Delinquency, 32,* 251–286.

Piquero, A. R., & Tibbetts, S. (1996). Specifying the direct and indirect effects of low self-control and situational factors in offenders' decision making: Toward a more complete model of rational offending. *Justice Quarterly, 13,* 481–510.

Pogarsky, G. (2002). Identifying "deterrable" offenders: Implications for research on deterrence. *Justice Quarterly, 19,* 431–453.

Pratt, T., & Cullen, F. T. (2000). The empirical status of Gottfredson and Hirschi's general theory of crime: A meta-analysis. *Criminology, 38,* 501–534.

Rahim, M. M., Seyal, A. H., & Rahman, M. N. A. (2001). Factors affecting soft-lifting intention of computing students: An empirical study. *Journal of Educational Computing Research, 24,* 385–405.

Rao, S. S. (2003). Copyright: Its implications for electronic information. *Online Information Review, 27,* 264–275.

Tibbetts, S. G. (1997). Shame and rational choice in offending decisions. *Criminal Justice & Behavior, 24,* 234–255.

Tibbetts, S. G., & Gibson, C. L. (2002). Individual propensities and rational decision-making: Recent findings and promising approaches. In A. R. Piquero & S. G. Tibbetts (Eds.), *Rational choice and criminal behavior: Recent research and future challenges* (pp. 3–24). New York, NY: Routledge Press.

Tibbetts, S. G., & Myers, D. L. (1999). Low self-control, rational choice, and student test cheating. *American Journal of Criminal Justice, 23,* 179–200.

Turner, M. G., & Piquero, A. R. (2002). The stability of self-control. *Journal of Criminal Justice, 30,* 457–471.

Wright, B. R. E., Caspi, A., Moffitt, T. E., & Paternoster, R. (2004). Does the perceived risk of punishment deter criminally prone individuals? Rational choice, self-control, and crime. *Journal of Research in Crime & Delinquency, 41,* 180–213.

Suing the Genie Back in the Bottle
The Failed RIAA Strategy to Deter P2P Network Users

10

MICHAEL BACHMANN

Contents

Introduction

June 2009. $1.92 million—that is the amount that a federal jury in Minneapolis ruled a 32-year-old mother of four to pay to six of the world's largest record companies. The verdict against Jammie Thomas-Rasset amounts to $80,000 for each of the 24 songs she was charged with sharing on the peer-to-peer (P2P) platform KaZaa in 2005 before KaZaa was transformed into a legal music download service (*Capitol Records, Inc et al. v. Thomas-Rasset*, 2009). For the young mother, this was the second trial of her case: In October 2007, a federal court in Chicago stunned the P2P community when it sentenced Thomas-Rasset to pay $220,000 for copyright infringements of the 24 songs—only an eighth of the sentence she received in the retrial of her case ("Music labels win $2 million," 2009).

Although proponents of P2P networks argue that it is highly unlikely that the defendant will ever be able to pay even a fraction of the grossly disproportionate sentence and that, if the record industry has accomplished anything in this trial, it was to terrorize potential music customers at great cost, industry spokespeople celebrated the outcome as a decisive victory in their battle against file sharers, who they blame for a $6 billion loss in revenue in the past few years (Sheffner, 2009).

Regardless of which assessment of the outcome a person chooses to believe, the trial presents the latest incident in an unprecedented legal campaign that the recording industry waged against individual users of P2P technology. During the last 6 years, the Recording Industry Association of America (RIAA) has filed, settled, or threatened legal actions against at least 30,000 American P2P users (Kravetz, 2008). To better understand the industry's decision to target potential consumers over the last 6 years, in this chapter we trace the appearance and development of P2P networks and their implications for the established music recording and distribution industry.

The History of P2P Networks

For the traditional recording industry, the emergence of the first P2P network software, Napster, was an upsetting event of unparalleled amplitude. Napster's pioneering new technology allowed its users to distribute and copy highly compressed (MP3-coded) music files at next to no cost (Mitten, 2002). Because of the media coverage that this software received and its user-friendly interface, Napster gained vast popularity. It rapidly accumulated an extensive selection of readily available music. Millions of users soon used Napster's network to share and exchange masses of copyright-protected files without explicit permission (Horrigan & Schement, 2002). The long-established recording industry was shocked by Napster's unprecedented facilitation of copyright infringements, and it reacted by filing the first lawsuit against a P2P network (Robinson & Halle, 2002).

The allegations upon which the lawsuit against Napster Inc. rested were based on the particular architecture of its network. Napster, a first-generation P2P network, used central, company-owned servers to create and manage directories and indexes of connected users and the music files that they provided. Although the actual file transfers were conducted directly among the users, these central servers established the connections among users and initiated the music file transfers. In their allegations, complainants argued that because of its centralized architecture, Napster functioned as a "listing service" that offered directories, indexes, a search engine, and links. Thereby, it actively facilitated the sharing of files. Plaintiffs declared Napster to be ultimately responsible for the copyright violations caused by its users. In this initial lawsuit, individual users were not accused of being responsible for the copyright violations. The initial strategy was to refrain from prosecuting individual P2P network users because the industry feared that the generalized criminalization of music consumers would trigger massive public relations predicaments. Instead, litigators argued that individual users were being victimized by the new technology (Spitz & Hunter, 2005). A decree was issued against Napster Inc. in March 2001, and Napster was ordered to prevent the trading of copyright-protected music on its network. It soon became obvious that the effective exclusion of copyright-protected music was technically impossible, so Napster had to discontinue its service in order to comply with the court order.

The RIAA had succeeded in court, but it turned out to be a "Pyrrhic victory" in that it created media attention for P2P networks, spread the idea of sharing files, and helped to spawn new networks (Wayne, 2004). By the time Napster was shut down, various new P2P networks had been released, all of which had learned from Napster's downfall. They were completely decentralized and were no longer restricted to just music files. Instead, these second-generation networks could be used to share any type of file format. The networks were based on different protocols and encrypted the shared data; some enterprises went as far as selling their businesses to obscure offshore companies (Matthew & Kirkhope, 2004; Merriden, 2001). All of these measures were designed to prevent the recording industry from shutting them down through legal actions.

Confronted with these new types of networks, the industry had to adjust its strategy. It became obvious that the campaign against the networks held little promise, so the revised strategy had to focus on the users of these networks. The new strategy was a two-pronged approach: Drastic legal punishments to deter "major offenders" (Weiss, Lamy, & Collins, 2003) were combined with new attempts to educate users and the public about the illegality of copyright infringements. The RIAA wanted to teach file sharers that their behavior was not just a petty offense but was tantamount to shoplifting (Denegri-Knott & Taylor, 2005).

The first wave of 1,600 subpoenas was sent out in fall 2003, only a few weeks after court rulings mandated that Internet Service Providers (ISPs) provide the identities of customers accused of illegal file sharing. At the same time, the first lawsuits against 261 "power users" were filed (Legon, 2004). The lawsuits were based on accusations of violating U.S. Copyright Law, particularly two of its amendments—the Digital Millennium Copyright Act (DMCA) and the No Electronic Theft (NET) Act. These two amendments allow the criminal prosecution of individuals accused of recording infringements, even when the activity is undertaken without the intent to derive monetary profit or commercial gain.

Around the same time as the lawsuits, the RIAA announced what Cary Sherman, its president at the time, called their "version of an olive branch" (Legon, 2004, para. 7). The industry group offered file traders the chance to "come clean" and avoid future lawsuits by admitting their misconduct, signing an affidavit to never infringe again, and deleting all of their illegally acquired files. The *Clean Slate Program*, as it was called, was designed to complement the industry's legal efforts in an attempt to reach out to file sharers. The dual purpose of this program was to simultaneously alleviate the impression that RIAA was engaging in strict confrontation with music consumers and justify the legal enforcement of the industry's interests.

The goal of this twofold strategy was ultimately to deter the mass of Internet users from signing on to P2P networks. By generating headlines, the RIAA sought to steer the focus of public discourse surrounding file sharing to the issue of copyright violation. A few months after the enactment of the Clean Slate Program, it was announced that the dual-tracked deterrence strategy had been a resounding success. In fact, it was declared so successful that the RIAA proclaimed that it had met the goal of educating the public. The industry decided to terminate the Clean Slate Program and limited the prosecution of users to sporadic lawsuits against single individuals (RIAA, 2003).

Indeed, a Pew Internet & American Life Project phone survey from November 2003 found that the lawsuits against music file traders "had a devastating impact on the number of those engaging in Internet peer-to-peer music sharing" (Rainie & Madden, 2004, p. 1). The study found that the percentage of Internet users who downloaded music files dropped from 29% (about 35 million users) to 14% (about 18 million). Even more drastically, the numbers of active music traders on any given day fell from 4% to 1%. Of those who continued sharing files, about 20% said they were doing so less often because they were afraid of being sued. Similar indicators of the campaign's successful short-term effect were found by Bhattacharjee, Gopal, Lertwachara, and Marsden (2006) in their tracking study of more than 2,000 P2P users. Bhattacharjee and colleagues (2006) found that the legal threats resulted in substantially lower levels of file sharing.

These findings suggested that the new campaign had been very successful. Yet, both studies were conducted only months after the campaigns were launched. In late 2003, the prospect of being sued was still on everybody's mind. However, several years down the road, the question must be asked regarding how sustained the generated impact was. How did the popularity of P2P networks develop since the time in which the lawsuits against users were filed? What do the most recent data on P2P communities reveal about the current composition of the P2P population? Finally, what, exactly, are the reasons why today's users discontinue using P2P networks, and which technical alternatives for obtaining music files are taking their place?

A review of the available literature on these questions has concluded that these questions have been answered only tentatively. In part because file-sharing communities are based on a relatively recent technical innovation, analyses of their social developments continue to be scarce. Moreover, most studies on the subject are of limited relevance for the previously posed questions because their concern is to frame the rise and fall of Napster in a particular theoretical context (Horrigan & Schement, 2002; Jones & Lenhart, 2004; Leyshon, Webb, French, Thrift, & Crewe, 2005; Marshall, 2004; Matthew & Kirkhope, 2004; Mitten, 2002; Robinson & Halle, 2002; Spitz & Hunter, 2005; Wayne, 2004).

One of the more recent studies on illegal file sharing was conducted by Hinduja (2005). The author administered surveys about engagement in P2P file sharing to undergraduate students at a midwestern university. The survey successfully tested the applicability of three main criminological theories but, due to its limited sample frame, was not able to examine the general population of file-sharing participants. To date, only Bhattacharjee and colleagues (2006) have conducted a representative examination of P2P communities shortly after the lawsuit campaign was launched.

In the present chapter, I seek to provide answers to the aforementioned questions by analyzing the most recent available data on file-sharing communities. I further use the data to scrutinize whether it is indeed appropriate to equate music downloading with file sharing, as is common practice in the literature. It is argued that music downloading and file sharing are two separate activities that coincide only when music files are shared. Various file formats are available on P2P networks today, and music is downloaded from multiple other sources. Probably because of the limitation of early file-sharing networks and the fact that the discussion over copyright issues has centered on music files for so long, the two activities continue to be treated as interchangeable in the extant literature.

Data

In this study, three different data sets from the Pew Internet & American Life tracking survey (Rainie & Madden, 2004) are analyzed. The surveys were designed to examine the Internet's role in everyday life in the United States, particularly the details of Internet use and its social impact. All three nationally representative data sets were collected through telephone interviews between March 2003 and January 2005. The data collection was based on a random digit sample frame of telephone numbers selected from telephone exchanges in the continental United States.

To compensate for the known biases in telephone interviews, the sample data were weighted in the analysis. The demographic weighting parameters for each dataset were derived from a special analysis of the most recently available *Annual Social and Economic Supplement* from the U.S. Census Bureau (2003). Using an iterative technique that simultaneously balances the distribution of all weighting parameters, I compared these parameters with the sample characteristics to construct representative sample weights.

In this chapter, data from three waves of the tracking survey are analyzed. The first survey was conducted between March and May 2003—before the RIAA launched its lawsuit campaign. The campaign contained 2,515 respondents, 1,555 of whom were Internet users. The second tracking survey was fielded between November and December 2003—shortly after the first wave of subpoenas and lawsuits were filed. During that time 2,013 adults in the United States were surveyed, 1,358 of whom were Internet users. The third survey is the latest file-sharing survey released by the Pew Internet & American Life Project (Rainie & Madden, 2004). It was conducted between January and February 2005 and contained 2,201 adult respondents, including 1,421 Internet users.

Measures

Independent Variables

Several sociodemographic characteristics of file sharers and music downloaders were examined—among them, gender, race, age, income, educational attainment, student status, Internet experience, and type of Internet connection. Student status was included on the basis of the common suggestion that file sharing is particularly prevalent among students (Hinduja, 2005). Internet experience and type of Internet connection were included as proxy measures of experience-based and technical accessibility to P2P networks. To render the analysis of different user types more meaningful, the variables age, income, educational attainment, and years of Internet experience were all recoded into grouped categories. The same coding procedure was applied to the variable years of Internet experience. A series of dummy variables was created for additional sociodemographic characteristics, including student status (1 = *full- or part-time students*), gender (1 = *males*), Internet connection (1 = *broadband connection*), and race. Race was measured with three indicator variables: White, African American, and Hispanic (the reference is White). Except for the income variable, all other variables contained only small amounts of apparently randomly missing data. These cases were simply excluded from the analysis. For the income variable, missing values are replaced via linear interpolation to avoid artificial reduction of the variance. The last valid value of the case before the missing value and the first valid value of the case after the missing value are used for the interpolation (Little, 1988; Schafer, 1997).

Dependent Variables

As mentioned previously, the practice of simply equating file sharing with music downloading remains common. The case argued here is that simply equating the two activities is inadequate because it ignores the fact that file sharing is not restricted to music files anymore. Many file sharers trade video, application, document, image, picture, or archive files but refrain from swapping music to avoid prosecution. Conversely, many individuals who download music do so from a variety of sources—among them, legal online music services such as iTunes or Amazon, friends' portable MP3 players, music-related websites, and search engines such as Baidu or even Google. In the present analysis, I examine file sharing and music downloading as two different activities. The separate analysis further enables a more detailed examination of the impact that the industry's lawsuit campaign had on only music downloading versus file sharing in general.

To measure file-sharing activity, I developed a question that asked respondents if they "share files from their own computer, such as music, video or picture files, or computer games with others online." File-sharing activity was recorded in the categories "Yes, I did this yesterday"; "Yes, I have done this, but not yesterday"; and "No, I have never done this." The first two categories were collapsed into one category for file sharers (1 = *file sharing*). To measure music downloading activity, I developed a question that asked participants if they "download music files onto their computer so they can play them at any time they want." Again, the response categories distinguished between having done this yesterday, ever, or never, and the categories were recoded into one category for music downloaders (1 = *have downloaded music*).

Two additional aspects were considered for further examination of the impact created by RIAA's lawsuit campaign. To reveal the relative importance that "being afraid to become indicted" had on the decision to stop downloading, I reviewed the reasons that were given for having discontinued music downloading. Second, the importance of alternative sources for obtaining music files was evaluated. The technical alternatives that have emerged since 2003 are an important consideration because the RIAA's campaign targeted only downloading through P2P networks but had no effect on the downloading of music files through other illegal sources.

The item measuring the reasons for discontinuing downloading music provided participants with the following alternatives:

- "I was afraid to get in trouble/I heard about the RIAA lawsuits."
- "I decided that it was wrong."
- "I was getting more viruses, pop-up ads, or having other computer problems."
- "I couldn't find the quality or type of files that I wanted."
- "I found other ways to get the music or movies I wanted."
- "My Internet service provider, school, or workplace warned me."

In addition, the open-answer option triggered the two common replies that it is "too time-consuming/too slow" and that the participant had just "lost interest."

The technical alternatives for obtaining files were asked in a series of separate questions. Respondents were asked whether they had ever downloaded music from any of the following sources: "a peer-to-peer network like KaZaA or Morpheus"; "an online music service such as iTunes or buymusic. com"; "someone's iPod or other MP3 player"; "other music-related websites, such as online music magazines or musicians' home pages"; or "e-mail or instant messages you receive." Each of the sources was dummy coded (1 = *respondent had ever downloaded from this source*).

Method

For the analysis, all three data sets were limited to only Internet users and were merged into one dataset. The exclusion of respondents who do not use the Internet reduced the sample sizes by approximately one third. Nevertheless, each data set still contained more than 1,300 observations. Also, all recoded subgroups remained considerably larger than 30 respondents—a circumstance that allowed generalizations to the population with only small error margins.

Results

Trends in Demographic Characteristics of P2P Community Members

Table 10.1 shows the changes in P2P communities between the three survey waves. The table reveals two very different patterns for file sharing and music downloading. The impact of the lawsuit campaign was as insignificant on file sharing as it was significant on music downloading. The only meaningful

Table 10.1 Weighted Sociodemographic Characteristics of Peer-to-Peer (P2P) Community Members

| Characteristic | Internet Users Who Share Files | | | | | Internet Users Who Download Music | | | | |
	Mar. 2003 % (N)	Nov. 2003 % (N)	Jan. 2005 % (N)	% Change Nov. 03–Mar. 03	Jan. 05–Nov. 03	Mar. 2003 % (N)	Nov. 2003 % (N)	Jan. 2005 % (N)	% Change Nov. 03–Mar. 03	Jan. 05–Nov. 03
All adults	20.7 (645)	20.3 (452)	24.5 (632)	−0.4	4.2***	29.0 (906)	14.5 (322)	21.6 (559)	−14.5***	7.1***
Men	20.9 (326)	21.0 (231)	22.5 (280)	0.1	1.5	32.5 (506)	18.3 (201)	24.9 (311)	−14.2***	6.6**
Women	20.4 (319)	19.7 (221)	26.4 (352)	−0.7	6.7***	25.6 (400)	10.8 (121)	18.6 (248)	−14.8***	7.8***
Whites	19.9 (456)	19.5 (330)	24.3 (463)	−0.4	4.8**	27.6 (643)	13.2 (219)	19.4 (372)	−14.4***	6.2***
African Americans	22.4 (60)	25.8 (54)	27.7 (60)	3.6	1.9	36.7 (98)	25.2 (52)	24.8 (54)	−11.5**	−0.4
Hispanics	26.3 (78)	22.1 (42)	23.1 (60)	−4.2	1.0	35.3 (105)	19.8 (37)	26.7 (70)	−15.5***	6.9
Age cohorts										
18–29 years	31.2 (250)	27.1 (145)	30.0 (192)	−4.1	2.9	52.4 (420)	27.8 (149)	40.2 (257)	−24.6***	12.9***
30–49 years	18.4 (262)	18.6 (192)	24.4 (283)	0.2	5.8***	26.6 (379)	13.1 (135)	18.5 (215)	−13.5***	5.4***
50+ years	15.3 (127)	18.1 (111)	20.7 (153)	2.8	2.6	11.8 (98)	6.0 (37)	11.0 (82)	−5.8***	5.0***
Household income										
Under $30,000	21.5 (149)	19.5 (87)	20.9 (123)	−2.0	1.4	37.5 (261)	20.8 (93)	26.1 (153)	−16.7***	5.3*
$30,000–$50,000	22.6 (196)	19.0 (115)	23.3 (160)	−3.6	4.3	28.0 (243)	13.7 (83)	19.2 (132)	−14.3***	5.5**
$50,000–$75,000	18.3 (117)	19.4 (94)	26.9 (132)	1.1	7.5**	26.7 (170)	9.9 (48)	16.2 (79)	−16.8***	6.3**
$75,000+	19.9 (182)	22.6 (156)	26.6 (218)	2.7	4.0	25.3 (232)	14.3 (99)	23.7 (194)	−11.0***	9.4***
Education										
Less than high school	25.2 (51)	33.1 (44)	19.8 (35)	7.9	−13.3**	39.0 (79)	23.5 (31)	31.1 (55)	−15.5**	7.6*
High school graduate	22.0 (202)	19.2 (126)	27.2 (211)	−2.8	8.0***	30.8 (283)	18.2 (119)	22.3 (172)	−12.6***	4.1*
Some college	23.6 (204)	20.7 (132)	22.1 (159)	−2.9	1.4	32.8 (283)	13.0 (83)	21.6 (155)	−19.8***	8.6***
College degree/more	16.7 (187)	18.6 (148)	24.9 (226)	1.9	6.3**	23.0 (258)	11.1 (88)	9.3 (175)	−11.9***	8.2***

(continued)

Table 10.1 Weighted Sociodemographic Characteristics of Peer-to-Peer (P2P) Community Members (continued)

	Internet Users Who Share Files			% Change		Internet Users Who Download Music			% Change	
Characteristic	Mar. 2003 % (N)	Nov. 2003 % (N)	Jan. 2005 % (N)	Nov. 03– Mar. 03	Jan. 05– Nov. 03	Mar. 2003 % (N)	Nov. 2003 % (N)	Jan. 2005 % (N)	Nov. 03– Mar. 03	Jan. 05– Nov. 03
Student										
Full or part time	31.6 (195)	31.5 (121)	28.7 (139)	−0.1	−2.8	48.5 (299)	21.1 (81)	37.3 (181)	−27.4***	16.2***
Not a student	17.8 (440)	18.0 (329)	23.6 (493)	0.2	5.6***	24.0 (593)	13.2 (240)	18.1 (378)	−10.8***	4.9***
Internet experience										
3 or fewer years	17.0 (130)	12.2 (58)	18.0 (36)	−4.8*	5.8*	28.0 (214)	12.9 (62)	17.9 (36)	−15.1***	5.0
4–6 years	23.5 (296)	18.4 (158)	20.1 (85)	−5.1*	1.7	29.8 (376)	13.6 (117)	19.0 (81)	−16.2***	5.4*
7 or more years	20.0 (219)	26.5 (236)	32.7 (189)	6.5***	6.2**	28.8 (316)	16.2 (144)	23.0 (133)	−12.6***	6.8***

$*p < .05$, $**p < .01$, and $***p < .001$.

decrease in file sharing during 2003 was found among less experienced user groups. These users were the only ones who refrained significantly more from sharing their files online ($p < .05$). The exact opposite was the case for experienced users. They showed highly significant increases in the percentage of file sharing ($p < .001$) between March and November 2003. The data suggest that (a) the legal campaign had hardly any effect on file sharing in general (more than 20% of all users continued to share) and (b) the overall rate of file sharing among Internet users has been increasing significantly since the end of 2003 ($p < .05$).

The trends in music downloading show a very different picture. The lawsuit campaign had a notable impact on music sharing. The overall fraction of music downloaders plummeted (it was halved to 14.5%) across all demographic groups in November 2003 ($p < .001$). Yet, the data from the latest survey show that the campaign's impact diminished significantly 2 years later. Since the end of 2003, the trend for music downloading has been picking up again. The overall popularity of downloading music files grew significantly between 2003 and 2005 ($p < .001$), even though it continued to remain at a lower level than before the campaign.

The two activities show very different patterns across the three survey waves. As opposed to file sharing, the curve in music downloading shows a consistent pattern for all groups. After the legal prosecution campaign was launched, music downloading dropped significantly across all sociodemographics. The pronounced decrease in music downloading was clear evidence for a successful short-term effect of the campaign. However, with the exception of African American respondents, the percentage of music downloaders went back up by 2005. This upward trend suggests that the impact of the campaign has been wearing off. Despite occasionally renewed media reports of new lawsuits, it appears that the deterrence effect has been diminishing.

Alternatively, the developments in file sharing demonstrate an inconsistent pattern. Clearly, the campaign did not have the same deterrence effect on file sharing in general. Even though file sharing became slightly less popular, overall, between March and November 2003 (it decreased only insignificantly by 0.4%), this development varied considerably across sociodemographic groups. Most notably, file sharing became even more popular in 2005 than it was in 2003.

Comparing the two activities in the March 2003 survey, one can see that a higher fraction of Internet users had downloaded music than had been sharing files. This finding might be a result of the fact that (a) at the time, many file-sharing programs did not require users to share their files in order to be able to download, and (b) many users already employed different sources to download music files.

The comparison of single sociodemographic groups reveals other interesting findings. The commonly held assumption that downloaders are disproportionally male (Jones & Lenhart, 2004) clearly must be relativized. A larger fraction of male users were downloading music files (25% of male participants compared with 19% of female participants), but the popularity of file sharing shows a reversed relation across genders. In 2005, female users were more likely to share their files.

The racial distribution of file sharers and music downloaders developed disparately, too. In the first wave of the survey, Hispanics had the largest fraction of file sharers among them (26% Hispanic compared with 20% White and 22% African American), but between 2003 and 2005, they developed into the group with the smallest percentage of file sharers. In 2005, African Americans had become the group with the largest fraction of file sharers among them (28% African American compared with 24% White and only 23% Hispanic). African Americans also turned out to be the group least affected in their music downloading activities. Although the fraction of African American music downloaders dropped from 37% before the lawsuits to 25% in November 2003, the decrease was even more significant for White users and Hispanic users.

Among all sociodemographic groups, age showed the largest differences from one subgroup to the next. As expected, the highest fractions of file sharers and music downloaders were in the youngest age group. The percentage of file sharers in this age group remained relatively stable over the course of the three surveys. At the same time, the proportion of file sharers among older people increased gradually. The increase of file sharers in the older cohorts is probably attributable to the fact that file-sharing networks came into existence approximately 6 years before the last survey wave, and many of the young people who shared their files early on moved into older age groups.

The differences between the age groups were even more pronounced for music downloading than they were for file sharing. Prior to the lawsuit campaign, more than half of the youngest group of users was downloading music (52%). In contrast, only 27% of the cohort between 30 and 49 years and 12% of the people 50 years or older used their Internet access to download music. The lawsuits temporarily reduced the fractions of music downloaders in all three age groups in the November 2003 survey by about 50% ($p < .001$). However, since 2003, the percentages of music downloaders have again increased significantly for all age groups ($p < .001$). In 2005, 40% of the younger Internet users, 19% of the middle-aged Internet users, and 11% of the older Internet users were again downloading music files. The large differences between age groups were not surprising—they simply reflected the greater interest that younger people have in music.

A counterintuitive pattern emerged among the distributions in the various income groups. In spring 2003, the two lower income segments had the highest percentage of file sharers among them; however, in 2005, the correlation between income and file sharing had reversed. In this survey, the lower income segment had the smallest fraction of file sharers, and the two higher income groups had amassed the highest percentage of file sharers. Still, the smallest income group maintained the largest fraction of music downloaders. A speculative explanation for this finding is that between 2003 and 2005, higher income groups were more likely to switch to a faster broadband connection, which allows them to share larger movie, software, or image files. Other data support this speculation. In 2005, 61% of households with an annual income of more than $75,000 had a broadband Internet connection at home, compared with only 33% of households with an annual income of less than $30,000. The slower modem connection in many lower income households limited their sharing activity to smaller files such as songs, texts, or pictures.

The two curves of the activities further show large differences between students and nonstudents. In early 2003, almost one third of all students were sharing files, and almost half of them were downloading music. Students were roughly twice as likely to engage in both file-sharing and music downloading activities than were nonstudents. Even in the 2005 survey, the percentage of students who were downloading music went back up close to the high level from before the lawsuit campaign. Alternatively, the percentage of students who were sharing their files was almost completely unaffected by the campaign. It was surprising to note that file-sharing activities decreased slightly among students between 2003 and 2005. A likely explanation for this slight decline is that many schools have begun blocking file-sharing ports in recent years.

The last sociodemographic characteristic included in the analysis was years of Internet experience. Here, only small differences appeared among groups. In 2005, the most experienced users were also the ones with the highest percentage of file sharing and music downloading among them. Although the fraction of file sharers among experienced users increased significantly between March and November 2003, it sharply decreased among the least experienced users. Clearly, users with the least experience were the ones most affected by the RIAA campaign. In this group, the percentage of music downloaders dropped from 28% to 13% after the lawsuits and increased only slightly by 2005. Obviously, the campaign clearly had the most profound and sustained impact on individuals who were less familiar with the details of file-sharing networks.

Reasons for No Longer Sharing Files and Technical Alternatives to P2P Networks

To gain a better understanding of the impact that the campaign had on music downloading and file sharing, in the second part of this analysis we examine the reasons that users provided for discontinuing their downloading of music through P2P networks and the alternatives that they chose instead. These items were not included in the 2003 surveys and could not be analyzed over time. Nevertheless, the results hold valuable information about the motives for quitting.

The breakdown of motives for quitting reveals that the fear of getting into trouble caused only one fourth of respondents to stop downloading music through P2P networks. An even lower percentage (10%) reported that they had been convinced that it was morally wrong to infringe copyrights by downloading music. The bulk of users who eventually refrained from downloading music through P2P networks did so because of practical reasons: Of the respondents, 15% reported that they stopped because they got more viruses, pop-up ads, or other PC problems; 4% were simply dissatisfied with the quality of the files; and 7% decided to switch to more convenient alternatives. Thirteen percent decided that downloading through P2P networks was too slow for them, and 6% said that they simply had lost interest in downloading music. These results show that, compared with issues related to the practicality of P2P networks, the RIAA campaign had a much smaller impact. The lawsuits against users were not the main deterrent causing users to stop downloading music. Pronounced as these results are, they still need further investigation because the variable in the Pew Internet & American Life Project survey (Rainie & Madden, 2004) suffered from large amounts of missing data, and some categories had only very few observations.

The second part of Table 10.2 shows the different sources used for downloading music files. Table 10.2 reveals that only 12% of users utilize P2P networks to download their music. In 2005, just as many (10%) indicated that they typically get their files from legal online music services. Another 6% said that they obtained their files from a friend's MP3 player. Nine percent said that they download their music from websites or blogs. An additional 9% said that they received their music through e-mails or instant messages from friends. Of note is that the RIAA's lawsuit campaign had targeted only a very small fraction of all illegal music file sources. It had no influence on the downloading of copyright-protected music from MP3 players; neither did it affect any distribution through e-mails or instant messages. What should be of concern to the industry is that, taken together, these sources were used by a larger percentage of users than were P2P networks.

Discussion and Conclusion

In summary, the conclusion can be drawn that music downloading and file sharing have to be understood as two separate activities that overlap only partially. The analysis of the very detailed Pew Internet & American Life Project (Rainie & Madden, 2004) data in this chapter revealed that the equation of

Table 10.2   Reasons for No Longer Downloading and Technical Alternatives to P2P Networks[a]

	Jan. 2005[b] % (N)
Reasons for no longer downloading[c]	
I was afraid to get in trouble/heard about the RIAA lawsuits.	26.1 (37)
I decided it was wrong.	10.6 (15)
I was getting more viruses, pop-up ads, and other PC problems.	15.5 (22)
I couldn't find the quality or types of files that I wanted.	4.2 (6)
I found other ways to get the music that I wanted.	7.0 (10)
My ISP, school, or workplace warned me.	0.7 (1)
Too time consuming.	7.4 (10)
I lost interest.	5.6 (8)
Other.	23.2 (33)
Sources for downloading music files[d]	
A P2P network such as KaZaA or Morpheus	12.3 (175)
An online music service such as iTunes or buymusic.com	10.3 (147)
Someone's iPod or other MP3 player	5.6 (80)
Other music-related websites	7.0 (100)
Music or movie blogs	2.1 (30)
E-mail or instant messages	8.5 (121)

RIAA, Recording Industry Association of America; PC, personal computer; ISP, Internet Service Provider; P2P, peer-to-peer.

[a] Unweighted percentages and total number of observations (in parentheses) are reported. Percentages may not add to 100 because of rounding.

[b] Unfortunately, these items were not asked in the 2003 surveys and cannot be compared over time.

[c] Only 142 former music downloaders provided reasons for no longer downloading. Counting all Internet users, the variable has 1,279 missing observations that were not imputed.

[d] The percentage of Internet users using the source to download music files is reported.

the two activities is ignorant of important differences and is likely to lead to false conclusions about either one. This important circumstance seems to have been overlooked, thus far, in the literature. An adequate assessment of the impact of legal prosecutions to prevent copyright violations through file sharing in P2P networks requires a separation of activities in the analysis. This might even hold true for the downloading of files other than music. So far, the Motion Picture Association of America (MPAA), a consortium representing the American movie industry, has refrained from pursuing the same strategy as that of the RIAA (Nhan, 2008).

The analysis in this chapter further showed that users are well-aware of who is targeting them. The RIAA's legal campaign affected merely the downloading of music, not the participation in file-sharing networks. On the contrary, P2P network participation was even more popular in 2005 than it was before the lawsuit campaign was launched. These findings suggest that the sharing of other file formats remained largely unaffected. The campaign was successful in slowing down the downloading of music but was not able to diminish the popularity of file-sharing networks overall. Moreover, the impact on music downloading seems to have been short lived. As the media attention to the lawsuits subsided, so did awareness among users. When looking at the reasons given for no longer downloading music, we must conclude that the RIAA's legal actions led only a small fraction of users to discontinue their music downloading. Practical reasons appear to be the main motivation behind users refraining from downloading music through P2P networks. Finally, the message that music downloading is morally wrong was heard and agreed on by only 1 in 10 Internet users. At large, the attempt to educate the public about copyright infringement being a condemnable misconduct has to be considered a failure, considering it was one of the most uncommon reasons cited quitting music downloading.

Already in 2005, alternative sources for downloading music played a more important role than did P2P networks. Some of these alternatives were legal distribution sources, but the majority of them also distributed files without having the appropriate copyrights. All of these sources have not been targeted by the RIAA's campaign and cannot be targeted with the same measures. This development will pose considerable difficulties for the RIAA's future battle against copyright violations. New sources, such as the Chinese search engine Baidu, are completely ignorant of copyright protections and have gained vast popularity in recent years.

Even though, in this chapter, we have produced some valuable insights to Internet users' reactions to the RIAA's lawsuits and a detailed assessment of the campaign's success, this study is limited in several ways. The January 2005 questionnaire contained only a very limited number of questions assessing users' attitudes and opinions about the legal enforcement of copyrights. A more detailed assessment of user opinions should be conducted. Future surveys need to include more detailed questions to shed light on the users' reception of the industry's copyright enforcement strategies. For example, one survey question could ask how familiar Internet users are with the current copyright laws and whether they perceive these laws as protecting the artists or mainly looking out for the interests of those selling their works.

Some other important considerations pertain to the degree to which users believe that copying or sharing of any type of electronic files for noncommercial purposes should be legal; the conditions under which they would be willing to pay for the music they download; the extent to which they purchase music after listening to the downloaded album; or how, exactly, they support their favorite artists. Today, the RIAA is no longer the only industry organization targeting illegal downloading. As more and more movies become distributed in P2P networks, the MPAA has joined the RIAA in its battle. In future studies, researchers should examine the differences between the strategies used by the two associations and the role that increasingly popular legal download alternatives play in the pirating of copyright-protected movie and music files.

References

Bhattacharjee, S., Gopal, R. D., Lertwachara, K., & Marsden, J. R. (2006). Impact of legal threats on online music sharing activity: An analysis of music industry legal actions. *The Journal of Law and Economics, 49*, 91–114.

Capitol Records, Inc et al. v. Thomas-Rasset, No. 0:06-cv-01497-MJD-RLE (U.S. Dist. Ct., S.E. Minn. 2009).

Denegri-Knott, J., & Taylor, J. (2005). The labeling game: A conceptual exploration of deviance on the Internet. *Social Science Computer Review, 23*, 93–107.

Hinduja, S. (2005). *Music piracy and crime theory*. New York, NY: LFB Scholarly Publishing.

Horrigan, J., & Schement, J. (2002). Dancing with Napster: Predictable consumer behavior in the new digital economy. *IT&Society, 1*, 132–160.

Jones, S., & Lenhart, A. (2004). Music downloading and listening: Findings from the Pew Internet & American Life project. *Popular Music and Society, 27*, 185–199.

Kravetz, D. (2008, September 4). File sharing lawsuits at a crossroads, after 5 years of RIAA litigation. *Wired*. Retrieved from http://www.wired.com/threatlevel/2008/09/proving-file-sh

Legon, J. (2004, January 23). 261 music file swappers sued; amnesty program unveiled. Retrieved from http://articles.cnn.com/2003-09-08/tech/music.downloading_1_riaa-amnesty-program-amnesty-program?_s=PM:TECH

Leyshon, A., Webb, P., French, S., Thrift, N., & Crewe, L. (2005). On the reproduction of the musical economy after the Internet. *Media, Culture & Society, 27*, 177–209.

Little, R. J. A. (1988). Missing data adjustments in large surveys. *Journal of Business & Economic Statistics, 6*, 287–296.

Marshall, L. (2004). The effects of piracy upon the music industry: A case study of bootlegging. *Media, Culture & Society, 26*, 163–181.

Matthew, D., & Kirkhope, J. (2004). New digital technologies: Privacy/property, globalization, and law. *Perspectives on Global Development and Technology, 3*, 437–449.

Merriden, T. (2001). *Irresistible forces: The business legacy of Napster and the growth of the underground Internet*. Oxford, England: Capstone.

Mitten, C. (2002). *Shawn Fanning: Napster and the music revolution*. Brookfield, CT: Twenty-First Century Books.

Music labels win $2 million in web case. (2009, June 18). *The New York Times*. Retrieved from http://www.nytimes.com/2009/06/19/business/media/19music.html

Nhan, J. (2008). It's like printing money: Piracy on the Internet? In F. Schmallager & M. Pittaro (Eds.), *Crimes of the Internet* (pp. 356–383). Upper Saddle River, NJ: Prentice Hall.

Rainie, L., & Madden, M. (2004). *Pew Internet Project and Comscore Media Metrix data memo: The impact of recording industry suits against music file swappers*. Washington, DC: Pew Internet & American Life Project.

Recording Industry Association of America. (2003, September 8). Recording industry begins suing P2P file sharers who illegally offer copyrighted music online.
Retrieved from http://www.riaa.com/newsitem.php?news_year_filter=&result
page=44&id=85183A9C-28F4-19CE-BDE6-F48E206CE8A1

Robinson, L., & Halle, D. (2002). Digitization, the Internet, and the Arts: eBay,
Napster, SAG, and e-Books. *Qualitative Sociology, 25,* 359–383.

Schafer, J. L. (1997). *Analysis of incomplete multivariate data.* New York, NY: Chapman
and Hall.

Sheffner, B. (2009). Damages of $1.9 million could backfire on music indus-
try. *Reuters.* Retrieved from http://www.reuters.com/article/musicNews/
idUSTRE55K07E20090621

Spitz, D., & Hunter, S. D. (2005). Contested codes: The social construction of Napster.
The Information Society, 21, 169–180.

U.S. Census Bureau. (2003). *Annual social and economic supplement.* Washington,
DC: Author. Retrieved from http://www.bls.census.gov/cps/asec/adsmain.htm

Wayne, M. (2004). Model of production: New media technology and the Napster file.
Rethinking Marxism, 16, 137–154.

Weiss, A., Lamy, J., & Collins, A. (2003). Recording industry begins suing P2P file
sharers who illegally offer copyrighted music online. Retrieved from http://
www.riaa.com/news/newsletter/090803.asp

Criminological Predictors of Digital Piracy
A Path Analysis

11

WHITNEY D. GUNTER

Contents

Introduction

When one thinks of crime, violent street crime typically comes to mind. In more recent years, white-collar crimes, environmental crimes, identity theft, and other crimes previously considered less important have at least shared the spotlight of America's interest with violent crime. Yet the growing threat of digital piracy is still often overlooked by the general population. Although digital piracy is resulting in billions of dollars in losses each year, it is given little more consideration than jaywalking by most people. The effectiveness of efforts to combat this crime could be greatly enhanced if it was known which factors cause individuals to engage in electronic copyright piracy.

This study assesses factors that potentially affect digital piracy among college students. Specifically, this study asks the question: Are social learning theories predictive of piracy behaviors? The importance of studying piracy has often been ignored in empirical studies. According to one study, copyright piracy in the U.S. software industry alone accounts for $6.8 billion in lost revenue each year (Business Software Alliance, 2006). Estimated losses in wages and tax revenue reflect similar importance. The music industry faces dire piracy problems as well, with the annual estimated sales for pirated music worldwide reaching $4.6 billion (International Federation of the Phonographic Industry, 2005). Moreover, this figure does not include the vast number of illegal files exchanged over the Internet without cost via peer-to-peer (P2P) file-sharing programs. The total number of media files transferred through these programs has reached over 27 billion annually (U.S. House of Representatives, 2004a). Although the legality of such files cannot be ascertained due to the private nature of the exchanges, a large portion of the transfers is nonetheless illegitimate.

The violation of law and loss of potential revenue to "big business" are not, in and of themselves, considered harmful by the average citizen. The impact of digital piracy, however, still has a severe impact. First, governments worldwide are already spending millions of dollars to combat copyright piracy. These attempts often specifically outline goals consistent with deterrence-based law enforcement (e.g., U.S. House of Representatives, 2004a). Empirical evidence of the antecedents of digital piracy would undoubtedly assist in these efforts. Furthermore, tax revenue would increase if sales and the industry's taxable profits likewise increase. One study indicated that a 10% decrease in the piracy rate would increase tax revenue by an estimated $21 billion in the United States alone (International Data Corporation, 2005).

Although using the word *piracy* to describe certain copyright violations has existed for centuries, it is a relatively new concept in terms of being a widespread phenomenon. With the digital revolution came a new form of theft known as *digital piracy*, which is the unauthorized and illegal digital reproduction of intellectual property. Given its recent conception, few studies have addressed the causes of digital piracy, and fewer still explicitly use a criminological theory as a foundation for research. The recent advancement of fast, easily accessible forms of electronic piracy has quickly outdated many of the few studies that have addressed this topic. More specifically, the rapid increase in popularity of P2P file-sharing software since 1999 has dramatically increased the accessibility of music and video files. Presently, the average individual with minimal experience and broadband Internet access, which is common on virtually all college campuses, can download a music file in under a minute (Cooper & Harrison, 2001).

In light of this recent, rapid increase in accessibility, piracy has become more widespread than ever before. The technological access provided to college students and prevalence of piracy at universities is well-documented and is often the target of government actions (Cooper & Harrison, 2001; U.S. House of Representatives, 2004b). Using survey data from college students from two mid-Atlantic higher learning institutions, in this study we empirically tested whether variables derived from social learning theories affect digital Internet-based piracy among college students. Some of the potential implications include more effective prevention strategies or the elimination of actions not consistent with the theoretical findings.

Social Learning Theories of Digital Piracy

Differential association (Sutherland & Cressey, 1960), one of the first social learning theories specifically developed to explain crime, views crime as a product of social interaction. According to this theory, crime is learned, and criminal actions are the end result of an individual's exposure to an excess of definitions favorable to the violation of law. *Definitions* include the motives, attitudes (rationalizations), and techniques (ability) that permit an individual to commit a crime, all of which are learned through association with others. According to differential association theory, the most powerful definitions come from intimate primary groups, such as family members and friends/peers. Secondary groups—such as government officials, entertainment industry representatives, university policies, and campaigns against piracy—generate less powerful definitions.

Modern social learning theories (Akers, 1985, 1998; Akers, Krohn, Lanza-Kaduce, & Radosevich, 1979; Burgess & Akers, 1966) describe the *social learning process* in greater detail, noting that it contains multiple concepts. The principal concepts of social learning include *differential association, definitions,* and *differential reinforcement* (Akers, 1985, 1998). The concept of differential association has remained quite similar to Sutherland's (Sutherland & Cressey, 1960) original description. Accordingly, *differential association* is the process by which people are exposed to normative definitions that are favorable or unfavorable to the violation of law. More specifically, this process usually involves direct contact with individuals engaging in deviant or criminal behaviors; however, normative aspects such as moral approval or the absence of disapproval of deviant or criminal behavior are also part of this process. Thus, the concept of differential association comprises both behavioral and attitudinal support for deviant or criminal acts.

In empirical studies of digital piracy, differential association has found some support relating to software piracy. Skinner and Fream (1997) tested differential association and found family and peer involvement to be predictive of piracy; however, these results are quite dated and are limited to only one distinct type of piracy. One other study from the pre-P2P era concluded that *social factors,* defined as "norms, roles, and values at the societal level that influences [sic] an individual's intentions to pirate software" (Limayem, Khalifa, & Chin, 1999, p. 125), were similarly related software piracy. The exact measure for this variable is unspecified but is implied to be peer activity and support of piracy. However, this study was limited to business undergraduates at a Canadian university, so its generalizablility to the United

States, where piracy rates are significantly lower (Business Software Alliance, 2006), is questionable.

More recently, several studies by Higgins and colleagues have found additional support for differential association. Several of these studies (Higgins, 2005; Higgins & Makin, 2004a,b; Higgins & Wilson, 2006; Higgins, Wolfe, & Marcum, 2008) included peer activity, which was measured through use of a six-item scale and for which statistical significance was found. In these studies, the behavior of study was again strictly limited to illegally copied software. All of these studies used various scenarios from a previous study (Shore et al., 2001) to describe the behavior to participants. However, one of the studies (Higgins & Makin, 2004b) used a shareware-based scenario in which an individual is asked to send a registration fee to the author but is not explicitly required to do so by law. Although scenarios about computer ethics are interesting, they do not necessarily measure actual engagement in illegal activities but, rather, a more abstract willingness to do so. Despite this limitation, these studies indicated that differential association may be an antecedent of digital piracy. Additional studies have also indicated support for this concept as a predictor of piracy (Higgins, Wilson, & Fell, 2005; Hinduja, 2006).

The second concept of social learning theory is that of definitions. According to the theories (Akers, 1985, 1998; Akers et al., 1979; Burgess & Akers, 1966; Sutherland & Cressey, 1960), the concept of *definitions* represents a variety of attitudes or meanings by an individual toward a specific behavior. These can include rationalizations for deviant or criminal acts, a general orientation toward the behavior, or an overarching moral evaluation of the behavior. In other words, definitions form the general moral belief that one has or that pertains to a specific act. Definitions, not being an innate part of an individual, are learned through the differential association process. Thus, definitions are both an outcome of differential association and an influence over behavior.

Similar to differential association, definitions have also received empirical support as being relating to digital piracy. Moreover, studies have shown that such a relationship holds true when definitions are operationalized as general moral beliefs toward piracy (Higgins, 2005; Higgins et al., 2005; Higgins & Wilson, 2006; Limayem et al., 1999), specific rationalizations for pirating behaviors (Higgins & Wilson, 2006; Skinner & Fream, 1997), and specific beliefs about crimes unrelated to piracy (Gopal, Sanders, Bhattacharjee, Agrawal, & Wagner, 2004). However, the relationship between differential association and definitions in the area of digital piracy remains untested.

Another key concept of social learning theory is differential reinforcement. According to the theories (Akers, 1985, 1998; Akers et al., 1979; Burgess & Akers, 1966; Sutherland & Cressey, 1960), *differential reinforcement* refers to the anticipated rewards or punishments for a specific act or behavior. These hypothetical consequences serve to encourage or inhibit the likelihood of an individual engaging in deviant behavior. This concept is actually quite similar to that of deterrence (Beccaria, 1764/1985), especially when more recent rational choice theories (e.g., Cornish & Clarke, 1986) are considered. These views similarly predict that perceived certain and severe punishment is likely to prevent a person from engaging in a criminal behavior. Differential reinforcement can include informal rewards and punishments beyond the criminal justice system, such as a negative reaction by friends or family. In the case of piracy, however, such informal reactions seem unlikely given the low severity ascribed to the crime of piracy and the overall prevalence of digital piracy. It is unlikely that there is much variation in positive reinforcement, as pirating for personal use does not involve rewards beyond getting the sought item without cost.

Differential reinforcement has not often been tested in relation to digital piracy. In fact, the Skinner and Fream (1997) study was the only criminological test to explicitly relate the concept to a form of piracy. The results of the study noted only nonsignificant relationships between differential reinforcement variables and software piracy. This finding, however, is not entirely applicable to modern piracy. First, the vast changes in technology and subsequent increase in piracy since 2000 would, in and of themselves, demand additional consideration before rejecting deterrence altogether. Second, the study defined the act being investigated as "knowingly used, made, or gave to another person a 'pirated' copy of commercially sold computer software" (Skinner & Fream, 1997, p. 504). Thus, the definition of *piracy* in this study was strictly limited to the sharing or copying of software among peers. This variation of piracy occurs in a setting even more private than Internet-based digital piracy and could easily result in different perceptions of punishment. Additionally, it was unclear whether the term *pirated* was defined to the participants.

Although theories of general deterrence and differential reinforcement are clearly different in many vital aspects, the operationalization process in studies of digital piracy has resulted in both theories being tested through measures of punishment severity and certainty. Thus, although deterrence is not interchangeable with differential reinforcement, the research applying these concepts to piracy is not unrelated. It is unfortunate that, despite an interest in applying deterrence to digital piracy (Sherizan, 1995), only one such study exists. In a test of software piracy (Higgins et al., 2005), empirical support for a link between deterrence and piracy was found for punishment certainty but not for severity. Similar to the Skinner and Fream (1997) study, Higgins and colleagues (2005) measured punishment and likelihood of pirating in terms of sharing a physical copy of software. As before, the private setting of in-person sharing radically changes the "chances of being caught" and will likely alter the potential offender's perceptions as well (Higgins et al., 2005, p. 173).

The Present Study

Using social learning theory, in this study we investigated three hypotheses. First, given that social learning theory predicts that imitation is the result of differential association, belief, and differential reinforcement (Akers, 1985, 1998; Akers et al., 1979; Burgess & Akers, 1966), it is expected that individuals with differential association, belief, and differential reinforcement supportive of piracy will be more likely to engage in piracy. More specifically, Sutherland and Cressey (1960) predicted that primary groups, including family and peers, generate more powerful messages than do secondary groups, such as government officials. Thus, it is expected that differential association, which involves primarily family and peers, will have a greater impact than would differential reinforcement, which involves societal forces.

Second, Sutherland and Cressey (1960) postulated that the differential association process includes the transmission of definitions, motives, and abilities. Therefore, it is expected that the effects of differential association will be mediated partially through belief and technical ability.

Third, primary groups may have influence over an individual's perceptions of rewards and punishments through the differential association process. Essentially, pirating friends may downplay the likelihood of getting caught and, therefore, differential association favorable to piracy will decrease perceptions of punishment.

Methodology

Data Collection and Sample

Data used in this research were collected through student surveys from two mid-Atlantic higher education institutions, one of which is a small, private, liberal arts college and the other a moderately sized public university. Prior research has postulated that perceptions of punishment and belief can best be ascertained through vignettes describing the criminal act being studied (Bachman, Paternoster, & Ward, 1992; Higgins & Makin, 2004a; Klepper & Nagin, 1989; Shore, et al., 2001). Therefore, participants were presented with several vignettes, each describing an individual committing a specific act of piracy. These vignettes were intentionally kept brief to minimize the introduction of mitigating circumstances in the hopes that the participant would respond to the crime rather than to the specific events surrounding the particular scenario. Questions following each vignette addressed the morality of the act, likelihood of punishment, severity of punishment, similarity to peer behavior, technical ability to engage in the act, and parental approval of the behavior (see the Appendix). To minimize confusion between piracy and legal downloading, participants were explicitly told prior to responding that the scenarios and questions in the questionnaire are not instances of legal downloading (e.g., iTunes, shareware, demos, etc.). Participants also were reminded of this on the questionnaire itself.

The sample for this study was a nonrandom sample of undergraduate college students enrolled in various classes during the spring 2006 semester. Thirteen classes were selected for the sample primarily based on their large enrollment figures but also for diverse topics and varying levels. From the 594 students asked to participate, 7 students opted to not participate, resulting in a total response rate of about 98%.

The demographics of the sample are displayed in Table 11.1. Also displayed are the institution demographics from the larger public university.

Table 11.1 Sample Demographics

Variables	% (N)	Population %
Gender		
Male	44.3 (260)	42.2
Female	55.7 (327)	57.8
Race/ethnicity		
White	86.7 (509)	83.1
Black	5.3 (31)	5.3
Hispanic	4.1 (24)	4.4
Asian	2.2 (13)	3.8
Other/mixed	1.7 (10)	3.3
Class year		
Freshman	30.7 (180)	28.8
Sophomore	28.1 (165)	25.1
Junior	19.9 (117)	23.0
Senior	21.1 (124)	23.2
Other	0.2 (1)	
Major		
Business-related	12.4 (73)	
Computer sciences	0.9 (5)	
Criminal justice	27.4 (161)	
Natural sciences	8.0 (47)	
Psychology	8.7 (51)	
Sociology	5.8 (34)	
Other social science	9.4 (55)	
Other	26.6 (156)	

Unfortunately, enrollment statistics from the private college were unavailable. The gender, race, and class year demographics are roughly representative of the institutions from which the sample was drawn. The participants' majors, however, were overrepresentative of the social sciences and underrepresentative of the computer sciences, despite the fact that three introductory computer sciences classes were included in the sample.

Variables

The dependent variables for this study were measured through the use of objective questions about the monthly average of violations for three types of piracy: music, software, and movies. The available responses were ordinal, ranged from one to four, and varied in description for each type of piracy. For music piracy, response options included 1 (*never*), 2 (*one to five songs per month*), 3 (*six to 15 songs per month*), and 4 (*more than 15 songs per month*). For software piracy, response options included 1 (*never*), 2 (*one to three programs per year*), 3 (*four to six programs per year*), and 4 (*more than seven programs per year*). Finally, for movie piracy, response options included 1 (*never*), 2 (*one to three movies per month*), 3 (*four to six movies per month*), and 4 (*more than seven movies per month*).

The analysis included six independent variables, each with three variations for each type of piracy in the vignette. We measured the first independent variable, peer involvement, in a manner similar to that used in previous studies (Skinner & Fream, 1997) by asking how many of the respondent's friends would do the described act (e.g., download music without paying for it). The possible responses were 1 (*none*), 2 (*few*), 3 (*about half*), or 4 (*most or all*). The second independent variable, parental approval, was measured with a Likert-type scale in response to asking if the respondents' parents would approve if they did the described act. The responses ranged from 1 (*strongly disapprove*) to 4 (*strongly approve*). These first two measures made up the differential association concept. Although theoretically, a scale could be compiled from the two measures, the reliability of such a scale would be unacceptably low (< .50), and we decided that comparing peer and parent variables' independent effects would yield more interesting results.

Two variables were derived from concepts associated with differential reinforcement. We measured reinforcement certainty by asking how likely it was that the described act would result in an individual being "caught and punished." Responses ranged from 1 (*extremely unlikely*) to 4 (*extremely likely*). Alternatively, we measured reinforcement severity by asking what the punishment would be if the fictional individual in the vignette were "caught." Responses included nothing, small fine, loss of Internet access, heavy fines/lawsuit, or jail/prison. These responses were later dichotomized to either

0 (*mild*) for responses of nothing, small fine, or loss of Internet access or 1 (*severe*) for heavy fines/lawsuit or jail/prison.[1]

The measure for technical ability is a straightforward question about the respondent's ability (yes or no) to do the described act. We measured the belief variable using a question similar to Higgins's (2005) morality measure ("How morally wrong is this behavior?") with responses of 1 (*not wrong*), 2 (*slightly wrong*), 3 (*moderately wrong*), and 4 (*very wrong*). The descriptive statistics for the main independent and dependent variables are displayed in Table 11.2. The correlation matrices for each of the three types of piracy indicated that none of the correlation coefficients for the seven variables used in the analyses exceeded .52, so we did not expect collinearity to be problematic.[2] Additionally, the variance inflation factors (VIFs) and tolerances also indicated no multicollinearity issues.

Analysis

Several of the hypotheses in the present study addressed mediating effects within the causal model. Although several techniques allow for the testing of such effects, path analyses as a part of structural equation modeling (SEM) were most appropriate in this instance. This allowed the direct, indirect, and total effects of exogenous and intervening variables to be analyzed and discussed. The initial model for the analysis is presented in Figure 11.1. Maximum likelihood (ML) is typically used for such analyses. This analysis, however, used weighted least squares mean and variance adjusted (WLSMV) to account for the ordinal nature of the dependent variables. The significance of a chi-square statistic has often been used to determine the strength of the model overall, yet this statistic is often problematic when using large samples. Therefore, in this analysis, we also consulted the comparative fit index (CFI) and root-mean-square error of approximation (RMSEA) to determine the overall fit of the model. The analysis was performed separately for each type of Internet piracy included in this study, and subsequent results were compared for any noteworthy differences.[3]

---

[1] Multiple methods of coding the severity variable were attempted, including using it as an ordinal variable as originally collected. Severity's effect in the models remained similar regardless of the coding method. The dichotomous version was chosen because it seemed most consistent with general deterrence theory, which indicates that severity's effect should not increase once the severity becomes more severe than the crime, and because "nothing," "small fine," and "loss of Internet access" all appear to be considered insignificant punishments based on prior research of piracy (e.g., Cooper & Harrison, 2001).

[2] Correlation matrices are not shown but are available from the author upon request.

[3] Each variable was measured with three observations—the minimum number of observations required for forming a latent construct and using true SEM. A bivariate analysis of the data, however, indicates that the different types of piracy measured in this study do not correlate sufficiently for such an analysis. The Cronbach's alpha for such a construct would be a mere .59. Therefore, forming a latent construct for a single SEM model would be unwarranted.

Table 11.2 Descriptive Statistics

Variable	M	SD	Min	Max
Peer involvement				
Music	3.65	0.640	1.00	4.00
Software	2.69	0.961	1.00	4.00
Movie	2.80	0.900	1.00	4.00
Parental approval				
Music	2.54	0.699	1.00	4.00
Software	2.38	0.749	1.00	4.00
Movie	2.36	0.740	1.00	4.00
Reinforcement certainty				
Music	1.90	0.633	1.00	4.00
Software	2.10	0.706	1.00	4.00
Movie	2.11	0.697	1.00	4.00
Reinforcement severity				
Music	0.57	0.496	0.00	1.00
Software	0.64	0.481	0.00	1.00
Movie	0.66	0.475	0.00	1.00
Belief				
Music	2.01	0.775	1.00	4.00
Software	2.26	0.829	1.00	4.00
Movie	2.19	0.787	1.00	4.00
Technical ability				
Music	0.94	0.234	0.00	1.00
Software	0.73	0.444	0.00	1.00
Movie	0.81	0.391	0.00	1.00
Piracy involvement				
Music	2.46	1.174	1.00	4.00
Software	1.41	0.686	1.00	4.00
Music	1.22	0.584	1.00	4.00

Min, minimum; Max, maximum.

Results

The results of the path analyses, including the direct, indirect, and total effects on the dependent variables, are presented in Table 11.3. The results for all direct paths in the analysis are displayed in Figures 11.2, 11.3, and 11.4. Looking first at the direct effects on digital piracy, measures of differential association from primary groups were powerful predictors of digital piracy of all types (standardized effects ranged from .11 to .23). Similarly, technical ability also displayed strong influence over the three forms of digital piracy (standardized effects ranged from .20 to .33). It is interesting to note that the effect of belief appears to change depending on the specific type of piracy. For

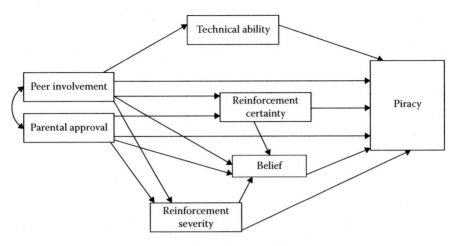

Figure 11.1 Theoretical model.

music piracy, belief has a substantively strong relationship (–.24) with piracy that rivals that of differential association measures (.19 and .11). With regard to software piracy, technical ability is no longer as influential (–.11) as differential association (.23 and .14) but still statistically significant. Conversely, belief has no significant impact on movie piracy. This is especially surprising considering that downloading movies requires more expertise than downloading music. The differential reinforcement variables, alternatively, hold the weakest impact on piracy, with no significant influence over the crime when controlling for the other social learning variables. Therefore, the hypothesis that social learning variables (differential association, technical ability, belief, and differential reinforcement) have a direct effect on digital piracy is supported. Differential reinforcement itself, however, is not empirically supported as a predictor of digital piracy.

The second hypothesis is that the effects of differential association are partially mediated through belief and technical abilities. Supporting this assertion, the indirect effects of differential association variables are found to be moderately strong. For music and software piracy, the indirect effects of parental approval (.08 and .10) rivaled those of the direct effects (.11 and .14) and were statistically significant. Similarly, peer involvement's indirect effects on music, software, and movie piracy (.10, .15, and .09) also significantly contributed to the total effect of peer involvement on the three forms of piracy. Of the effects of differential association on digital piracy, only the indirect effect of parental approval on movie piracy was insignificant. Therefore, it seems that these indirect effects are powerful enough to lend some credibility to the notion that differential association's effect is mediated through belief and ability.

The third hypothesis of this study is that differential association favorable to piracy will decrease perceptions of punishment. The results indicate that parental approval has significant direct effects on perceptions

Table 11.3 Standardized Regression Coefficients for Final Path Analysis Models

Variable	Music Piracy			Software Piracy			Movie Piracy		
	Direct	Indirect	Total	Direct	Indirect	Total	Direct	Indirect	Total
Peer involvement	.19*	.10*	.30*	.23*	.15*	.38*	.21*	.09*	.30*
Parental approval	.11*	.08*	.19*	.14*	.10*	.24*	.23*	.01	.25*
Reinforcement severity	.07	-.02*	.04	.05	-.02	.03	.05	-.01	.04
Reinforcement certainty	.01	-.06*	-.05	-.10	-.11*	-.21*	.05	-.04*	.01
Belief	-.24*		-.24*	-.11*		-.11*	-.07		-.07
Technical ability	.20*		.20*	.33*		.33*	.33*		.33*
r^2		.242			.413			.312	
χ^2/df		1.252			1.212			1.302	
CFI		.995			.997			.995	
RMSEA		.021			.019			.023	

CFI, comparative fit index; RMSEA, root-mean-square error of approximation.

*$p < .05$.

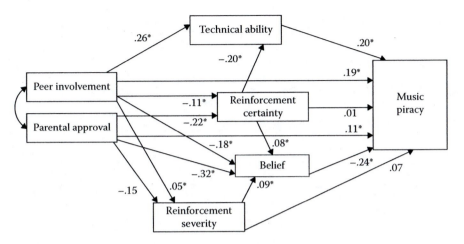

Figure 11.2 Final model for music piracy.
*p < .05

of reinforcement certainty (−.22 to −.32), as does peer involvement (−.11 to −.24). Interestingly, the effects of peer involvement and parental support on reinforcement severity are relatively weak and nonsignificant. Although this evidence gives support to this hypothesis in general, it is clear that such a relationship gravitates toward punishment certainty rather than severity.

Overall, the models explain 24.2% of the variation in movie piracy, 41.3% of that in software piracy, and 31.2% of that in movie piracy. Despite the large sample size, all of the chi-square statistics, ranging from 1.21 to 1.30, are too low to reject the null hypothesis that the data fit the models

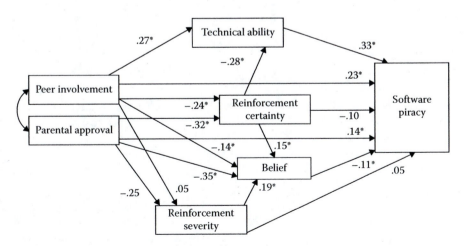

Figure 11.3 Final model for software piracy.
*p < .05

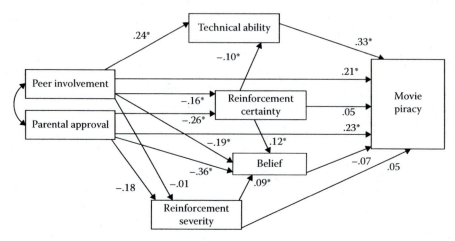

Figure 11.4 Final model for movie piracy.
*p < .05

perfectly. Similarly, the CFI statistics (.995 to .997) are well above the required .95, indicating a significant improvement over a baseline comparison. The RMSEA statistics (.019 to .023) are also well within acceptable values.[4]

Discussion and Conclusion

In this study, we investigated the empirical validity of differential association and deterrence as applied to multiple forms of digital piracy. As predicted by social learning theory (Akers, 1985, 1998; Akers et al., 1979; Burgess & Akers, 1966), differential association predicted digital piracy in that college students with peers engaging in piracy and parents supportive of piracy were more likely to engage in piracy themselves. This finding is consistent with several prior studies that have noted a strong relationship between peers and piracy (e.g., Higgins & Makin, 2004a; Higgins & Wilson, 2006; Hinduja, 2006; Limayem et al., 1999; Skinner & Fream, 1997). However, in this study we have shown that such an effect is not limited solely to peers and extends to parents as well. Furthermore, differential association theory (Sutherland & Cressey, 1960) also predicts the effects to be mediated

---

[4] As is common with many SEM-based models, minor modifications to the theoretically derived model were made to improve its fit. The paths from reinforcement certainty to technical ability were freed, as recommended by the modification indices. Although not initially predicted in this study's model, such a relationship is consistent with literature on piracy and the theory used. Depending on the direction of the relationship, an individual might not seek the ability to commit a crime that he or she considers not worthy of the risk involved, or an individual with the technical ability to pirate may have an increased awareness of the anonymity involved and, therefore, knows that detection is unlikely. The direction for the path in this model was arbitrary but could theoretically flow in either direction or reciprocally.

through motives, beliefs, and ability. Although motives were beyond the scope of this study, significant indirect effects were observed through belief and ability. Additionally, it was hypothesized that perceptions of punishment would be influenced by differential association with pirating peers and parents supportive of piracy. The empirical evidence examined here is supportive of this postulation.

Conversely, the effects of differential reinforcement were statistically and substantively weak. The effects of perceptions of severity and certainty of punishment only rarely were statistically significant and were consistently weak—a finding consistent with prior studies of deterrence and differential reinforcement (Higgins et al., 2005; Skinner & Fream, 1997). These mixed results were obviously not enough to conclude that there is an effect by reinforcement, but they were also not weak enough to definitively reject the notion that reinforcement may have some effect. With the simplicity of the measurement and analysis of this study, it is entirely possible that the poor relationships were the result of oversimplification in operationalizing severity and certainty.

Another noteworthy finding was the discrepancy between types of piracy. Although the overall conclusion that differential association is a strong predictor of piracy and that differential reinforcement variables are weak or nonpredictors remains the same for all three types of piracy in this study, several differences were observed. Thus, different forms of piracy likely have similar causes and correlates. However, it would be erroneous to assume that such findings are identical without empirical verification.

The largest policy implication that can be derived from this study is the importance of social learning and belief. Obviously, the social learning process cannot be stopped altogether, but what is being learned can be altered if the environment changes. Attempting to sway the moral beliefs of college student to antipiracy stances could result in exponentially growing antipiracy beliefs. The effectiveness of programs designed to sway opinions is not guaranteed, but the data at least show that prosocial beliefs may prevent piracy.

Conversely, the deterrence factor so often discussed by government officials and the victimized industries did not receive much support; however, this is not necessarily a definitive conclusion. The number of individuals who reported punishment being unlikely or extremely unlikely was consistently higher than the number of people engaged in the activity. If everyone believes that punishment is unlikely, then the variance must be explained by other concepts. These data cannot predict what would happen should punishment become more certain. Rather, the data showed that perceptions are presently so far removed from certain that a deterrent effect is not present even among most nonpirating students. In other words, deterrence theory cannot find empirical support—even if it is applicable to piracy—if the vast majority of respondents have correctly assessed that the certainty and severity of punishment is minuscule. Therefore, the policy implication for deterrence is that if a deterrence effect is possible, it will take a radical change in tactics to become powerful enough to actually deter.

Several limitations to this study must also be addressed. First, we measured peer activity and parental support using data reported by only the respondent. Given the number of cases involved and anonymity being guaranteed, it was unfeasible to contact parents and peers to confirm the validity of the reported support and activity. Although it is unlikely that participants intentionally lied in their responses, it is entirely possible that their responses reflected inaccurate perceptions of parental support and peer activity. For parental support, students may be unaware of their parents' stance on what is typically considered to be a minor crime. Thus, they may have selected (guessed) an answer representative of their own philosophy. The same concern exists for peer activity, but at least here, it appears that popular answers for peer activity coincide with popular answers for self-involvement in piracy activities.

Second, the data used in this study were cross-sectional. Therefore, these results cannot truly claim to explain causality without establishing time order. Although it seems unlikely that one would select peers on the basis of a relatively minor and typically considered "secretive" part of one's life, these data do not disprove such a notion. Time order would be a greater concern had punishment certainty and severity been significant predictors of piracy, considering that experimenting with piracy could increase awareness of the anonymity involved and become a reciprocal relationship. Finally, the items used to measure the variables were quite simplistic. Because a one-item measure is rarely as valid or reliable as a multiple-item measure, it may be more accurate to use scales or indices for more abstract concepts, such as belief.

Future researchers should attempt to overcome these limitations. In addition to using longitudinal data, assessing the validity of peer/parent measures, and importing more complex constructs, researchers should expand the theory to surpass the limited model used in this study. Modern and complete versions of social learning theory would be especially interesting to apply to Internet piracy and the learning process. Furthermore, research must distinguish between differing types of piracy. What may be true and well-established for peers copying software may very well be undocumented and different for illegal, anonymous music downloads. Additionally, although it appears that P2P programs are becoming a permanent part of technology, the Internet is ever changing and must be studied as such. The high number of individuals who report having high-speed access and the technical ability to download music illegally are evidence of how theory can be affected through technological evolution in even a relatively short period of time.

Appendix: Questions and Responses Used in Analysis

Participants were presented with each of the following vignettes separately:

1. Daniel considers buying a new CD but instead decides to download the songs for free.
2. John considers buying software but instead decides to download it for free.
3. Hector considers buying a movie but instead decides to download it for free.

How morally wrong is this behavior?
- ☐ It is not wrong
- ☐ Slightly wrong
- ☐ Moderately Wrong
- ☐ Very wrong

If [name] continues this behavior, how likely is it that [name] will be caught and punished?
- ☐ Extremely unlikely
- ☐ Unlikely
- ☐ Likely
- ☐ Extremely likely

What would be [name]'s punishment if he were caught?
- ☐ Nothing
- ☐ A small fine or paying for the songs
- ☐ Loss of Internet access
- ☐ Heavy fines or a lawsuit
- ☐ Jail or prison

How many of your friends would do what [name] did?
- ☐ None of them
- ☐ A few of them
- ☐ About half
- ☐ Most or all of them

Do you believe you have the technical ability to do what [name] did?
- ☐ Yes
- ☐ No

If you did what [name] did, would your parents approve of your actions?
- ☐ Strongly Approve
- ☐ Approve
- ☐ Disapprove
- ☐ Strongly Disapprove

Before the following questions were administered, students were informed that "The following questions address piracy (downloading files *without* the permission of the copyright owner). Files legally transferred for free (samples, shareware, public domain, etc.) are exempt."

On average, how often do you download **music** without paying for it?
  ☐ Never
  ☐ 1–5 songs per month
  ☐ 6–15 songs per month
  ☐ More than 15 songs per month

On average, how often do you download **movies** without paying for them?
  ☐ Never
  ☐ 1–3 movies per month
  ☐ 4–6 movies per month
  ☐ More than 7 movies per month

On average, how often do you download **software** without paying for it?
  ☐ Never
  ☐ 1–3 programs per year
  ☐ 4–6 programs per year
  ☐ More than 7 programs per year

References

Akers, R. L. (1985). *Deviant behavior: A social learning approach.* Belmont, CA: Wadsworth.

Akers, R. L. (1998). *Social learning and social structure: A general theory of crime and deviance.* Boston, MA: Northeastern University.

Akers, R. L., Krohn, M. D., Lanza-Kaduce, L., & Radosevich, M. (1979). Social learning and deviant behavior: A specific test of a general theory. *American Sociological Review, 44,* 636–655.

Bachman, R., Paternoster, R., & Ward, S. (1992). The rationality of sexual offending: Testing deterrence/rational choice conception of sexual assault. *Law & Society Review, 26,* 343–372.

Beccaria, C. (1985). *Essay on crimes and punishments* (H. Paolucci, Trans.). New York, NY: Macmillan. (Original work published 1764)

Burgess, R. L., & Akers, R. L. (1966). A differential association-reinforcement theory of criminal behavior. *Social Problems, 14,* 128–147.

Business Software Alliance. (2006, May). *Third Annual BSA and IDC Global Software Piracy Study.* Retrieved from http://www.bsa.org/globalstudy/upload/2005%20 Piracy%20Study%20-%20Official%20Version.pdf

Cooper, J., & Harrison, D. M. (2001). The social organization of audio piracy on the Internet. *Media, Culture & Society, 23,* 71–89.

Cornish, D., & Clarke, R. V. (1986). *The reasoning criminal: Rational choice perspectives on offending.* New York, NY: Springer-Verlag.

Gopal, R. D., Sanders, G. L., Bhattacharjee, S., Agrawal, M., & Wagner, S. C. (2004). A behavioral model of digital music piracy. *Journal of Organizational Computing and Electronic Commerce, 14*, 89–105.

Higgins, G. E. (2005). Can low self-control help with the understanding of the software piracy problem? *Deviant Behavior, 26*, 1–24.

Higgins, G. E., & Makin, D. A. (2004a). Does social learning theory condition the effects of low self-control on college students' software piracy? *Journal of Economic Crime Management, 2*, 1–22.

Higgins, G. E., & Makin, D. A. (2004b). Self-control, deviant peer association, and software piracy. *Psychological Reports, 95*, 921–931.

Higgins, G. E., & Wilson, A. L. (2006). Low self-control, moral beliefs, and social learning theory. *Security Journal, 19*, 75–92.

Higgins, G. E., Wilson, A. L., & Fell, B. D. (2005). An application of deterrence theory to software piracy. *Journal of Criminal Justice and Popular Culture, 12*, 166–184.

Higgins, G. E., Wolfe, S. E., & Marcum, C. D. (2008). Digital piracy: An examination of three measurements of self-control. *Deviant Behavior, 29*, 440–460.

Hinduja, S. (2006). *Music piracy and crime theory*. New York, NY: LFB.

International Data Corporation. (2005, December). *Expanding the frontiers of our digital future: Reducing software piracy to accelerate global IT benefits*. Retrieved from http://www.bsa.org

International Federation of the Phonographic Industry. (2005). *The recording industry 2005 commercial piracy report*. Retrieved from http://www.ifpi.org

Klepper, S., & Nagin, D. (1989). Tax compliance and perceptions of the risks of detection and criminal prosecution. *Law & Society Review, 23*, 209–240.

Limayem, M., Khalifa, M., & Chin, W. W. (1999). Factors motivating software piracy: A longitudinal study. In P. De & J. I. DeGross (Eds.), *International Conference on Information Systems: Proceedings of the 20th International Conference on Information Systems* (pp. 124–131).

Sherizan, S. (1995). Can computer crime be deterred? *Security Journal, 6*, 177–181.

Shore, B., Venkatachalam, A. R., Solorzano, E., Burn, J. M., Hassan, S. Z., & Janczewski, L. J. (2001). Shoplifting and piracy: Behavior across cultures. *Technology in Society, 23*, 563–581.

Skinner, W. F., & Fream, A. M. (1997). A social learning theory analysis of computer crime among college students. *Journal of Research in Crime and Delinquency, 34*, 495–518.

Sutherland, E. H., & Cressey, D. R. (1960). *Principles of criminology* (6th ed.). Philadelphia, PA: Lippincott.

U.S. House of Representatives. (2004a). *Piracy Deterrence and Education Act of 2004* (Report No. 108-700). Washington, DC: U.S. Government Printing Office.

U.S. House of Representatives. (2004b). *Peer to peer piracy on university campuses: An update* (Serial No. 112). Washington, DC: U.S. Government Printing Office.

Change of Music Piracy and Neutralization

An Examination Using Short-Term Longitudinal Data

12

GEORGE E. HIGGINS
SCOTT E. WOLFE
CATHERINE D. MARCUM

Contents

Introduction

The Internet—and the increased use of the personal computer (PC) in recent years—has provided a refuge for a multitude of computer-based crimes (Adler & Adler, 2006; Hinduja, 2004). One of the most challenging computer-related crimes to law enforcement and the economy has been intellectual property piracy. PCs and the Internet enable individuals to find, copy, and use intellectual property without providing any payment for it (Higgins,

Wolfe, & Marcum, 2008). Digital piracy is one form of intellectual property piracy that has been increasing in recent years (International Federation of Phonographic Industries [IFPI], 2008).

Gopal, Sanders, Bhattacharjee, Agrawal, and Wagner (2004) defined *digital piracy* as the illegal act of copying digital goods, software, digital documents, digital audio (including music and voice), and digital video for any reason other than to back up without explicit permission from and compensation to the copyright holder. The Internet facilitates digital piracy because it allows the crime to take place in a context that is detached from the copyright holder (Wall, 2005). For instance, the Internet provides a sense of confidentiality and anonymity. This is especially true for digital music piracy that is committed through a multitude of modus operandi (e.g., compact disc [CD] burning, peer-to-peer [P2P] networks, local area network [LAN] file sharing, digital stream ripping, and mobile piracy [see http://www.ifpi.org for a discussion of these techniques]). A problem with digital piracy is that the anonymity and confidentiality provides the pirate with a sense that the crime is victimless. However, music piracy is far from a victimless crime and has been described as "the greatest threat facing the music industry today" (Chiou, Huang, & Lee, 2005, p. 161).

Piracy has wreaked havoc on digital music sales, which have been increasing in recent years. In 2007, digital music sales accounted for an estimated $2.9 billion in record company revenues and represented 15% of the total music market (IFPI, 2008). The fluidity of digital music markets allows them to grow but allows the piracy market to grow, as well. Simon Gunning, the senior vice president of digital at EMI (United Kingdom and Ireland) said, "The music industry is way ahead of other media, broadcast and online companies in getting our content out there, yet, ironically, we are behind when it comes to getting paid for it" (IFPI, 2008, p. 11). The IFPI (2006) estimated that 20 billion songs were illegally downloaded in 2005. Further, losses from worldwide digital music piracy in the U.S. music industry alone were projected at $3.7 billion (IFPI, 2008). The lost revenue results in loss of jobs and poor legitimate market stability.

Digital piracy of music is not confined to one country but, rather, is an international issue. This criminal behavior is pervasively global and has affected markets in Mexico, Brazil, Spain, the Netherlands, and China (IFPI, 2008). Specifically, an estimated 2.6 billion illegal music downloads occurred in Mexico in 2007 and another 1.8 billion occurred in Brazil (IFPI, 2008). In at least two countries, the music piracy problem has also resulted in the underperformance of the legitimate music market in Spain and the Netherlands (IFPI, 2008). The Spanish Ministry of Culture conducted a study showing that 13% of Spaniards had illegally downloaded music in 2007. Additionally, China has only a $74 million legitimate music market because of the effects of a digital music piracy rate of over 99% (IFPI, 2008).

The international nature of digital piracy has led to legislation that attempts to reduce this behavior. Copyright laws in the United States attempt to protect intellectual property such as digital music. Specifically, the Piracy and Counterfeiting Amendments Act made digital piracy a copyright violation, and the No Electronic Theft Act declared the distribution of copyrighted materials via the Internet a felony (Koen & Im, 1997).

Although in many countries, music piracy is acknowledged as a criminal activity, Hinduja (2007) has argued that individuals may not view music piracy as a crime. However, the legal statutes clearly show that it is a criminal behavior. The research on music piracy has indicated that it is a primarily male endeavor (Higgins, 2007; Hinduja, 2003). Some researchers have shown that music piracy is a behavior that is performed primarily by younger individuals (Hinduja, 2003). However, the theoretical explanations of music piracy are not very plentiful in the empirical literature. A theoretical explanation of music piracy would be helpful because it would allow researchers to organize their data in a rational way that can contribute to the development of policies that curb this behavior. We do acknowledge that others have used several theoretical perspectives to understand music piracy (Higgins, 2005), but we chose to examine the changes with a specific theory that would provide insight about the decision-making process—this theory is known as *neutralization*. We believe that the neutralization theory can provide some information concerning an individual's perceptions that music piracy is not a form of criminal behavior. Sykes and Matza (1957) addressed the rationale as to why individuals would seemingly shirk the idea of social constraints so that they can commit deviant or criminal behavior. To clarify, the legal, moral, and ethical issues are not completely disavowed, but individuals who engage in digital piracy momentarily relieve themselves from these dictates so that they may feel released to perform the behavior of interest. This means that these individual may use verbal or cognitive cues to convince themselves of the acceptability or properness of the behavior regardless of society's views. Once this process takes place, the individual is free to perform the behavior without acquiring a permanent criminal persona or identity because the individual has adequately neutralized the feelings of the dominant society toward the behavior. In short, because of neutralization, the typical social controls that inhibit deviant and criminal behavior are inoperable; thus, the individual feels free to violate the conventions of society (Sykes & Matza, 1957). The neutralization process takes place through the use of the following five main techniques.

1. *Denial of responsibility (i.e., "It is not my fault.")*: The action that was performed was not the fault of the individual performing the behavior.

2. *Denial of injury (i.e., "No harm resulted from my actions."):* This technique negates the behavior because no particular harm has been produced by such behavior.
3. *Denial of victim (i.e., "Nobody got hurt."):* This is the assumption that the victim deserves the consequences of the action.
4. *Condemning the condemners (i.e., "How dare they judge me, when they are just as criminal or hypocritical?"):* The behavior is not produced by the individual but, rather, is produced in retaliation of the hypocrisy and moral failings of the individuals who disapprove.
5. *Appeal to a higher a loyalty (i.e., "There is a greater and higher cause."):* The behavior is performed to help not only the individual performing the behavior but others, as well.

These techniques provide individuals with the information and the thought process necessary to garner freedom from conventional social constraints so that criminal and deviant activity may take place.

The empirical literature shows support for neutralization theory. Maruna and Copes (2004) presented the partial support that neutralization has with several different forms of behavior. In relation to the present study, neutralization theory has been applied to different forms of music piracy and computer crime. Goode and Cruise (2006) used responses from 28 individuals to examine the role of neutralization and cracking. Although this study has a substantial problem with sample size, the results of this research indicate that crackers have different mean levels of the neutralization techniques. Hinduja (2007) used cross-sectional responses from 507 college students to examine the role of neutralization and software piracy. The author's results show that the techniques of neutralization have a weak link to software piracy. On the basis of these findings, the intuitive link between neutralization, music piracy, and computer crime does not seem to have a substantial amount of support in the literature. Although these studies contribute to our understanding, they do not address all of the areas concerning neutralization and music piracy. For instance, Maruna and Copes (2004) argued that longitudinal studies could test whether reductions in the use of neutralizations over time predicts a reduction in criminal activity. We believe that this may be the case for music piracy. Thus, more study in the area of neutralization and music piracy is necessary because a gap exists in this area. Further, these earlier studies of neutralization and music piracy are unable to discuss how the changes that take place in neutralization can influence the changes that take place in music piracy. Figure 12.1 presents the hypothesized links that are being examined in the present study.

This particular view allows for an important investigation to take place that focuses on the causal sequencing of neutralization—that is, the longitudinal focus of neutralization may be able to address the issue of music piracy persistence or desistance. This implies that neutralization occurs only as an

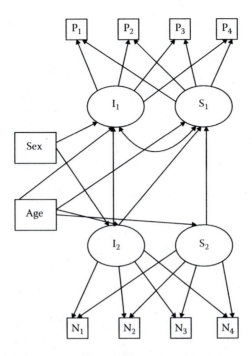

Figure 12.1 Structural equation model for neutralizations and music piracy.

after-the-fact rationalization that may create the conditions for future behavior. This allows neutralization to be a theory that accommodates both persistence in crime and desistence from crime. Maruna and Copes (2004) argued that researchers examining neutralization and crime should consider this perspective in their studies. This call implies that researchers should focus on longitudinal designs that make this possible.

The purpose of the present study was twofold. Through this study, we aimed to provide an understanding of (a) the changes in neutralization and music piracy and (b) how the changes in neutralization influence the initial point and changes in music piracy. The results from this study can be seen as uniquely informing the two literatures—that is, the music piracy literature is lacking in understanding of the initial point and changes in the behavior. The results can be seen as informing the literature on neutralization by providing an understanding of the initial point and changes in this particular measure. The results of this study may be used to inform policy to reduce instances of music piracy.

Method

Sample and Procedures

This study used a short-term longitudinal design in which low self-control and gender were measured at Time 1 and the digital piracy and intentions were measured every week for 4 weeks (i.e., Time 1 through Time 4). Some may argue that the short time in capturing the data may be a disadvantage because it could be triggering the changes. Maruna and Copes (2004) argued that neutralizations are dynamic cognitive processes. However, we have not been able to uncover any quantitative evidence showing that neutralizations require a substantial amount of time for change. Therefore, we see our design as an advancement of the quantitative empirical literature.

The sample comprised undergraduate students who resided in the College of Arts and Sciences and the Justice Administration Department at a university in the eastern United States. The courses chosen for this study were those open to all majors and those courses in which the instructor agreed to allow the study to take place during class. The researchers informed the students of their rights for participation or nonparticipation in the classroom. Specifically, the researcher instructed the students that their participation in the study was voluntary, anonymous, and confidential. After the researcher explained the rights as respondents and gave the respondents a letter stating these rights and procedures, 25 students refused to take part in the study. Before completing the surveys, the students were given instructions on how to develop their own identification codes so that the surveys may be linked across administrations. Specifically, the identification code included a combination of the instructor's name, the section number, and the student's birthday. The present study used data collected over the course of 4 weeks: Week 1 ($n = 292$), Week 2 ($n = 202$), Week 3 ($n = 213$), and Week 4 ($n = 185$).

Measures

The dependent measures (i.e., digital piracy) and the independent measures (i.e., neutralization, age, and gender) are presented in this section.

Dependent Measure

The dependent measure consisted of a single item of digital piracy. For all 4 weeks, the students reported—using an open-ended response format—how many times in the past week they had downloaded music without paying for it and had used sites such as iTunes.

Neutralization

The measure of neutralization is a composite measure that uses six items to capture the techniques of neutralization (i.e., the six items can be found in the Appendix). The students used a five-point Likert-type scale ranging from 1 (*strongly disagree*) to 5 (*strongly agree*) to mark their responses. Higher scores on this measure meant that more individuals neutralized their digital piracy.

Additional Control Measures

Age was open-ended and was used as a continuous measure. In the present study, gender was measured as 0 (*female*) or 1 (*male*).

Results

Table 12.1 shows the descriptive statistics for the sample and the distribution for the variables. The sample was 46% male ($M = 21$ years of age). The results were relatively consistent with the individuals at the institution from which the data were drawn. Even though the sample and population were similar, the differences do not allow us to conclusively say that our sample was representative of the university from which it came, making our study a preliminary investigation.[1]

The correlations showed that the connections among the variables were in their predicted directions. For instance, all of the piracy measures (i.e., P1 through P4) and neutralization (N1 through N4) had reasonable amounts of shared variance, indicating that changes that can be found in a trajectory model were possible. Thus, the data now turned to the latent trajectory modeling.

To address the purpose of this study, we conducted a latent trajectory analysis (Muthen & Muthen, 1998–2004). The issue of missing data is consistently problematic with longitudinal studies (Brame & Paternoseter, 2003); consequently, in the present study, we were not able to falsify the hypothesis that the data were missing at random, using Little's (1988) coefficient. In the missing data, we did not show any statistically significant differences for those who pirated and those who did not pirate. Because we were not able to falsify the hypothesis that the data were missing at random, we decided to correct for missing data. We used a correction procedure similar to that used in Higgins (2007).

To correct the missing data, in the present study, we used all of the information in maximum likelihood in the latent trajectory model (LTM) estimations (see Allison, 2003, for comparisons of full information maximum likelihood and imputations) that is operationalized in Mplus 4.2 (Muthen & Muthen, 1998–2004). For an adequate fit of the models, the chi-square statistic should not be statistically significant (Hu & Bentler, 1999). However, given that the total sample size may lead to excessive power of the chi-square

---

[1] As a result of clerical error, we were not able to use our measure of major. Therefore, we were not able to draw solid conclusions about the sample's representativeness of the university as a whole. We do not see this as a fatal flaw to our data. In fact, if neutralization is to be a general theory, it should hold regardless of the group being studied. Thus, in our view, the representativeness of the data is not in question for testing the theoretical links that we have hypothesized, but this does reduce the generalizability of the results. Therefore, we see our study as providing preliminary information at best.

Table 12.1 Bivariate Correlation Matrix (n = 300)

	M	1	2	3	4	5	6	7	8	9	10
1. P1	2.18	1									
2. P2	.87	.25*	1								
3. P3	.70	.17*	.30*	1							
4. P4	.19	.10	.36*	.29*	1						
5. N1	13.16	.07	.22*	.21*	.12*	1					
6. N2	12.51	.07	.16*	.07	.12*	.25*	1				
7. N3	10.22	.08	.16*	.19*	.16*	.13	.07	1			
8. N4	9.27	−.07	.06	.20*	.16*	.32*	.28*	.20*	1		
9. Gender	.46	.14*	.17*	.11	.14*	−.03	−.01	.11	.06	1	
10. Age	21.16	−.10	−.10	−.05	−.06	−.06	−.08	−.08	.01	.03	1

*$p = .05$.

test, three additional fit statistics were used to evaluate the model fit: the root–mean-square error of approximation (RMSEA), the confirmatory fit index (CFI), and the standardized root-mean of the residual (SRMR). Hu and Bentler (1999) provided the standards for proper fit of these statistics: The RMSEA should be below .08, the CFI should be equal to or above .95, and the SRMR should be below .05. Based on these standards, all of the models tested using these data have adequate levels of fit.

The first step in the analysis was to test for the presence of change in music piracy and neutralization over the 4-week period. Two LTMs were estimated— one for music piracy and one for neutralization. The basic LTM comprises two latent factors, with the repeated measures of the construct over time as the indicators. Conceptually, this model is a confirmatory factor analysis (CFA) model. The first latent factor defines the intercept of the growth curve such that the factor loadings of the repeated measures are set to 1.0, which represents the identification point of the LTM at Time 1. This is held constant so that a metric for the development of LTM can be provided (see Bollen & Curran, 2006, for a complete discussion of this issue). Without this metric, the LTM would not be able to converge for proper results. The second latent factor defines the slope of the growth curve and represents the trajectory's rate of change over time. The means of these latent intercept and slope factors represent the group growth parameters and are overall measures of the intercept and slope for all participants. The variances of the latent factor reflect the variation of each individual around the overall group growth parameters. This estimation of variance makes this model a random coefficients model.

Music Piracy

A two-factor LTM as described previously was estimated for the four repeated measures of music piracy. The model was found to fit the observed data well:

$\chi^2(x) = 4.55$, $p = .47$, CFI $= 1.00$, RMSEA $= .00$, SRMR $= .03$. The significant slope factor ($M = -.36$) indicated that the overall group reported decreases in music piracy over the 4-week period. Using equally spaced factor loadings (0, 1, 2, 3), the decrease was linear. The variance components for the slope (1.12) and the intercept (11.32) factors indicated that there were significant individual differences in both initial levels and change of music piracy over the 4-week period. Finally, the negative correlation between the intercept and the slope ($r = -.94$, $p < .05$) indicated that there was an inverse link between the initial point and the change over the 4-week period (i.e., individuals who reported high levels of music piracy at Time 1 tended to report lower levels of music piracy at Time 4).[2]

Neutralization

A second two-factor LTM as described previously was estimated for the four repeated measures of neutralization. The model was found to fit the observed data well: $\chi^2(x) = 9.72$, $p = .05$, CFI $= .95$, RMSEA $= .07$, SRMR $= .05$. The significant mean slope factor (-1.38) indicated that the overall group reported decreases in neutralization over the 4-week period. The factor loadings were developed to reflect a linear decrease over the 4-week period. The variance component for the slope (1.76) and the intercept (19.98) indicated that there were significant individual differences in both the initial levels and the change in neutralization over the 4-week period. Finally, the correlation between the slope and the intercept factors is statistically significant ($r = -1.60$, $p < .05$), which indicated that there was an inverse link between the slope and the intercept. (i.e., individuals who reported high levels of neutralization at Time 1 tended to report lower levels of neutralization at Time 4). This may be a result of the students' not seeing this as a moral behavior where they have to relinquish their identity in order to perform the behavior—that is, after performing the behavior, the students may see music piracy as normal behavior (Hinduja, 2007).

Combined LT

The two LTMs presented here indicated that there were negative linear changes in both music piracy and neutralization and that there were

---

[2] We performed the same analysis using the count function for Mplus (Muthen & Muthen, 1998–2004). We substantively found the same results. Following Nagin's (2005) suggestions with count data issues, we paid attention to the Bayesian information criterion (BIC) for the count runs and compared it to that which came from our original findings. In addition, we paid attention to convergence issues. We did not find convergence issues with the data in our original runs, count runs, or simulations. Although not completely representative of our population, the data did not seem to bias our results. Therefore, we feel confident in the LTMs that we present in this study. Interested readers can obtain these results upon request from the first author.

significant individual differences in changes over time. To further explore the individual variation around the group trajectories, the LTM for music piracy and neutralization was estimated simultaneously and regressed on respondent age and gender.

The a priori model was estimated so that age and gender predicted both the intercept and slope factors for respondent music piracy and neutralization. The structural parameters were estimated so that the intercept factor of neutralization predicted the intercept and slope factors of music piracy. In addition, the slope factor of neutralization also predicted the slope factor of music piracy. These structural paths between the intercept and slope factors represented longitudinal prospective prediction over time and tested whether earlier information about one measure is predictive of later changes in the other measure. To further specify, the model, gender, and age were hypothesized to account for the intercepts of neutralization and digital piracy as well as the slope factors of neutralization and digital piracy. To clarify, male participants were more likely to neutralize and pirate music, and our results showed that they demonstrated changes in both measures. Finally, younger individuals were more likely to neutralize and pirate music, whereas younger individuals were more likely to change in both areas.

In this study, $\chi^2(x) = 44.63$, $p = .05$, CFI $= .94$, RMSEA $= .04$, and SRMR $= .05$. Gender was associated with the initial level and the change in music piracy, but it was not associated with the initial level of or change in neutralization. Age was not associated with the initial levels or change of music piracy or with neutralization. Table 12.2 presents a decomposition of the standardized effects in this particular model. Of key interest is the fact that the initial level of neutralization has a link with the initial level of music piracy (.50). This indicates that the neutralization of the behavior is important for initial music piracy. Further, the initial level of neutralization has a link with the change in music piracy (−.48). Thus, the findings from these results indicate that neutralization has a link with the initial level of, and the changes in, music piracy. This advances our understanding of the

Table 12.2 Decomposition of Standardized Effects

	Endogenous Variable			
Casual Variable	Intercept Piracy	Slope Piracy	Intercept Neutralization	Slope Neutralization
Intercept neutralization	.50* (.14)	−.45* (.04)		
Slope neutralization		.10 (.08)		
Gender	.26 (.56)	−.25* (.20)	.06 (.95)	.29 (.43)
Age	−.02 (.06)	.00 (.02)	−.22 (.09)	.19 (.04)

For each cell, beta weights are followed by standard errors in parentheses. *$p = .05$.

connection between neutralization and music piracy. To clarify, neutralization can be viewed as a theory of crime desistance—that is, as the neutralizations changed, the individuals changed their music piracy.

It is interesting to note that the attrition rate for this data is high. However, we performed the analysis using the complete data for all 185 respondents[3] and the entire sample. Our results were robust. To be certain, we performed simulation analyses ($n = 1,000$ datasets) for each of these models using all of the observations and the 185 observations and found little or no bias in the estimates, standard errors, and fit statistics (Muthen & Muthen, 2002). Therefore, we feel confident in presenting results for the entire sample.

Discussion

Use of the Internet permits easy accessibility to an abundance of information and entertainment, including digital music. Digital music sales in 2008 provided the music industry with $2.9 billion in revenues (IFPI, 2008). However, the convenient and impassive access of this intellectual property provides a conducive environment for theft of the music. According to Sykes and Matza (1957), individuals can participate in this type of criminal behavior by neutralizing their behavior. The purpose of this study was to provide an understanding of how changes in neutralization affect music piracy as well as the initial point and future changes of music piracy.

Those who participated in music piracy at Week 1 were less likely to participate in music piracy at Week 4. Moreover, the latent trajectory models of neutralization and music piracy were changing systematically over time, and the functional form of the change for both models was linear. There were significant individual differences in the initial status and changes over time in each model. Earlier levels of music piracy were significantly related to later levels of music piracy. This finding is similar to the changes that were found by Higgins (2007) in an examination of digital piracy. However, in this study, initials levels of neutralization were not significantly related to later levels of neutralization. These findings provide modest support for the changes in music piracy, but they do not support the changes in neutralization.

As discussed previously, the second purpose of this study was to provide a better understanding of the link between changes in neutralization and music piracy. We conducted a dual trajectory model that controlled the influences of gender and age to investigate the relationship between these simultaneous changes in the two behaviors. This model shows that the initial level and changes of neutralization have a direct influence on the initial level and change in music piracy. Because no other study in the literature provides

---

[3] Not shown here but available from the first author on request.

any type of longitudinal examination of the relationship between neutraliza-tion and this type of criminal behavior, we can confirm Maruna and Copes's (2005) prediction about the importance of this finding.

The findings of the present study indicated that individuals will take a "holiday" from social controls to allow themselves to pirate music without developing a pirating identity. In other words, using different forms of neu-tralization performs a self-serving purpose for the respondents who partici-pated in digital piracy, as they detached themselves from the criminality of the behavior. This is especially true for male participants and younger mem-bers of the sample, as both populations were more likely to neutralize their behavior and to pirate music.

As the study progressed, the findings indicated that the rate of digital piracy and neutralization simultaneously decreased. It is probable that after continued participation in the study, respondents reflected on the criminal-ity of their behavior, as they were consistently reminded of that possibility through their weekly participation in the study. When the participation in the deviant behavior decreased, the need to neutralize (or justify) the behav-ior was also smaller (Hinduja, 2007). This demonstrates that education about this issue—and a friendly push toward moral conscience—decreases the likelihood of criminal behavior.

These unique results suggest that policies may be developed to reduce instances of music piracy. In particular, the results suggest that to reduce instances of music piracy, the manner in which individuals perceive the behavior is the key to reducing the instances of music piracy. The value of properly using the Internet to acquire music media needs to be instilled so that the moral "holiday" that is necessary to perform music piracy is reduced. If the illegality of this behavior is reinforced to youth before participation in this behavior, the likelihood that they will participate in music piracy, espe-cially on a regular basis, is diminished. This sort of moral development can occur through educational programs with a specific curriculum that points toward reducing the neutralizations as well as understanding the detriment that participation in such behavior can cause.

Although the results of this study are unique to the literature and the results point to policy implications, the study is not without limits. In this study, we used the student body of only one college to collect our data. However, important results in the music piracy and neutralization literatures come from studies with similar samples (Higgins, 2007; Hinduja, 2007); therefore, the value of this data is considerable. In regard to the research design, we used a comparatively short longitudinal study. Although close repetition of the study may indicate a bias in the results, we believe that this is a strength rather than a weakness. The short time period allows the observer to begin seeing what actually occurs in the patterns of piracy. Others may wish to perform daily inquiries about how piracy takes place.

It is important to note that the composite measures of neutralization may be an issue, considering these measures do not take into account a wide variety of the larger content of domains that is possible for neutralization (Murana & Copes, 2004). However, the psychometric properties of our measures indicated that they shared enough variance to be considered one measure. As this study is the first of its kind, it makes a significant contribution to the literature, providing insight into how the neutralization process involves criminality.

The limitations of this study, as well as the need for further investigation in this area, encourage the necessity for future research. Obviously, a lengthier study with increased points of data collection would provide further insight into the affect of neutralization on music piracy as well as the usage of other measures of neutralization. However, and more important, these findings indicate the potential for using neutralization measures to explain other types of cyber criminality, such as identity theft and other types of piracy. The Internet enables any person to detach him- or herself from reality, in turn not placing a human face on the victim of his or her criminal behavior. In the future, researchers should conduct similar studies to determine whether the same link exists between a change in neutralization and a change in the cyber criminality of choice.

Conclusions

Despite its limitations, the present study provides evidence that the level of neutralization used by a potential music pirate affects the piracy that actually occurs. Participants in music piracy are often misguided about their perceptions of the harm that is caused through participation in this behavior—as well as the responsibility that resides with them. This perception, and a lack of education in this subject area, increases the likelihood of participation in this "victimless" crime. The findings of this study are extremely important: This study is the first of its kind, and it provides insight into a potential solution to the increasing problem of music piracy.

Appendix

1. The entertainment industry exaggerates the impact of not paying for downloading music from the Internet.
2. Profit is emphasized above everything else in the entertainment industry.
3. The government overly regulates the downloading of music.
4. It is all right to download music without paying for it because CDs nowadays don't have good songs.

5. I think it is OK to use copied music for entertainment.
6. I see nothing wrong in giving friends copies of my music in order to foster friendship.

References

Adler, P., & Adler, P. A. (2006). The deviance society. *Deviant Behavior: An Inter-disciplinary Journal, 27*, 129–147.

Allison, P. D. (2003). Missing data techniques for structural equation models. *Journal of Abnormal Psychology, 112*, 545–557.

Bollen, K. A., & Curran, P. J. (2006). *Latent curve models: A structural equation perspective*. Hoboken, NJ: John Wiley & Sons, Inc.

Brame, R., & Paternoster, R. (2003). Missing data problems in criminological research: Two case studies. *Journal of Quantitative Criminology, 19*, 55–78.

Chiou, J. S., Huang, C. Y., & Lee, H. H. (2005). The antecedents of music piracy: Attitudes and intentions. *Journal of Business Ethics, 57*, 161–174.

Gopal, R., Sanders, G. L., Bhattacharjee, S., Agrawal, M., & Wagner, S. (2004). A behavioral model of digital music piracy. *Journal of Organizational Computing and Electronic Commerce, 14*, 89–105.

Goode, S., & Cruise, S. (2006). What motivates software crackers? *Journal of Business Ethics, 65*, 173–201.

Higgins, G. E. (2007). Digital piracy: An examination of low self-control and motivation using short-term longitudinal data. *CyberPsychology & Behavior, 10*, 523–529.

Higgins, G. E., Wolfe, S. E., & Marcum, C. D. (2008). Digital piracy: An examination of three measurements of self-control. *Deviant Behavior: An Interdisciplinary Journal, 29*, 440–460.

Hinduja, S. (2003). Trends and patterns among online software pirates. *Ethics and Information Technology, 5*, 49–61.

Hinduja, S. (2004). Perceptions of local and state law enforcement concerning the role of computer crime investigative teams. *Policing: An International Journal of Police Strategies & Management, 27*, 341–357.

Hinduja, S. (2007). Neutralization theory and online software piracy: An empirical analysis. *Ethics and Information Technology, 9*(3), 187–204.

Hu, L. T., & Bentler, P. M. (1999). Cutoff criteria for fit indexes in covariance structure analysis: Conventional criteria versus new alternatives. *Structural Equation Modeling, 6*, 1–55.

International Federation of Phonographic Industries (IFPI). (2006). *The Recording Industry 2006 piracy report: Protecting creativity in music*. Retrieved from http://www.ifpi.org

IFPI. (2008). *IFPI digital music report 2008*. Retrieved from http://www.ifpi.org

Koen, C. M., & Im, J. H. (1997). Software piracy and its legal implications. *Security Journal, 31*, 265–272.

Little, R. J. A. (1988). Missing data in large surveys. *Journal of Business and Economic Statistics, 6*, 287–301 (with discussion).

Maruna, S., & Copes, H. (2004). Excuses, excuses: What have we learned from five decades of neutralization research? In M. J. Tonry (Eds.), *Crime and justice 2004–2008* (pp. 1–100). Chicago, IL: University of Chicago Press.

Muthen, L. K., & Muthen, B. O. (2002). How to use a Monte Carlo study to decide on sample size and determine power. *Structural Equation Modeling, 9*, 599–620.

Muthen, L. K., & Muthen, B. O. (1998–2004). *Mplus users' guide* (3rd ed.). Los Angeles, CA: Muthen and Muthen.

Nagin, D. S. (2005). *Group-based modeling of development.* Boston, MA: Harvard University Press.

Sykes, G., & Matza, D. (1957). Techniques of neutralization: A theory of delinquency. *American Sociological Review, 22*, 664–670.

Wall, D. S. (2005). The Internet as a conduit for criminal activity. In A. Pattavina (Ed.), *Information technology and the criminal justice system* (pp. 78–94). Thousand Oaks, CA: Sage Publications.

Digital File Sharing
An Examination of Neutralization and Rationalization Techniques Employed by Digital File Sharers

13

ROBERT MOORE

Contents

Introduction

Digital file sharing, which is also occasionally referred to as *peer-to-peer (P2P) file sharing* or *digital piracy*, refers to the downloading of movies, music, or software via the Internet or via a P2P network (Higgins, Wolf, & Marcum, 2008; Holsapple, Iyengar, Jin, & Rao, 2008). Over the last decade, the issue of digital file sharing has seen a dramatic increase in interest from legislators as well as legal, economics, and criminological experts (Berger, 2001;

Oberholzer & Strumpf, 2005; Rochelandet & LeGuel, 2005; Higgins, 2007; Hinduja, 2007). Although interest in the topic has grown dramatically and more scholarly works are now addressing the phenomenon, there is still some confusion concerning the terminology used when addressing file sharing. Some researchers refer to the act of sharing files via the Internet or P2P networks as *digital piracy*, whereas others refer to the act as *intellectual property theft*. For many people, the term *piracy* may invoke an image of financial gain; however, in terms of technological techniques, *digital piracy* has been defined as "the purchase of counterfeit products at a discount to the price of the copyrighted product, and illegal file sharing of copyrighted product over peer-to-peer computer networks" (Hill, 2007, p. 9). Through the use of this definition, the concept of financial gain is removed from consideration. Although the term *digital file sharing* is used throughout this chapter, note that the terms *digital piracy*, *digital file sharing*, and *intellectual property theft* have become synonymous throughout the majority of the scholarly literature.

W hy has there been such a dramatic increase in interest regarding digital file sharing? It is possible that the interdisciplinary fascination with file sharing could be attributed to the fact that the Recording Industry Association of America (RIAA) and the Motion Picture Association of America (MPAA) have begun aggressive legal actions against users of digital file sharing software rather than launching legal attacks against the manufacturers of file sharing software—a phenomenon that has attracted both scholarly and nonscholarly interest. The RIAA and MPAA claim that the technology is responsible for lagging sales of compact discs (CDs) and digital video discs (DVDs) around the world (Pomerantz, 2005). However, economic researchers have obtained varying results when studying the financial impact that file-sharing software has had on the sales of CDs and DVDs. At least one report claimed that more than $33 billion in lost sales of CDs and DVDs in 2004 was attributed to file sharing (Pomerantz, 2005). However, Oberholzer and Strumpf (2005) as well as Rochelandet and LeGuel (2005) claim that digital file sharing affects the purchase of CDs and DVDs only minimally if at all. This is not to say that there is no evidence that file sharers are transferring copyrighted materials via the Internet and P2P networks, but reports such as these do make it difficult to place a price on the behavior. After all, estimates by Ouellet (2007) found that as many as 2.6 billion digital files are being illegally transferred every month; however, these estimates provide insight into only how popular the behavior is—not how economically damaging the behavior may be for the RIAA and MPAA.

Regardless of whether financial harm can be proven, there is still a need to better understand the motives and rationales of digital file sharers—even more so if, in fact, there are more than 2 billion copyrighted digital files shared each month. The RIAA and the MPAA have resolved to solve the problem through the use of lawsuits against known file sharers. However, the best approach to dealing with file sharers may call for an approach that does not involve the threat of civil or criminal lawsuits. Learning how to deal with digital file sharers likely will involve gaining a better understanding of why individuals support the use of file-sharing software to the extent that they would engage in the illegal sharing of over 2 billion files per month. In this chapter, I examine the evolution of digital file sharing and how it is believed that digital file sharers are using neutralization techniques, such as those espoused by Sykes and Matza (1957), to minimize any guilt that they may have about regularly engaging in criminal behavior. First, however, it is important to briefly address the evolution of digital file sharing and to examine past studies in which researchers have attempted to explain criminal behavior through the use of neutralization techniques.

Brief History of File Sharing

The technology behind P2P networking was originally designed to aid businesses in sharing network resources; however, in the late 1990s, a student who had dropped out of college developed a version of the software that would allow for the trading of music files. The individual reportedly developed the software after he became disillusioned with the complexity of trading music files via Internet Relay Chat (IRC) and other complex file-sharing programs (Berschadsky, 2000). He named the software Napster, and its design enabled users to combine P2P networking protocols with the newly developed MP3 algorithm, resulting in greater file compression and faster transfers of digital music files between users (Carey & Wall, 2001).

The capabilities of the Napster software were highlighted in a news magazine, and file sharing rapidly began to gain popularity. It is my opinion that one other factor contributed greatly to Napster's rapid growth in popularity—the decreasing cost of CD-writing devices. Around the same time that the Napster software was gaining popularity, the cost of CD-writing hardware was also decreasing. More computers were being released with CD writers that enabled users to make their own data and music CDs. Thus, users could now download music files faster—thanks to the Napster software—and then make personal CDs that could be played away from the computer, meaning that, perhaps, people felt a decreased need to purchase commercial CDs. Public outrage concerning the use of file-sharing software was highlighted after several very popular rock bands spoke out against Napster. The most notable critic among musicians was the band Metallica, who went so far as to develop television ads informing users of the illegal nature of the activity and asking fans to not share their music. At the height of Napster's popularity, it was estimated that as much as 87% of the files being traded were in violation of copyright law (Berger, 2001). Because of the increased publicity

concerning the software as well as the increase in its use, lawsuits were ultimately filed against the company manufacturing the Napster software.
Initially, the software company attempted to fight the charges. However, in
the end, their defense was unsuccessful, and the company was forced to shut
down. Users had to search elsewhere for their file-sharing software (Freeman,
Coats, Rafter, & Given, 2002).

It was determined that Napster was responsible for the files being shared
through the use of their software because the software's design required that
all searches for musical files be routed through a central server maintained
by the company that manufactured the Napster software. Ultimately, the
company was found responsible for ensuring that no copyright violations
took place through the use of their software (*A&M Records, Inc. v. Napster,
Inc.*, 2001). Digital file-sharing software programs released in the wake of
Napster's demise have attempted to avoid a similar result by removing the
central server feature, meaning that requests are no longer routed through
the manufacturer's computers. Releasing the software in this format has,
thus far, allowed the companies to deny responsibility for how the software
has been used (Freeman et al., 2002; *Metro-Goldwyn-Mayer Studios, Inc. v.
Grokster Ltd*, 2004).

With newer file-sharing programs thus far avoiding legal liability through
removal of the central server feature, the RIAA has begun to apply legal suits
against individual file sharers. Even more recently, the MPAA has filed civil
suits against file sharers who download, share, or distribute copyrighted
movies in a digital format (Rupley, 2004). Increasing access to high-speed
Internet services means that users today can transfer digital movie files—
often larger than digital music files—at reasonable speeds. The RIAA and
the MPAA each have begun an aggressive awareness campaign to inform
file sharers that they are engaging in illegal behavior and that, if caught, they
will be subject to civil or criminal prosecution. However, the success of these
lawsuits has been questioned, as studies have indicated that there has been
very little, if any, decrease in file-sharing activities as a result of the awareness
campaigns (Green & Sager, 2004). If individuals are now informed that digital file sharing is illegal and that file sharers could be held legally responsible,
what could explain why individuals continue to engage in behavior that they
know to be both criminal and potentially costly? Perhaps the answer lies in
the theory of *neutralization*, whereby individuals neutralize any guilt associated with criminal behavior in order to engage in an act that they know to
be illegal. *Techniques of neutralization* may provide an individual with the
ability to temporarily remove guilt for their behavior and, thereby, enable a
file sharer to continue engaging in behavior that he or she knows is illegal.
Before discussing the use of neutralization techniques by digital file sharers,
it is important to first briefly discuss how the theory has been applied to other
delinquent or criminal behaviors in the past.

The Evolution of Neutralization Theory

In 1957, Gresham Sykes and David Matza released a theory to address how juvenile delinquents countered feelings of guilt associated with delinquent behaviors. Prior to the release of this theory, the commonly held belief was that juveniles adhered to a code of values and beliefs that was distinct from those of the larger population. Sykes and Matza disagreed, arguing that on many occasions, delinquents could adhere to the same beliefs and norms of the general population; only when juveniles engaged in certain acts would the individual move from a state of lawfulness to a state of unlawfulness. Matza (1964) would later term this process of moving from law abider to law breaker as *drifting*. These two theorists believed that when juveniles drifted into unlawful behavior, they would use a series of justifications allowing them to neutralize any guilt associated with their delinquent behaviors— behaviors that are now referred to as *techniques of neutralization* (Sykes & Matza, 1957).

In reaching this conclusion, Sykes and Matza (1957) determined that there were five techniques that juveniles would use to neutralize any guilt associated with a delinquent behavior. These techniques were termed *denial of responsibility, denial of injury, denial of victim, condemnation of the condemners,* and *appeal to higher loyalties.* Each term is explained in the paragraphs that follow.

Denial of responsibility involves more than a mere refusal to accept legal responsibility for one's actions, as in the case of the juvenile who claims that he or she is being wrongly accused. Individuals who apply this technique are those who refuse to believe that they had a choice about whether to engage in the delinquent behavior. Individuals who use this technique believe that factors beyond their control have led them to the point in their life where they must engage in the delinquent behavior (Sykes & Matza, 1957). An example of denial of responsibility might be the juvenile delinquent who claims that he had no choice but to engage in a particular delinquent act and who blames his participation on the fact that he comes from a bad neighborhood.

Denial of injury is the neutralization technique used by individuals who feel that their delinquent behaviors cause no harm or injury to the individuals who are affected by their delinquent behavior. Even if there is actual harm, the individual may attempt to negate the harm by claiming that the victim could afford the injury, therefore invoking a belief that there is no true injury involved in their behavior (Sykes & Matza, 1957). *Denial of victim* is closely related to denial of injury. Users of this technique claim that there are no victims or that any victims of delinquent behaviors are not truly victims because they deserved whatever harm was caused to them.

The fourth technique of neutralization is *condemnation of the condemn-ers*, whereby individuals attempt to justify their delinquent behaviors on the grounds that any victims of their activity are hypocrites for complaining about the individual's behavior. These individuals may feel that those who complain about being victimized are the same individuals who would engage in the same harmful behaviors if given the opportunity.

The final technique discussed by Sykes and Matza (1957) is the *appeal to higher loyalties*. Individuals who use this technique of neutralization may recognize that their behaviors are inappropriate but continue to justify the behavior on the grounds that their immediate social or familial group may have needed their behavior at the time. An example of this technique might be the individual who engages in a physical altercation and then justifies their behavior by the belief that one should always help a friend who is involved in a fight.

Over the last 5 decades since Sykes and Matza (1957) released their theory, the techniques of neutralization have been discussed by a variety of researchers and have been applied to a very diverse collection of criminal and delinquent behaviors. Eliason and Dodder (1999) have examined neutraliza-tion techniques used by individuals who illegally hunt deer, Levi (1981) has examined the use of these techniques by a contract killer and self-professed hit man, and Dabney (1995) has examined the use of neutralization tech-niques by those who steal medical supplies. More recently, neutralization techniques have been examined in relation to the act of copying commercial software and musical discs (Hinduja, 2007). Agnew (1985) has even exam-ined neutralization techniques in relation to a crime victim's perceptions of victimization.

As a result of these and other studies, at least five additional neutraliza-tion techniques have been developed. One such technique is the metaphor of the ledger, whereby an individual argues that unacceptable behavior was acceptable because the person had built up a reserve of good deeds (Klockars, 1974). Put simply, the individual claims that he or she has been a law-abiding citizen for his or her entire life and, as such, deserves to commit one law-breaking behavior. Coleman (1994) proposed three additional neutralization techniques: denial of the necessity of the law, the claim that "everybody else is doing it," and the claim of entitlement. The first of these, denial of the neces-sity of the law, claims that a particular law is unreasonable and does nothing to benefit the greater good of society. As such, the individual argues that the law does not have to be obeyed in all situations. The second additional neutralization technique—the claim that everybody else is doing it—refers to the belief that so many people are disobeying the law that the law has, in effect, become no longer valid. The third additional technique—the claim of entitlement—refers to an individual's belief that because of something in his or her life, he or she has a right to engage in a particular behavior and should not feel any guilt about doing so (Coleman, 1994). Minor (1981) also proposed an additional neutralization technique known as the defense of necessity: This technique claims that although an individual's behavior may be inappropriate, it was necessary in order to prevent an even greater criminal or delinquent act.

In studying neutralization techniques, researchers have noted that several important considerations must be made when determining whether neutralization techniques can be applied to delinquent or criminal behaviors. First, there is the fact that for neutralization techniques to be used by individuals, the individual must believe that there is something wrong with his or her behavior. If there is no belief that the one's behavior is wrong, then there is likely no guilt to neutralize (Copes, 2003). Second, there is the temporal issue that involves exactly when an individual applies the neutralization techniques—either before or after the individual engages in delinquent or criminal behaviors. According to Conklin (2004), if the techniques are applied prior to the individual engaging in the delinquent act, then the technique would be referred to as a *neutralization technique*, whereas application of the technique after engaging in a delinquent act would be referred to as a *rationalization technique*.

Digital file sharing, like many ongoing delinquent or criminal activities, may make the temporal consideration of neutralization techniques less important. The distinction of whether a file sharer attempts to minimize guilt beforehand (neutralization) or after the fact (rationalization) becomes less important if the individual continues to engage in file sharing on a regular basis—evidence of which I have found in earlier studies and discussions with university students on the topics of digital file sharing and the legality of the behavior. In many cases, students would indicate an understanding of the illegal nature of digital file sharing yet at the same time indicate a strong level of support for the activity; many students indicated that even though the activity was illegal, they would still continue to engage in the behavior.

The Present Study

The data in this study were collected through in-person interviews with 44 university students who were identified during an earlier research project that I and a colleague conducted (see Moore & McMullan, 2004). At the time of the initial study, participants were informed that a second study involving interviews would take place. Forty-five individuals originally indicated a willingness to take part in the interviews. However, during the course of the interview process one participant withdrew for personal reasons. We decided to interview university students because (1) university students most often have ready access to computers, and (2) university students may be more likely to engage in file sharing of music and movies (Higgins, 2007; Hinduja, 2007; Moore & McMullan, 2004).

Using a semistructured interview format, interviews were conducted at each participant's home university. These interviews ranged in length from approximately 30 min to 90 min and consisted of a few demographic questions concerning age, gender, file-sharing activities (i.e., the frequency with which they shared digital files and their favorite types of files to be shared), theft of traditional forms of music and movies (i.e., CDs and DVDs) from retail stores, and their views on the legality of file sharing.

The mean age for participants was 21 (standard deviation [SD] = 2.07), with the youngest participant being 18 years of age and the oldest participant being 29 years of age. Much like the demographics of participants in some earlier studies, there were more men ($n = 30$) than there were women ($n = 14$), although the fact that these participants were selected on a voluntary basis should prevent readers from placing too much emphasis on the variable of gender. After all, it may just be that male participants feel more comfortable talking about their file-sharing activities than do their female counterparts.

In considering the illegal nature of file sharing, 100% ($n = 44$) of participants indicated that they were aware that digital file sharing was illegal, yet they continued to engage in the behavior. When asked about the theft of traditional forms of media such as stealing a music CD or a DVD from a store, 96% of participants ($n = 42$) indicated that they would never engage in physical shoplifting, and the remaining 4% ($n = 2$) indicated that they had either shoplifted or would shoplift CDs or DVDs if given the opportunity. Of the different types of digital files that were shared via digital means, music was overwhelmingly the number one primary choice for participants (91%; $n = 40$). The sharing of digital movie files was second (7%; $n = 3$), and only one individual (2%) indicated that their primary reason for using digital file-sharing software was to download or share software programs (i.e., Adobe Photoshop, Microsoft Word, Microsoft Windows, etc.). It should be noted that the term *primary* was used because many participants downloaded multiple file types. Just because a participant indicated that he or she shared primarily music files does not mean that the individual never shared movie files or software files; it simply meant that on most occasions, they shared only music files.

Neutralization and Rationalization Techniques

Participants in this study provided evidence of the use of 6 of the 10 techniques of neutralization when justifying their digital file-sharing behaviors. Many of the participants indicated support for multiple techniques of neutralization, but each participant indicated primary support for one of six techniques. The most commonly encountered neutralization techniques were denial of injury, denial of victim, and "everybody else is doing it," with less support being found for condemnation of the condemners, metaphor of the ledger, and entitlement. In the next section, I examine each of the six neutralization techniques used by participants.

Denial of Injury

The denial of injury technique was the most commonly encountered technique (57%; $n = 25$). Participants who indicated support for this neutralization technique generally felt that there was no harm done to the music industry or the movie industry when they engaged in digital file sharing. In fact, there was some support for the belief that file sharing was actually helpful to CD sales because it allowed consumers to preview albums and then decide which albums to go out and purchase. One participant stated, "Artists will benefit from file sharing because my friends and I download music from the file-sharing program and then we go out and purchase the CD."

Should this be the case, then, if in fact a good argument could be made for the legality of digital file sharing? The reality is that although some participants indicated support for the denial of injury as a means of justifying the use of digital file-sharing software, only one participant indicated that they had, in fact, purchased CDs after sharing music files. The majority indicated that they had, in fact, purchased few (or, in many cases, not even one) CDs since they began file sharing. Some participants actually stated that they had a list of CDs that they had become interested in thanks to file sharing and that they would purchase the CDs on this list when they graduated and got good jobs—an optimistic if not doubtful belief. Yet another participant indicated that although he did not purchase more CDs as a result of file sharing, he did, in fact, attend more concerts after engaging in digital file sharing. This participant shared the following thoughts:

> I listen to artists' songs off of the file-sharing program and then I get more excited about seeing them perform live. I read somewhere that musicians make their money off concerts, so I think file sharing is actually helping the artists.

Madden (2004) put forth a similar argument in claiming that lesser known musicians have benefited from digital file sharing because of the fact that consumers might download a musical track for free before they would pay for a track from an unknown artist. These artists then hope that individuals will enjoy the downloaded songs and then come to the artists' concerts and watch them perform live, thereby allowing the artists to make money from their music. It does seem that there are some individuals in the industry who believe this, considering the fact that newer, lesser known musicians have seemingly embraced digital file sharing (Madden, 2004).

Denial of Victim

Closely related to the denial of injury technique is the second most commonly encountered neutralization technique—the denial of victim. Sixteen percent (*n* = 7) of participants indicated primary support for the denial of victim neutralization technique. Participants who closely associated with this technique appeared to have trouble acknowledging that there was a financial victim to consider when engaging in digital file sharing. Respondents indicated the following opinion:

> Recording artists are not victimized by this type of activity. I only download music CDs from artists who are no longer a part of the top 100. These individuals aren't selling CDs anymore, so they are not harmed when I download their music.

Individuals who indicated use of this neutralization technique failed to consider that even though artists are no longer on *Billboard*'s Top 100, they are still victims who suffer from the trading of musical files because they do not receive any compensation.

Everybody Else Is Doing It

The "everyone else is doing it" neutralization technique was also employed primarily by 16% (*n* = 7) of participants. I was actually surprised by these results, expecting more individuals to associate with this technique. In examining the responses of individuals who closely associated with this technique, I observed two evenly balanced beliefs: First, because many of their friends were downloading music, it has become more acceptable to download music and movie files. Second, because there are so many people sharing digital files online, there is less chance of getting caught engaging in the activity. Respondents shared the following insights:

> Why should I worry about sharing music on the Internet? After all, there are so many people [engaging in] online sharing [of] songs that I sometimes have trouble downloading my one or two songs that I am looking for. I sometimes wish that there were fewer people online.

> There were almost two million individuals online last night sharing files. I never allow more than 20 or 30 songs to be listed in my shared folder. Think about it, if the recording industry was going to go after someone then who

> would they go for? Me, the guy with the 20 songs or the guy with 2,000 songs?
> I read they get paid by the song, so I would hardly be worth their time.

> Almost everyone I know downloads music. If it were truly wrong then why
> would so many people be allowed to get away with it?

Previous research on digital file sharing has examined the impact of control theories and deterrence theories as tools to control the file-sharing phenomenon (Higgins, 2007; Higgins, Wilson, & Fell, 2005). The previous statements seemingly would provide support for continued studies in the areas of control and deterrence theories. By looking to these theories, researchers might better understand the impact that the likelihood and severity of punishment may have on a person's decision to engage in digital file sharing. Yet another participant indicated that with more individuals engaging in file sharing, it is only a matter of time before digital file sharing will have to become legalized behavior. Although such a belief is interesting, it is my opinion that unregulated digital file sharing is not an option that the RIAA or the MPAA has seriously considered in their fight against digital file sharing.

Condemnation of the Condemners

A small percentage of participants (7%; $n = 3$) indicated primary support for the condemnation of the condemners technique of neutralization. These individuals indicated that although harm is committed by file sharing—a fact that these participants readily accepted—the individuals in the music and movie industry are hypocritical in their reactions to the problem. These persons felt as though the music and movie industries have had numerous opportunities in the past to reach out to consumers, and each time, they have actually alienated consumers more than they have attracted them to their products. The participants perceived this alienation as even more justification for downloading movies and, to a lesser degree, music. This perception was evidenced by statements such as the following:

> I love the advertisements before some movies start now, where they have some
> stage worker come out and claim that they are the ones who lose money when
> people download movies. Hollywood wants me to think that this poor guy is
> suffering. They want me to feel bad, yet I don't see any of them taking a pay cut
> to help this poor guy out.

These advertisements have been played at the beginning of several motion pictures as a means of trying to explain to file sharers that their file-sharing activities may not hurt the actors or the directors, but their behaviors are hurting the stage hands and the makeup artists. What was possibly intended as a means of instilling guilt into the minds of file sharers may, in some cases, be responsible for developing further animosity toward the MPAA—animosity that individuals have used to justify continued file-sharing behaviors.

Metaphor of the Ledger

One participant's interview responses led me to associate the participant with the metaphor of the ledger neutralization technique. This individual felt that throughout his life, he had always followed the law and had avoided criminal activity. Therefore, it was his belief that he had somehow built up a reserve of goodness—a reserve that should allow society to forgive him for his one habit of sharing copyrighted files via P2P networks. This individual shared the following thoughts:

> I have never broken the law in my life. Sure, I may download a few movies and songs on my computer, but I would never steal anything from Wal-Mart or Target. If this is my only bad habit, then I think I should be allowed to engage in the activity.

This individual indicated that he would never shoplift a CD or a DVD, yet he continually stated that he felt it was OK to engage in digital file sharing—thus, not only showing support for the metaphor of the ledger technique but also continuing to show that some individuals have trouble equating virtual activities to physical activities. Although one may engage in virtual shoplifting through digital file sharing, that individual fails to equate the behavior to physical shoplifting from retail stores.

Entitlement

One individual provided the most unique response of the study when he indicated why he continued to engage in file sharing despite numerous reports indicating that the activity was illegal. The individual's response appeared to be most closely associated with the entitlement technique of neutralization. This person felt that he deserved to be able to download all the music and movies he desired when using his computer's Internet connection, which he paid a monthly fee to use. The individual expounded on this belief in the following manner:

> I pay my monthly Internet bill. Whatever I can get for $29.95 is what I believe that I have a right to download. It may be illegal, but it shouldn't be available to me if they don't want me to have it.

Although this particular response was provided by only one participant, it is a dangerous representation of a mentality that if the government does not prevent you from obtaining something, then it must be acceptable, on some level. When it comes to regulating the Internet, it could be argued that there is no possible method for securing the entire World Wide Web. The belief of this one individual is reminiscent of an earlier mindset that I encountered in the past when discussing file sharing among friends and colleagues—that is, the belief that file sharing could not be illegal because it was so readily available. However, lawsuits by the music and movie industries have apparently cleared up this confusion, as all of the individuals in the present study indicated their awareness of the illegal nature of the act—even if they also indicated no intent to stop engaging in the behavior.

Discussion

All participants in the present study ($N = 44$) indicated primary support for at least one of six neutralization techniques, with many of the participants indicating support for multiple neutralization techniques. In considering why participants most closely associated themselves with these techniques, there are a number of things to consider. First, there is the perceived anonymity of Internet behaviors. Without face-to-face contact, there may be a sense of freedom and a loosening of inhibition in a person's activities (Bell, 2001; Rowland, 2003; Suler, 2004). As such, it may be harder for a person who engages in digital file sharing to understand that there are victims to digital file sharing as well as injuries to those who own the copyrighted materials. File sharers may have an image of the musician or actor being surrounded by wealth and fortune. As such, the file-sharing individual may develop a belief that his or her digital file sharing is not truly harming anyone in the industry—a belief that fails to consider those behind the scenes who do lose money because of digital file sharing. Because the file sharer's behavior does not bring him or her face to face with the persons that their behaviors harm, it may be easier for file sharers to neutralize or rationalize away any guilt associated with their behavior.

Some participants indicated that the government should do a better job of regulating access to the materials if they are truly causing someone harm. The problem is that regulating the Internet is extremely difficult, given the fact that the network is worldwide—although the United States may have strict intellectual property laws, other countries may not. Additionally, it would be almost impossible for the government to step in and regulate file sharing through technological means. The RIAA and the MPAA have recognized this reality following the lawsuits against manufacturers of file-sharing software. These entities have now responded by filing numerous public lawsuits to involve university students and nonstudents. These lawsuits may have made the public more aware of the fact that digital file sharing is illegal

(Banerjee, 2004); however, there have been little data to support a belief that these lawsuits have reduced file sharing. The file-sharing software manufacturers have also avoided serious punishment. Although the government and the RIAA were able to stop Napster, subsequent legal attempts to attack the availability of the software have met with limited success. The reason for this is because the courts have ruled that the software cannot be completely illegal, as there are some legitimate, legal uses for P2P networking technology (*Metro-Goldwyn-Mayer Studios, Inc. v. Grokster Ltd*, 2004).

On the basis of these study results, two facts have become apparent. First, digital file sharing is an activity that does not appear to be slowing down or stopping. Participants in the present study repeatedly indicated that they knew their behavior was illegal and that they ran a risk of being civilly charged with copyright infringement. However, these individuals also indicated that they would likely continue to engage in digital file sharing despite their awareness of these issues. Second, this study found initial support for the belief that digital file sharers use one or more of a variety of neutralization techniques to regulate any guilt associated with their digital file sharing. If individuals can remove the guilt associated with violations of copyright infringement, then it stands to reason that these individuals will continue to engage in the act of digital file sharing.

How, then, can the RIAA and the MPAA hope to better control copyright violations? Perhaps educational programs can be designed not to focus on guilt (e.g., the MPAA advertisement related to the harm caused to crew members) but, rather, to focus on education and awareness of the behavior. Another approach proposed by Higgins and colleagues (2005) involves gaining a better understanding of deterrence and how punishment severity could be used to regulate digital file sharing. If researchers can find the exact threshold for affecting a file sharer's behavior, then perhaps arguments could be made to decrease—although, likely, never completely abolish—digital file sharing.

Need for Future Research

The results of the present study provide initial evidence that neutralization techniques are used by digital file sharers; however, there is a need for more research on this topic. Perhaps research with a larger sample size and a quantitative research instrument would enable even better understanding of how prevalent the use of neutralization techniques may be among digital file sharers. The present study was qualitative, and although smaller sample sizes are acceptable because of the in-depth data collected from interviews, there is still a need for more quantitative studies on the topic of digital file sharing. Hinduja (2007) used a quantitative instrument and found some initial support for the use of neutralization techniques; however, the data were collected prior to the initiation of civil lawsuits against users. Thus, it is possible that data collected after the launching of these civil lawsuits may reveal new and important conclusions. In future studies, researchers should consider moving beyond the realm of university students. Although the earlier statements concerning the value of using a university student population still hold true, it is also important that researchers gain a better understanding of how nonstudents use neutralization techniques—if, in fact, they use them at all. Several of the students in the present study indicated that they used digital file sharing as a means of gaining access to materials (movies, music, software, etc.) that they could not afford while they were in college. Although none of the respondents indicated any initial support for this neutralization technique—that is, defense of necessity—the responses of some participants in this study were close to what one would expect to uncover from someone making such a claim. A small percentage (7%; $n = 3$) indicated that they could not afford to purchase music CDs or DVDs, attend as many movies as they wanted to attend, or purchase certain software that they may have needed for their university coursework. Extending this research into the realm of working adults would allow researchers to gain better insight into the mindset of digital file sharers. A complete understanding of the digital file sharer is more important than ever in the development of strategies to better control digital piracy and digital file sharing.

Conclusion

Digital file sharing continues to be a fascinating topic of interest across many disciplines. As the technology has developed and the legal system has evolved, rates of file sharing have remained relatively steady. Although individuals who engaged in file sharing during the early days of Napster may have been able to argue that they were unaware of the illegal nature of their behavior, today's file sharers appear to understand that the behavior is illegal and potentially costly. Yet, they continue to engage in the act of sharing copyrighted movie, music, and other digital media files. In response, the RIAA and the MPAA have initiated civil lawsuits against file sharers, but the effectiveness of such tactics has been questioned because the lawsuits have not significantly slowed the rate of file sharing. It would appear that the RIAA and MPAA are not likely to accept file-sharing technology, so the answer to controlling digital piracy must lie in gaining a better understanding of what drives individuals to engage in digital file sharing. The present study has shown that file sharers understand that they are wrong in sharing copyrighted materials, but they seem to neutralize their guilt, thereby allowing them to continuously engage in the behaviors. Recent educational ads focused on making file sharers feel guilty are then destined to fail, as any guilt is neutralized both before and after a user engages in file-sharing activities. It appears that controlling digital file sharing does not lie in changing statutes or improving technological security features but, rather, in changing human rationale when it comes to digital file sharing—a daunting but necessary task for criminological, economic, and legal researchers.

References

Agnew, R. (1985). Neutralizing the impact of crime. *Criminal Justice and Behavior, 12*, 221–239.

A&M Records, Inc. v. Napster, Inc., 239 F.3d 1004 (9th Cir. 2001)

Banerjee, S. (2004). P2P users get more elusive. *Billboard, 116*, 5–6.

Bell, M. (2001). Online role-play: Anonymity, engagement and risk. *Educational Media International, 38*, 251–260.

Berger, S. (2001). The use of the Internet to "share" copyrighted material and its effect on copyright law. *Journal of Legal Advocacy & Practice, 3*, 92–105.

Berschadsky, A. (2000). RIAA v. Napster: A window into the future of copyright law in the Internet age. *John Marshall Journal of Computer and Information Law, 18*, 755–789.

Carey, M., & Wall, D. (2001). MP3: The beat bytes back. *International Review of Law, Computers & Technology, 15*, 35–58.

Coleman, J. (1994). *The criminal elite: The sociology of white collar crime.* New York, NY: St. Martin's Press.

Conklin, J. (2004). *Criminology.* New York, NY: Pearson Allyn & Bacon.

Copes, H. (2003). Societal attachments, offending frequency, and techniques of neutralization. *Deviant Behavior: An Interdisciplinary Journal, 24*, 101–127.

Dabney, D. (1995). Neutralization and deviance in the workplace: Theft of supplies and medicines by hospital nurses. *Deviant Behavior: An Interdisciplinary Journal, 16*, 313–331.

Eliason, S., & Dodder, R. (1999). Techniques of neutralization used by deer poachers in the western United States: A research note. *Deviant Behavior: An Interdisciplinary Journal, 20*, 233–252.

Freeman, V., Coats, W., Rafter, H., & Given, J. (2002). Revenge of the Record Industry Association of America: The rise and fall of napster. *Villanova Sports and Entertainment Law Journal, 9*, 35–56.

Green, H., & Sager, I. (2004, November 22). File sharers: Can they be scared away? *Business Week, 39*(09), 16.

Higgins, G. (2007). Digital piracy, self-control theory, and rational choice: An examination of the role of value. *International Journal of Cyber Criminology, 1*, 33–55.

Higgins, G., Wilson, A., & Fell, B. (2005). An application of deterrence theory to software piracy. *Journal of Criminal Justice and Popular Culture, 12*, 166–184.

Higgins, G., Wolfe, S. & Marcum, C. (2008). Digital piracy: An examination of three measurements of self-control. *Deviant Behavior, 29*, 440–460.

Hill, C. W. (2007). Digital piracy: Causes, consequences, and strategic responses. *Asia Pacific Journal of Management, 24*, 9–25.

Hinduja, S. (2007). Neutralization theory and online software piracy: An empirical analysis. *Ethics and Information Technology*, *9*, 187–204.

Hinduja, S. (2008). Deindividuation and internet software piracy. *Cyberpyschology and Behavior*, *11*, 391–398.

Holsapple, C., Iyengar, D., Jin, H., & Rao, S. (2008). Parameters for software piracy research. *Information Society*, *24*, 199–218.

Klockars, C. (1974). *The professional fence*. New York, NY: Free Press.

Levi, K. (1981). Becoming a hit man: Neutralization in a very deviant career. *Urban Life*, *10*, 47–63.

Madden, M. (2004). Artists, musicians and the Internet. Washington, DC: Pew Internet & American Life Project. Retrieved from http://www.pewinternet.org/Reports/2004/Artists-Musicians-and-the-Internet/Summary-of-Findings.aspx

Matza, D. (1964). *Delinquency and drift*. New York, NY: Wiley.

Metro-Goldwyn-Mayer Studios, Inc. v. Grokster Ltd, 380 F.3d 1154 (9th Cir. 2004).

Minor, W. (1981). Techniques of neutralization: A reconceptualization and empirical examination. *Journal of Research in Crime and Delinquency*, *18*, 295–318.

Moore, R., & McMullan E. (2004). Perceptions of peer-to-peer file sharing among university students. *Journal of Criminal Justice and Popular Culture*, *11*, 1–19.

Oberholzer, F., & Strumpf, K. (2005). *The effect of file sharing on record sales: An empirical analysis*. Retrieved from http://www.unc.edu/~cigar/papers/Filesharing_June2005_final.pdf

Ouellet, J. (2007). The purchase versus illegal download of music by consumers: The influence of consumer response towards the artist and music. *Canadian Journal of Administrative Sciences*, *24*, 107–119.

Pomerantz, D. (2005). Hang the pirates. *Forbes*, *175*, 96–97.

Rochelandet, F., & LeGuel, F. (2005). P2P music sharing networks: Why the legal fight against copiers may be inefficient. *Review of Economic Research on Copyright Issues*, *2*, 69–82.

Rowland, D. (2003). Privacy, freedom of expression and cyberslapps: Fostering anonymity on the internet. *International Review of Law, Computers & Technology*, *17*, 303–312.

Rupley, S. (2004, December 28). Making movies, taking movies. *PC Magazine*, *23*, 19.

Sykes, G., & Matza, D. (1957). Techniques of neutralization: A theory of delinquency. *American Sociological Review*, *22*, 664–670.

Suler, J. (2004). The online disinhibition effect. *CyberPsychology & Behavior*, *7*, 321–326.

Cyber Victimization

IV

Cyber-Routine Activities

14

Empirical Examination of Online Lifestyle, Digital Guardians, and Computer-Crime Victimization

KYUNG-SHICK CHOI

Contents

Introduction

The recent rise in cyber crime affects everyone because society has become so dependent on computer technology in almost every aspect of life. The effects of cyber crime are most harmful in the banking and financial industries, where computers are used to send and receive funds and where thousands of business transactions are processed every day. This dependency on technology has increased opportunities for computer criminals to engage in illegal behavior, jeopardizing the safety of individuals and organizations every time a computer is turned on.

Precise statistics on the number of computer crimes that occur and the revenue loss caused by these criminals is impossible to know for several reasons. First, most computer crimes go undetected. Second, few computer crimes are ever reported to authorities (Standler, 2002). Policing in cyberspace is very difficult, especially because the sophistication of these cyber criminals has greatly increased. These criminals have many tools at their disposal; most crimes occur through the use of anonymous re-mailers, the use of encryption devices, and the accessing of third-party systems, making it difficult for law enforcement to find and prosecute the perpetrator (Furnell, 2002; Grabosky & Smith, 2001; Yar, 2005). The damages that these cyber criminals cause—and will cause in the future—have been underestimated by the general population.

Because most people are not clear about the differences between cyber crime and computer crime, it is necessary to draw a distinction between the two terms. *Cyber crime* is defined as "crime that involves computers and networks, including crimes that do not rely heavily on computers" (Casey, 2000, p. 8). It has also been defined as "computer-mediated activities which are either illegal or considered illicit by certain parties and which can be conducted through global electronic networks" (Thomas & Loader, 2000, p. 3). Cyber crimes cover many categories of crime on the World Wide Web, including "computer-assisted crimes" and "computer-focused crimes" (Furnell, 2002, p. 22).

Computer crime is different from cyber crime in that no special computer skills are needed to commit a computer-assisted crime. Criminals can use web-based chat-rooms, Microsoft Network (MSN) messenger, or e-mail to communicate with potential victims. The criminal only has to gain the potential victim's trust and then the criminal can gain access to valuable personal information. The computer then becomes the tool that an offender uses to commit a crime of fraud or a confidence scam (Casey, 2000). Although a criminal does not need special computer skills to commit a computer crime, he or she usually needs to have more than a basic level of computer knowledge to commit crimes successfully (Carter & Katz, 1997).

For the purposes of this study, *computer criminals* are defined as individuals who commit illegal or unwanted invasions of someone else's computer. Hence, the focus of this study is on individual victimization that occurs through computer crimes, particularly computer hacking, including the implanting of computer viruses. Originally, the term *hacking* was defined as computer experts accessing systems, programs, and private networks in order to discover vulnerabilities and to develop ways to correct the problems; however, the term has been expanded recently, now referring to any unauthorized access with "intent ... to cause damage, steal property (data or services), or simply leave behind some evidence of a successful break-in" (NW3C, 2003, p. 1).

The number of individuals falling victim to computer criminals is on the increase. According to Flanagan and McMenamin (1992), the cost of computer crime runs anywhere between $500 million and $5 billion per year, with security breaches in 2000 increasing by 54% over that number in 1999 (McConnell International, 2000). These increasing numbers suggest that computer crime will only get worse if there is no attempt to find a way to halt the computer hacking. Specifically, the general population still has not recognized the dangers and seriousness of computer crime. This may partially explain why an individual's online lifestyle patterns—coupled with a lack of security software—increase a computer criminal's opportunities to victimize others.

Study Purpose

The specific purpose of this study was to examine the factors responsible for computer-crime victimization. Through the use of lifestyle-exposure theory and routine activities theory, an individual's online lifestyle and the presence of installed computer security software on the individual's computer are examined. Additionally, this study was conducted to argue that Cohen and Felson's (1979) routine activities theory is actually an expansion of Hindelang, Gottfredson, and Garofalo's (1978) lifestyle-exposure theory. Cohen and Felson (1979) reported that one of the main concepts in the lifestyle-exposure theory is lifestyle variables, which the authors refer to in routine activities theory as their target suitability component. These lifestyle variables contribute to potential computer-crime victimization. An individual's daily routine activities in cyberspace, including those at home and at work, increase the possibility of that individual becoming a victim of computer crime. Another important tenet in routine activities theory is that of the *capable guardian*—that is, the computer security software used by an individual to protect themselves against such victimization.

This chapter begins with a discussion of the theoretical perspectives behind computer-crime victimization and then moves to a presentation of the method, analysis, findings, and a discussion of the findings. The chapter concludes with a discussion of limitations of the study and recommendations for further study.

Theoretical Perspectives

Hindelang and colleagues' (1978) lifestyle exposure theory and Cohen and Felson's (1979) routine activities theory were developed during the time in which the criminal justice system began to emphasize victimization issues (Williams & McShane, 1999). In the early 1970s, criminologists shifted their focus away from studies on the criminal offender to the impact of crime on victims (Karmen, 2006). The growth of victimization theories was facilitated by the creation of "the self-report survey" and the emergence of national victimization studies in 1972 (Karmen, 2006, p. 51). Both the life-style-exposure theory and the routine activities theory were introduced based on the evidence of "the new victimization statistics" and as a part of a ratio-nal theoretical perspective embedded in sociological orientation (Williams & McShane, 1999, p. 235). These two theories are ideally suited for explaining why certain individuals are more likely to become victims of crime because of the activities, interactions, and social structure of their lifestyles.

Previous research (Hindelang et al., 1978) has indicated that an individual's daily lifestyle, both at the job and at home, often contributes to victimization. Hindelang and colleagues (1978) also suggested that a person's social role and social position influence that person's lifestyle patterns, and a person's lifestyle contributes to the decision to engage in certain activities. Thus, choosing to engage in risky activities is often a rational choice on the individual's part.

Three main factors are thought to predict whether an individual is victimized (Cohen & Felson, 1979). First, there must be an interested offender. Second, there must be an opportune target for victimization. Third, there must be the absence of a capable guardian that would protect the individual from such an attack. All three factors must be combined in order for victimization to occur. Thus, an absence of any one of these three components either decreases the likelihood of victimization or eliminates the possibility of victimization.

Routine activities theory and lifestyle-exposure theory have both been widely applied to explain criminal victimization. Much research has supported the use of both theories with predatory and property crimes (Cohen & Felson, 1979; Felson, 1986, 1988; Kennedy & Forde, 1990; Massey, Krohn, & Bonati, 1989; Miethe, Stafford, & Long, 1987; Roncek & Maier, 1991; Sherman,

Gartin, & Buerger, 1989). Although the two theories enjoy empirical support in criminology research, these theories have failed to present testable propositions regarding certain offenders and victims' conditions, making it impossible to make accurate predictions about crime (Meier & Miethe, 1993). Additionally, little research has focused on the problem of individual computer-crime victimization (Kowalski, 2002; Moitra, 2005).

It is argued here that routine activities theory is simply an expansion of the lifestyle-exposure theory espoused by Hindelang and colleagues in 1978. Routine activities theory can be seen as a theoretical expansion of lifestyle-exposure theory because it includes the main factor of lifestyle-exposure theory as well as the individual's vocational and leisure activities. Cohen and Felson (1979) included this factor or tenet into what they termed the *suitable target tenet* and added both a motivated offender and the lack of a capable guardian. Hence, it is hypothesized here that an individual becomes a suitable victim because of his or her vocational and leisure activities. Cohen and Felson (1979) suggested that an individual's lifestyle reflects his or her social interaction and social activities. These activities help create a target suitable for a motivated offender.

There is a common theme between the two theories, with routine activities theory offering two more factors—capable guardianship and motivated offender. Thus, it is suggested here that the two theories are not separate theories: Routine activities theory is simply an expansion of lifestyle-exposure theory. In this study, then, I applied routine activities theory but with the recognition that lifestyle-exposure theory provides a more complete explanation of the suitable target tenet found in routine activities theory.

The factor of capable guardian, one of the three tenets of routine activities, contributes to the new computer-crime victimization model in this project. This research assumes that offenders who have suitable targets are given situational factors. This is especially true in cyberspace, where motivated computer criminals look for suitable targets such as individuals who use the Internet without adequate computer security (Yar, 2005). Felson (1998) reported that there are four main criteria for target suitability: (a) the value of the target of crime, (b) the inertia of crime target, (c) the physical visibility of crime target, and (d) the accessibility of crime target. These four criteria are referred to as *value, inertia, visibility, and accessibility* (VIVA). The problem occurs when an individual accesses the Internet and that individual's personal information attracts a motivated computer criminal. When that computer criminal uses a sophisticated cyber attack, the inertia of the crime target becomes almost weightless in cyberspace (Yar, 2005). The motivated computer criminal is able to target victims and commit offenses because of the visibility and accessibility within the cyber environment (Yar, 2005). Hence, in this study, I hypothesized that of the three elements of routine activities theory, the most important one in controlling computer-crime victimization is the level of capable guardianship. An individual increases his or her online safety by using a target-hardening strategy—that is, an individual equips their computer with adequate security software and ensures that the software on the computer remains updated. Equipping the computer with computer security is a crucial component in reducing computer criminal opportunities in the new theoretical model.

In this study, I hypothesized that individuals who (a) have computer lifestyles that include visiting unknown websites or downloading software from websites in order to gain free MP3 files or free software programs, or (b) click on icons without precaution are most likely to be victimized by computer criminals. An individual's level of job and home activities can either increase or decrease that person's victimization in the physical world. As Hindelang and colleagues (1978) reported, both vocational and leisure activities are the most significant factors in a lifestyle that directly influence the level of victimization risk. Vocational (job) and leisure (home) activities translate into the level of target suitability attributed to Felson's (1998) VIVA assessment.

In addition, this research followed Mustaine and Tewksbury's (1998) argument that people who engage in delinquent lifestyle activities are likely to become victimization targets "because of their anticipated lack of willingness to mobilize the legal system" (p. 836). Individuals often underestimate their risk by failing to consider whether their vulnerability is increased by the websites they select and whether they have protected themselves with the needed security (Mustaine & Tewksbury, 1998).

To examine how lifestyle activities may affect an individual's victimization, in this study, I analyzed the online behaviors of college students, focusing on what website they visited on the Internet, what their behaviors are on the Internet, and how they protect themselves while they are on the Internet. To achieve the study's goals, self-reports from college students were analyzed using structural equation modeling (SEM). This study followed a format similar to that used by Gibbs, Giever, and Higgins (2003) to divide a self-report measure of deviance into multiple measures to satisfy the minimum requirements for SEM.

Method and Analysis

This study was divided into three phases: In Phase 1, sampling techniques and procedure of the sample were presented. In Phase 2, psychometric properties of scales were examined on two main factors: (a) digital guardian and individuals' online lifestyle, and (b) computer-crime victimization. Phase 3 of the analysis included the measurement and structural models derived from the combination of the two victimization theories tested. Through use of SEM, the causal relationships among digital guardian, online lifestyle, and computer-crime victimization indexes were assessed, focusing on whether digital-capable guardianship and online lifestyle directly affect computer-crime victimization.

Phase 1: Sample and Procedure

In spring 2007, students in nine liberal studies classes at a university in the Pennsylvania State System of Higher Education (PaSSHE) were given a self-report survey designed to measure the main constructs of routine activities theory. The students were selected through a stratified-cluster, random-sample design. A list of all available liberal studies classes available in spring 2007 were entered into a computer through use of the Statistical Package for the Social Sciences (SPSS) software. The lists were stratified by class level, and a proportionate subsample of classes was randomly selected through use of SPSS.

The random number generator of SPSS chose nine of these general studies classes, based on class level, for inclusion in the sample. Three-hundred forty-five respondents took part in the study. However, only 204 surveys were completed fully, so those 204 surveys were analyzed for the purposes of this study.

There were two specific requirements for participating in the study: First, the student must be enrolled in a general studies class; and second, the student must use his or her own personal computer or laptop.

After entering 10 predictors (two observed variables from the digital-capable guardianship latent variable, three observed variables from the online lifestyle latent variable, three observed variables from the online victimization latent variable, and two demographic variables) with a power of .95 and a medium effect size of $f = .15$ into the G*Power program, I computed the total sample ($N = 172$) at the .05 alpha level. Thus, threats to statistical conclusion validity were not an issue in this research. Surveying a minimum of 172 students allowed for a large enough sample from which to ensure that the sample size accurately represented the student population at PaSSHE.

I used a self-report survey instrument to investigate the computer-crime victimization patterns among the university student population. Using university students in this study provided several advantages. First, university students are expected to be literate and experienced in completing self-administered, self-report instruments. Second, because the price of owning a computer has decreased and because most students are required to complete their assignments via computer, students are constantly using a computer for their work and entertainment. Additionally, it is assumed that young people are more likely adopters of technology than are older generations (Internet Fraud Complaint Center [IFCC], 2003).

Phase 2: Properties of Measures

Digital Guardian

Each digital guardian has its own distinctive function to protect a computer system from computer criminals. There are three common digital-capable guardians available to online users: antivirus programs, antispyware programs, and firewall programs. Each type of digital guardian has its own distinctive function. *Antivirus programs* monitor whether computer viruses have gained access through digital files, software, or hardware; if the antivirus computer software finds a virus, the software attempts to delete or isolate it to prevent a threat to the computer system (Moore, 2005). *Firewall programs* are designed to prevent computer criminals from accessing the computer system over the online network; however, unlike the antivirus software, firewalls do not detect or eliminate viruses (Casey, 2000). *Antispyware programs* are mainly designed to prevent spyware from being installed on the computer system (Casey, 2000). Spyware intercepts users' valuable digital information such as passwords or credit card numbers as a user enters them into a web form or other application and sends that information to the computer criminal (Ramasastry, 2004).

Before administration of the self-report survey, all participants were supplied with a pre-survey guideline that provided definitions of the three digital guardian measures and asked the participants to examine their personal or laptop computer so that they could determine, prior to participation in the actual survey, whether they had any of the digital guardian measures already installed on their computers. The purpose of the pre-survey guideline was to ensure content validity in the portion of the actual survey focusing on the digital guardian measure.

It was hypothesized that the level of capable digital guardianship, in the form of installed computer security systems, will differentiate the level of computer-crime victimization. Hence, the number of installed software security programs were measured so that the level of digital-capable guardianship could be determined.

The first observed variable consisted of three items that asked the respondents to state what types of computer security they had on their own computer prior to participation in the survey. The three items were based on a dichotomous structure, which was identified as 0 (*absence of security*) or 1 (*presence of security*). The possible range for the number of installed computer security programs was between 0 (*absence of computer security*) and 3 (*presence of antivirus, antispyware, and firewall software*). The mean computer security score for this sample was 2.6 (SD = .73, skewness = −1.96, kurtosis = 3.37).

The internal consistency coefficient of .62 indicates an undesirable range of Cronbach's alpha based on DeVellis's (2004) reliability standards.

However, the item–total correlations (Item 1, $\alpha = .40$; Item 2, $\alpha = .43$; and Item 3, $\alpha = .44$) were respectable, with all three items above the acceptable level of .30.

The second observed variable also consisted of three items with a series of three visual analogues by asking the participants to indicate, on a 10-cm response line, their responses regarding each of the three main computer security measures. Their level of agreement with each statement was identified by asking whether they had the specific computer security program on their personal or laptop computers during the 10-month period. Each line had a range of 0 to 10, with the total possible range for this capable guardian scale between 0 and 30 ($M = 22.3$, SD = 7.65, skewness = $-.99$, kurtosis = .25).

The findings showed that this digital guardian scale had an adequate alpha coefficient of .70, which was sufficient for research purposes. All three scale items (Item 1, $\alpha = .50$; Item 2, $\alpha = .52$; and Item 3, $\alpha = .55$) performed well and sufficiently met the acceptable levels of item–total correlation. The unidimensionality of the scales was confirmed by Cattell's scree test with principal components factor analysis using a varimax rotation.

Online Lifestyle

It was hypothesized that a user's online lifestyle is a substantial factor in minimizing computer-crime victimization. Individual online lifestyle was measured by three distinct observed variables: (a) vocational (job) and leisure (home) activities on the Internet, (b) online risky leisure activities, and (c) online risky vocational activities. For the first measure of online lifestyle, eight survey items—along with their item–total correlations—made up the Vocational and Leisure Activities scale. Respondents were asked to indicate, on a 10-cm response line, their level of agreement or disagreement with each statement. The items were anchored by 0 (*strongly agree*) and 80 (*strongly disagree*) at the upper limit. Higher scores reflect higher online vocational and leisure activities ($M = 53.62$, SD = 11.22). The scale based on eight items had satisfactory skewness and kurtosis levels, and the assessment of principal factor analysis and a *Scree test* validated the scale items as a unitary construct.

For the measures of two categories of online risky lifestyle, each of four survey items was designed to rate the respondents' online leisure and vocational activities that are risky. Similar to other online lifestyle scales, respondents were asked to indicate, on a 10-cm response line, their level of agreement or disagreement with each statement. The terms *strongly agree* and *strongly disagree* anchor the response line.

The possible aggregate range for the Risky Leisure Activities scale is from 0 to 40. The mean of the first Risky Leisure Activities score for this sample is 16.02 (SD = 8.93). The second category of online risky activities consisted of four items, so the possible aggregate range for the Risky Vocational Activities scale is also from 0 to 40. Both categories have met the appropriate levels of skewness and kurtosis for SEM analysis, and the results (based on principal components factor analysis and a scree test) suggested that each scale item consists of a unitary construct.

Computer-Crime Victimization

Three computer-crime victimization items were developed for this study. In the current project, I have adapted the construct of corporate computer-crime victimization to delineate individual-crime victimization.

The Computer-Crime Victimization scale consists of three distinct observed variables: (a) total frequency of victimization, (b) total number of hours lost, and (c) total monetary loss. In terms of data quality, the descriptive statistics imply conditions of severe non-normality of data that are one of the violations in SEM assumptions. The three computer-crime victimization scales contained extreme values of skewness and kurtosis, and the reliability coefficient indicated poor variability and low item–scale correlations because of strong outliers. In order to adjust a highly skewed distribution to better approximate a normal distribution, the original items were transformed— ratio level—to a Likert-type scale format based on four possible responses; I applied this format by using a recoding process and minimizing the magnitude of outliers.

The existing scales from the *2004 Australian Computer Crime and Security Survey* (Australian Computer Emergency Response Team, 2005) were adapted for use in this study. In the first item (i.e., "During the last 10 months, how many times did you have computer virus infection incidents?"), the original responses were coded to the scales of 0 to 3 (0 = *none*, 1 = *1–5 times*, 2 = *6–10 times*, 3 = *more than 10 times*). In the second item (i.e., "During the last 10 months, approximately how much money did you spend fixing your computer due to computer virus infections?"), the original responses were labeled to a scale from 0 to 3 (0 = *$0*, 1 = *$1–$50*, 2 = *$51–$100*, 3 = *more than $100*). In fact, there were no specific guidelines of monetary loss in the survey, so this category of the scales was developed based on the distribution of responses from participants and the adaptation of the survey structure. In the third item (i.e., "During the last 10 months, approximately how many hours were spent fixing your computer due to the virus infections?"), the original values were transformed to a scale of 0 to 3 (0 = *0 hr*, 1 = *1–12 hr*, 2 = *13–84 hr*, 3 = *more than 84 hr*). In the *2004 Australian Computer Crime and Security Survey* (Australian Computer Emergency Response Team, 2005), the time it took to recover from the most serious incident based on day, week, and month period was estimated. In this study, I adapted this time period by calculating 12 hr per 1 day for fixing the computer; therefore, Responses 1, 2, and 3 represent an hourly basis for days, weeks, and months, respectively.

After changing to the Likert-type format, the values of skewness and kurtosis significantly decreased. In addition, both Cronbach's alpha and item–total correlation values significantly improved. Even though the transformation to the Likert-type format could not achieve appropriate normal distribution, it offered the minimal acceptance of skewness and kurtosis levels for SEM analysis.

The computer-crime victimization scales also met the basic measurement criteria for SEM after the application of transformation to Likert-type scale. The scales have acceptable reliability ($\alpha = .66$), acceptable item–total correlations, and acceptable skewness and kurtosis levels; in addition, the observed variables are unidimensional.

Phase 3.1: Measurement Model

I examined nine fit indices in order to determine the model fitness of the measurement model (see Table 14.1). Table 2 from Gibbs et al. (2003) indicated the fit indices, their justifications, and standards. Five indexes of absolute fit are reported: chi-square, adjusted chi-square, root-mean-square residual (RMR), root-mean-square error of approximation (RMSEA), and global fit index (GFI). In addition, I also present the Tucker–Lewis Index (TLI), the comparative fit index (CFI), the parsimonious goodness of fit (PGFI), and the expected cross-validation (ECVI) in order to measure relative fitness by comparing the specified model with the measurement model.

Three of five measures of absolute fit (adjusted chi-square, RMSEA, and GFI) sufficiently met their standards. Because the probability value of the chi-square test was smaller than the .05 level, the test result indicates

Table 14.1 Selected Fit Indexes for the Measurement Model

	Model Fitness	Index	Value	Standard Point
1.	Absolute fit	Chi-square (χ^2)	34.47 ($df = 18$) $p = .011$	$p > .05$
2.	Absolute fit	Normal chi-square (χ^2/df)	1.915	<3
3.	Absolute fit	Root-mean-square residual (RMR)	1.73	Close to 0
4.	Absolute fit	Root-mean-square error of approximation (RMSEA)	.07	$<.10$
5.	Absolute fit	Goodness-of-fit index (GFI)	.96	.90
6.	Incremental fit	Tucker–Lewis index (TLI)	.95	Close to 1
7.	Incremental fit	Comparative fit index (CFI)	.97	Close to 1
8.	Parsimony	Parsimony goodness-of-fit index (PGFI)	.48	Larger value = better fit
9.	Comparative fit	Expected cross-validation index (ECVI)	.35	Smaller value = better fit

the rejection of the null hypothesis that the model fits the data. However, such a rejection based on the chi-square test result was relatively less substantial compared to other descriptive fit statistics because the chi-square test is very sensitive to sample size and non-normal distribution of the input variables (Hu & Bentler, 1999; Kaplan, 2000; Kline, 1998). Thus, examining other descriptive fit statistics would be of substantive interest to this project.

Even though there was no absolute RMR standard, the obtained RMR value of 1.70 appeared to be high because an RMR of 0 indicates a perfect fit. The CFI and TLI, which compare the absolute fit of the specified model to the absolute fit of the measurement model, also sufficiently met the standard for appropriate model fit. Although the PGFI and ECVI do not have precise standards, the guideline of Gibbs and colleagues (2003) suggests that these obtained values are very close to good model fit. Despite the fact that it is very difficult to construct a model that fits well at first, the measurement model has acquired the overall good model fit. Therefore, the measurement model fits well, based on the suggested descriptive measures of fit.

Figure 14.1 indicates that the digital guardian latent variable has statistically significant unstandardized regression coefficients. The negative statistical relationship between the digital guardian and crime victimization is illustrated by the statistically significant unstandardized regression coefficient of −.75. The standardized coefficient of −.74 also reveals that the digital guardian is the most substantial factor on computer-crime victimization. Among digital guardian–observed variables, standardized

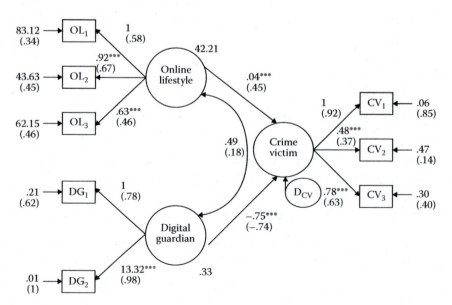

Figure 14.1 Measurement model.

coefficients indicate that (a) how well-equipped one's computer is with a number of computer security software programs, and (b) how long the computer security software has been present on one's computer has an equally substantial impact on minimizing computer-crime victimization. These findings sufficiently support the routine activities theoretical component—that is, capable guardianship—by emphasizing the importance of computer security that contributes to the reduction of computer-crime victimization.

The research findings showed a strong relationship between the online lifestyle factor and computer-crime victimization. The unstandarized path coefficient of .04 revealed that a substantial, statistically significant relationship exists between the online lifestyle factor and computer-crime victimization. The unstandarized coefficients of online lifestyle confirmed that the online users, who spend significant time and engaged in risky online behaviors in cyberspace, are likely to be victimized. In addition, the standardized coefficient of .67 indicates that risky online leisure activities (visiting unknown websites, downloading games, music, and movies) provide the most substantial contribution to computer-crime victimization among online lifestyle categories. It is a very important finding because previous research has failed to identify certain types of online risky behaviors that are more susceptible to other online behaviors.

It was hypothesized that there would be an interaction effect among two factors, digital-capable guardianship and online lifestyle, which would directly contribute to the level of computer-crime victimization. Surprisingly, the results indicated that there was little correlation among two latent variables. Although the covariance between digital guardian and online lifestyle indicator suggested positive covariance, the result was insignificant ($p = .056$). Thus, the findings showed that there was no interaction effect between personal online lifestyle and equipping computer-security features on personal desktop or laptop computers.

Phase 3.2: Structural Model

Similar to the measurement model, the probability value of the chi-square test ($p = .005$) was less than the .05 level. As stated in the measurement model, such a rejection based on the chi-square test result appeared to be due to sample size. Three measures of absolute fit (adjusted chi-square, RMSEA, and GFI) met or exceeded their standards. The obtained RMR value of 3.03 was higher than that of the measurement model, indicating that the structural model did not offer a perfect fit. The CFI, TLI, PGFI, and ECVI values were similar to those of the measurement model, which sufficiently met the standard for an appropriate model. Although the structural model was unable to convey an adequate fit for the model compared to the measurement

Table 14.2 Selected Fit Indexes for the Structural Model

	Model Fitness	Index	Value	Standard Point
1.	Absolute fit	Chi-square (χ^2)	38.392 ($df = 19$) $p = .005$	$p > .05$
2.	Absolute fit	Normal chi-square (χ^2/df)	2.02	<3
3.	Absolute fit	Root-mean-square residual (RMR)	3.03	Close to 0
4.	Absolute fit	Root-mean-square error of approximation (RMSEA)	.07	<.10
5.	Absolute fit	Goodness-of-fit index (GFI)	.96	.90
6.	Incremental fit	Tucker–Lewis index (TLI)	.94	Close to 1
7.	Incremental fit	Comparative fit index (CFI)	.96	Close to 1
8.	Parsimony	Parsimony goodness-of-fit index (PGFI)	.50	Larger value = better fit
9.	Comparative fit	Expected cross-validation index (ECVI)	.36	Smaller value = better fit

model, the structural model had acquired the overall good model fit for the purposes of the research (see Table 14.2).

The structural model also provided empirical support on the components of routine activities theory (see Figure 14.2)—that is, individuals who have not installed computer security programs or who use the Internet frequently and engage in risky online behaviors are more likely to be victims of computer crime than are those individuals who regularly maintain and update their computer security program, who use the Internet less often, and who avoid engaging in risky online behavior.

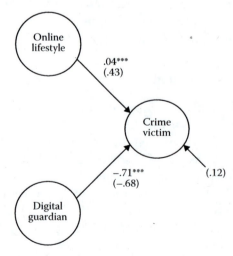

Figure 14.2 Structural model.

Findings

In this study, I investigated a new theoretical model that was derived from Hindelang and colleagues' (1978) lifestyle-exposure theory and Cohen and Felson's (1979) routine activities theory. The conceptual model advanced that digital-capable guardianship and online lifestyle both directly influence computer-crime victimization. The central measurement model in this study was shown to be superior, as indicated by comparisons of structural coefficients and measures of fit.

Computer crimes are a significant threat to Internet users. Computer criminals cause significant monetary loss for their victims as well loss of productivity in the workplace. These losses occur when criminals are able to obtain personal information that gives them access to the victim's computer (Grabosky & Smith, 2001). The findings from this study are valuable for policy recommendations. First, the findings show that college students who overlook their computer-oriented lifestyle in cyberspace or who fail to download the proper security software are more likely to become victims of cyber crime. Second, the findings show that differential lifestyle patterns are linked directly with being victimized in cyberspace. The findings in this research show that the presence of computer security is the most important element in protecting an individual from cybercrime. The same finding has been suggested by McQuade (2006), who suggested that "routine activities theory has important implications for understanding crimes committed with or prevented with computers, other IT devices, or information systems" (p. 147).

The results of this study also show that establishing prosocial views of promoting adequate online lifestyle and downloading effective computer security reduce the possibility of computer-crime victimization. These finding have been largely ignored by criminal justice crime-prevention programs. And although the number of computer users increases daily, computer crime–prevention programs are not fully available to online users (Moitra, 2005). In fact, computer crime–prevention programs can be categorized as school-based crime-prevention programs because some colleges and universities offer introductory and specialized courses in computer-crime and information security issues (McQuade, 2006).

Some researchers have suggested that the best way to minimize computer crime is through the incorporation of public awareness, formal education, and professional training (McQuade, 2006). Any program geared toward preventing computer crime needs to provide online users with general knowledge on information security and valuable tips on how to avoid crime victimization. Programs also should emphasize laws and regulations that cover cyber crime in order to empower online users. Finally, programs also should alert students to the types of lifestyle behavior that predict victimization (Moitra, 2005).

Discussion

This study was the first attempt to create a computer-crime victimization model based on routine activities theory. Routine activities theory was described in the main body of this chapter using a combination of Hindelang and colleagues' (1978) lifestyle-exposure theory and Cohen and Felson's (1979) routine activities theory.

There has been much criticism on previous computer crime–related research on the basis of the issue of "generalizable data." Additionally, the small sample sizes used in qualitative studies also have been criticized for having potentially biased outcomes (Moitra, 2005). The present research accomplished its main goals and contributes to the literature by using and integrating two criminological victimization theories with the empirical assessment of SEM in order to uncover computer-crime victimization. Through use of the lifestyle-exposure theory, the daily living style, and the computer-oriented lifestyle in cyberspace, the present research developed one of the main tenets in the model. Routine activities theory helped reveal that a capable guardian reconstructed with a digital-capable guardian provided computer security in this research. Thus, the findings of this study suggest that online lifestyle and digital guardianship are essential aspects of a model that delineates patterns of computer-crime victimization.

Limitations and Directions for Future Studies

There are a number of limitations to this study. Although the results accurately reflect a university's student population, the results may not be generalized to the entire university population in the state of Pennsylvania or in the United States. In the future, when selecting potential universities for study, researchers should consider the level of computer technical support and the student population size at the university. Any future research should include diverse sites that represent the geographic and demographic characteristics of the entire university population in the United States.

Another limitation of this study was that it was impossible to completely measure computer security. There may have been some error with the measurement of digital guardianship because some participants might not remember when they first downloaded security products on their computers.

For future studies, it is important that the researcher be aware of this problem and attempt to identify specific dates of individual computer security installations from the participants' computer systems. Doing such a check would increase the quality of computer security measurement.

Because the study looked at content validity regarding computer security, it is possible that the study's participants did not understand the computer security definitions or precise functions of the computer security software. A lack of understanding could have lead to underreporting or overreporting and, thus, could have affected the content validity of the study. I did attempt to increase the precision of measurement regarding these components by giving a pre-survey guideline, but that attempt was not infallible.

Criminology literature acknowledges that demographic factors are related to general crime victimization in the physical world. However, this relationship has not been completely revealed. There was no focus in this study on the relationship between cyber crime and demographic factors. Hence, it is important that future research include an assessment of causal relationships between demographic variables (age, race, and gender) and cyber crime factors. Future research should also focus on how demographic variables are statistically associated with variables such as fear of cyber crime, digital-capable guardianship, online lifestyle activities, and computer-crime victimization.

It should be noted that criminology literature has used other theories to explain risk-taking behavior. Early in the literature, some researchers believed that some personalities were more likely to exhibit risk-taking behaviors. Lyng (1990) delineated five terms for the two modal types (risk seeker vs. risk averter) from the early literature: (a) the *narcissistic* versus the *anaclitic*, (b) the *extrovert* versus the *introvert*, (c) the *schizoid* versus the *cycloid*, (d) the *counterphobic* versus the *phobic*, and (e) the *philobatic* versus the *ocnophilic*. Additionally, researchers used other terms such as *stress-seekers* (Klausner, 1968), *sensation-seekers*, and *eudaemonists* to identify individuals who seek high-risk experiences (Lyng, 1990, p. 853). However, these studies, were never able to convey adequate empirical validity because they were not able to explain casual factors in risk-taking behaviors (Lyng, 1990).

Future studies also need to focus on why individuals continue to exhibit online risky behaviors even when they are aware of the potential dangers in doing so. Additionally, future researchers need to develop more precise scales to measure computer security and online users' behaviors in order to investigate other theoretical perspectives for delineating a true crime victimization model.

Appendix A: Digital Guardian Items and Quality of Measures

Item–Total Correlations for Digital Guardian (Number of Security):
Three Items

Item		Item–Total Correlation	α if Item Deleted
1.	Did you have antivirus software on your computer during the last 10 months?	.40	.55
2.	Did you have antispyware software on your computer during the last 10 months?	.43	.42
3.	Did you have firewall software on your computer during the last 10 months?	.44	.41

Cronbach's alpha (α) = .62.

Item–Total Correlations for Digital Guardian (Duration of Having Security):
Three Items

Item		Item–Total Correlation	α if Item Deleted
1.	I always had antivirus software on my computer during the last 10 months.	.50	.64
2.	I always had antispyware software on my computer during the last 10 months.	.52	.60
3.	I always had firewall software on my computer during the last 10 months.	.55	.56

Cronbach's alpha (α) = .70.

Principal Components Analysis (Varimax Rotation)
of Digital Guardian: Number of Security

Factor	Eigenvalue
1	1.69
2	.68
3	.63

Principal Components Analysis (Varimax Rotation)
of Digital Guardian: Duration of Having Installed
Security

Factor	Eigenvalue
1	1.88
2	.59
3	.52

Appendix B: Online Lifestyle Items and Quality of Measures

Item–Total Correlations for Vocational and Leisure Activities: Eight Items

Item		Item–Total Correlation	α if Item Deleted
1.	I frequently checked my e-mail during the last 10 months.	.33	.64
2.	I frequently used an instant messenger (e.g., MSN, AOL, etc.) to communicate with people during the last 10 months.	.37	.62
3.	I frequently spent time downloading materials from the Internet during the last 10 months.	.34	.63
4.	I frequently spent time shopping on the Internet during the last 10 months.	.21	.66
5.	I frequently spent time on the Internet to entertain myself during the last 10 months.	.55	.57
6.	I frequently viewed or watched news on the Internet during the last 10 months.	.30	.64
7.	I frequently sent e-mails to people during the last 10 months	.26	.64
8.	I frequently spent time on the Internet when I was bored during the last 10 months.	.54	.58

Cronbach's alpha (α) = .66.

Principal Components Analysis (Varimax Rotation) of Vocational and Leisure Activities

Factor	Eigenvalue
1	2.58
2	1.32
3	1.16
4	.92
5	.65
6	.57
7	.50
8	.31

Item–Total Correlations for Risky Leisure Activities: Four Items

Item		Item–Total Correlation
1: B10	I frequently visited websites that were new to me during the last 10 months.	.31
2: B12	I frequently downloaded free games from any website during the last 10 months.	.69
3: B13	I frequently downloaded free music that interested me from any website during the last 10 months.	.66
4: B14	I frequently downloaded free movies that interested me from any website during the last 10 months.	.67

α = .73.

Item–Total Correlations for Risky Vocational Activities: Four Items

Item		Item–Total Correlation
1: B15	I frequently opened any attachment in the e-mails that I received during the last 10 months.	.72
2: B16	I frequently clicked on any web-links in the e-mails that I received during the last 10 months.	.77
3: B17	I frequently opened any file or attachment I received through my instant messenger during the last 10 months.	.63
4: B18	I frequently clicked on a pop-up message that interested me during the last 10 months.	.41

$\alpha = .80$.

Principal Components Analysis (Varimax Rotation) of Risky Leisure Activities

Factor	Eigenvalue
1	1.96
2	.91
3	.61
4	.52

Principal Components Analysis (Varimax Rotation) of Risky Vocational Activities

Factor	Eigenvalue
1	2.32
2	.84
3	.55
4	.30

Appendix C: Computer-Crime Victimization Items and Quality of Measures

Descriptive Qualities of Computer-Crime Victimization Measures

Name of Scale	N	M	SD	Skewness	Kurtosis
Frequency of virus infection	204	3.85	21.45	9.54	97.88
Monetary loss	$204	$17.85	$75.95	$6.50	$49.39
Hour loss	204	6.23	13.69	3.89	18.33

Descriptive Qualities of Computer-Crime Victimization Measures: Likert-Type Format

Name of scale	N	M	SD	Skewness	Kurtosis
Frequency of virus infection	204	.65	.63	.92	1.98
Monetary loss	204	.25	.74	3	7.76
Hour loss	204	.58	.80	1.14	.27

Item–Total Correlations for Computer-Crime Victimization

Item		Item–Total Correlation
1.	During the last 10 months, how many times did you have computer virus infection incidents?	.28
2.	During the last 10 months, approximately how much money did you spend fixing your computer due to computer virus infections?	.24
3.	During the last 10 months, approximately how many hours were spent fixing your computer due to the virus infections?	.29

Cronbach's alpha (α) = .26.

Item–Total Correlations for Computer-Crime Victimization: Likert-Type Format

Item		Item–Total Correlation
1.	During the last 10 months, how many times did you have computer virus infection incidents?	.55
2.	During the last 10 months, approximately how much money did you spend fixing your computer due to computer virus infections?	.35
3.	During the last 10 months, approximately how many hours were spent fixing your computer due to the virus infections?	.53

α = .66.

Principal Components Analysis (Varimax Rotation) of Computer-Crime Victimization: Likert-Type Format

Factor	Eigenvalue
1	1.81
2	.76
3	.43

Appendix D: Correlations and Covariances Between Observed Variables

	DG1	DG2	OL1	OL2	OL3	CV1	CV2	CV3
DG1	1							
	.536							
DG2	.785 (**)	1						
	4.395	58.538						
OL1	.178 (**)	.181*	1					
	1.466	15.576	125.939					
OL2	.146 (*)	.112	.412 (**)	1				
	.955	7.667	41.232	79.731				
OL3	.006	−.019	.268 (**)	.272 (**)	1			
	.038	−1.318	26.751	21.633	79.064			
CV1	−.423 (**)	−.615(**)	.064	.187 (*)	.266 (*)	1		
	−.195	−2.965	.454	1.050	1.488	.397		
CV2	−.183 (**)	−.317 (**)	−.042	.094	.143 (*)	.312 (**)	1	
	−.099	−1.801	−.352	.623	.944	.146	.550	
CV3	−.147 (*)	−.334 (**)	.106	.227 (**)	.176 (*)	.590 (**)	.296 (**)	1
	−.076	−1.822	.845	1.440	1.111	.265	.157	.507

The top value in each cell is the correlation coefficient. The value below it is the variance or covariance.
* Correlation is significant at the .05 level (two-tailed).
** Correlation is significant at the .01 level (two-tailed).

References

Australian Computer Emergency Response Team. (2005). *2004 Australian computer crime and security survey.* Retrieved from http://www.auscert.org.au/render.html?it=2001

Carter, L. D., & Katz, J. A. (1997). *Computer crime: An emerging challenge for law enforcement.* East Lansing: Michigan State University.

Casey, E. (2000). *Digital evidence and computer crime.* London, England: Academic Press.

Cohen, L. E., & Felson, M. (1979). Social change and crime rate trends: A routine activity approach. *American Sociological Review, 44,* 588–608.

DeVellis, R. (2004). *Scale development.* London, England: Sage.

Felson, M. (1986). Routine activities, social controls, rational decisions, and criminal outcomes. In D. Cornish and R. Clarke (Eds.), *The reasoning criminal* (pp. 302–327). New York, NY: Springer Verlag.

Felson, M. (1998). *Crime and everyday life: Insights and implications for society* (2nd ed.). Thousand Oaks, CA: Pine Forge Press.

Flanagan, W., & McMenamin, B. (1992). The playground bullies are learning to type. *Forbes, 150,* 184–189.

Furnell, S. (2002). *Cyber crime: Vandalizing the information society.* London, England: Addison Wesley.

Gibbs, J. J., Giever, D., & Higgins, G. E. (2003). A test of the Gottfredson and Hirschi general theory of crime using structural equation modeling. *Criminal Justice and Behavior, 30,* 441–458.

Grabosky, P., & Smith, R. (2001). Telecommunication fraud in the digital age: The convergence of technologies. In D. Wall (Ed.), *Crime and the Internet* (pp. 23–45). London, England: Routledge.

Hindelang, M. J., Gottfredson, M. R., & Garoffalo, J. (1978). *Victims of personal crime: An empirical foundation for a theory of personal victimization.* Cambridge, MA: Ballinger.

Hu, L., & Bentler, P. M. (1995). Evaluating model fit. In R. H. Hoyle (Ed.), *Structural equation modeling: Concepts, issues, and applications* (pp. 76–99). Thousand Oaks, CA: Sage.

Internet Fraud Complaint Center. (2003). *IFCC 2002 Internet fraud report.* Washington, DC: Government Printing Office. Retrieved from http://www.ic3.gov/media/annualreport/2002_ifccreport.pdf

Kabay, M. E. (2001). *Studies and surveys of computer crime.* Retrieved from http://www.mekabay.com/methodology/crime_stats_methods.pdf

Kaplan, D. (2000). *Structural equation modeling: Foundations and extensions.* Thousand Oaks, CA: Sage.

Karmen, A. (2006). *Crime victims.* Thousand Oaks, CA: Thomson Higher Education.

Kennedy, L. W., & Forde, D. R. (1990). Routine activities and crime: An analysis of victimization in Canada. *Criminology, 28,* 137–151.

Klausner, Z. (1968). *Why men take chances.* New York, NY: Anchor.

Kline, R. B. (1998). *Principles and practices of structural equation modeling.* New York, NY: Guilford Press.

Kowalski, M. (2002). *Cyber-crime: Issues, data sources, and feasibility of collecting police-reported statistics.* Ottawa, Ontario, Canada: Statistics Canada.

Lyng, S. (1990). Edgework: A social psychological analysis of voluntary risk taking. *The American Journal of Sociology 95,* 851–886.

Massey, J., Krohn, M., & Bonati, L. (1989). Property crime and the routine activities of individuals. *Journal of Research in Crime and Delinquency, 26,* 378–400.

McConnell International. (2000). *Cyber crime ... and punishment? Archaic laws threaten global information.* Washington, DC: Author.

McQuade, S. C. (2006). *Understanding and managing cyber crime.* Boston, MA: Pearson/Allyn and Bacon.

Meier, R., & Miethe, T. (1993). Understanding theories of criminal victimization. *Crime and Justice 17,* 459–499.

Miethe, T., Stafford, M., & Long, J. S. (1987). Social differentiation in criminal victimization: A test of routine activities/lifestyle theories. *American Sociological Review 52,* 184–194.

Moitra, S. D. (2005). Developing policies for cyber crime. *European Journal of Crime, Criminal Law and Criminal Justice, 13,* 435–464.

Moore, R. (2005). *Cyber crime: Investigating high-technology computer crime.* Philadelphia, PA: LexisNexis.

Mustaine, E., & Tewksbury, R. (1998). Predicting risks of larceny theft victimization: A routine activity analysis using refined lifestyle measures. *Criminology, 36,* 829–857.

Ramasastry, A. (2004). *Can Utah's new antispyware law work?* Retrieved from http://www.cnn.com/2004/LAW/06/03/ramasastry.spyware/index.html

Roncek, D. W., & Maier, P. A. (1991). Bars, blocks, and crimes revisited: Linking the theory of routine activities to the empiricism of hot spots. *Criminology, 29,* 725–753.

Sherman, L. W., Gartin, P. R., & Buerger, M. E. (1989). Hot spots of predatory crime: Routine activities and the criminology of place. *Criminology, 27*(2), 27–55.

Standler, B. R. (2002). *Computer crime.* Retrieved from http://www.rbs2.com/ccrime.htm

Thomas, D., & Loader, B. D. (2000). Introduction—Cyber crime: Law enforcement, security and surveillance in the information age. In D. Thomas & B. Loader (Eds.), *Cyber crime: Law enforcement, security and surveillance in the information age* (pp. 1–14). London, England: Routledge.

Williams, F. P., & McShane, M. D. (1999). *Criminological theory.* Upper Saddle River, NJ: Prentice Hall.

Yar, M. (2005). The novelty of 'cybercrime': An assessment in light of routine activity theory. *European Journal of Criminology, 2,* 407–427.

Adolescent Online Victimization and Constructs of Routine Activities Theory

15

CATHERINE D. MARCUM

Contents

Introduction

The idea of an electronic global communication system originated from J. C. R. Licklider of the Massachusetts Institute of Technology (MIT) in the early 1960s (Licklider & Clark, 1962, as cited in Leiner et al., 2003). His idea of a "galactic network" entailed an internationally connected set of computers that allowed for easy accessibility to information. Now known as the *Internet*, this intercontinental information highway has enabled people of all ages—especially youths—to drastically expand their social circles and improve their ability to communicate with friends and family (Roberts, Foehr, Rideout, & Brodie, 1999; Rosenbaum et al., 2000). Unfortunately, young Internet users are often unable to participate in online activities without the annoyance of uninvited communication from other online users.

Several studies on youths' Internet use found that increasing numbers of young people are experiencing the following types of victimization while using computer-mediated communication (CMC) methods: (a) unwanted exposure to sexual material, (b) sexual solicitation, and (c) unwanted nonsexual harassment (Mitchell, Finkelhor, & Wolak, 2003, 2007; O'Connell, Barrow, & Sange, 2002; Quayle & Taylor, 2003; Sanger, Long, Ritzman, Stofer, & Davis, 2004; Wolak, Mitchell, & Finkelhor, 2002, 2003, 2004, 2006, 2007; Ybarra, Mitchell, Finkelhor, & Wolak, 2007). However, a majority of these studies are descriptive in nature; thus, there is a lack of rigorous research indicating which online behaviors may increase the likelihood of victimization.

Roncek and Maier (1991) suggested that routine activities theory is excellent for the examination of predatory or exploitative crimes, which are precisely the types of deviant behavior examined in this study. According to the *routine activities theory*, three elements must be present in order for a crime to occur: (a) exposure to motivated offenders; (b) a suitable target; and (c) lack of capable guardianship (Cohen & Felson, 1979).

The purpose of this study was to investigate Internet usage in a sample of college freshmen and to consider their experiences with online victimization through variables representing the three constructs of routine activities theory. It was expected that this study would provide a significant contribution to the literature on adolescent online victimization, considering the overall lack of explanatory research on this topic.

Adolescent Internet Use and Victimization

Past empirical research demonstrated that Internet use by youth has increased drastically in the past 10 years (Izenberg & Lieberman, 1998; Lenhart, Rainie, & Lewis, 2001; Nie & Erbring, 2000; Rainie, 2006). Numerous studies have been conducted to examine the frequency and purposes of Internet use by adolescents (Beebe, Asche, Harrison, & Quinlan, 2004; Lenhart et al., 2001; Mitchell et al., 2003). Research suggests that the rate of Internet use in the United States is increasing, with adolescents becoming heavier users than adults (Subrahmanyam, Kraut, Greenfield, & Gross, 2001).

The communication media available on the Internet have contributed to increased Internet use (Clemmitt, 2006; Kirkpatrick, 2006; Lamb & Johnson, 2006; Rosen, 2006; Simon, 2006; Stuzman, 2006). Often referred to collectively as *social technology* (Lamb & Johnson, 2006), these Internet media have enabled people of all ages (especially youths) to expand their social circles and improve their ability to communicate with friends and family in an inexpensive manner (Roberts et al., 1999). The term *social technology* generally refers to CMC devices that connect people for personal and professional information sharing. The use of CMC methods enables ease in the workplace, educational setting, or home, allowing individuals to communicate effortlessly with others (Simon, 2006). Although there are numerous ways to communicate and socialize with CMCs, in this study, I focused on the following media: chat rooms, instant messaging, e-mail, and social networking websites. It is unfortunate that with the beneficial use of these CMC methods comes the increased possibility of online victimization.

Researchers in multiple studies have recognized that increasing numbers of young people are experiencing victimization while using CMC methods; however, very few have attempted to explain why this is happening. Of the few explanatory studies performed, those using data from the Youth Internet Safety Survey (respondents were between the ages of 10 and 17 years) found that the use of chat rooms, discussion of sexual topics with online contacts, and a tumultuous relationship with family or friends increased the odds of online victimization (Mitchell, Finkelhor, & Wolak, 2007; Wolak et al., 2007; Ybarra et al., 2007). Furthermore, using data from the high school senior and college freshmen time period, Marcum (in press) found that increased exposure to motivated offenders and provision of personal information to online contacts also increased the likelihood of online victimization.

In more recent empirical studies, researchers examined the effect of different forms of protective measures on adolescent online victimization. Fleming, Greentree, Cocotti-Muller, Elias, and Morrison (2006) and Marcum (in press) found that the installation of filtering and blocking software had no effect on users' exposure to inappropriate materials, behaviors, and online victimization. Lwin, Stanaland, and Miyazaki (2008) further explored protective measures through a quasiexperimental study of 10- to 17-year-olds in regard to their experiences with Internet monitoring and mediation by parents. These authors found that active monitoring of Internet behavior by parents decreased youths' likelihood of participation in risky behaviors online and their exposure to inappropriate materials. However, Lwin et al. (2008) noted that the effectiveness of active monitoring decreased as the adolescent became older, which may be a foreshadowing of the results found in the present study, considering the age of the sample.

As stated before, there are few explanatory studies in the literature that attempt to assess the factors of online victimization. The literature is anemic in regard to studies that use a strong theoretical basis to examine these online outcomes. In the next section, a brief summary is provided of the theoretical framework used in the present research to better investigate contributory factors that increase or decrease the likelihood of online victimization.

Routine Activities Theory

Society and its activity patterns are in a constant state of transformation (Madriz, 1996), especially with the development of new technology. For example, daily activities of children have evolved from bicycles and dolls to video games and the Internet. Rainie (2006) reported that 87% of youths are currently using the Internet, and that number is likely to grow. Yet, as innovative technologies emerge, new methods of victimization also accompany these developments (Mitchell et al., 2003; O'Connell et al., 2002; Sanger et al., 2004; Wolak et al., 2004, 2006).

Routine activities theory has proven itself to be useful in explaining different types of criminal victimization. This theory states that three components are necessary in a situation in order for a crime to occur: (a) a suitable target, (b) lack of a capable guardian, and (c) a motivated offender (Cohen & Felson, 1979). Moreover, crime is not a random occurrence; it follows regular patterns that require these three components.

Based on an examination of the relevant literature, routine activities theory has been supported on both the macro and micro level (Arnold, Keane, & Baron, 2005; Gaetz, 2004; Schreck & Fisher, 2004; Spano & Nagy, 2005; Tewksbury & Mustaine, 2000). Although not as plentiful as micro-level research, macro-level investigations of routine activities theory have revealed empirical support for the components of the theory. In particular, it has been shown that lack of guardianship in areas with large amounts of traffic from nonresidents having no ties to the area has produced a significant effect on crime rates in neighborhoods (Roncek & Maier, 1991). Moreover, the lack of guardianship and the risky lifestyles of city residents have a significant relationship with victimization (Cao & Maume, 1993; Cook, 1987; Forde & Kennedy, 1997; Sampson, 1987). An examination of countries in different continents revealed support for the theory by demonstrating how not only a lack of guardianship but also the crossing of paths with a motivated offender as a suitable target increases the likelihood of victimization (Tseloni, Wittebrood, Farrell, & Pease, 2004).

Micro-level studies use individual-level data, which allow for analysis of factors that apply specifically to individuals rather than to large groups. Literature on offending behavior indicated unstructured peer interaction, and lack of parental supervision reflected a lack of guardianship that was a significant predictor of criminal offending (Bernburg & Thorlindsson, 2001; Schreck & Fisher, 2004; Sasse, 2005). Personal and property crime victimization studies suggested that a person's routine activities—such as participating in leisure activities away from the home and other lifestyle choices—significantly increase the likelihood of victimization (Arnold et al., 2005; Cohen & Cantor, 1980; Gaetz, 2004; Moriarty & Williams, 1996; Mustaine & Tewksbury, 1999; Spano & Nagy, 2005; Tewksbury & Mustaine, 2000; Wooldredge, Cullen, & Latessa, 1992). Domain-specific models were noted to better explain routine activities in a specific environment (Mustaine & Tewksbury, 1999; Wang, 2002; Wooldredge et al., 1992). Finally, studies revealed that drug and alcohol consumption is a significant predictor of sexual victimization of females (Mustaine & Tewksbury, 1999; Schwartz et al., 2001).

Early tests of routine activities theory—a theory that researchers often use to examine different types of victimization—focused on the importance of the environment as a vital component of interaction between criminal offenders and victims (Cohen & Felson, 1979). This is particularly relevant to the research in this study because the environment—cyberspace—is a necessary factor that must be present in order for the user to both participate in online activities and become a victim of harassment or other online crime. Cyberspace, which thrives on the possibilities of the unknown, also provides the opportunity for users to engage in activities without the presence of a capable guardian. This is true for both the offender and the victim, as both parties potentially can participate in deviant behaviors without guardianship present (Danet, 1998; Jones, 1999).

According to Felson (1987), lack of behavioral controls encourages willingness to participate in criminal activity, and motivated offenders will place themselves in areas that have an abundance of suitable targets. In this study, I examined how the routine activities of adolescents affect their likelihood of online victimization.

Method

Research Design

The purpose of this study was to investigate Internet usage in a sample of freshmen enrolled in 100-level courses as well as to consider their experiences with online victimization. To fully examine the topic, I developed the chosen methodology under the concepts and propositions of routine activities theory, which has been used many times in the past to explain various types of victimization. In this study, I used a survey that I anticipated would produce a more complete understanding of adolescents' Internet use and victimization.

Surveys were administered to enrolled freshmen in spring 2008, with a focus on their frequency and types of Internet use as well as experiences with different types of Internet victimization. It is important to note that because the students who were polled were college freshmen, we asked them to recall information from their senior year of high school. Recalling accurate information from the past may be difficult for respondents, which, in turn, would affect the validity of the findings. However, because this study asked questions that limit the scope of recall (less than 1 year earlier), the reliability and validity of the findings generally will be greater than those of a study asking for information that is farther in the past.

Through administration of the survey, I measured the three central elements of routine activities theory. The first element evaluated was *exposure to motivated offenders*, which occurred through the examination of independent variables representing general usage of the Internet and specific modes of CMC. This study asserts that general use of the Internet, including the use of various CMCs, exposes users to potential motivated offenders online, as the chances of interaction between the user and the offender are reasonably high.

We first asked students questions regarding their general usage of the Internet as high school seniors. Next, I asked questions based on the types of activities performed online, accompanied by a set of pre-selected responses. Students were asked to mark the Internet activities that they performed as a high school senior, if any. These activities included, research, gaming, planning travel, website design, shopping, socializing with others, and/or "other." We also questioned respondents about the type of social networking websites they used as a high school senior, if any. In general, if more motivated offenders inhabit one particular site more often than another, the respondent may increase his or her chance of victimization by using that site.

The second element of routine activities theory evaluated was *target suitability*, which occurred through the examination of independent variables representing behaviors that indicate attractiveness as a suitable target for victimization. Survey questions addressed this concept by asking respondents to reveal their behaviors regarding privatization of a social networking website as well as personal information that they gave to people online and posted on their social networking website.

The final element of routine activities theory assessed the *lack of capable guardianship*. Independent variables represent the amount of monitoring experienced by respondents as high school seniors and their experiences with protective measures while using the Internet. Frequencies for categorical independent variables and descriptive statistics for continuous independent variables in the model are presented in Tables 15.1, 15.2, and 15.3.

Sample

The population for the present research included all freshmen enrolled in a 100-level course at a mid-sized university in the northeastern United States during the spring 2008 academic term. To obtain a representative sample of freshmen, I developed a sampling frame of all 100-level courses potentially available to freshmen at the main campus in spring 2008, along with the respective sections available for each course. Course sections were randomly selected, and permission was requested from the professor of the course to

Table 15.1 Frequencies for Categorical Variables Representing Independent Variables (N = 483)

Variable	N	%
Activities performed on the Internet		
Research (n = 482)		
No	23	4.8
Yes	459	95.2
Gaming (n = 482)		
No	223	46.3
Yes	259	53.7
Planning travel (n = 482)		
No	326	67.6
Yes	156	32.4
Website design (n = 482)		
No	406	84.2
Yes	76	15.8
Shopping (n = 482)		
No	193	40.0
Yes	289	60.0
Socializing with others (n = 482)		
No	47	9.8
Yes	435	90.2
Other (n = 481)		
No	429	89.2
Yes	52	10.8
Use of e-mail (n = 482)		
No	91	18.9
Yes	391	81.1
Use of instant messaging (n = 482)		
No	93	19.3
Yes	389	80.7
Use of chat rooms (n = 482)		
No	442	91.7
Yes	40	8.3
Use of social networking sites (n = 482)		
No	89	18.5
Yes	393	81.5
Social networking site used		
MySpace (n = 480)		
No	178	37.1
Yes	302	62.9

(*continued*)

Table 15.1 Frequencies for Categorical Variables Representing Independent Variables (N = 483) (continued)

Variable	N	%
Facebook (n = 480)		
No	180	37.5
Yes	300	62.5
Other (n = 480)		
No	464	96.7
Yes	16	3.3
Used a nonprivatized social networking site (n = 481)		
No	244	50.7
Yes	237	49.3
Information posted on social networking site[a]		
Age (n = 481)		
No	120	24.9
Yes	361	75.1
Gender (n = 481)		
No	91	18.9
Yes	390	81.1
Descriptive characteristics (n = 481)		
No	355	73.8
Yes	126	26.2
Picture(s) of yourself (n = 481)		
No	98	20.4
Yes	383	79.6
Telephone number (n = 481)		
No	452	94.0
Yes	29	6.0
School location (n = 481)		
No	221	45.9
Yes	260	54.1
Extracurricular activities (n = 481)		
No	191	39.7
Yes	290	60.3
Goals/aspirations (n = 481)		
No	337	70.1
Yes	144	29.9
Sexual information (n = 481)		
No	471	97.9
Yes	10	2.1
Emotional/mental distresses/problems (n = 481)		
No	451	93.8
Yes	30	6.2

Table 15.1   Frequencies for Categorical Variables Representing Independent Variables (N = 483) (continued)

Variable	N	%
Family conflicts (*n* = 481)		
No	474	98.5
Yes	7	1.5
Other (*n* = 481)		
No	455	94.6
Yes	26	5.4
Communicate with strangers online (*n* = 479)		
No	272	56.8
Yes	207	43.2
Personal information to others (*n* = 482)		
No	382	79.3
Yes	100	20.7
Information given to person(s) online[b]		
Age (*n* = 482)		
No	381	79.0
Yes	101	21.0
Gender (*n* = 482)		
No	378	78.4
Yes	104	21.6
Descriptive characteristics (*n* = 482)		
No	425	88.2
Yes	57	11.8
Picture of yourself (*n* = 482)		
No	422	87.6
Yes	60	12.4
Telephone number (*n* = 482)		
No	444	92.1
Yes	38	7.9
School location (*n* = 482)		
No	439	91.1
Yes	43	8.9
Extracurricular activities (*n* = 482)		
No	416	86.3
Yes	66	13.7
Goals/aspirations (*n* = 482)		
No	439	91.1
Yes	43	8.9
Sexual information (*n* = 483)		
No	468	97.1
Yes	15	3.1

(continued)

Table 15.1   Frequencies for Categorical Variables Representing Independent Variables (N = 483) (continued)

Variable	N	%
Emotional/mental distresses/problems (n = 482)		
No	467	96.9
Yes	15	3.1
Family conflicts (n = 482)		
No	467	96.9
Yes	15	3.1
Other (n = 482)		
No	480	99.6
Yes	2	0.4
Location of computer use		
Home (n = 481)		
No	34	7.1
Yes	447	92.9
Living room/family room (n = 475)		
No	281	59.2
Yes	194	40.8
Your bedroom (n = 475)		
No	320	67.4
Yes	155	32.6
Parent/guardian's bedroom (n = 475)		
No	467	98.3
Yes	8	1.7
Other room (n = 475)		
No	394	82.9
Yes	81	17.1
School computer lab (n = 480)		
No	458	95.4
Yes	22	4.6
Friend's home (n = 480)		
No	474	98.7
Yes	6	1.3
Coffee shop (n = 480)		
No	480	100.0
Yes	0	0.0
Other (n = 480)		
No	472	98.3
Yes	8	1.7
In same room		
Parent/guardian (n = 481)		
No	256	53.2
Yes	225	46.8

Table 15.1   Frequencies for Categorical Variables Representing Independent Variables (*N* = 483) (continued)

Variable	N	%
Friend (*n* = 481)		
No	223	46.4
Yes	258	53.6
Teacher/counselor (*n* = 481)		
No	415	86.3
Yes	66	13.7
Sibling (*n* = 481)		
No	258	53.6
Yes	223	46.4
Someone else (*n* = 481)		
No	429	89.2
Yes	52	10.8
No one (*n* = 481)		
No	275	57.2
Yes	206	42.8
Restrictions online		
Time spent online (*n* = 480)		
No	404	84.2
Yes	76	15.8
Viewing of adult websites (*n* = 480)		
No	309	64.4
Yes	171	35.6
Use of CMCs (*n* = 480)		
No	453	94.4
Yes	27	5.6
Other (*n* = 480)		
No	467	97.3
Yes	13	2.7
No restrictions (*n* = 480)		
No	216	45.0
Yes	264	55.0
No active monitoring (*n* = 478)		
No	184	38.5
Yes	294	61.5
Active monitoring (*n* = 478)		
No	411	86.0
Yes	67	14.0
Unsure of active monitoring (*n* = 478)		
No	361	75.5
Yes	117	24.5

(continued)

Table 15.1   Frequencies for Categorical Variables Representing Independent Variables (N = 483) (continued)

Variable	N	%
No filtering/blocking software (*n* = 478)		
No	291	60.9
Yes	187	39.1
Filtering/blocking software (*n* = 478)		
No	239	50.0
Yes	239	50.0
Unsure of filtering/blocking software (*n* = 478)		
No	426	89.1
Yes	52	10.9

[a] Independent variables listed as "Information posted on social networking websites" were combined into one variable termed "SNWInfo" for statistical analysis.
[b] Independent variables listed as "Information given to person(s) online" were combined into one variable termed "ProvidedInfo" for statistical analysis.

administer the survey to the class of students. This process continued until a sample of 483 freshmen (out of the 744 surveys collected) was collected for analysis.

In regard to the demographics of the sample, approximately 40% of the respondents were male. This is comparable to the entire freshman population at this university (42.6% male). Also, much like the freshmen population, the majority of the sample (83.7%) was White and non-Hispanic. Finally, 51.3% of respondents were 18 years of age, and the remaining members were 19 years of age (this information was not available for the population).

Table 15.2   Descriptive Statistics for Recoded Continuous Variables Representing Exposure to Motivated Offenders (N = 483)

Variable	Min	Max	M	SD
Hours per week on the Internet (*n* = 479)	0	35	15.14	8.97
Hours per week on e-mail (*n* = 479)	0	4	1.29	1.06
Hours per week on IM (*n* = 480)	0	15	4.39	4.09
Hours per week in chat rooms (*n* = 480)	0	1	0.08	0.27
Hours per week of use of social networking websites (*n* = 477)	0	15	4.05	3.79

Three dependent variables were examined in this particular study. Respondents were asked if, during their high school senior year, they had received the following from a person online: sexually explicit material (e.g., pornography), nonsexual harassment (e.g., unwanted e-mails, instant messages), and sexual solicitation (e.g., request for either online or offline sexual interaction). Dependent variables for this study were measured as dichotomous variables. Frequencies for categorical dependent variables are presented in Table 15.3.

Table 15.3   Frequencies for Categorical Variables Representing Dependent Variables (N = 483)

Variable	N	%
Received unwanted sexually explicit material (n = 473)		
No	365	77.2
Yes	108	22.8
Received harassment in nonsexual manner (n = 468)		
No	324	69.2
Yes	144	30.8
Received solicitation for sex (n = 470)		
No	425	90.4
Yes	45	9.6

Analysis

Data obtained through administration of the survey were analyzed in different manners through various techniques. Because I initially measured the dependent variables as a dichotomy, I used logistic regression models to assess relationships between the independent variables and the likelihood of victimization. Because of the large number of independent variables measured in this study, I used stepwise logistic regression to determine the appropriate variables to assess in the models. In multivariate analysis, some variables can have a statistically significant effect only when another variable is controlled, which is called a *suppressor effect*. As a result, backward elimination was selected as the method of stepwise regression, whereby all possible variables are initially contained in the model, and there is less risk of ruling out variables involved in suppressor effects.

Another step that I took to enhance the discovery of potential relationships was to relax the $p < .05$ criterion for retention of variables in the models. The criterion for retention of variables in this study was set at .20 to better reveal any possible statistically significant relationships. Furthermore, linear probability models first were used to identify any possible problems with multicollinearity through the use of tolerance statistics and variance inflation factors. These factors were found to be normal and, therefore, were not an issue in this study.

Results

Table 15.4 contains the logistic regression estimates for the dependent variable "receipt of sexually explicit material." The high school senior time period model was shown to explain a range of 12.3% to 18.3% of the variation in the dependent variable. Respondents who shopped online (Shop) and those

Table 15.4   Logistic Regression Estimates for the Dependent Variable of Receipt of Sexually Explicit Material (N = 483)

Variable	B (SE)	Exp(B)
Travel	−0.456 (0.269)	0.634
Design	0.477 (0.305)	10.611
Shop	0.812 (0.263)	20.253**
OtherActivity	0.592 (0.357)	10.808
ChatHour	0.774 (0.393)	20.169*
ProvidedInfo	0.107 (0.046)	10.113*
ParInRm	0.446 (0.237)	10.562
OthInRm	0.489 (0.357)	10.630
RestrictTime	0.498 (0.303)	10.645
Sex	−0.436 (0.242)	0.646
White	−0.750 (0.297)	0.472*
GPA	−0.222 (0.109)	0.801
Privileges	0.142 (0.043)	10.153**
Constant	−10.464 (0.440)	0.231**

−2 log-likelihood = 467.669; model χ^2 = 62.651; Cox & Snell R^2 = .123; Nagelkerke R = .183.
*p < .05, **p < .01, and ***p < .001.

who used chat rooms 1 or more hr per week (ChatHour) were over two times more likely to be victimized, and those who provided various types of information to online contacts also were more likely to receive sexual material. In addition, two control variables emerged as significant predictors. First, respondents who were White (White) were less likely than minorities to receive sexually explicit material online ($B = -0.750$, $p < .05$). Second, respondents whose parents more often took away privileges (Privileges) during the high school senior time period were more likely to be victimized ($B = 0.142$, $p < .01$). The temporal ordering of the latter relationship may be important to consider, as it is possible that when respondents received sexually explicit material, parents then took away computer privileges.

Table 15.5 presents the logistic regression estimates of the dependent variable "receipt of nonsexual harassment" during the high school time period. The variables retained at the .20 level were shown to explain 15.7% to 21.9% of the variation in the dependent variable during the college freshman time period model. Socializing online (Social) continued to increase the likelihood of nonsexual harassment ($B = 1.537$, $p < .05$). Furthermore, hours per week spent using e-mail (EmHours) now emerged as a variable that significantly increased the likelihood of this type of victimization ($B = 0.232$, $p < .05$). Providing various types of personal information to online contacts (ProvidedInfo) was the most statistically significant predictor of nonsexual harassment ($B = 0.178$, $p < .001$). Finally, the only significant control variable

Table 15.5 Logistic Regression Estimates for the Dependent Variable of Receipt of Nonsexual Harassment (N = 483)

Variable	B (SE)	Exp(B)
Shop	0.344 (0.221)	10.410
Social	10.537 (0.631)	40.651*
EmHours	0.232 (0.111)	10.261*
IMHours	0.048 (0.028)	10.049
ProvidedInfo	0.178 (0.043)	10.195***
LivRm	−0.391 (0.221)	0.677
SchLab	−10.420 (0.809)	0.242
RestrictCMC	0.767 (0.459)	20.152
DKActMon	−0.331 (0.256)	0.718
Sex	0.381 (0.240)	10.464
GPA	−0.181 (0.112)	0.835
Grades	0.154 (0.089)	10.167
Succeed	−0.184 (0.075)	0.832*
Constant	−20.707 (0.872)	0.067**

−2 log-likelihood = 525.572; model χ^2 = 82.029***; Cox & Snell R^2 = .157; Nagelkerke R^2 = .219.
*p < .05, **p < .01, and ***p < .001.

in the model was "placing importance on succeeding in school." Respondents who had a stronger desire to succeed in school (Succeed) were less likely to receive nonsexual harassment (B = −0.184, p < .05).

Finally, the full logistic regression model examining the last type of victimization analyzed in this study, *receipt of sexual solicitation*, is presented in Table 15.6. Variables retained at the .20 level were shown to explain 15.4% to 30.0%[1] of the variation in the dependent variable. Two independent variables were statistically significant predictors, along with three control variables. Providing personal information to online contacts (ProvidedInfo) had the most highly significant impact on this type of victimization—it increased the likelihood of receipt of sexual solicitation by approximately 38%, Exp(B) = 1.377, for each type of information provided. Main use of the Internet in locations noted as "Other Place" (OthPl; i.e., not in the parent's or friend's home, or school computer lab) also significantly increased this likelihood (B = 2.196, p < .05). With regard to the control variables, respondents who reported that they could share thoughts and feelings with friends (ShareFriends; B = −0.228, p < .05) and those who had greater respect for their teachers (RespectTeachers; B = −0.214, p < .05) were significantly less

---

[1] There is a notable spread between the Cox and Snell residuals and Nagelkerke R^2 in this model. After careful evaluation of the model, I believe that the reason for this spread is the low number of respondents who experienced this dependent variable (n = 45) compared with the total sample.

Table 15.6 Logistic Regression Estimates for the Dependent Variable of Receipt of Sexual Solicitation (N = 483)

Variable	B (SE)	Exp(B)
Gaming	−.567 (.343)	.567
Social	1.366 (1.089)	3.919
SNWHours	.081 (.044)	1.085
ProvidedInfo	.320 (.055)	1.377***
OthPl	2.196 (.949)	8.988*
FriInRm	.605 (.349)	1.831
SibInRm	−.630 (.347)	.532
RestrictTime	−.761 (.511)	.467
ShareFriends	−.228 (.089)	.796*
RespectParents	.203 (.125)	1.225
RespectTeachers	−.214 (.098)	.080*
Succeed	.146 (.082)	1.157
Nag	−.122 (.072)	.885
Privileges	.143 (.071)	1.153*
Constant	−3.214 (1.484)	.040*

−2 log-likelihood = 265.676; model χ^2 = 80.393***; Cox & Snell R^2 = .154; Nagelkerke R^2 = .300.
*$p < .05$, **$p < .01$, and ***$p < .001$.

likely to receive sexual solicitation online. In addition, a respondent whose parents more often took away privileges (Privileges) was more likely to receive sexual solicitation online (B = 0.143, $p < .05$). Again, this could indicate that privileges were removed as a result of inappropriate online behaviors or that conflict with parents actually influenced the likelihood that a respondent would be in a position to receive sexual solicitation online.

Discussion and Conclusion

Daily use of the Internet is a customary behavior for so many Americans, whether it is for socialization, research, or various other activities. Considering the idea for the Internet was conceived in 1962 (Leiner et al., 2003) and did not become a familiar facet of businesses and homes until the early 1990s (Sanger et al., 2004); this new commodity of communication has become a prevalent mainstay in American homes. Becaue of its easy accessibility and availability, the frequency of Internet use has increased in all age groups; however, Internet use by adolescents has had the largest increase in use than any other age group.

Today's adolescents have grown up using the Internet, and, in turn, are extremely familiar with the multiple opportunities for use that are available online. Youths are especially involved in online socialization using various methods of CMC such as e-mail, chat rooms, instant messaging, and social networking websites. Moreover, not only are more adolescents using the Internet to socialize, but they are also spending more time online (Izenberg & Lieberman, 1998; Nie & Erbring, 2000). It is unfortunate that although the use of CMCs can produce positive interactions and help users develop enjoyable relationships, when young people spend extensive amounts of time online, they are also placing themselves at an increased risk for victimization.

The purpose of this study was to further investigate past Internet use in a sample of college freshmen as well as to consider their experiences with online victimization. To more fully examine this topic area, I developed the chosen methodology under the concepts and propositions of routine activities theory, which has been used many times in the past to explain various types of victimization. Because few researchers have attempted to provide an explanation for adolescent online victimization, in this study, I employed a survey that had a theoretical basis, with the anticipation of coming to a more complete understanding of adolescents' Internet use and victimization.

Examination of the data showed that behaviors that increased exposure to motivated offenders had a sizeable impact on the likelihood of victimization. Consistent with the findings of Wolak and colleagues (2007), respondents in this study reported that participation in certain activities while online—as well as amplified used of CMCs—increased the likelihood of victimization through receipt of sexual material as well as nonsexual harassment. These results, which indicated that exposure to motivated offenders increased a person's likelihood of experiencing victimization, are also consistent with previous victimization research using routine activities theory.

Examination of the data also showed that behaviors that increased target suitability had a large impact on the likelihood of victimization. In fact, participating in behaviors that increased target suitability was shown to have the largest effect on dependent variables. Supporting findings by Mitchell and colleagues (2007), this study indicated that communicating with people online and providing personal information to online contacts increased the likelihood of all three types of victimization measured in the study for respondents during the high school senior time period.

These findings were analogous with previous studies examining victimization through routine activities theory. Multiple studies have found that decreasing a person's target suitability in turn decreases his or her likelihood of becoming a victim of crime (Felson, 1986; Horney, Osgood, & Marshall, 1995; Schreck & Fisher, 2004). For example, Arnold and colleagues (2005) discovered that if a respondent's main activities are drinking and other leisure activities, his or her level of target suitability is increased and, in turn, they are more likely to be a victim of crime. Moreover, Wang (2002), during his examination of causal factors associated with bank robberies, determined that banks who presented themselves as suitable targets (i.e., excessive amounts of cash and located close to a major highway) were more likely to be robbed.

Unlike the other two constructs of routine activities theory, protective measures taken during Internet use (measured under the theoretical construct of "lack of capable guardianship") had a minimal effect on the dependent variables measured in the study. Findings from this study indicated that protective software had no significant effect on victimization for survey respondents. Contrary to what was expected of the findings, the use of filtering and blocking software did not appear to decrease victimization for the respondents. Conversely, some respondents who were unsure if the software was present were more likely to be victimized; in other words, although there was a possibility that software was present to filter unwanted materials, respondents were still more likely to receive some type of sexual material.

Little support was found for the theory that online restrictions given to respondents would decrease the likelihood of victimization online, as only one type of restriction (the viewing of adult websites) had a statistically significant effect on the victimization. High school seniors who had been given this type of restriction were less likely to be victimized online, whereas college freshmen were not affected. Furthermore, little support was found for the expectation that adolescents who were monitored while online were less likely to be victimized.

The findings of this study were not similar to those of previous studies examining victimization through routine activities theory, as past research revealed that uses of protective measures—which decreased lack of capable guardianship—decreased the likelihood of victimization (Cao & Maume, 1993; Cook, 1987; Sampson, 1987). Wang (2002; mentioned previously) discovered that banks that increased security and employed armed security guards were less likely to be robbed. Tseloni and colleagues (2004), in their study on victimization through burglary, found further support: He discovered that single-parent families were more likely to have their homes burglarized due to a lack of guardianship.

Policy Suggestions

The findings of this study indicated that respondents who spent an increased amount of time using the Internet and specific CMCs (in turn exposing their likelihood of encountering a motivated offender) were more likely to be victimized. Nevertheless, it would be futile to attempt to develop prevention programs that encourage youths to reduce their use of the Internet. Use of the Internet is often necessary for educational purposes, and many youths use the

Internet to socialize and connect with others. In fact, after the administration of the first Youth Internet Safety Survey, Wolak et al. (2002) determined that over half of the respondents (55%) reported using chat rooms, instant messages, and e-mail to communicate with people they had never met, with the hopes of forming relationships. Rather than encourage youths to stop socializing on the Internet, it would be more effective to educate youths on the dangers that are present online so they become aware of the potential for victimization.

Adolescents using the Internet should be educated so that they restrict their participation in online communication only to people whom they know and trust. Many of the respondents in this study reported that they communicated with and provided personal information to people they met online as well as participated in offline relationships with these online contacts. In other words, these youths were revealing personal information to complete strangers (i.e., people who may intend to prey upon a vulnerable population) and were likely to continue the virtual relationship offline through various modes of communication, often in person. Although none of the respondents in this study reported participating in unwilling sexual relationships with people whom they met online, past research has shown that there are adolescents who are physically victimized by such contacts (Kendall, 1998; Tarbox, 2000). If adolescents limit their online communication to people they know, the risk of offline victimization should be lower.

With limited past research available, in this study, I sought to generate greater understanding about the relationships between (a) Internet behaviors and activities (representing the three constructs of routine activities theory) and (b) online victimization and relationship formation. Providing personal information to online contacts and communicating with people whom an individual has met only online (variables representing the theoretical construct of "target suitability") were the strongest and most consistent predictors of online victimization. Moreover, use of certain CMCs (variables representing the theoretical construct of "exposure to motivated offenders") also was shown to predict certain types of victimization. However, variables representing the third construct of routine activities theory—that is, lack of capable guardianship—were not shown to be strong or consistent predictors of online victimization of youths.

From the knowledge gained through this study, it is my hope that more effective policies and programs can be developed for the education of youth and families about protecting themselves while online. Youths should be aware of who they are conversing with online and should refrain from providing any type of personal information to people whom they do not know or trust. Regardless of the preferred solution by parents, the reality is that as children get older and become more independent, they become more technologically savvy and, therefore, are able to participate in online communication without the watchful eye of a parent or guardian. Adults have the responsibility to make youths aware that predators come in many forms—not just the stereotypical "creepy old man" preying on little children on the playground. This especially is true on the Internet, where offenders can create multiple identities and employ these identities to prey on young online users. The main goal is not to create paranoia but, rather, to foster intelligent awareness.

Finally, there is ample of opportunity for future research in this area. Surveying a wider age range of adolescents, as well as those in different geographical areas, would add to the knowledge base. Also, further investigation of the use of social networking websites and the offending behaviors of adolescents, as well as their familiarity with deceptive Internet practices, will advance our knowledge of the online behaviors and experiences of adolescents. With this knowledge, better protective measures and policies can be developed to keep adolescents safe online.

Limitations of the Study

A sample of adolescents was chosen for this study because past research has shown that youths between the ages of 12 and 17 years are at a high risk for online victimization (Mitchell et al., 2003; O'Connell et al., 2002; Sanger et al., 2004; Wolak et al., 2002, 2004, 2006). The ideal sample for this particular study includes respondents who fall into this age group. However, based on human subject issues that would have been encountered while trying to survey this group, college students who were legally able to participate in research (without parental consent) were chosen. The sample included adolescents ages 18 and 19 years and lacked the inclusion of younger adolescents.

A second limitation regarding the representativeness of this sample is based on the geographical area from which the sample was drawn. The mid-sized university in the northeastern United States is located in a rural area, and many of its students originate from surrounding rural areas. This limited the number of students from urban and suburban settings in the sample, thereby decreasing the general ability of the findings. Nonetheless, because this study was one of the few explanatory studies performed in this topic area, issues of recall and geographical location did not prevent a significant contribution from being made to the knowledge and understanding of potential causes of adolescent online victimization.

A final issue involved the wording of survey items, specifically pertaining to the measurement of persons in the room with the respondent during Internet use. The variable representing having a person in the room designated as "other" during Internet use was shown to be a significant predictor. However, a qualitative response to elaborate on the identity of the person designated as "other" was not available in the survey. Considering this was shown to be a significant independent variable, it should be investigated further in the future.

References

Arnold, R., Keane, C., & Baron, S. (2005). Assessing risk of victimization through epidemiological concepts: An alternative analytic strategy applied to routine activities theory. *Canadian Review of Sociology and Anthropology, 423,* 345–364.

Beebe, T., Asche, S., Harrison, P., & Quinlan, K. (2004). Heightened vulnerability and increased risk-taking among adolescent chat room users: Results from a statewide school survey. *Journal of Adolescent Health, 35,* 116–123.

Bernburg, J., & Thorlindsson, T. (2001). Routine activities in social context: A closer look at the role of opportunity in deviant behavior. *Justice Quarterly, 18,* 543–567.

Cao, L., & Maume D. (1993). Urbanization, inequality, lifestyles and robbery: A comprehensive model. *Sociological Focus, 26,* 11–26.

Clemmitt, M. (2006). Cyber socializing. *CQ Researcher, 16*(27), 1–34.

Cohen, L., & Cantor, D. (1980). The determinants of larceny: An empirical and theoretical study. *Journal of Research in Crime and Delinquency, 17,* 140–159.

Cohen, L., & Felson, M. (1979). Social change and crime rate trends: A routine activity approach. *American Sociological Review, 44,* 588–608.

Cook, P. (1987). Robbery violence. *Journal of Criminal Law and Criminology, 78,* 357–376.

Danet, B. (1998). Text as mask: Gender, play, and performance on the Internet. In S. G. Jones (Ed.), *Cybersociety 2.0: Revisiting computer-mediated communication and community* (pp. 129–158). Thousand Oaks, CA: Sage.

Felson, M. (1986). Linking criminal choices, routine activities, informal control, and criminal outcomes. In D. B. Cornish & R. V. Clarke (Eds.), *The reasoning criminal: Rational choice perspectives on offending* (pp. 119–128). New York, NY: Springer-Verlag.

Felson, M. (1987). Routine activities and crime prevention in the developing metropolis. *Criminology, 25,* 911–932.

Fleming, M., Greentree, S., Cocotti-Muller, D., Elias, K., & Morrison, S. (2006). Safety in cyberspace: Adolescents' safety and exposure online. *Youth & Society, 38,* 135–154.

Forde, D., & Kennedy, L. (1997). Risky lifestyles, routine activities, and the general theory of crime. *Justice Quarterly, 14,* 265–289.

Gaetz, S. (2004). Safe streets for whom? Homeless youth, social exclusion, and criminal victimization. *Canadian Journal of Criminology and Criminal Justice, 46,* 423–455.

Horney, J., Osgood, D., & Marshall, I. (1995). Criminal careers in the short-term: Intra-individual variability in crime and its relation to local life circumstances. *American Sociological Review, 60,* 655–673.

Izenberg, N., & Lieberman, D. (1998). The web, communication trends, and children's health: How the children use the web. *Clinical Pediatrics, 37,* 335–340.

Jones, S. (1999). *Doing internet research.* London, England: Sage.

Kendall, V. (1998). The lost child: Congress's inability to protect our teenagers. *Northwestern University Law Review, 92,* 1307–1315.

Kirkpatrick, M. (2006, May 17). Top 10 social networking sites see 47 percent growth. *Thesocialsoftwareweblog.* Retrieved from http://socialsoftware.weblogsinc.com

Lamb, A., & Johnson, L. (2006). Want to be my friend? What you need to know about social technologies. *Teacher Librarian, 34*(1), 55–57.

Leiner, B., Cerf, V., Clark, D., Kahn, R., Kleinrock, L., Lynch, D., … Wolff, S. (2003). A brief history of the Internet. *Internet Society.* Retrieved from http://www.isoc.org/internet/history/brief.shtml

Lenhart, A., Rainie, L., & Lewis. O. (2001). *Teenage life online: The rise of the instant-message generation and the internet's impact on friendships and family relationships.* Washington, DC: Pew Internet and American Life Project. Retrieved from http://www.pewinternet.org/~/media//Files/Reports/2001/PIP_Teens_Report.pdf.pdf

Lwin, M., Stanaland, A., & Miyazaki, A. (2008). Protecting children's privacy online: How parental mediation strategies affect website safeguard effectiveness. *Journal of Retailing, 84,* 205–217.

Madriz, E. (1996). The perception of risk in the workplace: A test of routine activity theory. *Journal of Criminal Justice, 24,* 407–412.

Marcum, C. D. (in press). Adolescent online victimization: Comparing genders through a test of routine activities theory. *Journal of Criminal Justice and Popular Culture.*

Mitchell, K., Finkelhor, D., & Wolak. J. (2003). The exposure of youth to unwanted sexual material on the internet: A national survey of risk, impact, and prevention. *Youth & Society, 34,* 3300–3358.

Mitchell, K., Finkelhor, D., & Wolak. J. (2007). Youth internet users at risk for the more serious online sexual solicitations. *American Journal of Preventive Medicine, 32,* 532–537.

Moriarty, L., & Williams, J. (1996). Examining the relationship between routine activities theory and social disorganization: An analysis of property crime victimization. *American Journal of Criminal Justice, 21,* 43–59.

Mustaine, E., & Tewksbury, R. (1999). A routine activities theory explanation for women's stalking victimization. *Violence Against Women, 5,* 43–62.

Nie, N., & Erbring. L. (2000). *Internet and Society: A preliminary report.* Stanford, CT: Stanford Institute for the Quantitative Study of Society.

O'Connell, R., Barrow, C., & Sange, S. (2002). *Young people's use of chat rooms: Implications for policy strategies and programs of education.* Preston, United Kingdom: University of Central Lancashire.

Quayle, E., & Taylor, M. (2003). Model of problematic Internet use in people with a sexual interest in children. *CyberPsychology and Behavior, 6,* 93–106.

Rainie, L. (2006). *Life online: Teens and technology and the world to come.* Speech to the annual conference of the Public Library Association, Boston, MA.

Roberts, D., Foehr, U., Rideout, V., & Brodie, M. (1999). *Kids and media @ the new millennium: A comprehensive analysis of children's media use.* Menlo Park, CA: The Henry J. Kaiser Family Foundation.

Roncek, D., & Maier, P. (1991). Bars, blocks, and crimes revisited: Linking the theory of routine activities to the empiricism of hot spots. *Criminology, 29,* 725–753.

Rosen, L. (2006). *Adolescents in MySpace: Identity formation, friendship, and sexual predators.* Dominguez Hills, CA: California State University.

Rosenbaum, M., Altman, D., Brodie, M., Flournoy, R., Blendon, R., & Benson, J. (2000). *NPR/Kaiser/Kennedy School Kids and Technology Survey.* Retrieved from http://www.npr.org/programs/specials/poll/technology/technology.kids.html

Sampson, R. (1987). Personal violence by strangers: An extension and test of the opportunity model of predatory victimization. *Journal of Criminal Law and Criminology, 78,* 327–356.

Sanger, D., Long, A., Ritzman, M., Stofer, K., & Davis, C. (2004). Opinions of female juvenile delinquents about their interactions in chat rooms. *Journal of Correctional Education, 55,* 120–131.

Sasse, S. (2005). Motivation and routine activities theory. *Deviant Behavior, 26,* 547–570.

Schreck, C., & Fisher, B. (2004). Specifying the influence of the family and peers on violent and victimization. *Journal of Interpersonal Violence, 19,* 1021–1041.

Schwartz, M., DeKeseredy, W., Tait, D., & Alvi, S. (2001). Male peer support and a feminist routine activities theory: Understanding sexual assault on the college campus. *Justice Quarterly, 18,* 623–649.

Simon, J. (2006). Computer-mediated communication: Task performance and satisfaction. *Journal of Social Psychology, 146,* 349–379.

Spano, R., & Nagy, S. (2005). Social guardianship and social isolation: An application and extension of lifestyle/routine activities theory to rural adolescents. *Rural Sociology, 70,* 414–437.

Stutzman, F. (2006). *Social networking on campus.* Chapel Hill, NC: University of North Carolina.

Subrahmanyam, K., Kraut, R., Greenfield, P., & Gross, E. (2001). New forms of electronic media: The impact of interactive games and the Internet on cognition, sociialization, and behavior. In D. G. Singer & J. L. Singer (Eds.), *Handbook of children's media.* (pp. 73–99). Thousand Oaks, CA: Sage.

Tarbox, K. (2000). *Katie.com.* New York, NY: Penguin Group.

Tewksbury, R., & Mustaine, E. (2000). Routine activities and vandalism: A theoretical and empirical study. *Journal of Crime and Justice, 23,* 81–110.

Tseloni, A., Wittebrood, K., Farrell, G., & Pease, K. (2004). Burglary victimization in England and Wales, the United States and the Netherlands. *The British Journal of Criminology, 44,* 66–91.

Wang, J. (2002). Bank robberies by an Asian gang: An assessment of the routine activities theory. *International Journal of Offender Therapy and Comparative Criminology, 46,* 555–568.

Wolak, J., Mitchell, K., & Finkelhor, D. (2002). Close online relationships in a national sample of adolescents. *Adolescence, 37,* 441–455.

Wolak, J., Mitchell, K., & Finkelhor, D. (2003). Escaping or connecting? Characteristics of youth who form close online relationships. *Journal of Adolescent Health, 26,* 105–119.

Wolak, J., Mitchell, K., & Finkelhor, D. (2004). Internet-initiated sex crimes against minors: Implications for prevention based on findings from a national study. *Journal of Adolescent Health, 35,* 11–20.

Wolak, J., Mitchell, K., & Finkelhor, D. (2006). *Online victimization of children: Five years later.* Washington, DC: National Center for Missing and Exploited Children.

Wolak, J., Mitchell, K., & Finkelhor, D. (2007). Unwanted and wanted exposure to online pornography in a national sample of youth Internet users. *Pediatrics, 119*, 247–257.

Wooldredge, J., Cullen, F., & Latessa, E. (1992). Victimization in the workplace: A test of routine activities theory. *Justice Quarterly, 9*, 325–335.

Ybarra, M., Mitchell, K., Finkelhor, D., & Wolak, J. (2007). Internet prevention messages: Targeting the right online behaviors. *Archives of Pediatric and Adolescent Medicine, 161*, 138–145.

Cyber Stalking
Typology, Etiology, and Victims

16

MICHAEL L. PITTARO

Contents

Introduction

The Internet has undergone rapid growth in this millennium in that it has promoted advances in just about every aspect of society and is available and accessible in practically every corner of the globe (Jaishankar & Uma Sankary, 2005; McFarlane & Bocij, 2003). The predicted benefits to society are incalculable. The Internet is primarily responsible for developing and enriching global commerce to previously inconceivable heights, fostering remarkable advancements in education and health care, and facilitating worldwide communication that was once perceived to be limited and costly (Jaishankar & Sankary, 2005; McFarlane & Bocij, 2003). However, the Internet, with its infinite size and previously unimaginable capabilities, has a dark side, too: It has opened windows of previously unknown criminal opportunities that not only challenge but also transcend all physical boundaries, borders, and limitations that work to detect, punish, and diminish what appears to be a growing social problem of global proportions. The Internet has literally become a fertile breeding ground for an entirely new and unique type of criminal offender hereafter known as the *cyber stalker*. The cyber stalker is one who uses the Internet as a weapon or tool, of sorts, to prey upon, harass, threaten, and generate fear and trepidation in his or her victims through sophisticated stalking tactics, which, for the most part, are largely misunderstood and, in some cases, legal.

Despite nearly a decade of prominent criminological research, there is no concise, universally accepted definition of traditional *stalking*, and to make matters worse, there is even less literature available in reference to cyber stalking (McFarlane & Bocij, 2003). Consequently, the cyber stalkers' behaviors, patterns, and tactics are largely misunderstood and—to a certain extent—unknown (Mustaine & Tewksbury, 1999). The term *cyber stalking* generally refers to the use of the Internet, e-mail, or other electronic communication device to create a criminal level of intimidation, harassment, and fear in one or more victims (Petrocelli, 2005; Reno, 1999). As mentioned, there is very little known about cyber stalking, but what is accepted is that cyber stalking behaviors can vary from a nonthreatening e-mail to a potentially deadly encounter between the stalker and the targeted victim (Hutton & Haantz, 2003). The obvious key to distinguishing traditional stalking from cyber stalking is that cyber stalkers rely predominantly on the Internet and other electronic communication devices to harass, threaten, and intimidate their targeted victims. Most cyber stalking behaviors are premeditated, are repetitious, and can be quite aggressive in their approach but only border on being truly illegal under current statutory law in most states (Hutton & Haantz, 2003).

Because cyber stalking is largely misunderstood, many people incorrectly assume that cyber stalking involves an element of sexual obsession; however, the research findings are not as conclusive in that regard (Mustaine & Tewksbury, 1999). Mustaine and Tewksbury (1999) proposed that *stalking* is a criminal offense motivated by interpersonal hostility and aggressive behaviors stemming from power and control issues rather than from material gain or sexual obsession. *Cyber stalking*, similar to traditional offline stalking, is fueled by rage, power, control, and anger that may have been precipitated by a victim's actions or, in some cases, the victim's inactions. The research suggests that the number of cyber stalking incidents will continue to mount, in part, because the Internet provides a safe haven in which an offender can theoretically hide and conceal his or her identity behind a veil of anonymity (Bowker & Gray, 2004). With anonymity, an offender can literally pretend to be someone completely different, which is similar to an actor who conjures up a convincing persona to persuade the audience that the actor's guise is, in fact, genuine (Bowker & Gray, 2004). The anonymity of the Internet also affords the perpetrator an opportunity to contact virtually anyone with Internet access, at any time, with little fear of being identified and even less fear of being arrested and prosecuted under the current legal system in many jurisdictions (Bowker & Gray, 2004).

Online Cyber Stalking Versus Traditional Offline Stalking

To some extent, cyber stalking is fundamentally an extension of traditional stalking, in which the offender uses a hi-tech modus operandi to commit the crime (Petherick, 2007). With cyberstalking becoming a growing criminological concern in contemporary society, the offender's behaviors and actions need to be examined in greater depth (Desai & Jaishankar, 2007). Bocij (2005) was one of the very first researchers to study the prevalence and impact of cyber stalking. Cyber stalking behaviors are similar to traditional stalking behaviors in many respects; however, cyber stalking—at least from a criminological and legal perspective—represents an entirely new form of deviant criminal behavior (Bocij & McFarlane, 2002). For one, both offender types—traditional and online—resort to tactics and behaviors that are primarily intended to harass, and in some cases, threaten or intimidate the victim (Petrocelli, 2005). As mentioned previously, traditional stalkers and cyber stalkers frequently react aggressively when confronted, scorned, rejected, or belittled by a victim (Bocij, 2005). The research suggests that cyber stalkers are demographically more in line with the stereotypical white-collar criminal offender as opposed to the street-level criminal offender. The overwhelming majority of cyber stalker offenders are middle- to upper-class Caucasian men with stable employment and firmly established ties to the community (Bocij & McFarlane, 2002).

Conversely, the research literature also suggests that many cyber stalkers have a prior criminal record, a history of substance abuse, or a personality disorder that directly or partly contributes to, and increases the likelihood of, such antisocial behaviors (Hutton & Haantz, 2003; Reno, 1999). Although this may be true in some cases, there is very little conclusive evidence to support this claim in all cases (Mustaine & Tewksbury, 1999). The figures cited throughout this report are purely speculative on the basis of limited empirical evidence in that the actual numbers or percentages can never be known because most crimes, especially cyber stalking crimes, go unreported or undetected, thereby contributing to the so-called dark figure of crime. In addition, scientific information in relation to cyber stalking is still in its infancy and is, therefore, anecdotal. The evidence collected thus far suggests that the cyber offender suffers from a personality disorder that may range from an abnormally high level of paranoia to delusional behaviors and thoughts that can consume him or her (Mullen, Pathe, Purcell, & Stuart, 1999).

As repeatedly mentioned, many of the behaviors displayed by cyber stalkers resemble those of traditional stalkers; however, many notable differences clearly distinguish the former from the latter. One of the most striking similarities is that both offender types are motivated by an insatiable desire and need to have power, control, and influence over the victim (Reno, 1999). If left unattended, these actions could conceivably escalate to a potentially volatile physical confrontation between the offender and the victim, even though many, including those in law enforcement, perceive cyber stalking to be relatively harmless (Reno, 1999).

Traditional stalking behaviors are fairly predictable in that the offender often follows the victim home, to work, or even to school, thereby making it somewhat effortless for investigators to track, apprehend, arrest, and subsequently prosecute the offender. Further, many stalkers resort to leaving harassing written messages at the victim's home or place of employment, and, in some cases, the offender makes threatening phone calls that are intended to provoke fear and intimidation in the victim, all of which can often be traced back to the perpetrator with relative ease (Reno, 1999). As stated, the aforementioned crimes typically leave a physical trail of evidence behind that will undoubtedly be used to assemble a criminal case against the offender. Another noteworthy comparison between the stalker and the cyber stalker is the distinctively high probability that both offender types had a prior intimate relationship, whether real or perceived, with the victim; however the cyber stalker is more inclined to choose his or her victims at random (Bocij & McFarlane, 2003; Reno, 1999). According to Reno (1999), nearly 50% of all cyber stalking incidents involved complete strangers who were initially contacted in some perceivably innocent manner via the Internet.

In fact, there has been a considerable increase in the number of stranger cases, particularly with cyber stalkers; the Internet grants cyber stalkers access to a vast amount of personal information with relative ease (Reno, 1999). Information that was once considered private and confidential a few decades ago can easily be accessed through a variety of brokerage websites that cater specifically to individuals innocently searching for friends or loved ones (Reno, 1999). Some of these websites are free, but the large majority will charge a small service fee in exchange for a person's name, phone number, address, social security number, date of birth, and other confidential identifying information (Reno, 1999). The majority of these brokerage sites were established to help people find friends and loved ones of the past, but like anything else, these sites are subject to abuse by those who want to use the service for diabolical reasons.

For example, on July 29, 1999, 21-year old Liam Youens of New Hampshire contacted Docusearch, an Internet-based investigation and information service, and requested information—specifically, the date of birth of Amy Lynn Boyer, a 20-year old woman with whom Youens had been obsessed ever since the two attended high school together (Electronic Privacy Information Center, 2006). Shortly after receiving the date of birth for several Amy Boyers—none of whom was the Amy Lynn Boyer sought by Youens—Youens once again contacted Docusearch for a second time to request Boyer's social security number and employment information, for which Youens was charged merely $45 (Electronic Privacy Information Center, 2006).

On September 8, 1999, Docusearch managed to obtain Boyer's employment information and address by having a subcontractor, Michelle Gambino, place a "pretext" call to Boyer (Electronic Privacy Information Center, 2006). *Pretexting* is the practice of collecting information about a person using false pretenses in which the caller often claims to be someone "official" calling in regard to some proclaimed legitimate purpose (Electronic Privacy Information Center, 2006). In this particular case, Gambino "pretended" to be affiliated with Boyer's insurance company in order to obtain employment verification information concerning Boyer's workplace address—all of these activities were conducted under the false pretense of facilitating the delivery of a fictitious overpayment refund (Electronic Privacy Information Center, 2006). The investigation later revealed that Youens paid Docusearch $109 for this information. On October 15, 1999, Youens, armed with a handgun and a map to Boyer's place of employment, drove to the dentist's office in Nashua, New Hampshire, where Boyer worked and fatally shot her—11 times—as she left work before turning the gun on himself in a senseless act that was quickly ruled a murder–suicide (Spencer, 2000).

To make matters worse, the investigation into Boyer's murder discovered that Youens had constructed and maintained a website, titled "Amy Boyer," for nearly 2 years prior to the murder. The website contained explicit details of how he had stalked her for years, how he felt about her, and, more alarmingly, how he planned to kill her (Spencer, 2000). On the website, Youens explained that he had fallen in love with Boyer in the eighth grade, that she had rejected him in high school, and, in response to the rejection, that he had written a detailed chronicle of why and how she must die (Spencer, 2000). An excerpt from the website reads, "When she gets in [to work], I'll drive up to the car blocking her in, window to window, then I'll shoot her with my Glock," which is, tragically, the way it occurred on October 15, 1999 (Spencer, 2000). How could Youens' rambling messages regarding his intentions to kill Amy Boyer go unnoticed? The existing laws, as will be seen, are virtually meaningless when the cyber stalkers are across states lines, especially when threats are only implied.

In response to Boyer's death, her mother and stepfather (Helen and Tim Remsburg) filed a wrongful death suit against Docusearch and the investigators with whom the agency subcontracted to obtain Boyer's personal information (Electronic Privacy Information Center, 2006). The suit claimed an invasion of privacy through intrusion upon seclusion; invasion of privacy through commercial appropriation of private information; violation of the Fair Credit Reporting Act; and violation of the New Hampshire Consumer Protection Act (Electronic Privacy Information Center, 2006). The Electronic Privacy Information Center filed an amicus brief on behalf of the Remsburgs, arguing that Docusearch should be held liable under all of the aforementioned claims.

In addition to the people-search websites via Google and other popular search engines, the Internet is host to a number of sites that specifically promote retaliation and revenge, which is, in essence, a cyber stalker's dream (Bocij, 2005). For instance, cyber stalkers who wish to send anonymous letters or e-mails can do so through a website called "The Payback" (http://www.thepayback.com), a site that purposely conceals and protects the sender's name and personal information (Bocij, 2005). There are also a number of radical extremist sites, including "The Avenger's Page," a site that encourages visitors to seek revenge and, in some instances, incite violence (Bocij, 2005).

Case in point, a Pennsylvania State Trooper was arrested on March 13, 2006 for posting five nude photographs of his former wife on a bondage and sadomasochistic website, apparently in order to seek revenge for a failed marriage. According to Christine Pittaro (personal communication, May 14, 2007), the crime victim/witness advocate for the District Attorney's Office of Northampton County, Pennsylvania, Luke Heller had worked as a trooper for approximately 14 years until the date of his arrest. In addition to creating a profile in his wife's name and posting the nude photographs, Heller also posted his wife's occupation as a schoolteacher and date of birth on the bondage website (Pittaro, 2007). A forensic examination of Heller's laptop computer revealed that the laptop had been used to post 5 of the 18 nude photographs of his ex-wife that were taken when the two were initially married (Iannace, personal communication, May 11, 2007).

The forensic examination, which was performed by State Trooper Paul Iannace, determined that Heller—posing as his ex-wife—posted explicit messages on the website, soliciting viewers to contact her to engage in violent sexual acts (Iannace, personal communication, May 11, 2007). This particular cyber stalking offense was unearthed after one of the website's visitors decided to contact Heller's ex-wife at her place of employment (Iannace, personal communication, May 11, 2007). Heller subsequently pleaded guilty to harassment for placing the images on the bondage site and agreed to quit the

Pennsylvania State Police in light of the criminal charges lodged against him (Iannace, personal communication, May 11, 2007).

One obvious difference between traditional stalking and cyber stalking is the geographic proximity between the offender and the victim. In a traditional stalking case, the offender and victim often live or work within relatively close proximity of one another, whereas cyber stalkers could be harassing the victim from the house across the street, from a coffee shop in another state, or even from another country (Reno, 1999). One of the many advantages that cyber stalkers have over traditional stalkers is that these offenders typically have a high level of computer proficiency and aptitude—essential skills that allow the stalker to take crucial steps toward avoiding detection (Hutton & Haantz, 2003). As stated, the anonymity of the Internet allows the cyber stalker to easily conceal his or her identity through a variety of inexpensive and simple tactics. For instance, cyber stalkers can connect to several different Internet service providers (ISPs), thereby creating a number of screen names, which makes it nearly impossible to track the origin of the e-mails (Reno, 1999).

Because there is rarely any physical contact between the cyber stalker and the victim, most police officers minimize the seriousness of such harassment and simply dismiss the victim's fears as nuisance complaints (Reno, 1999). However, cyber stalking can be just as threatening and frightening as being followed and watched by a traditional stalker in one's neighborhood (Reno, 1999). Cyber stalking behaviors like those of sexual offenders such as the peeping Tom voyeur may simply be a prelude to other dangerous disturbed behaviors, some of which may end in violence (Bocij, 2005; Reno, 1999). The level of danger is elevated further if the offender has a criminal record, a history of substance abuse, or a psychological disorder, all of which predispose the offender to violence (Bocij, 2005).

Even though most stalkers act alone, the Internet has made it much easier for cyber stalkers to conspire and encourage third parties to harass victims in chat rooms, discussion boards, and within Internet public forums (Reno, 1999). In fact, researchers have coined the term *stalking by proxy* to describe the process in which cyber stalkers encourage others such as family members and friends to aid in harassing the victim (Bocij & McFarlane, 2003). Some cyber stalkers have even been known to hire private investigators to follow and report on the victim's daily activities and whereabouts (Bocij & McFarlane, 2003). Cyber stalkers also may use private investigators to obtain additional personal information on the victim that may not be readily available on the Internet, as in the case of Amy Lynn Boyer (Bocij & McFarlane, 2003).

The Internet as a Medium for Online Predatory Behavior

The Internet is particularly appealing to cyber stalkers and other online predators simply because many users are drawn to its relatively inexpensive cost, ease of use, and, as previously mentioned, anonymity in seeking out victims and avoiding detection (Reno, 1999). Cyber stalking behaviors are often misunderstood and confused with other online predatory behaviors, including those of sexual offenders who seek out children purely for sexual gratification (Dombrowski, LeMasney, Ahia, & Dickson, 2004).

As mentioned, not all cyber stalking incidents are motivated by sexual obsession. However, one cannot discount the fact that the Internet has become a virtual playground for sex offenders because it provides predators with easy access to literally tens of thousands of children and presents a completely new and unique way to groom a child from afar (Dombrowski et al., 2004). This is particularly frightening considering that nearly 30 million children have regular access to the Internet in the United States alone with little to no parental supervision (Dombrowski et al., 2004). Adolescents, in particular, tend to be the most vulnerable group in light of the group's collective sexual curiosity and continuous exploration with pornography websites (Dombrowski et al., 2004). A number of websites such as MySpace (http://www.myspace.com) allow adolescents to post and exchange personal and often sensitive information about one another. What these adolescents fail to recognize or accept is that this information is publicly accessible to anyone who visits the site, including those who prey upon children (Dombrowski et al., 2004). MySpace and other social networking websites have security measures in place, but there is no foolproof way to truly secure access to a potential smorgasbord of victims, given today's computer-savvy offenders.

Prevalence

As of February 2002, 54% of all Americans accessed the Internet on a regular, consistent basis, and more than half of all households in the United States had contracted with an ISP at home (Schneider, 2003). In the United States alone, more than 80 million adults and 10 million children have access to the Internet, whether it be at home, work, school, or one of the many emerging wireless provider locations (Reno, 1999). As with any crime, there is no practical, truly scientific way of predicting with 100% accuracy the prevalence of cyber stalking in the United States (Reno, 1999). It is surprising that criminologists and other researchers have only recently begun to gather information on cyber stalking behaviors, trends, and patterns (Reno, 1999). Nevertheless, the most recent findings have unveiled some fascinating information, but these findings should be approached with a degree of caution because the information has been compiled and evaluated only on a relatively small scale (Reno, 1999). The anecdotal evidence presented thus far suggests that cyber stalking is a serious societal problem that warrants further review and attention, particularly because cyber stalking—by all measurable accounts—is on the rise (Reno, 1999).

For the purpose of gaining a true understanding and practical insight into the extent of cyber stalking, it would be best to study the behaviors associated with traditional stalking offenders, considering that many of those same behaviors overlap with those of cyber stalkers (Reno, 1999). Because California leads the nation in the number of cyber stalking cases, it would be best for researchers to make California the focal point for future research (Reno, 1999). This approach would be similar to that used by sociologists in the 1920s, who were interested in studying the relationship between immigration demographics and Chicago's rising crime rates, a movement that eventually led to the birth of the Chicago School of Criminology (Barkan, 2006). What makes California so unique? There must be a logical reason to explain why the majority of cyber stalkers emanate from California, and it needs to be explored.

E-Mail as a Means of Harassment

Research findings strongly suggest that cyber stalkers use e-mail as the primary means of harassing and threatening victims, far more than any other electronic communication device (Petrocelli, 2005). E-mail allows an offender to repeatedly transmit harassing, threatening, hateful, or obscene messages, including pictures, videos, or audio (Petrocelli, 2005). In rare instances, cyber stalkers were known to purposely transmit electronic files that contained a hidden computer virus, which was intended to damage the victim's electronic files and spread the virus to others in the victim's address book (Hutton & Haantz, 2003). In some cases, cyber stalkers use the victim's e-mail address and other personal information to subscribe to or purchase books, magazines, or other Internet services without the victim's knowledge or consent (Hutton & Haantz, 2003).

As such, it appears that revenge and retaliation are the key components of cyber stalking (Hutton & Haantz, 2003). As noted, cyber stalkers have been known to send the victim's private information to websites that cater specifically to pornography in the hopes that the site will continuously inundate the victim with obscene e-mail messages and pop-ups, as noted in the Heller case that was mentioned earlier in this report (Hutton & Haantz, 2003). A clever cyber stalker will frequently use computer programs that are specifically designed to repeatedly send enormous amounts of explicit e-mails at regular or random intervals (Reno, 1999). Moreover, this offender is also likely to use anonymous re-mailers that make it virtually impossible for ISPs, law enforcement, or victims to trace the e-mails' point of origin (Reno, 1999).

According to Ogilvie (2000), cyber stalking patterns often replicate those of traditional stalking behaviors in that the intent is often to establish a relationship or mend a previously established relationship, whether real or perceived. The introduction of spyware has enabled cyber stalkers to purchase inexpensive software that was created specifically to notify the perpetrator whenever the victim is online (Petrocelli, 2005). All the cyber stalker needs, in most cases, is the victim's screen name (Petrocelli, 2005). The victim could conceivably block such messages, but it is highly likely that the computer-savvy cyber stalker will eventually find a way around the block. Victims are then forced to change ISPs or create another screen name.

Cyber stalkers often enter discussion boards, chat rooms, and the like, for attention or merely for companionship (Stephens, 1995). Once contact has been initiated, the cyber stalker continues to befriend the victim. In many cases, the cyber stalker perceives that a "relationship" exists when one does not. In other words, the cyber stalker truly believes that a relationship exists, even though the victim may have innocently responded to an offender's question in a chat room or discussion board (Stephens, 1995). However, if the offender believes that the relationship has been jeopardized in any way, the cyber stalker may launch into a full-fledged campaign to ruin the victim's reputation, financial credit, or personal identity (Stephens, 1995).

Discussion forums are typically sites on which Internet users post opinions and comments on one or more subjects. However, discussion boards can also be a place for cyber stalkers to post harmful, negative personal information about the victim, including the victim's name, address, phone number, e-mail address, and other private information (Petrocelli, 2005). The term *cybersmearing* is used to refer to the posting of embarrassing or humiliating rumors about the victim in a chat room, newsgroup, or bulletin board (Bocij & McFarlane, 2003). The most common form of cybersmearing is the posting of false sexual innuendos about the victim (Petrocelli, 2005). This online verbal abuse can also take the form of chat harassment or what is commonly referred to in the cyber world as *flaming*, in which the victim is belittled or demeaned in a live public forum (The National Center for Victims of Crime, 2004).

Typology and Etiology of Cyber Stalking and Victims

Typology of Cyber Stalkers

McFarlane and Bocij (2005) conducted one of the most exhaustive studies on cyber stalkers and stalking victims. Four distinct types of cyber stalkers emerged from the data. There have been other studies, but in my opinion, these other studies pale in comparison to this particular study. According to McFarlane and Bocij, the four types include the *vindictive cyber stalker*, the *composed cyber stalker*, the *intimate cyber stalker*, and the *collective cyber stalker* (McFarlane & Bocij, 2005).

According to McFarlane and Bocij (2005), the *vindictive cyber stalker* is one that is particularly malicious. It was found that offenders in this group threatened and harassed victims far more often than did offenders in the other three groups (McFarlane & Bocij, 2005). Offenders in this group were more likely to use a number of spiteful tactics intended to continuously harass victims through excessive spamming, e-mail bombing, and identity theft (McFarlane & Bocij, 2005). Vindictive cyber stalkers were the only group of the four to purposely use *trojans* to access the victim's computer and deliberately infect the computer with a destructive virus (McFarlane & Bocij, 2005). The group members' computer skills and proficiency ranged from medium to high, and there was some indication that mental illness was present on the basis of the bizarre, disturbing content that was often transmitted to victims (McFarlane & Bocij, 2005). I would place Liam Youens in this particular category based on Youens' bizarre behaviors, obsession with stalking, and eventual murdering of Amy Lynn Boyer.

The *composed cyber stalker* targets victims in a calm, poised, and unruffled manner (McFarlane & Bocij, 2005). The primary purpose of the harassment is to cause constant distress to the victim through a variety of threatening behaviors (McFarlane & Bocij, 2005). I would place former State Trooper Luke Heller in this particular category, mostly on the basis of media reports detailing the crime and interviews with those intimately familiar with the case.

The primary objective of the *intimate cyber stalker* is to establish a relationship with an intended target on the basis of infatuation and obsession (McFarlane & Bocij, 2005). The members of this group were the most diverse, in that some were once personally involved with the victim while others were simply infatuated with a targeted individual (McFarlane & Bocij, 2005).

Collective cyber stalkers, as the name implies, consist of two or more individuals who pursue the same victim (McFarlane & Bocij, 2005). This group's computer skills are exceptionally high when compared with those of the other three cyber stalker types (McFarlane & Bocij, 2005).

Etiology of Stalking

Possible Psychological Explanation

As mentioned earlier, one commonly held myth is that cyber stalkers commit such crimes because of some type of mental abnormality (Bocij & McFarlane, 2003). Granted, most of the literature findings to date suggest that this may be true; however, some of the studies—with the exception of those pertaining to Bocij and McFarlane (2003)—suggest that stalkers suffer from *de Clerambault's syndrome*, an erotomanic type of delusional disorder that is formally identified and defined in the *Diagnostic and Statistical Manual of Mental Disorders* (DSM-IV, 4th ed.) (American Psychiatric Association, 1994;

Dressing, Henn, & Gass, 2002). This syndrome is used to explain the obsessive and compulsive behaviors of those individuals who truly believe they are in an intimate relationship with the victim (Dressing, Henn, & Gass, 2002). Other studies suggest that stalking is not the result of a mental disorder but, rather, a behavioral disorder that stems from various psychopathological conditions, including paranoid and delusional disorders (Dressing, Henn, & Gass, 2002). However, this is not always the case with cyber stalkers. Cyber stalkers tend to be emotionally distant loners who simply want to seek the attention and companionship of another (Hutton & Haantz, 2003). The problem lies in the fact that these individuals often become obsessed or infatuated with the victim, but the victim does not reciprocate those same feelings and perceptions about the relationship (Hutton & Haantz, 2003).

Social Learning Theory

What is known is that both online and offline stalkers are driven by an underlying desire to exert some type of power and control over the targeted victim (Reno, 1999). If cyber stalking were to be approached from a behaviorist's perspective, the starting point would be citing the early research of B. F. Skinner (1953), who drew from the psychological research concerning classical and operant conditioning (Barkan, 2006). In *classical conditioning*, the frequency of an exhibited behavior is often contingent upon the amount of external positive reinforcement received (Barkan, 2006). In *operant conditioning*, certain behaviors are often repeated when rewarded and, therefore, are positively reinforced (Barkan, 2006). If the same behavior is met with a negative response, the behavior is likely to diminish because a reward is not present (Barkan, 2006). If a stalker makes contact with the victim and that victim engages in a discussion, whether positive or negative, the stalker is likely to repeat the action. Therefore, it may be best to ignore the stalker rather than offer a negative response. Exhibitionists often display similar behaviors. Exposing one's genitals to an innocent victim is likely to elicit a response—albeit a shocked one. Even though the response is typically negative, the behavior is still reinforced and, therefore, is sought in all subsequent incidents.

Rational Choice Theory

Rational choice theory suggests that individuals—who, in this case, would be cyber stalkers—freely choose to commit a crime after weighing the prospective rewards against the potential risks (Barkan, 2006). Rational choice theory can be integrated with *routine activities theory*, which assumes that individuals will commit a crime if there is a motivated offender, a suitable target, and the absence of guardians capable of preventing the offense from being successfully committed (Barkan, 2006; Mustaine & Tewksbury, 1999). In other words, the cyber stalker, as a motivated offender, will seek out and stalk a victim (a "suitable target") in the absence of capable guardianship, which, in this situation, is through the anonymity of the Internet, which provides protection against detection. According to Mustaine and Tewksbury (1999), women may be suitable targets because cyber stalking victimization is not yet taken seriously by society nor has it received the attention it deserves from the criminal justice system. Stalking via the Internet allows the offender to stalk at a relatively remote distance, yet the offense can still inflict the same type of fear and harassment in the victim, as if the victim were in a direct, face-to-face encounter with an offender.

Because rational choice theory assumes that cyber stalkers will calculate the risks before committing a crime, it also assumes that such behaviors could be deterred if the risks were certain and the punishment were severe (Barkan, 2006). At the present time, there is no true deterrent against such behaviors. The risk of detection is low, and even if the cyber stalker's identity is revealed, the threat of being arrested, prosecuted, and found guilty of such crimes is exceptionally low, thereby making cyber stalking a relatively safe and attractive crime to commit. Based on what has been presented, it appears that routine activities theory, at least as an outgrowth of rational choice theory, can have a significant amount of explanatory potential in future criminological studies.

Treatment

Rosenfeld (2003) was the first researcher to conduct an empirical study on the relationship between stalkers and recidivism. The findings, although limited to traditional stalkers, determined that roughly 50% of those studied reoffended. The strongest predictors of recidivism include the presence of a personality disorder, particularly one that involves antisocial, borderline, or narcissistic behaviors, which are collectively referred to as *Cluster B personality disorders* (Rosenfeld, 2003). The combination of a personality disorder and a history of substance abuse further increased the risk of reoffending (Rosenfeld, 2003). This is consistent with the findings associated with other criminal offender groups. Based on experience, those offenders with a history of mental illness and substance abuse have a higher than normal probability of reoffending.

Unfortunately, there are several obstacles to treating this disorder. First, finding a qualified mental health professional who acknowledges this condition and specializes in this type of treatment may be a cumbersome task to accomplish (King, 1996). The literature on cyber stalking is scarce at best, and the studies that have been done were based on comparatively small sample populations. From what has been researched, it is doubtful that mental health professionals have even a general understanding of cyber stalking behaviors and are less likely to know how to approach and treat this particular offender. The Internet is one of the most resourceful advancements in technology to have ever been created by humankind, but it also has a malevolent side to it that cannot be discounted. Clinicians have only recently begun to understand the dangers associated with the Internet.

Cyber Stalking Victims

Like most traditional crimes, cyber stalking knows no boundaries. Anyone can become a stalking victim, whether it is random or predicated on poor judgment when one releases personal information on the Internet. Even though most of the evidence is anecdotal, it strongly suggests that the majority of cyber stalkers are men and the majority of victims are women; however, there have been several highly publicized cases of females stalking men and same-sex stalking (Reno, 1999). Unlike male stalkers, female stalkers are more inclined to stalk and harass ex-partners and are less likely to stalk strangers (Purcell, Pathe, & Mullen, 2001). Female stalkers also are more likely to target other females in the hopes of establishing an intimate relationship with the victim (Purcell et al., 2001). According to Purcell and colleagues (2001), female stalkers are very similar to male stalkers in regard to demographic profiles and psychiatric status; however, male stalkers are more likely to have a history of criminal offense or substance abuse (Purcell et al., 2001).

As noted, virtually anyone can become a victim, but certain demographic groups are more at risk than others, such as women, juveniles, newcomers to the Internet, and other particularly vulnerable groups (Hutton & Haantz, 2003). In a 2002 study conducted by the online victim advocacy group known as Working to Halt Online Abuse (WHOA, 2003), 71% of cyber stalking victims were women, and 59% of that group had some type of previous relationship with the stalker (Hutton & Haantz, 2003). A prior relationship, whether real or perceived, seems to be the catalyst for cyber stalking, particularly when the victim attempts to end the relationship (Reno, 1999).

A 2001 research study concluded that 61% of cyber stalking victims were Caucasian, 3.9% were Asian, and 1.6% were African American (McFarlane & Bocij, 2003). These findings should be approached with a degree of caution because the survey data were confined to the United States and consisted of only a minimal number of respondents (McFarlane & Bocij, 2003). However, several follow-up studies have revealed similar findings in that the majority of victims were Caucasian women between the ages of 18 and 30 years (McFarlane & Bocij, 2003).

Nearly four out of five victims are female, and female individuals are eight times as likely to be the stalking victims of ex-partners or acquaintances (Hutton & Haantz, 2003). Because of the different levels of online harassment, some victims may not report the harassment to law enforcement for one reason or another (Hutton & Haantz, 2003). It has been speculated that the majority of cyber stalking victims do not report being victimized for one of two reasons. First, the victim may feel that the behavior is not serious enough to warrant the attention of the police. Second, the victim does not believe that law enforcement will take the matter seriously (Reno, 1999). It is unfortunate that when a victim does report a cyber stalking incident to law enforcement, many law enforcement agencies simply advise the victim to come back if the perpetrator confronts them or makes a threatening statement offline (Reno, 1999). As of this writing, there are only a small number of online victim advocacy groups available to assist, support, and advise cyber stalking victims (Pittaro, personal communication, May 14, 2007).

In response to being stalked, some cyber stalking victims may experience abrupt changes in sleeping and eating patterns, nightmares, hypervigilance, anxiety, helplessness, and fear for his or her safety (The National Center for Victims of Crime, 2004). *Hypervigilance* is often associated with post-traumatic stress disorder (PTSD) whereby the victim, when in a state of fear, lashes out inappropriately through aggressive and, at times, violent behavior (Bocij, 2005).

Very rarely do brief episodes of stalking cause distress in the victim; however, there have been a number of stalking incidents that have extended for weeks, months, or even years (Mullen, 2003). The frequency of such communication greatly increases the risk of a potential physical assault (Mullen, 2003). Victimization also may lead to vandalism—but not necessarily vandalism in the traditional sense of the term. *Vandalism* is typically associated with traditional stalking but can also take place in cyberspace. For instance, an offender may use vandalism to damage the victim's personal computer data with the assistance of a computer virus or a trojan horse program, as mentioned earlier (Bocij & McFarlane, 2003). There are a number of Internet websites that will happily provide interested parties with information on a victim (Reno, 1999).

Legal and Social Issues of Cyber Stalking

Unique Challenges for Law Enforcement

According to Petrocelli (2005), cyber stalking crimes present a unique challenge to law enforcement, particularly to those departments that lack the expertise or resources to investigate and prosecute cyber stalkers. Local law enforcement is at a particular disadvantage as result of jurisdictional limitations (Petrocelli, 2005). For example, a stalker may be in another city, county, state, or even country, thereby making it difficult if not entirely impossible for law enforcement to investigate and prosecute the offender (Petrocelli, 2005). The anonymity of the Internet also places the cyber stalker in a truly advantageous position over law enforcement investigators (Reno, 1999). Petrocelli (2005) claims that some victims went to the police for help but were ill advised, with the police telling them to simply turn the computer off and the harassment would stop. Clearly, this is an inappropriate response and is quite unrealistic, considering that most individuals have come to rely on the Internet, both professionally and personally. Thankfully, some of the larger metropolitan police departments such as Los Angeles and New York City have created units that deal specifically with computer-related crimes (Petrocelli, 2005). In response to the growing number of cyber stalking cases, the Federal Bureau of Investigation (FBI) has created a number of computer crime squads, in which agents are schooled and experienced in cyber stalking investigations (Petrocelli, 2005). The FBI has, in turn, offered to assist local and state law enforcement in tracking and prosecuting cyber stalkers (Petrocelli, 2005).

Most cyber stalkers have turned to cable service providers as the preferred ISP because the Internet connection speeds are far faster and reliable than the antiquated dial-up connections (Reno, 1999). One apparent obstacle in investigating an alleged cyber stalking incident is that the Cable Communications Policy Act of 1984 requires law enforcement agencies to obtain a court order if requesting personal information on a cable subscriber (Reno, 1999). To complicate matters further, the cable company is required to notify the suspect, in advance, that law enforcement officials have requested an inquiry into the suspect's records (Reno, 1999). The warning could conceivably jeopardize the entire investigation if a suspect attempts to destroy all evidence that is even remotely connected to the alleged cyber stalking incident.

Regrettably, there are a number of websites that allow users to set up free e-mail accounts with little personal information. Even though the site requires the individual to list identifying information, it rarely authenticates that the personal information provided is accurate, thereby hindering law enforcement efforts further (Reno, 1999). Moreover, a number of e-mail servers will purposefully remove identifying data for a small fee, making it extremely difficult for law enforcement to trace the account (Reno, 1999). Many cyber stalkers who subscribe to such a service will pay with either a money order or some other nontraceable form of payment to avoid detection (Reno, 1999).

Antistalking Legislation in the United States

To date, all 50 states and the District of Columbia have adopted criminal stalking statutes (Reno, 1999). As of 2010, 47 states have enacted cyber stalking laws within existing stalking or harassment laws (National Conference of State Legislatures, 2010). According to Reno (1999), Title 18 U.S.C. 875(c) makes it a federal crime to transmit any interstate or foreign commerce containing a threat that is intended to injure another person. The penalty for violating the law is a prison sentence punishable up to 5 years and may include a fine of up to $250,000 (Reno, 1999). One glaring problem with the federal law is that the communication must specifically include a direct rather than implicit threat to harm another. Cyber stalking communication does not always include a specific message in which the perpetrator threatens to harm the victim.

The basic foundation of criminal law requires the following two elements to be present for a crime to have been committed: *actus reus* and *mens rea* (Dennison & Thomson, 2002). *Actus reus*, or the "act," requires that certain behaviors take place; *mens rea*, or the "guilty mind," requires that the offender intended to cause harm. A third element requires that there be a victim. Establishing *actus reus* is not as difficult as establishing *mens rea*, whereby the state (prosecution) must prove that the perpetrator intended to cause harm (Dennison & Thomson, 2002). Dennison and Thomson (2002) found that it was easier to prove intent in ex-intimate relationships than it was in stranger or acquaintance cases.

In certain situations, cyber stalking may be prosecuted under 47 U.S.C. 223, a federal statute that makes it a crime to use a telephone or any other communication device to harass or threaten any person (Reno, 1999). The statute is somewhat easier to apply to cyber stalking cases because, unlike Title 18 U.S.C. 875(c), it includes both harassment and threats (Reno, 1999). Fortunately, *harassment* is such a vague term that it includes virtually any behavior that may be interpreted as a nuisance. Even though it does not mention cyber stalking specifically by name, the Interstate Stalking Act of 1996 makes it a crime for anyone to travel from one state to another with the intent to injure or harass that person (Reno, 1999). The problem with enforcing this law lies in the language used in the legislation, which states that the offender must physically travel across the state line; clearly, this rules out most cases of Internet harassment (Reno, 1999). In addition to other statutes cited here, The Violence Against Women Act of 2000 made cyber stalking part of the federal interstate stalking statute and, thus, a federal crime (The National Center for Victims of Crime, 2004).

Cyber Stalking State Statutes

According to Reno (1999), the first traditional stalking law was enacted slightly more than a decade ago in 1990, when California passed a law making stalking a criminal offense. As in the federal laws that have been cited in this report, most traditional stalking laws require that the perpetrator make a direct threat to injure or, in some way, harm the victim or victims (Reno, 1999). However, some state laws will prosecute an offender if the behavior or conduct displayed constitutes an implied threat (Reno, 1999). Because most state laws require a direct threat of harm to the victim, many perpetrators can avoid arrest and prosecution in the absence of a direct threat. In other words, the harassment can continue as long as the stalker does not directly threaten the victim or the victim's family with bodily injury, which appears to be the case in the Heller example cited earlier (Reno, 1999). In addition to criminal sanctions, some states allow the victim to file a civil suit against the harasser for injuries, including defamation, slander, pain and suffering, or lost income (Hutton & Haantz, 2003).

Societal Intervention and Prevention

Law enforcement officials have suggested that to prevent becoming a victim, people should choose gender- and age-ambiguous screen names and, if possible, avoid posting personal information in web profiles (Petrocelli, 2005). Most importantly, people should be extremely cautious when meeting with an individual that he or she met online. Petrocelli (2005) suggests that if a meeting is to take place, it should be done in a public location, and it is strongly advisable to bring a friend along. Cyber stalking victims should always inform the perpetrator that the communication is unwanted and request that it cease immediately (Petrocelli 2005); this act aids later in the investigation of cyber stalking, should the victim ever pursue a legal case against the offender. It is also advisable to save all unaltered and unedited communication from the perpetrator that could be used as prosecutorial evidence (Petrocelli, 2005). Establishing a pattern of harassment is paramount to the investigation and success of prosecution (Hutton & Haantz, 2005).

Victims can also purchase software to block, squelch, or ignore unwanted electronic communication; to do so, they should contact their ISP, considering most ISPs have established policies in the online agreement prohibiting such abuse of services (Hutton & Haantz, 2003). The ISP can immediately terminate the offender's service for violating this policy without fear of legal recourse by the offender (Hutton & Haantz, 2003). However, the reality of the situation is that most ISPs have concentrated more on helping their customers avoid spam, unwanted pop-ups, and virus protection rather than protecting customers against online harassment (Hutton & Haantz, 2003). The problem lies in the fact that complaint procedures are often hard to locate and somewhat vague, resulting in inadequate follow-up on such complaints (Reno, 1999). Victims also may consult one of the many victim advocacy groups such as WHOA (http://haltabuse.org) or CyberAngels (http://www.cyberangels.org) for assistance, support, and advice on cyber stalking (Petrocelli, 2005). According to McFarlane and Bocij (2003), CyberAngels is arguably the best-known Internet safety agency and one of the largest victim advocacy groups in the world.

Discussion and Conclusion

The literature on cyber stalking is still in its infancy; however, the incidence of cyber stalking is expected to increase as the Internet becomes even more popular than it is today, especially among society's youth (Hutton & Haantz, 2003). Simply stated, much of modern life cannot be performed as effectively without continuous access to the World Wide Web (Hutton & Haantz, 2003). Even though law enforcement is faced with a series of obstacles, there is hope. Law enforcement at the federal, state, and local levels must unite, share, and disseminate intelligence information. With proper training and guidance, law enforcement investigators can often trace, with some accuracy, an electronic trail that has been left behind by the cyber stalker (Reno, 1999). Metaphorically speaking, leaving an electronic trail is the equivalent of a burglar who leaves behind a fingerprint at the crime scene (Reno, 1999). With a little work, the electronic trail can often be traced back to its initial point of origin.

In the interim, law enforcement can resort to investigative strategies and tactics that have proven to be effective in traditional stalking situations (Reno, 1999). Former Attorney General Janet Reno suggested that law enforcement refer to an annual report generated by the Attorney General's Office to Congress titled *Stalking and Domestic Violence* (Reno, 1999) for additional insight into stalking behaviors. Additionally, it is strongly suggested that law enforcement form a cooperative partnership with ISPs, considering both are ultimately working toward the same goal—eradicating online harassment.

Still, not all the law enforcement training and support in the world can replace good old-fashioned education by informing citizens of the dangers associated with the Internet. Unfortunately, online harassment is only one of the many detrimental components to the Internet. Reno (1999) recommended that states review existing stalking statutes to include a section on cyber stalking. Pennsylvania is one of a handful of states that does not have a separate statute or subsection to address cyber stalking, therefore making it incredibly difficult to prosecute such offenses.

Contrary to critics of cyber stalking literature, cyber stalking is a growing problem that transcends international boundaries (Bocij & McFarlane, 2002). Granted, the inaccuracies stem from the media's false depiction of cyber stalking as a problem of epidemic proportion (Bocij & McFarlane, 2002). However, the number of cases is increasing and is expected to continue rising over the next decade (Bocij & McFarlane, 2002). In other words, the attention that cyber stalking has recently received is warranted and genuine—and is worthy of further criminological research (Bocij & McFarlane, 2002).

References

American Psychiatric Association. (1994). *Diagnostic and statistical manual of mental disorders* (4th ed.). Washington, DC: Author.

Barkan, S. (2006). *Criminology: A sociological understanding* (3rd ed.). Upper Saddle River, NJ: Prentice Hall.

Bocij, P. (2005). Reactive stalking: A new perspective on victimization. *The British Journal of Forensic Practice, 7,* 23–45.

Bocij, P., & McFarlane, L. (2002). Cyber stalking: Genuine problem or public hysteria? *Prison Services Journal, 140,* 32–35.

Bocij, P., & McFarlane, L. (2003). Seven fallacies about cyber stalking. *Prison Service Journal, 149,* 37–42.

Bowker, A., & Gray, M. (2004). An introduction to the supervision of the cybersex offender. *Federal Probation, 68*(3), 3–9.

Dennison, S. M., & Thomson, D. M. (2002). Identifying stalking: The relevance of intent in commonsense reasoning. *Law and Human Behavior, 26,* 543–558.

Desai, M., & Jaishankar, K. (2007, February). *Cyber stalking victimization of girl students: An empirical study.* Paper presented at the 2nd International and 6th Biennial Conference of the Indian Society of Victimology, Chennai, India.

Dombrowski, S. C., LeMasney, J. W., Ahia, E. C., & Dickson S. A. (2004). Protecting children from online sexual predators: Technological, psychoeducational, and legal considerations. *Professional Psychology, 35,* 65–73.

Dressing, H., Henn, F. A., & Gass, P. (2002). Stalking behavior: An overview of the problem and a case report of male-to-male stalking during delusional disorder. *Psychopathology, 35,* 313–319.

Electronic Privacy Information Center. (2006, June 15). *The Amy Boyer case.* Retrieved from http://www.epic.org/privacy/boyer

Hutton, S., & Haantz, S. (2003). *Cyber stalking.* Retrieved from http://www.nw3c.org

Jaishankar, K., & Uma Sankary, V. (2005). Cyber stalking: A global menace in the information super highway. *ERCES Online Quarterly Review, 2*(3). Retrieved from http://www.erces.com/journal/articles/archives/volume2/v03/v02.htm

King, S. A. (1996). *Is the Internet addictive, or are addicts using the Internet?* Retrieved from http://webpages.charter.net/stormking/iad.html

McFarlane, L., & Bocij, P. (2003). Cyber stalking: Defining the invasion of cyberspace. *Forensic Update, 1*(72), 18–22.

McFarlane, L., & Bocij, P. (2005). An exploration of predatory behaviour in cyberspace: Towards a typology of cyber stalkers. *First Monday, 8.* Retrieved from http://firstmonday.org

Mullen, P. E. (2003). Multiple classifications of stalkers and stalking behavior available to clinicians. *Psychiatric Annals, 33,* 650–656.

Mullen, P. E., Pathe M., Purcell R., & Stuart, G. W. (1999). Study of stalkers. *The American Journal of Psychiatry, 156,* 1244–1250.

Mustaine, E. E., & Tewksbury, R. (1999). A routine activity theory explanation for women's stalking victimizations. *Violence Against Women, 5*(1), 43–62.

National Conference of State Legislatures. (2001, February). *Public Internet/private lives.* Retrieved from http://www.ncsl.org/programs/pubs/201net.htm

National Conference of State Legislatures. (2010). *State computer harassment or "cyber stalking" laws.* Retrieved from http://www.ncsl.org/IssuesResearch/ TelecommunicationsInformationTechnology/CyberstalkingLaws/tabid/13495/ Default.aspx

Ogilvie, E. (2000). *Cyber stalking.* Retrieved from http://www.aic.gov.au/documents/ 4/7/A/%7B47A7FA60-8EBF-498A-BB9E-D61BC512C053%7Dti166.pdf

Petherick, W. (2007). *Cyber stalking.* Retrieved from http://www.trutv.com/library/ crime/criminal_mind/psychology/cyberstalking/1.html

Petrocelli, J. (2005). Cyber stalking. *Law & Order, 53*(12), 56–58.

Purcell, R., Pathe, M., & Mullen P. E. (2001). A study of women who stalk. *The American Journal of Psychiatry, 158,* 2056–2061.

Reno, J. (1999). *1999 report on cyber stalking: A new challenge for law enforcement and industry.* Retrieved from http://www.usdoj.gov/criminal/cybercrime/ cyberstalking.htm

Rosenfeld, B. (2003). Recidivism in stalking and obsessional harassment. *Law and Human Behavior, 27,* 251–265.

Schneider, J. P. (2003). The impact of compulsive cybersex behaviours on the family. *Sexual and Relationship Therapy, 18,* 1468–1479.

Skinner, B. F. (1953). *Science and human behavior.* New York, NY: Macmillan.

Spencer, S. (2000, March 23). *An online tragedy.* Retrieved from http://www.cbsnews. com

Stephens, G. (1995). Crime in cyberspace. *The Futurist, 29*(5), 24–29.

The National Center for Victims of Crime. (2004). *Cyber stalking.* Retrieved from http://www.ncvc.org/ncvc/main.aspx?dbName=DocumentViewer&Document ID=32458

Working to Halt Online Abuse (WHOA). (2003). *Top six locations of harassers.* Retrieved from http://www.haltabuse.org

Online Social Networking and Women Victims[1]

17

DEBARATI HALDER
K. JAISHANKAR

Contents

[1] This chapter was originally published as an article in *Temida Journal*. Reference as follows: Halder, D., & Jaishankar, K. (2009). Cyber socializing and victimization of women. *Temida—The Journal on Victimization, Human Rights and Gender, 12*(3), 5–26. The authors sincerely thank Vesna Nikolić-Ristanović, editor-in-chief of *Temida*, for providing permission to reprint this article.

Introduction

Socialization through social networking websites (SNWs) has become a favorite hobby for "gizmo freaks"[2] who are self-supporting, educated, independent, modern women of the 21st century. Social networking websites help users make new virtual friends and offer the promise to reconnect with old friends and relatives. Most women who use this new method of socialization see it as a stress reliever. Cyber socializing through SNWs help women users to share with like-minded friends their emotional needs, personal problems, culinary skills, and tips for child care and health care, including pregnancy and post pregnancy issues. These women users discuss these "needs," tips, and even their "mood swings" with their virtual friends who become "emotional comfort zones" for them either by writing on walls of some group/community forums or on the walls of their friends' profiles. Fraim (2006) defines *cyber socialization* as the "computerized interaction with known or unknown individuals for the purpose of research, entertainment, establishment of friendships or relationships due to feelings of loneliness, and sexual gratification" (p. 3). Internet socializing is "electronic interaction" (Fraim, 2006) with virtual friends through chat rooms, e-mails, forums (created by domain hosts such as Google, Yahoo, etc.), and SNWs.

Even though SNWs have opened a wide window for socializing, they have also opened the flood gates for various crimes against women in cyberspace. It is unfortunate that even though European Union (EU) conventions on cyber crimes established strict rules to control content-related offences, child pornography and identity theft–related offenses for securing e-commerce have proliferated.

The authors of the EU conventions, as well as the world leaders who are parties to the EU conventions, never considered victimization of women in cyberspace to be as big an issue as other crimes such as child pornography or hacking. Therefore, women victims remained as a secondary concern for all developed cyber-savvy nations. This lacuna is clearly evident in the growing number of criminal incidents targeting women on SNWs. Ongoing psychological and legal research on perilous cyber behavior and its after effects established that SNWs raise more dangers than do traditional Internet chat rooms (Clemmitt, 2006), which literally gives women a "chilling effect" (Citron, 2009, p. 378). These crimes do not limit themselves only to traditional cyber crimes such as hacking, pornography, stalking, or hate crimes. They can evolve into various traditional yet new forms of cyber crimes against women, which await a more involved study.

---

[2] A person who loves to use many contemporary gadgets such as computers, iPods, mobile phones, and so forth.

In this chapter, we discuss the victimizing effect of a typical segment of Web 2.0—namely, SNWs—on women netizens.[3] This chapter is limited to the victimization of women on cyber SNWs and does not cover victimization in other cyber socializing tools such as e-mails, blogs, online chatting, and so forth—even though we agree that victimization on SNWs also leads to victimization in other cyber socializing components.

The chapter is presented in four parts. In the first part, we discuss cyber socializing, the growth of hi-tech crimes targeting women members of SNWs, and the need for conceptualizing such offenses. In the second part, we establish the typology and pattern of victimization of women who use SNWs. In the third part, we discuss the emotional and physical risk factors of women who use SNWs. In the fourth part, we establish reasons for the victimization of women who use SNWs and the growth of such victimization.

Cyber Socializing and the Growth of Hi-Tech Crimes

The concept of *cyber socializing* dates back to the mid-1970s, when e-mail was invented. Even though it was mainly used for scientific and academic interactions (Clemmitt, 2006), usage of e-mail and Internet communications for commercial interactions and personal conversations as well as chatting gained tremendous popularity by the 1990s. The traditional Internet chat rooms can be divided into two categories: (a) chat rooms for normal interactions and (b) chat rooms used solely for sexual purposes, in which users can log on and enjoy either a "sex chat" (i.e., with a single partner) or a "group sex chat" (i.e., with more than two users). Some chat rooms also show pornographic pictures. However, these chat rooms never reveal an individual's private information publicly. Early on, these sex chats attracted teens and young adults, but soon they started to lose their appeal (Clemmitt, 2006).

Adult Internet use as a sexual as well as nonsexual form of entertainment (Morahan-Martin, 2000) started getting popularity challenges from the SNWs, on which communication became more transparent. On SNWs, users can create their own "profiles," providing their names, residences, schooling and college information, and likes and dislikes to find new friends or to relocate long-lost friends. These SNWs were able to attract teen girls as well as women because they felt that the danger of unknown sexual predators or problems of privacy was less significant on these SNWs. But, mostly, they

[3] The term *netizens* was coined by Michael Hauben. "A Netizen is a person who is, literally, a citizen of the internet. They are people who enjoy the freedoms of using the web (and all other related systems such as newsgroups, email and so on) and understand that it provides a whole new level of communication ability" (http://www.netizens.ws).

remained oblivious of the fact that their identities could be used maliciously (Clemmitt, 2006), thus making them potential victims for online sexual assault, stalking, identity theft (Finn & Banach, 2000), cyber gender harassment (Citron, 2009), Internet infidelity (Whitty, 2005), and even domestic violence by a suspicious spouse or even ex-spouse. Popularity of social networking reached its highest peak with the ushering-in of the new millennium in 2000. Simultaneously, at this time, the United States saw a severe clash of wills involving the fundamental freedoms of speech and expression. The United States also saw the evolution of modern ideologies of liberalization due to Web 2.0 developments in transparent Internet communications via different mediums such as blogs, open discussion forums, interactive websites, and, especially, SNWs. This led to the inevitable global growth of sexual harassment (Moraham-Martin, 2000) in cyberspace.

Problems Involved in Conceptualizing Cyber Offenses That Target SNW Users

The 10th United Nations Congress on the Prevention of Crimes and Treatment of Offenders, which was held in Vienna in 2000, made the first move toward recognizing the universal need for preventive measures against cyber crimes. The declaration in Vienna regarding cyber crime preventive measures was well developed in the Council of Europe's Convention on Cyber Crime, held in Budapest in 2001. Even though several cyber offenses were defined from criminological perspectives in as early as the 1970s and 1980s, it was only after the EU convention on cyber crime (2001) that these offenses were universally "criminalized." It could be said that the hacking of e-mails, personal data, and personal computer systems was one of the earliest concepts of cyber offenses, which was brought under the category of "criminal offenses against computer system" by the EU Convention in 2001.[4] However, the resolutions of the EU Convention were drafted mainly to protect e-commerce and not to prevent attacks on human privacy and dignity. But cyber victimization of ordinary Internet users via racial and other various types of hatred—violence, sexual abuse of adult women, including typical gender harassments like stalking, threatening to mutilate her virtual identity—had already started gaining momentum since 2000, and it was rising rapidly due to easy access to the targeted women's personal information, easy ways to communicate through SNWs, and absence of any proper preventive legal measures. On the whole, other than hacking, unauthorized

---

[4] See Chapter II, Section 1 of the EU Convention on Cybercrimes (2001) available at http://conventions.coe.int/treaty/en/treaties/html/185.htm

access to computer content, and child pornography, no cyber offense was legally defined or recognized.

By 2001, many cyber-savvy countries had begun adopting the draft definitions of *cyber crimes* and the preventive measures that were projected by the 2001 EU Convention. But the convention—as well as the nations who adopted the convention to establish their own domestic laws in hopes of preventing cyber crimes—failed to note that cyber crimes should not be restricted only to the offenses of hacking, child pornography, or cyber economic frauds. Rather, this "cancer" has spread well beyond these offenses, destroying the ordinary adult Internet user's peace, as well; thus, the definition of *cyber crimes* should be extended to protect the typical adult Internet user. The other "traditional" offenses that were identified by ongoing researchers as "cyber crimes targeting individuals" are stalking (Basu & Jones, 2008; Ellison & Akdeniz, 1998; Jaishankar & Uma Sankary, 2005), phishing, e-mail spoofing (Halder & Jaishankar, 2008), morphing (Halder & Jaishankar, 2008; Nash, 2008), cyber bombing (which is often used in relation to terrorism), cyber flame war (abusive/hate speech), cyber cheating (impersonation), cyber fraud (which is often used in relation to monetary crimes), cyber sex, and issues of cyber privacy, including cyber child pornography (Jaishankar, Halder, & Ramdoss, 2008). Compared with cyber child pornography, which was dealt with by the 2001 EU Convention, and identity theft, which was dealt with by the 2001 and 2005 EU Conventions, none of the previously mentioned cyber offenses got universally accepted legal definitions—nor did they get universal criminal sanctions. We assert that this was the main reason for cyber victimization of women. The concept of online sexual harassment remained completely unidentified. Along with the few offenses as demarcated by the EU conventions, different cyber savvy nations extended/stretched already existing definitions of penal offenses targeting human dignity and privacy to suit the needs of protecting only their own cyberspace.

Universally, *cyber stalking* has never been legally defined. In the United States, stalking has been treated as an extended version of the traditional physical notion of stalking, only with the aid of digital technology. A good example would be the provisions in the Violence Against Women and Department of Justice Reauthorization Act of 2005, which address crimes such as stalking. Section 226 1A of Title 18 of the United States Code, which was amended by Section 114 of the Violence Against Women and Department of Justice Reauthorization Act of 2005, has redefined *stalking* in the following way:

[T]ravels in interstate or foreign commerce or within the special maritime and territorial jurisdiction of the United States, or enters or leaves Indian country, with the intent to kill, injure, harass, or place under surveillance with intent to kill, injure, harass, or intimidate another person, and in the course of, or as a result of, such travel places that person in reasonable fear of the death of, or serious bodily injury to, or causes substantial emotional distress to that person, a member of the immediate family (as defined in section 115) of that person, or the spouse or intimate partner of that person; or (2) with the intent – (A) to kill, injure, harass, or place under surveillance with intent to kill, injure, harass, or intimidate, or cause substantial emotional distress to a person in another State or tribal jurisdiction or within the special maritime and territorial jurisdiction of the United States; or (B) to place a person in another State or tribal jurisdiction, or within the special maritime and territorial jurisdiction of the United States, in reasonable fear of the death of, or serious bodily injury to – (i) that person; (ii) a member of the immediate family (as defined in section 115) of that person; or (iii) a spouse or intimate partner of that person; uses the mail, any interactive computer service, or any facility of interstate or foreign commerce to engage in a course of conduct that causes substantial emotional distress to that person or places that person in reasonable fear of the death of, or serious bodily injury to, any of the persons described in clauses (i) through (iii) of subparagraph (B).

To accommodate the needs of digital stalking, various U.S. states have made their own stalking laws. But none have defined *cyber stalking* or drawn its legal boundaries. The term has been used as a synonym for *cyber harassment* in many U.S. state laws. For instance, the Michigan criminal code [Stalking: Section 28.643(8). Definitions. Sec. 411h. (1993)] included in its definition of *harassment* "conduct directed toward a victim that includes repeated or continuing unconsented contact, that would cause a reasonable individual to suffer emotional distress, and that actually causes the victim to suffer emotional distress."

Because the term *cyber harassment* has not been legally defined anywhere, the term has been very broadly applied to include various online disturbances. However, after Megan Taylor Meier's suicide,[5] the term *cyber bullying* has attracted proper legal attention in the United States and has been well defined.[6] Still, whether the definition and the law can be stretched to cover bullying incidents inflicted upon adult women remains a debatable issue. It is unfortunate that cyber bullying is still considered a "behavioral fault" in many countries such as India and that no legal definitions are available to prevent such behavior.

It is deplorable that the majority of cyber offenses targeting individual users of SNWs, including women, have remained topics relegated to

---

[5] Megan Taylor Meir was an American teenager who became a victim of cyber bullying and committed suicide. "Megan committed suicide after an internet hoax went terribly wrong. Cyber Bullying played a key part in her mental state" (http://hubpages.com/hub/Trolls-Among-Us-2).

[6] The U.S. Congress passed the Megan Meir Cyber Bullying Prevention Act of 2008 to prevent the bullying of children in cyberspace.

theoretical discussions and have failed to attract any legal prescription. New types of online offenses are emerging every day, but most of these offenses are generalized under a broad concept that often over looks the inherent nature of the crime. For instance, *cyber harassment* has been used as a holistic term for other cyber offenses such as cyber stalking or even cyber defamation. According to emerging research on the nature of cyber crimes (Halder & Jaishankar, 2008), each of these three terms differs from the other. Due to less—or a complete lack of—awareness of the "digital" or "cyber" version of traditional offenses (i.e., offenses that were once committed only in the physical world, such as stalking), SNWs are becoming hubs of criminal activity cyber offenders use to target individual Internet users.

Typology and Patterns of Victimization of Women on SNWs

Women on SNWs are victimized in different patterns by the abuser, who can be an individual or even a group of individuals. The abuser can be either male or female, and the offenses can be either sexual or nonsexual in nature. The type of victimization differs depending on various factors—for example, the woman's sexuality, ideologies, marital status, profession and professional commitments, regularity of participation in some chosen groups, language, or popularity within a given group.

In most cases, male harassers attack the victim for sexual purposes (e.g., morphing, using her image for pornographic purposes, cyber stalking) and nonsexual purposes (e.g., harassment, bullying). However, female perpetrators typically victimize individuals for ideological differences, hatred, or revenge. Such attacks may not be sexual in nature.

Based on these aforementioned criteria, the typology of the offenses against the women victims on SNWs is framed as follows:

1. *Cyber verbal abuse by groups of perpetrators expressing hatred.* Citron (2009) best describes this as a "cyber mob attack" (p. 93) where a female member of the SNW may be attacked by a group of perpetrators both on the community wall as well as in her own message board.
2. *Cyber defamation targeting the individual self* (Citron, 2009; Halder & Jaishankar, 2008). Emotional breakups may lead the male member to spread lies about the female member to other members through his own posts, community walls, and so forth.
3. *Cyber stalking.* The female member is stalked in all the groups she joins and her friends' walls are constantly watched in hopes of seeing her posts, her own write-ups, and her activities online (Basu & Jones, 2008; Ellison & Akdeniz, 1998; Jaishankar & Uma Sankary, 2005).

4. *Morphing* (Nash, 2008; Halder & Jaishankar, 2008). Photographs of the female SNW member are taken from personal albums and are morphed for pornographic purposes by using parts of the photos—for instance, the head, or the torso from the waist to the breasts.

5. *Cloning.* Victimizers create cloned profiles or fake profiles of female victims by stealing the female member's personal information. The cloned profile presents the original profile in such a strikingly similar manner that people are duped. The cloned profile then asks the friends of the original member to become his or her friend, thus going a step farther in victimization by cracking into other members' privacy as well (vs. using only the original member's information for evil purposes). Female members of the most popular SNWs such as Facebook, MySpace, and Orkut often face this problem (Halder, 2007).

6. *Cyber obscenity* (Citron, 2009). The victim's photograph is used, morphed so that the victim appears to be posing in obscene postures, and then distributed on the Internet. The harasser may also post obscene messages to her wall. Cyber obscenity also can be practiced by way of hacking the profile of the female member: Once the harasser hacks in, he or she morphs the original photographs posted on the woman's profile page and then uses the profile name and information as well as the morphed photographs to send obscene messages to the "friends" of the original profile owner and also to a wider audience.

7. *Hacking.* Particular targets are chosen, and their profiles are hacked. Their personal information is used for evil purposes. The harasser may even distribute open invitations for having sex with the profile owner at her home address (Halder & Jaishankar, 2008).

8. *Cyber harassment.* This may include constant messaging to the profile owner's wall or personal e-mail address (Halder, 2007), which is shown in the profile; regular peeping in as a visitor and leaving messages on her wall; continuously sending requests for friendship; joining groups of which she is a member; constantly posting messages disagreeing with her; and so forth (Citron, 2009).

9. *Virtual rape* (Citron, 2009; Whitty, 2005). This is a violent type of cyber victimization in which the targeted woman is taken up by a harasser. He either posts constant messages such as "I will rape you," "I will tear you up," "your Internet identity will be f...ed off," and so forth, or particular community members may "mob attack" the targeted female with such words, which successfully generates more enthusiasm among other unrelated members to comment on the victim's sexuality. The profile owner then becomes a hot topic for erotic discussions, vulgar name calling, and so forth.

10. *Banning a female member and restraining her from expressing her views.* This generally happens in a male-dominated group or community in which the moderator, owner, or group members may victimize the targeted female member by banning her for her own feminist ideologies even through the group or the community could have been created for letting people express their own ideologies. The reason could be that the majority of group members may be antifeminist or some individual members dislike the straightforwardness of the female members in discussing the problems of women in everyday life.

11. *Cyber bullying and name calling* (Citron, 2009; Halder & Jaishankar, 2008). The harasser may constantly bully the target on the SNW, both on her wall as well as in the groups or communities of which either he or she is a member. Even though this is a gender-neutral cyber offense, women are most commonly the chosen targets for their sexuality, emotional breakups, or even domestic violence. The ex-spouse or ex-lover constantly bullies the woman to vent his anger in public.

12. *Domestic violence and cyber flame.* As mentioned previously, separated partners may take up membership on SNWs to vent their anger against the female member. In such cases, the ex-partner starts bullying the woman first and then provokes her to have "online fights" (Citron, 2009; Southworth, Finn, Dawson, Fraser, & Tucker, 2007).

13. *Impersonation and cheating.* SNWs give wide options for creating profiles under pseudonames as well as hiding one's real age, gender, and other information. Further, creation of multiple profiles of the same individual using different e-mail addresses is also possible on SNWs. This gives the opportunity for mischief mongers to impersonate and flirt with female members (Halder & Jaishankar, 2008; Whitty, 2005). The harasser drags the victim into an emotional relationship, and she is encouraged to share her secrets and even have erotic chats with the harasser. When the victim finally pressures him to meet her in person, he either blackmails or cheats the victim. Additionally, impersonation and cheating can happen for financial reasons on SNWs. The harasser may promise the victim some online or offline monetary gain by showing his fake credentials and, thereby, dupe the victim later.

14. *Blackmailing and threatening.* This happens because the personal information of women SNW members is easily available. "Jilted lovers," ex-spouses, mischief mongers, and stalkers may threaten and blackmail the woman for various reasons, which may even lead the SNW administrators to shut down her profile. This can even have an offline effect, in which miscreants may physically threaten and blackmail the woman with the secrets that she may have shared with her friends on SNW groups or communities.

The Emotional and Physical Risk Factors of Women Members of SNWs

The Emotional Suffering

Finn and Banach (2000) stated that even though the Internet helps women to better their physical and mental health, it is not hazard free. The risks involve loss of privacy, disinhibited communication, online harassment, and stalking. The Internet has grown faster than the laws governing it. Döring (2000) pointed out that the biggest danger of Internet socializing lies in cyber sex, which leaves a deep, never-ending traumatic effect on women users. The word *cyber sex* is used by Doring (2000) as a compact term to cover online sexual harassment, cyber prostitution, or virtual rape and emphasizes that liberalization of women further encourages them to become victims of cyber sex. Hence, women users must learn from other victims' past experiences to protect themselves from online sexual abuse (Doring, 2000).

Whitty (2005) affirmed that cyber socializing can usher in emotional relationships between men and women, in which women then become victims of cyber cheating. Even though in some cases, cyber cheating may not have the same significant impact on real life as that of offline cheating, Whitty expressed fear that this may give birth to offline revenge-taking mentality. Southworth and colleagues (2007) pointed out that cyber socializing breeds domestic violence as well as violence against women in the way of cyber stalking, online abusive behavior, and gender harassment. They succinctly put that "ever-changing and increasingly inexpensive technologies make it easier than ever before for abusers to monitor and control their victims" (p. 844). They also emphasize an urgent need to build support groups to prevent and protect such online harassment of women, fearing that the current laws are insufficient. Citron stated that that social networking can breed many instances of gender harassment such as cyber hate speech, cyber bullying, and morphed photographs (Citron, 2009).

Ellison and Akdeniz (1998) reported that the phenomenon of cyber stalking and online harassment looks to be the focus of the next Internet-related moral panic. They explained that the transnational nature of cyberspace should encourage actions by individual governments and international organizations to have a profound effect on the rights of law-abiding Internet users, or *netizens*, around the world. These authors contend that successful cyber regulation cannot be achieved at the cost of fundamental freedoms of speech and privacy.

Halder (2007) noted that social networking websites such as Orkut pose a threat to Indian women's privacy as users. Many women register themselves as members without reading the privacy policies or being aware of the safety tips of such websites. The victims often become trapped due to their own negligence. As such, when a cloned profile is created of the victim or her morphed photograph flashes up in her own wall or in the scrapbooks of others—or even when she is informed of her harassment by other users—a sense of guilt and shame engulfs her. The experience becomes more traumatic when the victim is refused any police help due to officials' nonrecognition of offenses or lack of awareness. Citron (2009) pointed out that cyber hate speech targeting women is more distressing than other online offenses. The trauma deepens when the harasser is anonymous, leaving no immediate solution to find out who he is and why is he attacking. Citron (2009) also showed how anonymous profile users can vandalize the social networking of women. Anonymous mob attacks (Citron, 2009) and anonymous postings on an individual user's wall or community walls (Citron, 2009) create more panic within women victims. Citron (2009) also feels that the broad concepts of U.S. freedom of speech—which are randomly followed by many social networking websites, attracting non-Americans as well—give a huge opportunity to Internet users to publish their thoughts as anonymous. This is well supported by SNWs, and users get enough freedom to hide under the term "anonymous" when they write comments in harsh, rude, or abusive languages on groups' or communities' walls. We agree that most of such publications are targeted against women. The perpetrator successfully insults the "target" in public and generates similar hatred among the group members, who then follow him in teasing or bullying the victim. Eventually, anonymity leads to greater dangers on the SNWs, such as stalking, threatening, and abusive posting by other members of the group.

The following case studies[7] show how cyber socializing creates emotional suffering.

Case Study 1

The victim and the perpetrator met via a SNW. Eventually, they started making regular postings to one another's wall and engaging in online chatting. They came to know about one another's families through photographs that were posted in the personal albums of the perpetrator and the victim. Eventually, they fell in love. The perpetrator was residing in a foreign country for his professional commitments and promised that he would marry the victim once he returned (within a year). After the stipulated date, when the victim contacted the perpetrator, he completely denied these "promises." When the victim tried to contact his family members, they shunned her off

---

[7] Some of these case studies were provided by Working to Halt Online Abuse (WHOA, http://www.haltabuse.org), where the first author is engaged as an Internet safety advocate. Other case studies were taken from the cases handled by the first author as the managing director for Centre for Cyber Victim Counseling (CCVC, http://www.cybervictims.org) with the victims' permission. Because of confidentiality issues, victims' identities are not disclosed.

and threatened her with dire consequences if she tried to meet the man. The victim felt cheated, emotionally broken, and publicly humiliated.

Case Study 2

The perpetrator was the former husband of the victim. Both were members of the same SNW. The perpetrator found the victim after conducting a random name search and started following her. He also found out the chosen communities where she was regularly participating and started stalking her. He started becoming a member of those same groups and contacted the friends of the victim only to harass her. The perpetrator started inquiring about her private life from the friends of those groups and humiliated her. The victim felt panicked, and her privacy was disturbed. She started sensing that somebody was always watching her in cyberspace, and she became averse to the use of technology.

Case Study 3

In this case, the victim's sibling was the perpetrator. She was a member of an SNW that encouraged people to talk about their emotional outbursts, mood swings, and so forth. Because the victim and her sibling were not on good terms, the perpetrator (sibling) used this SNW to tell the wider audience that the victim was the "main cause" for her failures in life and defamed her in every possible way. The members started believing the perpetrator and started abusing the victim in every possible way. The victim felt humiliated and emotionally distressed.

The Physical Threat

The other danger that crops up with cyber socializing is offline threats created by online rendezvouses. In many instances, women victims become friends of other individual profile owners whom they have never met in real life. The problem starts when the online relationship turns unpleasant. These individuals, who can be either male or female, may have come to know about the victim's real life from the victim herself and, later, constantly use such information to threaten her. The victim remains in constant danger of being physically harmed by the perpetrator (Whitty, 2005) if the victim and the perpetrator stay in the same locality or even in the same state. The following case study shows how online socialization can create a physical threat to a victim.

Case Study

The victim and the perpetrator became friends via an SNW. The local members of the SNW group used to meet weekly at a city pub to chit-chat and also to celebrate members' birthdays, anniversaries, and so forth. The victim became the target of the perpetrator after an emotional relationship (as was "presumed" by the perpetrator) did not ever materialize. The perpetrator threatened the victim by telephone, stating that at the next weekly meeting in the pub, she would be physically assaulted by him and his followers.

Reasons for the Growth of Victimization of Women in Cyber Socialization

Easy Availability of Victims' (Women's) Personal Information

SNWs are created to let other people know the existence of the profile owner. Hence, users give away their vital information such as residential address, marital status, age, phone numbers, likes, dislikes, and so forth. Even though many SNWs provide options for using pseudonames and publication of such information as only "optional," many first-time registrants, including women, float their personal information on the web through these SNWs without actually knowing the dangerous effect of doing so. This gives harassers a huge opportunity to victimize the targets.

Ignorance and Negligence of the Users

Halder and Jaishankar (2008) have pointed out that women are prone to all sorts of cyber crimes such as hacking, stalking, morphing, cyber cheating, cyber defamation, and cyber sexual abuse. SNWs have become breeding grounds for such crimes. The question that haunts researchers is, "Why are women the targeted majority in the SNWs?" Among several factors that push women to become victims on SNWs, the ignorance of the policy guidelines and safety measures stands out first and foremost. The SNWs presently give wide options to protect oneself from being harassed in various modes such as setting up security measures, locking personal albums and message boards, blocking the harasser, preventing nonmembers from seeing one's personal information, preventing unknown persons from writing on one's message board, blocking and banning individuals from communities and groups, and hiding one's profile from an Internet search.[8] Halder (2007) cautions that the majority of women join the SNWs without checking any such safety measures.

Halder (2007) did a small study with a small sample size of 20 on the awareness of female members of Orkut, a popular social networking website.

---

[8] Popular SNWs such as Facebook, MySpace, Orkut, Hi5, and so forth give wide options in their privacy policies for users to exercise all of the safety measures such as locking the album, hiding profile visitors, banning unwanted "friends," and removing unwanted messages from one's scrapbook. But often, users simply cannot resist showing photographs of themselves, their families, or their homes to other "friends" whom they may have never met.

The author found that most respondents never read the policy guidelines before registering with the SNW; many checked available safety tips only after they were victimized themselves or after hearing of friends' experiences; and almost all of them have personal photographs posted, even though they know the displaying of photographs is not very safe on a public SNW. A majority have turned on their security button and "locked" their albums and message book only after they had experienced some sort of harassment. Some had their profile "cloned" (i.e., their personal information was used to dupe their friends). These cloned profiles sent friend requests to the already existing friends with the statement "I have deleted my older account; please accept me now." Some had their profiles hacked and their photographs used for pornographic purposes. These women users (whose profiles were either cloned or hacked) had deleted the old account themselves and had created fresh accounts. Some had reported abuse to the Orkut authorities; some felt that these incidents did not warrant being reported to the authorities. Many of the respondents indicated that they know posting personal photographs is not safe, but they continue to do so anyway.

Many of the respondents indicated that they do not trust friends from Orkut whom they have never met, but at the same time, they feel comfortable in sharing their interests, photographs, or personal secrets with those friends whom they have seen on Orkut for a longer period and who had been fairly active in the groups and communities of which they are members. However, a majority of them do not know that sharing of such information can bring in more problems by way of a third party peeping on the wall or message board of one of the two friends; this third party may not be a common friend among both parties. The problems that may arise are creating a fake profile with available information or even blackmailing the women with her secrets. Some women had seen their photographs in another person's album—a person who is in no way connected to them. But they did not report this incident to the authorities. Some women had verbal disagreements between groupmates and suspected that their profiles were cloned or even hacked by such people. Only two of the respondents had any idea that they have a legal right to preserve their privacy on the SNW, and almost all of them had experienced either major or minor harassments on the SNW.

Scheming Ways to Hide One's Real Identity Under Camouflaged Profiles

The ever-expanding freedom of speech and expression in the United States has fostered the right to be anonymous on SNWs (Citron, 2009). Even so, the SNWs allow a user to change his or her pseudoname and address regularly. Although this step was taken by the SNWs for the benefit of the members—so that members could change their physical and geographical location and at the same time save themselves from perpetrators—this has encouraged the perpetrators to commit a crime and hide under a new identity. These hide-and-seek (Jaishankar, 2008) games by the perpetrators put women members of SNWs at increased risk.

Lackadaisical Response of the SNWs

In most cases, cyber socializing becomes dangerous because of the SNWs' nonchalant response. Most SNWs have an option to report any abuse of their services. This includes reporting of cyber harassment, cyber bullying, cyber threats, and cyber pornography. But, in most cases, SNWs have their own policies to treat the post as defamatory or harassing. For example, the site AdultFriendFinder.com allows members to post seminude images of women, make lewd remarks about female members by their male friends, and even send pornographic pictures to fellow members.[9] Similarly, ventyouranger. com encourages members to vent their frustrations and anger toward a particular individual who may not be a member of the group.[10] On the contrary, SNWs such as Facebook, MySpace, and Orkut consider such written expressions "unwanted"; such offenses can be banned but only if the website authorities deem it an offense. For instance, if a woman is constantly targeted for cyber bullying, or the perpetrator creates fake profiles, the website directs the complainant to lodge a complaint with the bullying messages or the cloned profile. The site also points out that the stipulated time for taking action can vary from 24 hr to 15 days.[11] But the impact of the offense may be such that the victim needs to take action within 24 hr; the victim either has to withdraw herself from the "societies" of which she is a member or has to cancel her entire profile to eliminate all the hazards. The delayed (or even nil) response from the website authorities increases the panic in the victim, and the harasser gets infinite opportunities to harm the victim's reputation within the stipulated time.

It is noteworthy that most of the SNWs declare in their privacy policies that they will not take any responsibility for any sorts of harassment caused to users by other users.[12] However, they do provide safety tips in the menu bar and warn users that their profile may be removed if it is reported that said profile is harassing others, creating a hate campaign, soliciting

[9] AdultFriendFinder.com is an SNW for adults that is registered in the United States.
[10] ventyouranger.com is an SNW for adults that is registered in the United States and encourages people to vent their frustrations and anger in public forums.
[11] SNW such as Orkut and Facebook stipulate a minimum of 24 hr to 15 days' time to take action against the abuser. See http://www.google.com/support/orkut/bin/answer.py?answer=57444 and http://www.facebook.com/safety
[12] This information was gathered from the privacy policies of SNWs such as Orkut, Facebook, and MySpace.

pornography, and so forth.[13] It is unfortunate that these guidelines are not followed properly.

Lack of Uniform Laws, Conventions, and Rules

As discussed earlier, the most common forms of abuse on the SNWs are not universally recognized by any uniform law, convention, or rules. Moreover, most of the SNWs are registered under U.S. laws, and they are immune from being sued as defamatory media by Section 230 of the Communication Decency Act of 1996. However, this creates bigger problem for victims, especially women. As decided by the *Miller v. California* (1973) case, the ideas of obscenity differ from society to society. The United States protects members of SNWs who are under age 18 years from cyber bullying by the Megan Meier Cyber Bullying Prevention Act (2008), and women are protected from cyber harassment or cyber stalking, which may result from domestic violence or broken emotional relationships, by the Violence Against Women Act and the Department of Justice Reauthorization Act of 2005. On the contrary, the United Kingdom does not have any compendium of laws that protects women from cyber offenses. However, there are some major laws—such as the Computer Misuse Act of 1990, Police and Justice Act of 2006, Sexual Offenses Act of 2003, the Prevention of Sexual Offences (Scotland) Act of 2005, the Protection From Harassment Act of 1997, and the Malicious Communications Act of 1988—that are widely used to prevent atrocities against women on the Internet. But the offenses are not legally defined; hence, perpetrators often escape punishment. Canada regulates the online victimization of women through specific chapters of the Canadian Criminal Code that are meant for both men and women—there are no special laws designed specifically to protect women. In India's Information Technology Act (the original statute from 2000 as well as the amended 2008 version), the law does not recognize many of the offenses that occur from online socializing—offenses such as cyber bullying, cyber harassment, profile cloning, and so forth. Thus, the lack of universal laws to regulate SNWs and the lack of legal recognition of offenses against women in cyberspace encourage the growth of online victimization of women.

Conclusion

The main aim of cyber socializing is to give users the opportunity to meet with old and new friends, increase networks, and socialize without actually going in person to the social gatherings. But this is not a hazard-free endeavor. The main drawback of cyber socializing is the uncertain reliability of the

---

[13]Ibid.

"virtual friend" with whom we meet every day on the SNWs. Additionally, many users treat cyber socializing as a space for overriding their freedom of speech and expression. This attracts many offenses such as cyber flame, cyber hate speech, and cyber bullying. Online socializing never remains risk free for women. A majority of the cyber crimes targeting women happen via SNWs (Citron, 2009; Halder & Jaishankar, 2008), but considering no society is crime free, online societies are no exception. Cyber crime exists, and it is growing in number (Wall, 2007) through SNWs, e-mail, online chat rooms, and so forth.

SNWs provide a wide range of social activities to be carried out in cyberspace; however, similar to traditional in-person interactions, online socializing carries its own share of vulnerabilities and risks. But the patterns may differ due to the hi-tech nature of the offenses. The attackers may or may not be known to the victims, and the reasons and motives behind victimization are mostly emotional issues. The harasser also uses the broader platform of cyberspace to victimize the target under camouflaged identities. Moreover, the current laws are not adequate: They are often not equipped to deal specifically with cyber offenses. For example, their wording (which addresses traditional offenses committed in "the real world") makes them not applicable to offenses committed in cyberspace. Additionally, these laws are still very much in development and continue to evolve. The fact that online cyber offenses are still not formally, specifically recognized in the laws directly contributes to increased incidents of victimization.

The two main reasons for the growth of online victimization of women on SNWs are (a) the absence of proper gender-sensitive universal cyber laws and (b) lack of awareness of the safety modes among users of SNWs. The SNWs are considered to be a large global platform on which users can express their ideologies, thoughts, and feelings about others. Every individual is supposed to use this platform at his or her own risk (Wall, 2007). It is unfortunate that there are fewer laws and policy guidelines to regulate cyberspace; this insufficiency gives full freedom to the perpetrators. This is a perfect example of how the ignorance of cyber social rules and norms—coupled with weak laws—can encourage criminals to turn to online socialization sites.

References

Basu, S., & Jones, R. (2008). Regulating cyber stalking. In F. Schmallager & M. Pittaro (Eds.), *Crimes of the Internet* (pp. 141–165). Upper Saddle River, NJ: Prentice Hall.

Citron, K. D. (2009). Cyber civil rights. *Boston University Law Review, 89*, 61–125. Retrieved from http://ssrn.com/abstract=1271900

Clemmitt, M. (2006). Cyber socializing. *CQ Researcher, 16*, 625–648.

Döring, N. (2000). Feminist views of cybersex: Victimization, liberation, and empowerment. *CyberPsychology and Behavior, 3*, 863–884.

Ellison, L., & Akdeniz, Y. (1998). Cyber-stalking: The regulation of harassment on the Internet. *Criminal Law Review*, December, 29–48.

Finn, J., & Banach, M. (2000). Victimisation online: The downside of seeking human services for women on the Internet. *CyberPsychology & Behavior, 3*(5), 785–796.

Fraim, L. N. (2006, September). *Cyber socialization: What's missing in my life?* Paper presented at The Nordic Youth Research Information Symposium, Stockholm, Sweden.

Halder, D. (2007, June). Cyber crime against women in India. *CyberLawTimes.com Monthly Newsletter, 2*(6). Retrieved from http://www.cyberlawtimes.com/ articles/103.html

Halder, D. (2008, September). *Privacy in Orkut: A hopeless story.* Retrieved from http://www.cyberlawtimes.com/articles/108.html

Halder, D., & Jaishankar, K. (2008). Cyber crimes against women in India: Problems, perspective and solutions. *TMC Academic Journal, 3*(1), 48–62.

Jaishankar, K. (2008). Space transition theory of cyber crimes In F. Schmallager & M. Pittaro (Eds.), *Crimes of the Internet* (pp. 283–301). Upper Saddle River, NJ: Prentice Hall.

Jaishankar, K., Halder, D., & Ramdoss, S. (2008). Pedophilia, pornography, and stalking: Analyzing child victimization on the Internet In F. Schmallager & M. Pittaro (Eds.), *Crimes of the Internet* (pp. 28–42). Upper Saddle River, NJ: Prentice Hall.

Jaishankar, K., & Uma Sankary, V. (2005). Cyber stalking: A global menace in the information super highway. *ERCES Online Quarterly Review, 2*(3). Retrieved from http://www.erces.com/journal/articles/archives/volume2/v03/v02.htm

Michigan Criminal Code, Stalking: Section 28.643(8). Definitions. Sec. 411h. (1993).

Miller v. California, 413 U.S. 15 (1973).

Morahan-Martin, J. (2000). Women and the Internet: Promise and perils [Editorial]. *CyberPsychology & Behavior, 3,* 683–691.

Nash, J. (2008). *Making women's place explicit: Pornography, violence, and the Internet* [Open education module]. Cambridge, MA: Berkman Center for Internet and Society, Harvard Law School.

Sara, E. B, (2008). Identity theft: Causes, correlates, and factors: A content analysis In F. Schmallager & M. Pittaro (Eds.), *Crimes of the Internet* (pp. 225–251). Upper Saddle River, NJ: Prentice Hall.

Southworth, C., Finn, J., Dawson, S., Fraser, C., & Tucker, S. (2007). Intimate partner violence, technology and stalking. *Violence Against Women, 13,* 842–856.

Wall, D. S. (2007). *Cybercrime: The transformation of crime in the information age.* Cambridge, MA: Polity.

Whitty, M. T. (2005). The realness of cyber cheating: Men's and women's representations of unfaithful Internet relationships. *Social Science Computer Review, 23,* 57–67.

Malware Victimization
A Routine Activities Framework

18

ADAM M. BOSSLER
THOMAS J. HOLT

Contents

Introduction

The Internet has dramatically altered the way we communicate, live, and conduct business around the world. These advancements have modified traditional activities—such as banking, dating, and shopping—into activities in which individuals interact with others but neither leave the house nor actually physically meet people (Newman & Clarke, 2003). The growth and penetration of computer technology in modern life has provided criminals with more efficient tools to commit crime, more accessible opportunities, and crimes that could not exist without cyberspace. Few criminologists, however, have empirically assessed the impact of computer technology on victimization. As a consequence, there is a lack of understanding in the ability of traditional theories of crime to account for the prevalence and potential reduction of cybercrime victimization. In particular, routine activities theory (Cohen & Felson, 1979) may be successful in this endeavor, as it has been traditionally used to examine how technological innovations affect crime patterns and victimization.

One of the more common and significant forms of cyber crime victimization is the destruction of data files due to malicious software (malware; Furnell, 2002; Taylor, Caeti, Loper, Fritsch, & Liederbach, 2006). Malware typically includes computer viruses, worms, and Trojan horse programs that alter functions within computer programs and files. Viruses can conceal their presence on computer systems and networks and can spread via e-mail attachments, downloadable files, instant messaging, and other methods (Kapersky, 2003; Szor, 2005; Taylor et al., 2006). Trojan horse programs also often arrive via e-mail as a downloadable file or an attachment that people would be inclined to open, such as files titled "XXX Porn" or "Receipt of Purchase." When the file is opened, it executes some form of malicious code (Furnell, 2002; Szor, 2005; Taylor et al., 2006). In addition, some malware is activated by visiting websites—particularly, pornographic websites—that exploit flaws in web browsers (Taylor et al., 2006). Although worms do not involve as much user interaction as other malware because of its ability to use system memory and to send copies of itself, humans can facilitate its spread by simply opening e-mails that have the worm code embedded into the file (Nazario, 2003).

Cyber criminals often use malware to compromise computer systems and automate attacks against computer networks (Furnell, 2002). These programs can disrupt e-mail and network operations, access private files, delete or corrupt files, and generally damage computer software and hardware (Taylor et al., 2006). The dissemination of viruses across computer networks can be costly for several reasons, including the loss of data and copyrighted information, identity theft, loss of revenue due to customer apprehension about website safety, time spent removing the programs, and losses in personal productivity and system functions (Symantec Corporation, 2003; Taylor et al., 2006). This is reflected in the dollar losses associated with malware infection. U.S. companies that participated in a recent Computer Security Institute (CSI) report lost approximately $15 million because of viruses in 2006 alone (CSI, 2007). An infected system in one country can spread malicious software across the globe and cause even greater damage because of the interconnected nature of computer systems. The Melissa virus, for example, caused an estimated $80 million in damages worldwide (Taylor et al., 2006). Thus, malware infection poses a significant threat to Internet users around the globe.

A large body of information security research explores the technical aspects of malicious software. These research efforts have placed special emphasis on the creation of software applications such as antivirus programs that can identify and contain malicious software on computer systems (Kapersky, 2003; PandaLabs, 2007; Symantec Corporation, 2003). If these programs are to work as effectively as possible, however, individual computer users must obtain, update, and use them regularly. Thus, in order to better understand the spread and prevention of malware, the exploration of a theoretical approach that focuses on human behavior, such as routine activities theory (Cohen & Felson, 1979), is necessary because of the role that human behavior and interactions play in the spread of malicious software. Routine activities theory has had significant success in accounting for traditional forms of offending and appears to apply to some online crimes, such as harassment or stalking (Holt & Bossler, 2009).

It is unclear as to whether routine activities theory can address forms of crime that are not based in physical time and space and that exist solely on computer systems, such as malware infection (see Choi, 2008). To address this gap in the literature, in this study we explored the prevalence and correlates of malware infection by examining hypotheses derived from routine activities theory. The findings illustrate the social dimensions of this computer-focused, technological crime. We conclude the chapter with policy implications focused on the connection between participation in computer deviance and victimization rather than simple target hardening.

Routine Activities Theory and Malware Victimization

According to Cohen and Felson's (1979) *routine activities theory* (RAT), direct-contact predatory victimization occurs with the convergence in both space and time of three components: a motivated offender, the absence of a capable guardian, and a suitable target. *Motivated offenders* are individuals and groups who have both the inclination and ability to commit crime for various reasons (Cohen & Felson, 1979). *Guardianship* refers to the capability of persons and/or objects that prevent the motivated offender from injuring or taking the target. Individuals are more likely to be victimized if they spend time in the presence of deviants or criminals, if they or their possessions are seen as valuable, and if no guardian is present to adequately protect the potential victims or their property. This perspective can aid in understanding the commission of crime by focusing on the way that daily routine activities affect capable guardianship and target suitability. For example, individuals typically leave their houses at approximately the same time every day to go to work or school, creating a predictable pattern that places them in public areas closer to motivated offenders and leaves their home unguarded. Thus, routine activities are important in understanding particular crimes, in that these offenses often separate individuals from the

safety of their home, the people whom they know and trust, and the possessions that they value.

RAT has had significant success in explaining a wide range of victimization types, such as burglary (Cohen & Felson, 1979; Coupe & Blake, 2006),
larceny (Mustaine & Tewksbury, 1998), vandalism (Tewksbury & Mustaine,
2000), physical assault (Stewart, Elifson, & Sterk, 2004), robbery (Spano &
Nagy, 2005), and fraud (Holtfreter, Reisig, & Pratt, 2008). Several scholars
have briefly discussed how RAT can apply to cyber crime as well (Grabosky,
2001; Grabosky & Smith, 2001; Newman & Clarke, 2003; Taylor et al., 2006;
see Yar, 2005, for a longer discussion). However, there are limited studies
testing the empirical validity of RAT in relation to the commission of cyber
crime. Specifically, Hinduja and Patchin (2008) found that computer proficiency and time spent online were positively related to cyber bullying victimization for adolescent Internet users. Similarly, Holt and Bossler (2009)
discovered that spending more time in online chat rooms and committing
computer deviance increased the odds of online harassment.

RAT may have some applicability to person-based forms of cyber crime,
although its applicability regarding property-based cyber crimes, such as
malicious software infection, is unclear. Malware can be classified as a form
of "cyber theft" if a criminal uses these programs to steal data or information (Wall, 2001). Malware infection does, in fact, share characteristics with
burglary in that malware infects and compromises computer systems in a
fashion similar to how burglars enter a dwelling. Burglars surreptitiously use
common or concealed points of entry to minimize the likelihood of detection (Wright & Decker, 1994). They also may use force to obviate locks or
other security measures to gain access. Most malicious software infects computers through a weakness, or vulnerability, in the system that allows the
code to covertly activate and take control of system processes (Taylor et al.,
2006). Malware can also disable antivirus programs and other security measures to ensure that its payload is delivered successfully, in much the same
way that a burglar can deactivate a security system (Kapersky, 2003). Given
the potential theoretical overlap between malware infection and traditional
crime—specifically, burglary—it would be helpful to consider how the three
components of RAT (i.e., proximity to motivated offenders, capable guardianship, and suitable targets) might also apply to malware.

Proximity to Motivated Offenders

When considering the applicability of RAT to cyber crime, it is vital to consider whether daily computer activities—legal or illegal—place individuals
in proximity to motivated offenders, similar to how daily activities place
individuals in closer proximity to motivated offenders in physical space.

A major difference between most forms of real-world crime and cyber crime is the removal of physical distance between the motivated offender and suitable target (Yar, 2005). A few motivated malware writers can have a substantial impact on a large number of victims without engaging in physical contact with the victims (Taylor et al., 2006). Therefore, the critical issue is not whether the potential victims are in close physical proximity to a malware writer but whether they are in close virtual proximity to an offender's tool. In addition, victims do not have to have a unique temporal interaction with malware in order for their computer to become infected (Taylor et al., 2006). In most cases, malware is either present for as long a period as possible on a specific website or file, or it can activate when a certain function is performed.

Therefore, the activities of the potential victims and the websites or files with which they come into contact are more important than the times of the activities. Although the amount of time online generally might increase the odds of malware infection, RAT research has found that specific leisure activities are more strongly correlated with traditional victimization rates than simply the number of times in which individuals leave their homes for leisure (Mustaine & Tewksbury, 1998, 2002). Thus, it may be more likely that the number of hours that one spends partaking in specific activities on the computer is more important in understanding malware infection. Individuals who spend more time on websites on which they download files, share personal information, or provide credit card information expose themselves to a variety of dangers that may increase their risk of malware victimization. In addition, individuals who own their own computers and use high-speed Internet connections may increase their risk of victimization. High-speed connections allow for greater and more rapid access to materials and file sharing (see Hinduja, 2001), thereby increasing contact with potentially infected files.

Considering the substantial link between offending and victimization in real-world environments (e.g., Mustaine & Tewksbury, 1998; Stewart et al., 2004), it is reasonable to suspect that a similar connection exists in virtual settings as well. For example, Holt and Bossler (2009) found that computer deviance increased the odds of online harassment victimization. Those who engage in computer deviance also may increase their risk of exposure to infected files and motivated offenders. Pirating software and media may be important correlates of malware infection because piracy involves constantly downloading and opening files of unknown origin. Visiting pornographic websites and viewing sexually explicit materials may increase exposure to malware because of viruses being hidden in these files as well (Szor, 2005). Finally, participating in hacker-like behaviors has been shown to increase the risk of victimization by other hackers (Holt, 2007), which could include the use of malicious software.

Absence of Capable Guardianship

Physical guardianship is argued to be as important in preventing digital crime as it is in preventing residential burglary (Grabosky & Smith, 2001). Most studies have found that the use of physical security devices—including burglar alarms, external lights, extra locks, and other security measures—reduces the risk of burglary and larceny victimization (Coupe & Blake, 2006; Cromwell & Olson, 2004; Miethe & McDowall, 1993). Even when offenders argue that they are not concerned with these physical guardians, they still typically choose houses without them. Other scholars, however, have argued that locks are not much of a deterrent for burglars. Once the decision has been made to burglarize a house, the lock simply becomes an obstacle for the burglar to address (Wright & Decker, 1994). Although studies have produced mixed results on the impact of preventative measures (see Mustaine & Tewksbury, 1998; Tseloni, Wittebrood, Farrell, & Pease, 2004), it appears that any target hardening that decreases opportunity and increases physical guardianship reduces the odds of victimization, especially burglary.

Grabosky and Smith (2001) argued that many forms of cyber crime victimization occur simply because of an absence of capable physical guardianship. Physical guardians are readily available on computer systems through antivirus software and similar programs (Kapersky, 2003; Mell, Kent, & Nusbaum, 2005; PandaLabs, 2007). These programs are expressly designed to reduce the likelihood of malware infection and data loss by either scanning and preventing infected files from being introduced to the system or identifying and removing malicious software if it already has infected the system (see Mell et al., 2005; Taylor et al., 2006). Thus, physical guardians in cyberspace work similarly to physical guardians in the real world.

Social guardianship "refers to the availability of others who may prevent personal crimes by their mere presence or by offering assistance to ward off an attack" (Spano & Nagy, 2005, p. 418). In fact, one of the primary characteristics of adequate guardianship, according to burglars, is whether a house is occupied (Coupe & Blake, 2006; Cromwell & Olson, 2004; Shover, 1996; Wright & Decker, 1994). Most burglars state that they would never intentionally burglarize a house if they knew someone was home. In addition, individuals can decrease their social guardianship by associating with delinquent friends—this association not only places an individual in closer proximity to motivated offenders but also reduces the likelihood of his or her friends intervening when others are being victimized (Zhang, Welte, & Wiecxorek, 2001).

A similar phenomenon appears to exist in cyberspace as well. Individuals who associate with friends who commit various forms of computer deviance increase their risk of being harassed online (Holt & Bossler, 2009). Presumably, delinquent friends are more likely to harass their friends and less likely to support and protect them in their online interactions. Considering how malware spreads across computer systems, the relationship between deviance and victimization exists for the spread of malicious software. Viruses and worms often identify and use e-mail address books to send copies of their program to others (Furnell, 2002; Nazario, 2003). If a close associate's computer is infected, possibly due to computer deviance, the malware may try to compromise other machines. As a result, friends who download music or view pornography online may increase the risk of malware distribution and infection for others.

Victims can also participate in their own guardianship by taking "evasive actions which encourage offenders to pursue targets other than their own" (Cohen & Felson, 1979, p. 590). Many victims of burglary are victimized because they have inadvertently provided valuable information to others, such as when they are going to be away from home or how to deactivate a security system (Cromwell & Olson, 2004). However, self-protective behaviors do not appear to decrease victimization when the individual knows the perpetrator, such as in many cases of sexual assault (Mustaine & Tewksbury, 2002; Schwartz, DeKeseredy, Tait, & Alvi, 2001). In these cases, the victim did not anticipate the need for self-protective measures.

Personal guardianship plays a role in cyber crime prevention as it can be considered the primary form of defense (Grabosky, 2001). Individuals need to be aware of the possible risks and consequences that cybercrime or malware can have on their computer system and of the basic preventive measures that one can take to decrease these risks (Grabosky & Smith, 2001). Individuals need to continuously update their physical guardianship tools, including antivirus programs and critical operating system updates (Mell et al., 2005; Szor, 2005). In addition, individuals should limit interactions with strangers, as doing so could increase the odds of different forms of online victimization (Ybarra, Mitchell, Finkelhor, & Wolak, 2007). Opening e-mails from unknown individuals or sources also increases the risk of victimization, as attachments may contain malware (Szor, 2005; Taylor et al., 2006). Gaining knowledge of computer technology may reduce the likelihood of victimization by providing the user with the ability to correctly identify any system anomalies or errors indicative of malware infection (Furnell, 2002; Taylor et al., 2006). Finally, individuals can protect themselves by using complex passwords that are changed regularly and by keeping these passwords private (Furnell, 2002; Nazario, 2003; Taylor et al., 2006).

Suitable Targets

In the context of RAT, suitable targets "can be any person or property that any offender would like to take or control" (Felson, 2001, p. 43). Research has found that in their decision making, offenders consider the possible rewards of offending as a more important factor than the potential consequences (Cromwell & Olson, 2004; Shover, 1996; Wright & Decker, 1994). Residents with a higher income who live in areas of general affluence or who visibly display signs of wealth, such as cars and electronics, are more likely to be victimized because burglars associate the value of the items within the houses with the wealth of the area (Coupe & Blake, 2006; Cromwell & Olson, 2004; Miethe & Meier, 1994; Osborn & Tseloni, 1998). Unlike burglary targets, it appears that everyone connected to the Internet—and their information—is a suitable target for most forms of malware, although malware can be used for targeted attacks as well (Newman & Clarke, 2003; Yar, 2005). Even when a specific individual or website is not directly targeted by a malware writer, it may be incidentally affected because of the connectivity of the Internet by the disruption of a specific major website. In other cases, the target is the disruption of the entire Internet itself, rather than any specific website (Newman & Clarke, 2003). As a result, there may be no gender, age, or race differences in target attractiveness relative to the risk of malware infection, considering computers and their contents—not individuals—are the primary targets.

The Present Study

The theoretical discussion in this chapter illustrates the linkages among online activities, guardianship, and malware infection using an RAT framework. In this study, we examined theoretical and literature-based risk and protective factors related to malware infection. We considered how the specific measures of routine computer use, computer deviance, physical guardianship, social guardianship, and personal guardianship were related to malware infection. These findings not only further the knowledge base on malware infection and the role of RAT in explaining the connection between technological developments and crime but also contribute to recent scholarship that examines RAT as a domain-specific theory (Holtfreter et al., 2008; Lynch, 1987; Mustaine & Tewksbury, 1997, 2002; Wooldredge, Cullen, & Latessa, 1992).

We used data from a self-report survey administered to 788 college students in 10 courses offered on a university campus in the southeastern United States between August and October 2006. Five of these 10 courses allowed students from every college to enroll, thereby increasing the representative nature of the sample by including students from all colleges within the university. The sample was 57% female (43% male) and was predominantly White (77.9%; 22.1% non-White). By comparison, the sample is quite similar to that of the larger university population (52.5% female and 47.5% male; 75% White and 25% non-White). Routine computer use makes up a major part of college students' lives. Because of this group's knowledge of computers and other electronic devices—and because of their risky online behaviors (see Hinduja, 2001; Skinner & Fream, 1997), including deviant behaviors (Higgins, 2005)—a college campus can be considered a "hot spot" of both computer crime and victimization. Therefore, a college campus is an appropriate place to understand how routine computer activities and precautions affect cyber crime.

Five-hundred seventy cases were analyzed in the full regression models. The largest proportion of missing data is because of respondents not answering the questions on gender and race, totaling 126 cases. Considering the emphasis placed on anonymity and the fact that the missing data respondents' malware victimization did not statistically differ from that of the data set analyzed, the most reasonable explanation for the missing data is because they were placed on the last page of a nine-page survey instrument used for a larger project. Furthermore, comparative analyses between the missing data respondents and the 570 cases that were analyzed revealed no pattern and few statistical differences.[1] Thus, we did not find any evidence that the missing data influenced our findings and overall conclusions.

Measures

Dependent Variable

Our dependent variable assessed whether respondents had lost computerized data due to malware infection (viruses, Trojan horses, or worms) in the last 12 months. We were not interested in the mere presence of malware on a computer but, rather, whether malware caused the loss of computerized data, which is a serious and costly type of cyber crime victimization (CSI, 2007; Taylor et al., 2006). In a single-item question, respondents were asked how many times over the past 12 months they had been sent a computer virus, worm, or Trojan horse program that destroyed their computerized data (options included never, 1–2 times, 3–5 times, 6–9 times, and 10 or more times). Over one third (36.1%) had lost computerized data because of malware over the last year (see Table 18.1). Although a large percentage of respondents had been victimized by malware at least once or twice (30%), few respondents

---

[1] The missing data respondents were as likely as the other respondents to be victimized by malware over the last 12 months. Additionally, no pattern emerged that clearly separated the missing data respondents from the cases analyzed regarding their computer routines. The missing data respondents spent more time on the computer for work or school ($x = 1.79$) and on social networking websites ($x = .22$) but less time in chat rooms ($x = 1.50$). Additionally, they were less likely to have a hardware firewall ($x = .32$), and all of them were African-American minority students.

Table 18.1 Pearson Correlation Matrix and Descriptive Statistics (N = 570)

	1	2	3	4	5	6	7	8	9	10	11	12	13	14	15	16	17
1 Malware vict.	—																
2 Ownership	-0.090*	—															
3 Dial-up	-0.053	0.003	—														
4 T-1	-0.110**	0.006	-0.063	—													
5 Shopping	0.021	-0.078	-0.076	-0.011	—												
6 Video games	0.000	-0.068	-0.107*	0.009	0.225**	—											
7 E-mail	0.003	-0.045	-0.077	0.022	0.284**	0.131**	—										
8 Chat rooms	0.086*	-0.177**	-0.055	-0.002	0.130**	0.191**	0.280**	—									
9 Downloading	0.057	-0.098*	0.027	0.075	0.240**	0.255**	0.376**	0.319**	—								
10 Programming	0.073	-0.062	0.094*	0.094*	0.096*	0.174**	0.163**	0.147**	0.250**	—							
11 Online bank.	-0.004	0.079	0.148**	-0.022	-0.213**	-0.060	-0.102*	-0.039	-0.082*	0.065	—						
12 MySpace	-0.055	0.126**	0.152**	0.052	-0.080	-0.019	-0.109**	-0.330**	-0.122**	-0.027	0.041	—					
13 Dev. behavior	0.136**	-0.148**	-0.088*	0.066	0.173**	0.303**	0.001	0.110**	0.359**	0.144**	-0.084*	-0.083*	—				
14 Pirating soft.	0.048	-0.103*	-0.057	0.029	0.163**	0.250**	0.024	0.067	0.253**	0.104*	-0.099*	-0.027	0.694**	—			
15 Pirating media	0.149**	-0.165**	-0.102*	0.048	0.154**	0.180**	-0.006	0.106*	0.324**	0.111**	-0.049	-0.119**	0.767**	0.439**	—		
16 Pornography	0.057	-0.042	-0.051	0.035	0.062	0.267**	-0.035	0.034	0.180**	0.076	-0.045	-0.033	0.651**	0.305**	0.295**	—	
17 Hacking	0.084*	-0.075	-0.020	0.032	0.110**	0.214**	0.057	0.081	0.243**	0.150**	-0.029	-0.054	0.571**	0.373**	0.325**	0.251**	—
18 Unauth. wire.	0.099*	-0.090*	-0.036	0.071	0.097*	0.121**	-0.002	0.081	0.199**	0.070	-0.062	-0.024	0.627**	0.305**	0.312**	0.208**	0.292**
19 Skill level	-0.007	-0.187**	-0.082*	0.078	0.178**	0.218**	0.058	0.069	0.243**	0.227**	-0.128**	-0.063	0.312**	0.292**	0.253**	0.205**	0.138**
20 Giving passwords	0.027	-0.046	0.017	0.042	-0.071	-0.030	-0.065	-0.002	-0.051	0.060	-0.038	0.018	-0.054	-0.042	-0.005	-0.097*	-0.066
21 Physical guard.	0.026	-0.001	-0.073	0.088*	0.117**	0.147**	-0.009	-0.020	0.141**	0.137**	-0.112**	-0.003	0.125**	0.160**	0.111*	0.065	-0.011
22 Antivirus	0.030	-0.026	-0.009	-0.014	0.078	0.015	0.043	0.020	0.071	0.010	-0.062	0.019	0.018	0.033	0.086*	-0.001	-0.113**
23 Spybot	0.026	-0.003	-0.111**	0.043	0.016	0.144**	-0.065	0.000	0.042	0.042	-0.007	0.004	0.099*	0.125**	0.066	0.056	0.028
24 Ad-aware	0.082	-0.029	-0.099*	-0.020	0.063	0.128**	0.010	0.010	0.110**	0.055	-0.129**	-0.005	0.135**	0.159**	0.084*	0.094*	0.061
25 Microsoft Upd.	0.019	-0.047	-0.070	0.053	0.092*	0.012	0.025	0.005	0.087*	0.106*	-0.102*	-0.024	0.060	0.060	0.056	0.068	-0.040
26 Security center	-0.034	0.084*	0.128**	-0.028	0.038	0.007	-0.058	0.036	0.064	0.061	0.036	-0.035	0.005	0.033	-0.008	-0.017	0.014
27 Software firewall	-0.012	0.021	-0.024	0.133**	0.025	0.064	-0.039	-0.072	0.051	0.088*	-0.057	0.019	0.025	0.051	0.060	-0.024	-0.026
28 Hardware firewall	-0.023	0.012	-0.021	0.103*	0.104*	0.122**	0.048	-0.046	0.074	0.104*	-0.049	0.009	0.078	0.084*	0.045	0.034	0.013
29 Social guard.	0.153**	-0.169**	-0.135**	0.042	0.114**	0.180**	-0.018	0.151**	0.256**	0.055	-0.086*	-0.188**	0.653**	0.438**	0.557**	0.458**	0.357**
30 Fr. pirate soft.	0.069	-0.149**	-0.090*	0.067	0.118**	0.136**	-0.030	0.113**	0.164**	0.037	-0.100*	-0.084*	0.504**	0.528**	0.369**	0.285**	0.272**

31 Fr. pirate media	0.120**	−0.178**	−0.127**	0.040	0.105*	0.085*	0.003	0.129**	0.227**	0.014	−0.088*	−0.230**	0.510**	0.278**	0.659**	0.205**	0.192**
32 Fr. pornography	0.152**	−0.102*	−0.096*	0.011	0.069	0.184**	−0.038	0.090*	0.199**	0.034	−0.062	−0.105*	0.523**	0.264**	0.310**	0.614**	0.206**
33 Fr. hacking	0.113**	−0.043	−0.080	−0.002	0.030	0.144**	0.023	0.127**	0.159**	0.116**	0.029	−0.131**	0.380**	0.242**	0.237**	0.213**	0.527**
34 Female	0.055	0.057	0.047	−0.049	0.010	−0.261**	0.161**	0.086*	−0.070	−0.005	−0.083*	−0.119**	−0.346**	−0.256**	−0.171**	−0.469**	−0.058
35 Employment	0.102*	0.035	0.014	−0.064	0.082	−0.017	−0.002	−0.112**	−0.029	−0.012	−0.133**	0.013	0.063	0.073	0.048	0.018	0.027
M	0.361	0.139	0.049	0.072	1.265	0.791	2.778	1.916	2.119	0.372	0.279	0.153	0.509	0.335	1.039	0.553	0.187
SD	0.481	0.346	0.216	0.259	1.107	1.232	1.283	1.758	1.376	0.774	0.449	0.360	0.596	0.763	1.201	1.040	0.502

Table 18.1 Pearson Correlation Matrix and Descriptive Statistics (N = 570) (continued)

	18	19	20	21	22	23	24	25	26	27	28	29	30	31	32	33	34	35
18 Unauth. wire.	—																	
19 Skill level	0.133**	—																
20 Giving passwords	0.012	-0.037	—															
21 Physical guard.	0.062	0.218**	-0.024	—														
22 Antivirus	-0.019	0.070	0.002	0.390**	—													
23 Spybot	0.055	0.091*	0.008	0.539**	0.078	—												
24 Ad-aware	0.057	0.168**	-0.005	0.487**	0.054	0.275**	—											
25 Microsoft Upd.	0.018	0.206**	-0.030	0.591**	0.176**	0.133**	0.130**	—										
26 Security center	0.010	0.007	-0.036	0.327**	0.027	0.078	-0.025	0.117**	—									
27 Soft. firewall	0.001	0.125**	-0.007	0.589**	0.118**	0.162**	0.136**	0.259**	0.023	—								
28 Hard. firewall	0.080	0.068	-0.020	0.557**	0.126**	0.127**	0.047	0.189**	0.156**	0.236**	—							
29 Social guard.	0.319**	0.214**	-0.059	0.059	0.011	0.041	0.126**	0.017	-0.049	0.017	0.020	—						
30 Fr. pirate soft.	0.248**	0.190**	-0.079	0.059	-0.012	0.067	0.120**	0.021	-0.015	-0.019	0.028	0.763**	—					
31 Fr. pirate media	0.229**	0.152**	-0.018	0.025	0.075	-0.007	0.074	0.005	-0.058	0.031	-0.032	0.801**	0.526**	—				
32 Fr. pornography	0.269**	0.198**	-0.028	0.051	0.011	0.042	0.092*	0.035	-0.074	-0.005	0.051	0.758**	0.367**	0.400**	—			
33 Fr. hacking	0.196**	0.067	-0.070	0.044	-0.093*	0.026	0.102*	-0.025	0.038	0.060	0.018	0.634**	0.381**	0.330**	0.432**	—		
34 Female	-0.126**	-0.249**	0.067	-0.090*	0.038	-0.153**	-0.157**	-0.010	0.040	0.009	-0.046	-0.315**	-0.253**	-0.126**	-0.410**	-0.110**	—	
35 Employment	0.048	0.068	0.005	0.066	0.032	0.058	0.047	0.004	0.047	-0.007	0.060	0.071	0.048	0.028	0.081	0.060	0.022	—
M	0.430	0.670	0.907	3.183	0.870	0.295	0.351	0.614	0.132	0.518	0.404	0.907	0.756	1.447	1.056	0.370	0.575	0.821
SD	0.899	0.569	0.291	1.576	0.336	0.456	0.478	0.487	0.338	0.500	0.491	0.694	0.914	1.124	1.069	0.579	0.495	0.604

* $p < .05$ (two-tailed);
** $p < .01$.

reported multiple malware victimization. Twenty-eight respondents (4.9%) reported three to five victimizations, whereas only five respondents (.9%) and two respondents (0.4%) respondents reported six to nine and 10 or more victimizations, respectively. Because of this severely limited variation, we dichotomized this measure (0 = no victimization; 1 = victimization) and used logistic regression to examine what activities and precautions predict whether an individual loses computerized data because of malware.

Routine Activities

Following past RAT research, which focused on domain-specific models, we incorporated direct and proxy measures of online routine activities to understand how the respondents use computer technology for work/school and personal needs. Respondents were asked who owned the computer (ownership) that they used most often (0 = you or your family; 1 = other, including friends, school, and employer) and to indicate the Internet connection speed of this computer. Two dummy variables (Dial-up and T-1) were included in the models, with DSL/cable modem being the comparison group. We treated connectivity as a lifestyle measure because of the demographic trends in the type of Internet connection used. Individuals living in rural rather than urban environments are more likely to use dial-up Internet connections due to the lack of high-speed service (Pew Internet & American Life Project, 2009). African Americans and those making less than $20,000 per year are also more likely to have dial-up connections, due in part to the higher cost of broadband connectivity (Pew Internet & American Life Project, 2009). Thus, individuals who desire faster connections are willing to pay for this lifestyle privilege. In fact, despite the recent economic downturn, the number of broadband users has increased as individuals have eliminated other services, such as cellular telephone connections, to maintain their high-speed connection (Pew Internet & American Life Project, 2009).

We directly assessed the amount of time respondents spent on specific computer activities by asking the respondents how much time they spent on the computer each week, on average, over the past 6 months for each of the following activities: (1) shopping/going to auction sites (shopping); (2) playing video games (video games); (3) checking e-mail (e-mail); (4) using either chatrooms, Internet Relay Chat (IRC), or instant messaging (IM; chat rooms); (5) downloading and uploading files (downloading files); and (6) programming (programming). The options included never, less than 1 hr, 1–2 hr, 3–5 hr, 6–9 hr, and 10 or more hr.[2] In addition, the use of online

---

[2] In order to examine whether spending time on the computer, in general, affects malware victimization, we also measured the number of hours per week spent on the computer for work or school and also outside of work or school. The options were fewer than 5 hr, 5-10 hr, 11-15 hr, 16-20 hr, and 21 or more hr. These two measures tap into two distinct

banking systems (online bank) and popular social networking websites (MySpace) were measured with the following questions, "I generally avoid using online banking systems" and "I generally avoid using websites like Facebook, MySpace, and classmates.com" (0 = no; 1 = yes). Note that a positive response means that they do not use online banking or these websites.

Deviant Behavior

In order to examine the relationship between deviant computer activities and data loss due to malware infection, we asked respondents how many times (with the options being never, 1–2 times, 3–5 times, and 6 or more times) they used a computer in the past 12 months to do the following activities:

1. Knowingly use, make, or give to another person a "pirated" copy of commercially-sold computer software
2. Knowingly use, make, or give to another person "pirated" media (music, television show, or movie)
3. Look at pornographic or obscene materials
4. Guess another's password to get into his/her computer account or files
5. Access another's computer account or files without his/her knowledge or permission to look at information or files
6. Add, delete, change, or print any information in another's computer files without the owner's knowledge or permission
7. Use someone else's wireless Internet connection without their authorization to surf the Web or otherwise access on-line content (Rogers, 2001; Skinner & Fream, 1997)[3]

To create our deviant behavior measure, we first averaged items 4, 5, and 6 to create a reliable hacking scale ($\alpha = .859$) that ranged from 0 to 3. Averaging these three items allowed the other deviance measures to have the same influence in the deviant behavior measure rather than having three of the seven items included in the scale be hacking related. Responses for the five items were then averaged, creating a reliable measure ($\alpha = .752$) that ranged from 0 to 3 ($M = .509$; $SD = .596$).[4]

---

aspects of how computer usage is integrated into the participants' daily lives, as indicated by a significant but low correlation between the two measures (Spearman = .255). These two measures were not statistically significant in any regression model.

[3] The survey's options actually separate the "6 or more" category into "6–9 times" and "10 or more times." The last two categories were collapsed because of limited responses in this largest category.

[4] The data set does not contain a question assessing whether the respondents have knowingly created or distributed malware with the intent to cause computer damage. Although we expected that the number of respondents who engaged in this behavior within the last year was minimal or nonexistent (see Rogers, 2001), we could not directly assess the

Guardianship

We included guardianship measures that were categorized as personal, physical, and social. We asked respondents to assess their skill level with computers and technology (skill level) so that such an assessment would serve as
a proxy measure of their ability to protect their computers and themselves
while interacting or performing various activities online. This assessment
was based on a three-point ordinal scale adapted from Rogers (2001), in which
0 = I can surf the 'net, use common software, but not fix my own computer
("normal"); 1 = I can use a variety of software and fix some computer problems I have ("intermediate"); and 2 = I can use Linux, most software, and fix
most computer problems I have ("advanced"). The modal category (56.8%)
was intermediate, with an additional 38.1% self-assessing their skills as normal and only 5.1% indicating advanced skills.[5] To further assess personal
guardianship, we also asked the respondents whether or not they protect
their passwords and other sensitive information (0 = no; 1 = I avoid giving
out my passwords for e-mail accounts or other sensitive information).

We assessed physical guardianship by asking respondents whether or not
(0 = no; 1 = yes) the computer that they use most often has updated antivirus
(Anti-virus), spybot (Spybot software), and Ad-Aware software (Ad-Aware
software). Additionally, we asked whether they go to or use Microsoft Update
(Microsoft Update) or America OnLine (AOL) or ISP-provided security centers (Security Center). Finally, we asked asked whether or not the computer
they use most often has software (software firewall) and/or hardware firewalls (hardware firewalls). Physical guardianship was measured by adding
these seven items together and creating an additive scale.

Although our Physical Guardianship scale has low reliability ($\alpha = .512$),
we operationalized this measure as an additive scale because we hypothesized
there would be a cumulative effect, meaning that the more types of physical
guardianship a person obtains and updates, the less likely he or she is to have
data lost due to malware (see Holtfreter et al., 2008, for a similar argument

---

link between malware creation/distribution and malware infection with this data set.
As the literature review illustrates, however, the deviant computer behaviors measured
for this study can place an individual at risk for victimization because criminals may
place malware within software, media, and pornographic websites. Additionally, engaging in hacking activities increases the risk of victimization from other hackers.

[5] It should be noted that our skill level measure acts as a proxy measure for personal guardianship, but it could also be interpreted as a computer usage measure and, therefore, be
considered a proxy for routine computer activity. We consider skill level to be a guardianship measure because we have controlled for various computer-related routine activities as
discussed earlier. Any possible effect that skill level has on victimization would mostly be
reduced to guardianship influences. The survey did provide a fourth option for this question: I am afraid of computers and don't use them unless I absolutely have to. Only one
student in the original data set and no student in the 570 cases analyzed identified their
skill level as remedial; these responses indicated that this sample is computer literate.

regarding additive scales). We also examined the independent effects of the seven items on malware victimization as a precaution that physical guardianship cannot be operationalized as an additive scale.

It is important to note that our assessment of physical guardianship may not accurately reflect the use of these programs by the respondents. Choi (2008) noted that respondents may not understand the definition or utility of protective software programs; thus, any attempt to explore their use must be carefully developed by researchers. Because we did not provide definitions for each type of program in the survey, we were careful to moderate our discussion of these variables in the findings of this study.

We assessed social guardianship by asking the respondents how many of their friends pirated software (fr. pirate software) or media (fr. pirate media), viewed pornographic or obscene material (fr. pornography), and hacked (fr. hacking) during the past 12 months (0 = none of them; 1 = very few of them; 2 = about half of them; 3 = more than half of them).[6] Similar to the measure assessing the respondents' involvement in hacking (hacking), the Friends' Computer Hacking scale (α = .882) also was created. We did this by averaging the respondents' answers to how many of their friends guess passwords; access computer accounts or files without permission; and add, delete, change, or print information without permission. We then created the Social Guardianship measure by averaging the scores for the four items (pirate software, pirate media, pornography, and hacking; α = .732). Finally, we statistically controlled for gender (0 = male; 1 = female) and employment status (0 = unemployment; 1 = part time/temp; 2 = full time).[7]

Results and Discussion

The correlation matrix (see Table 18.1) illustrates that most routine activities on the computer, as well as personal and physical guardianship, are not corre-

---

[6] The original survey question also contained the option all of them. Only a small number of respondents reported that all of their friends pirated software or hacked computers. Thus, we combined the all of them option with the more than half option. We also ran the models with the nonrecategorized items, and the models were substantively similar to the results presented in Table 18.2.

[7] We also examined race and age, as these demographics have been related to traditional victimization. For race, respondents could identify themselves as White, African American, Hispanic, Asian, or "other racial/ethnic group." Hispanics, Asians, and "other racial/ethnic group" made up only 2.8%, 5.3%, and 3.2%, respectively, of the cases analyzed. We ran full models with dummy variables for each group, but no racial group was significantly related to malware infection. Age was a four-point ordinal scale (0 = 19 years; 1 = 20–21 years; 2 = 22–25 years; 3 = 26 years and up) and was not statistically related to malware victimization in our models. Thus, to simplify the models, we excluded these two demographics (race and age) from our full models presented in Table 18.2.

lated with data loss from malware victimization.[8] However, the hypothesized relationships between both deviant computer behavior (r = .136) and lack of social guardianship (r = .153) with malware victimization are supported. Although pirating software and viewing online pornography are not correlated with malware victimization, pirating media (r = .149), hacking (r = .084), and unauthorized access to the Internet (r = .099) are also statistically correlated—albeit weakly—with malware victimization. Furthermore, "friends' pirate software" is the only item from the Social Guardianship measure that is not correlated with data loss from malware victimization. Although the matrix does not indicate strong relationships between legitimate computer activities and malware victimization, these univariate analyses provide enough evidence to further explore our hypotheses via multivariate analyses.

We estimated logistic regression models with data loss caused by malware victimization as the dependent variable (see Holtfreter et al., 2008; Schreck, 1999).[9] Logistic regression is an appropriate technique for these analyses because our dependent variable is dichotomous and skewed. For our main analyses, we ran two models (see Table 18.2). Model A contains the items as described in the Measures section, meaning that the components of RAT are represented as constructs. In Model B, we do not use the general constructs but, rather, use the specific items that made up the scales. Researchers have traditionally used RAT as a framework to understand how specific behaviors and conditions are related to victimization rather than creating scales of the concepts themselves. This traditional approach does not directly test the theory but has the benefit of identifying how specific behaviors are related to victimization, leading to clearer policy implications (Mustaine & Tewksbury, 1998). Thus, our two-model strategy allows us to examine the utility of using RAT as a framework to understand malware victimization (Model A) as well as to understand how specific activities and precautions affect one's likelihood of victimization (Model B).

[8] We provide a full correlation matrix, including all of our measures for models A and B, because of the exploratory nature of our study and to provide the reader and future researchers as much information as possible regarding the correlates of malware victimization.

[9] The correlation matrix illustrates some moderately strong correlations between some of the independent variables [for example, deviant behavior and social guardianship (r = 0.653) and pirating media and friends pirating media (r = 0.659)]. Multicollinearity, however, was not an issue for the models. No VIF was over 10 and no tolerance level fell below .2. In Model A, deviant behavior (tolerance of .478 and VIF of 2.091) and social guardianship (tolerance of .525 and VIF of 1.906) met acceptable standards. In Model B, pirating media (tolerance of .384 and VIF of 2.606) and friends pirating media (tolerance of .421 and VIF of 2.374) were acceptable as well. Additionally, including measures for both downloading files and media piracy did not cause problems. Models ran without the downloading files measure produced substantively similar results to the findings presented in Table 2.

Table 18.2 Logistic Regression Predicting Data Loss from Malware Infection

	Full Model A (n = 570)			Full Model B (n = 570)			Male (n = 242)	Female (n = 328)
	B	SE	Exp (B)	B	SE	Exp (B)	Exp (B)	Exp (B)
Routine activities								
Ownership	-.480	.295	.619	-.435	.298	.647	.901	.564
Dial-up	-.622	.471	.537	-.527	.485	.590	1.381	.411
T-1	-1.221**	.446	.295	-1.161**	.453	.313	.464	.220*
Shopping	-.023	.091	.977	-.020	.093	.981	1.073	.926
Video games	-.072	.085	.930	-.059	.087	.943	.904	1.149
E-mail	-.049	.084	.952	-.049	.086	.952	.823	1.023
Chat Rooms	.078	.060	1.081	.078	.061	1.081	.888	1.175*
Downloading files	.000	.082	1.000	-.019	.084	.981	1.257	.823
Programming	.212	.126	1.236	.228	.130	1.256	1.607*	1.046
Online bank	.163	.217	1.177	.191	.222	1.211	.930	1.454
MySpace	.123	.289	1.130	.093	.298	1.097	.771	1.315
Dev. behavior	.384	.218	1.468	—	—	—	—	—
Pirating software	—	—	—	-.079	.162	.924	.772	.893
Pirating media	—	—	—	.240*	.116	1.271	1.492*	1.238
Pornography	—	—	—	-.042	.126	.959	.977	.477*
Hacking	—	—	—	.063	.242	1.065	1.761	.621
Unauth. wireless	—	—	—	.109	.110	1.115	1.084	1.200
Personal guardianship								
Skill level	-.237	.185	.789	-.264	.190	.768	.610	.972
Giving passwords	.179	.322	1.196	.098	.330	1.103	.896	1.252

(continued)

Table 18.2 Logistic Regression Predicting Data Loss from Malware Infection (continued)

	Full Model A (n = 570)			Full Model B (n = 570)			Male (n = 242)	Female (n = 328)
	B	SE	Exp (B)	B	SE	Exp (B)	Exp (B)	Exp (B)
Spybot software	—	—	—	.056	.217	1.057	.787	1.349
Ad-aware software	—	—	—	.378	.206	1.459	1.317	1.693
Microsoft update	—	—	—	.082	.208	1.085	1.543	.946
Security Center	—	—	—	-.187	.294	.829	.821	.835
Software firewall	—	—	—	-.009	.201	.991	.718	1.201
Hardware firewall	—	—	—	-.128	.203	.880	.831	.792
Social guardianship	.358*	.178	1.430	—	—	—	—	—
Fr. Pirate software	—	—	—	.007	.141	1.007	1.168	.924
Fr. Pirate media	—	—	—	-.061	.132	.941	.794	1.020
Fr. Pornography	—	—	—	.363**	.133	1.438	1.548*	1.584*
Fr. Hacking	—	—	—	.004	.214	1.004	.713	1.483
Demographics								
Female	.495*	.221	1.641	.602*	.248	1.827	—	—
Employment	.359*	.157	1.431	.350*	.160	1.418	2.033**	1.265
Constant	-1.760**	.524	.172	-1.865**	.568	.155	-2.029*	.280
Pseudo R²	.111			.138			.257	.192

Full model A: $\chi^2 = 48.215$***; $-2LL = 697.597$.
Full model B: $\chi^2 = 60.456$***; $-2LL = 685.357$.
Male model: $\chi^2 = 49.365$; $-2LL = 257.776$.
Female model: $\chi^2 = 49.954$; $-2LL = 386.980$.
Shaded cells illustrate significant difference ($z \geq 1.96$) between partitioned model.
* $p \leq .05$; ** $p \leq .01$**.

Some readers might be concerned that our full Model B, male model, and female model do not have enough cases for the number of measures included and that Type II error is present. In other words, would some of the nonsignificant results be significant if we had either more cases or fewer independent variables? There are no accepted rules for the number of cases needed per independent variable in logistic regression (i.e., 30 cases per measure). Instead, the issue is whether the results are stable depending on the number of variables included in the models. We illustrate the stability of our models two different ways. First, we provide a full correlation matrix (see Table 18.1) illustrating that many of the measures were not significantly correlated with malware victimization even at the zero-order level. Thus, even when only one independent variable is being examined, most of the measures are not significantly related. Second, and most important, we conducted further analyses not reported in the text. Following past traditional routine activities research, we ran full and reduced models to examine the stability of the models. Similar to the work of Mustaine and Tewksbury (1998, 2002), we included all of our measures into the regression model. All measures that were not significant at $p < .205$ were excluded, and the models were rerun. Specifically, we were examining whether measures that were not previously significant would be significant when fewer measures were in the models. In addition, we also ran models that contained only the measures that pertained to each construct (i.e., guardianship). The findings did not substantively differ in any of the extra models. Thus, the findings presented in Table 18.2, and our conclusions based off of these models, are not affected by the number of measures included in our models.

These regression models indicate that neither computer ownership nor legitimate computer-related activities, such as chat rooms and e-mail, appear to have an influence on the risk of data loss caused by malware infection. The only routine activity measure statistically related to data loss from malware infection is having T-1 Internet connection speed. The coefficient sign is negative, meaning that individuals who have faster, more efficient access to the Internet are less likely to get viruses, worms, and Trojans than are individuals with DSL/cable connections. Although we originally conceived of connectivity as a lifestyle factor, because of the demographic correlates of connectivity and the ability to access websites faster, the observed relationship between connectivity and the likelihood of malware infection may be a result of protective factors related to one's Internet connection. High-speed users, particularly on T-1 connections, are more likely to use the university as their ISP (see Hinduja, 2001). Large institutions are more likely to have significant filtering and firewalls in place to protect users than are those individual users at home on dial-up or DSL modems. This insularity may play a role in reducing the risk of infection. Additionally, dial-up users are more likely to be affected by unique forms of malicious software designed to subvert the modem that connects the computer to the Internet (Nazario, 2003). There is, however, a need for future research to explore and disentangle the operationalization of connectivity as either a guardianship or lifestyle measure.

We had argued that Internet connectivity is a lifestyle measure because individuals with faster connections can access websites more effectively and efficiently. In addition, the authors of previous research found that Internet connectivity is related to socioeconomic factors such as race, income, and whether individuals live in rural areas (Pew Internet & American Life Project, 2009). Because we found that connectivity is related to malware victimization, this would suggest that connectivity could mediate the effects of socioeconomic factors on malware victimization. This does not appear to be the case, however, with our data set. Although T-1 connectivity is significantly correlated with malware victimization ($r = -.11$), race, gender, and age are not related to our connectivity or victimization measures. Employment status is correlated with victimization ($r = .10$) but is not related to connectivity. Individuals with more computers skills are less likely to have dial-up ($r = -.08$), but skill level is not related to malware victimization. In addition, when all of the measures discussed here, with the exception of the connectivity measures, are included in a logistic regression model with malware victimization as the dependent variable, only employment status is significant, $Exp(B) = 1.43$. When both connectivity measures are included in the model, the effects of employment status do not change substantively, $Exp(B) = 1.40$. Thus, these zero-order correlations and regression models do not indicate that connectivity mediates any possible effects of demographics on malware victimization. At the same time, our findings could be limited to those of a college sample. Of the 570 students, only 28 (4.9%) had dial-up and 41 (7.2%) had T-1. Thus, a more representative sample of the U.S. population could show that Internet connectivity does mediate the effects of demographics on malware victimization because there would be more variation in the connectivity measure. Clearly, this is an important issue for future researchers to investigate.

Spending time performing illegitimate computer activities was also not a strong predictor of malware infection. The only form of personal deviance that increased the risk of malware infection was pirating media. Such behavior is particularly prevalent among college students and young people who regularly use computers (Gopal, Sanders, Bhattacharjee, Agrawal, & Wagner, 2004; Higgins, 2005; Hinduja, 2001). Those who pirate media make suitable targets for malware writers because piracy requires individuals to open files for their own benefit. Motivated offenders can easily conceal their malware to appear as a music or movie file that an individual would want to download (Szor, 2005; Taylor et al., 2006). Although hacking and unauthorized use of someone else's wireless Internet connection were correlated with malware infection (see Table 18.1), they were not significant in the fuller model after controlling for other routine computer activities. Thus, these findings illustrate the importance of including measures covering multiple forms of computer deviance in order to avoid model misspecification.

Personal and physical guardianship played small roles in explaining whether the respondent's primary computer was infected by viruses, worms, or Trojans leading to data loss. Strong computer skills and careful password management—what we termed *personal guardianship*—did not reduce the threat of malware victimization. Furthermore, malware infection was not influenced by physical guardianship. This finding is contrary to the current understanding of malware protection, considering that antivirus software and firewalls are made to stop computer infiltration and infection by viruses, worms, and Trojans. The cross-sectional design of our study could possibly nullify a significant negative relationship between physical guardianship measures and malware infection. If respondents purchased antivirus programs and firewalls as a preventive measure before and after victimization, physical guardianship would have a nonsignificant effect in a cross-sectional design. This logic, however, assumes that the theoretical negative relationship between physical guardianship and infection is so small that the relationship could be nullified by only a few victims purchasing physical guardianship after victimization.

Our models also indicated that associating with friends who view online pornography increases the risk of malware infection. Peers who view pornography online may increase the risk of malware infection because these programs can spread to other computers through e-mail address books or other techniques (Szor, 2005). As a consequence, their actions place all individuals in their social network at risk of victimization. At the same time, no relationship was identified between (a) friends who pirate software, pirate media, and commit "hacker-like" behaviors, and (b) malware victimization. This is surprising, given the relationship between respondents' pirating media and victimization as well as the connection between peers who engage in piracy and individual pirating behavior (Higgins, 2005; Skinner & Fream, 1997).

Finally, some demographic correlates of malware infection were found. Individuals who were employed were at a higher risk of malware victimization, supporting the traditional literature in which employment can be a risk factor for youth because it increases exposure to deviant others (Wright & Cullen, 2004). Being female increased the odds of malware victimization by 1.827 times. Of the females, 38.4% had lost data because of malware over the last 12 months, as compared with 33.1% of the males. Because the literature implies that computers, in general, are the primary targets for malware writers and not specific groups (i.e., females), we partitioned the model by gender and ran equality-of-coefficient tests (see Paternoster, Brame, Mazerolle, & Piquero, 1998) to examine whether routine activities and guardianship factors influence male and female victimization differently (see Table 18.2). These additional tests found no differences regarding the effects of guardianship on malware victimization. The only factor that was significant in at least one of the two models and statistically different in comparison to the other model was the number of hours that the respondent spent using chat rooms, IRC, or IM. For every one-unit increase in the chat room measure, the odds of female malware victimization increased by 1.175 times. This finding supports previous research that finds female users who engage in computer-mediated communications face a greater risk of online harassment and cyberstalking than do male users (Bocij, 2004; Finn, 2004; Holt & Bossler, 2009). In fact, malware has been used by harassers to install back-door programs and do serious harm to their intended target's computer (see Bocij, 2004; Finn, 2004). Thus, malware—or, at least, the use of it—might not be as indiscriminate as it appears.

Conclusions and Policy Implications

In the original presentation of RAT, Cohen and Felson (1979) wrote that "it is ironic that the very factors which increase the opportunity to enjoy the benefits of life also may increase the opportunity for predatory violations" (p. 605). Since 1990, the rise of the personal computer and the Internet has provided enormous advantages to society. At the same time, it has also provided more opportunities for motivated offenders to victimize individuals in brand-new ways. RAT has historically been fruitful in providing a useful framework to understand how technological shifts affect a wide variety of criminal offenses. However, criminologists have been slow to examine how routine computer activities and guardianship affect cyber crime. We addressed this gap by conducting an exploratory analysis of RAT to account for a computer-focused crime: malware infection.

Our findings provide partial support for the application of RAT to data loss from malicious software. Spending more time on computer activities that are theoretically related to malware infection—such as online shopping, e-mailing, and participating in chat rooms—did not increase the odds of victimization. Yet, individuals who engaged in media piracy were at an increased risk of victimization. In addition, those whose peers viewed pornography in cyberspace were at a significant risk of malware infection. The behavior of oneself and one's peers increases the risk of victimization largely because of the ways in which malware spreads across systems. These are excellent vectors for a motivated offender to distribute malicious code, considering media and pornographic files are attractive packages that many individuals would want to open (Furnell, 2002; Szor, 2005; Taylor et al., 2006). Thus, the findings suggest that the relationship between crime and victimization in the real world may be replicated in online environments.

Computer software that has been created specifically to decrease malware victimization had no significant impact on this sample. Our findings support recent studies on malicious software that highlight the difficulty of security measures to prevent malware infection (see PandaLabs, 2007). Almost 25% of personal computers around the world that use a variety of security solutions have malware loaded into their memory, compared with 33.28% of unprotected systems (PandaLabs, 2007). In addition, we did not find that different forms of personal guardianship decreased victimization. These results may, however, be a consequence of our assessment of protective software. Choi (2008) recommends careful measurement and elaboration of security software concepts to respondents in order to properly address their use. As we did not use such information in the course of this study, it is possible that the findings of this analysis are measurement related. Thus, future researchers should explicitly define and clearly assess the influence of protective software on the risk of malware victimization (see also Choi, 2008).

These findings are quite similar to those of other RAT studies that used college samples in which guardianship measures were primarily not significant (Mustaine & Tewksbury, 1998; Schwartz et al., 2001). These studies argued that taking safety precautions was not effective when the victimization experienced was caused by friends and not strangers. Physical guardianship measures will not be as effective in decreasing malware infection because these tools are most useful for addressing victimization caused by strangers rather than by friends. Thus, these findings do not support target hardening as the strongest protection tool to decrease the probability of data loss from malware in a college sample. Instead, individuals must be aware of the possible consequences of their behavior and that of their peers and attempt to change their behavior. This is easier said than done, considering that past research has illustrated the difficulty of individuals changing their behavior even when they understand the risks involved (Reisig, Pratt, & Holtfreter, 2009).

These findings strongly support the role that criminology can play in developing a framework to understand and prevent malware infection. Malware infection will not be decreased substantially through a single approach based solely on criminology or information technology. A two-pronged approach—that is, physical target hardening through security solutions and behavioral changes based on RAT—should have a role in future programs and policies meant to decrease the damage caused by malware. The continued examination of the behavioral correlates of malware infection using a RAT framework is vital.

A key policy implication from this study is the need for greater awareness of the connection between computer deviance and malware victimization.

The significant concentration of media piracy among young people, coupled with the increasing sophistication and efficacy of malware, suggests that this population is extremely susceptible to victimization. Most media campaigns against piracy focus on the significant financial harms caused by this crime (Higgins, 2005). However, these campaigns may have little impact, as piracy is largely perceived to have little effect on the artists and greater benefits for the individual (see Gopal et al., 2004; Higgins, 2005; Hinduja, 2001). Instead, antipiracy campaigns need to focus on the risk to individuals and their peers who download media illegally. Considering the significant volume of piracy that occurs in dorms on college campuses (see Higgins, 2005; Hinduja, 2001), educating students and computer security personnel on the risks of piracy may be an important preventive tool to decrease the risk of computer crime victimization on college campuses.

A further practical implication may be to expand the regulatory power of system administrators to withhold service. Currently, system administrators can cut Internet connectivity to computer systems that are suspected of malicious activity or violations of terms of service. Those who use large amounts of bandwidth for piracy purposes also may be tied to the spread of malicious software across networks. Thus, regular monitoring of Internet use for potential piracy, and selective removal of those users, may help to minimize the occurrence of infection. Although such a measure may be helpful, it would require great technical resources for administrators, as ISPs have very large customer populations. Improving the automated monitoring protocols that can detect and remove anomalous traffic may be a key to helping combat the problem of malicious software.

Although this exploratory study increases our knowledge of cyber crime, further study is needed to elaborate and expand on the issue of malicious software infection. Specifically, we used a convenience sample of college students from a single university, populated primarily by individuals from the same state. Although college samples have been used extensively for criminological theory testing (see Payne & Chappell, 2008, for a review of the use of college samples in criminological research), the representative nature of this study is limited. The characteristics of how malware spreads indicate that our findings would be generalizable to other universities around the country. In addition, we assessed whether the respondents had experienced a severe form of malware victimization by asking whether they had lost computerized data. This method does not capture information on malware that caused other forms of victimization, such as identity theft, or malware that is present but benign. Future research should use more direct and specific measures of malware infection to triangulate the reality of malware on a system, such as diminished functionality and identification by antivirus programming (see Choi, 2008; PandaLabs, 2007). Researchers also must use measures to identify the time at which antivirus and other protective software programs were placed on a computer system. Finally, our study explored the applicability of only routine activities theory to malware infection and did not examine the influences of concepts from other theories, such as self-control or rational choice theories. Clearly the participation in risky computer activities is an indicator of low self-control as well as behavior that places individuals in closer proximity to motivated offenders. Such explorations can improve understanding of cyber crime victimization and the applicability of traditional theories of crime to account for victimization in virtual environments.

References

Bocij, P. (2004). *Cyberstalking: Harassment in the Internet age and how to protect your family.* Westport, CT: Praeger.

Choi, K. C. (2008). Computer crime victimization and integrated theory: An empirical assessment. *International Journal of Cyber Criminology, 2,* 308–333. Retrieved from http://cyber.kic.re.kr/data/Kyungchoiijccjan2008.pdf

Cohen, L. E., & Felson, M. (1979). Social change and crime rate trends: A routine activity approach. *American Sociological Review, 44,* 588–608.

Computer Security Institute. (2007). *Computer crime and security survey.* Retrieved from http://i.cmpnet.com/v2.gocsi.com/pdf/CSISurvey2007.pdf

Coupe, T., & Blake, L. (2006). Daylight and darkness targeting strategies and the risks of being seen at residential burglaries. *Criminology, 44,* 431–464.

Cromwell, P., & Olson, J. N. (2004). *Breaking and entering: Burglars on burglary.* Belmont, CA: Wadsworth.

Felson, M. (2001). *Crime and everyday life* (3rd ed.). Thousand Oaks, CA: Sage.

Finn, J. (2004). A survey of online harassment at a university campus. *Journal of Interpersonal Violence, 19,* 468–483.

Furnell, S. (2002). *Cybercrime: Vandalizing the information society.* Boston, MA: Addison-Wesley.

Gopal., R. D., Sanders, G. L., Bhattacharjee, S., Agrawal, M., & Wagner, S. C. (2004). A behavioral model of digital music piracy. *Journal of Organizational Computing and Electronic Commerce, 14,* 89–105.

Grabosky, P. N. (2001). Virtual criminality: Old wine in new bottles? *Social and Legal Studies, 10,* 243–249.

Grabosky, P., & Smith, R. (2001). Telecommunication fraud in the digital age: The convergence of technologies. In D. Wall (Ed.), *Crime and the internet* (pp. 29–43). London, England: Routledge.

Higgins, G. E. (2005). Can low self-control help with the understanding of the software piracy problem? *Deviant Behavior, 26,* 1–24.

Hinduja, S. (2001). Correlates of Internet software piracy. *Journal of Contemporary Criminal Justice, 17,* 369–382.

Hinduja, S., & Patchin, J. W. (2008). Cyberbullying: An exploratory analysis of factors related to offending and victimization. *Deviant Behavior, 29,* 129–156.

Holt, T. J. (2007). Subcultural evolution? Examining the influence of on- and off-line experiences on deviant subcultures. *Deviant Behavior, 28,* 171–198.

Holt, T. J., & Bossler, A. M. (2009). Examining the applicability of lifestyle-routine activities theory for cybercrime victimization. *Deviant Behavior, 30,* 1–25.

Holtfreter, K., Reisig, M. D., & Pratt, T. C. (2008). Low self-control, routine activities, and fraud victimization. *Criminology, 46,* 189–220.

Kapersky, E. V. (2003). *The classification of computer viruses.* Bern, Switzerland: Metropolitan Network BBS.

Lynch, J. (1987). Routine activity and victimization at work. *Journal of Quantitative Criminology, 3,* 283–300.

Mell, P., Kent, K., & Nusbaum, J. (2005). *Guide to malware incident prevention and handling: Recommendations of the National Institute of Standards and Technology.* Gaithersburg, MD: National Institute of Standards and Technology.

Miethe, T., & McDowall, D. (1993). Contextual effects in models of criminal victimization. *Social Forces, 71,* 741–760.

Miethe, T. D., & Meier, R. F. (1994). *Crime and its social context: Toward an integrated theory of offenders, victims, and situations.* Albany, NY: State University of New York Press.

Mustaine, E. E., & Tewksbury, R. (1997). The risk of victimization in the workplace for men andwomen: An analysis using routine activities/lifestyle theory. *Humanity & Society, 21,* 17–38.

Mustaine, E. E., & Tewksbury, R. (1998). Predicting risk of larceny theft victimization: A routine activity analysis using refined lifestyle measures. *Criminology, 36,* 829–857.

Mustaine, E., & Tewksbury, R. (2002). Sexual assault of college women: A feminist interpretation of a routine activities analysis. *Criminal Justice Review, 27,* 89–123.

Nazario, J. (2003). *Defense and detection strategies against Internet worms.* Norwood, MA: Artech House.

Newman, G., & Clarke, R. (2003). *Superhighway robbery: Preventing e-commerce crime.* Cullompton, United Kingdom: Willan Press.

Osborn, D. R., & Tseloni, A. (1998). The distribution of household property crimes. *Journal of Quantitative Criminology, 14,* 307–330.

PandaLabs. (2007). *Malware infections in protected systems.* Retrieved from http://research.pandasecurity.com/blogs/images/wp_pb_malware_infections_in_protected_systems.pdf

Paternoster, R., Brame, R., Mazerolle, P., & Piquero, A. (1998). Using the correct statistical test for the equality of regression coefficients. *Criminology, 36,* 859–866.

Payne, B. K., & Chappell, A. (2008). Using student samples in criminological research. *Journal of Criminal Justice Education, 19,* 175–192.

Pew Internet & American Life Project. (2009). *Home broadband adoption increases sharply in 2009 with big jumps among seniors, low-income households, and rural residents even though prices have risen since last year.* Retrieved from http://www.pewinternet.org/Press-Releases/2009/Home-broadband-adoption-increases-sharply-in-2009.aspx

Reisig, M. D., Pratt, T. C., & Holtfreter, K. (2009). Perceived risk of internet theft victimization: Examining the effects of social vulnerability and impulsivity. *Criminal Justice and Behavior, 36,* 369–384.

Rogers, M. K. (2001). *A social learning theory and moral disengagement analysis of criminal computer behavior: An exploratory study* (Unpublished doctoral dissertation). Manitoba University, Canada.

Schreck, C. J. (1999). Criminal victimization and low self-control: An extension and test of a general theory of crime. *Justice Quarterly, 16,* 633–654.

Schwartz, M. D., DeKeseredy, W. S., Tait, D., & Alvi, S. (2001). Male peer support and a feminist routine activities theory: Understanding sexual assault on the college campus. *Justice Quarterly, 18,* 623–649.

Shover, N. (1996). *The great pretenders: Pursuits and careers of persistent thieves.* Boulder, CO: Westview Press.

Skinner, W. F., & Fream, A. M. (1997). A social learning theory analysis of computer crime among college students. *Journal of Research in Crime and Delinquency, 34,* 495–518.

Spano, R., & Nagy, S. (2005). Social guardianship and social isolation: An application and extension of lifestyle/routine activities theory to rural adolescents. *Rural Sociology, 70,* 414–437.

Stewart, E. A., Elifson, K. W., & Sterk, C. E. (2004). Integrating the general theory of crime into an explanation of violent victimization among female offenders. *Justice Quarterly, 21,* 159–181.

Symantec Corporation. (2003). *Symantec Internet security threat report.* Retrieved from http://eval.symantec.com/mktginfo/enterprise/white_papers/ent-whitepaper_symantec_internet_security_threat_report_iv.pdf

Szor, P. (2005). *The art of computer virus research and defense.* Upper Saddle River, NJ: Addison-Wesley.

Taylor, R. W., Caeti, T. J., Loper, D. K., Fritsch, E. J., & Liederbach, J. (2006). *Digital crime and digital terrorism.* Upper Saddle River, NJ: Pearson Prentice Hall.

Tewksbury, R., & Mustaine, E. (2000). Routine activities and vandalism: A theoretical and empirical study. *Journal of Crime and Justice, 23,* 81–110.

Tseloni, A., Wittebrood, K., Farrell, G., & Pease, K. (2004). Burglary victimization in England and Wales, the United States, and the Netherlands: A cross-national comparative test of routine activities and lifestyle theories. *British Journal of Criminology, 44,* 66–91.

Wall, D. S. (2001). Cybercrimes and the Internet. In D. S. Wall (Ed.), *Crime and the Internet* (pp. 1–17). New York: Routledge.

Wooldredge, J., Cullen, F., & Latessa, E. (1992). Victimization in the workplace: A test of routine activities theory. *Justice Quarterly, 9,* 325–335.

Wright, J. P., & Cullen, F. C. (2004). Employment, peers, and life-course transitions. *Justice Quarterly, 1,* 183–205.

Wright, R., & Decker, S. H. (1994). *Burglars on the job: Street life and residential break-ins.* Boston, MA: Northeastern University Press.

Yar, M. (2005). The novelty of cybercrime. *European Journal of Criminology, 2,* 407–427.

Ybarra, M. L., Mitchell, K. J., Finkelhor, D., & Wolak, J. (2007). Internet prevention messages: Targeting the right online behaviors. *Archives of Pediatric Adolescent Medicine, 161,* 138–145.

Zhang, L., Welte, J. W., & Wiecxorek, W. F. (2001). Deviant lifestyle and crime victimization. *Journal of Criminal Justice, 29,* 133–143.

Legal and Policy Issues of Cyber Crimes

V

Fatwas Chaos Ignites Cyber Vandalism

Does Islamic Criminal Law Prohibit Cyber Vandalism?

19

ALAELDIN MANSOUR MAGHAIREH

Contents

Introduction

[C]yber vandalism is religiously permitted because it is a digital weapon used against the enemy of Islam who are defaming the Islam, the prophet Mohammad, and Muslims. (Al-Azhar Al-Sharif's Fatwa, Egypt, 2008)

Fatwa and Islamic criminal law are concepts that have become somewhat common in recent years. A *fatwa* is a religious verdict given by a knowledge-able (qualified) person (*mufti*), a Council of Muftis, or a scholar of distinction on subjects connected with Shariah[1] (Hasan, 2006) on a troubling religious issue that has only recently emerged in Muslim society (Ramadan, 2006). For this reason, in every Muslim country, there is a mufti or a Council of Muftis

---

[1] *Shariah* is the pathway to fulfill the will of Allah. It is a comprehensive collection of rules, principles, teachings, and disciplines derived from the main sources of Islam, the Qur'an and the Sunnah.

who are appointed by the government to issue a fatwa on an emerging matter to consider whether the matter is Islamically acceptable. For example, in Egypt, the Al-Azhar Al-Sharif is responsible for issuing fatwas. In Saudi Arabia,[2] the official Council of Senior Scholars, which is headed by Sheikh Abd Al-Aziz Ibn Abdallah Aal-Sheikh, issues fatwas. However, not all fatwas are issued by authorized muftis or scholars. Several notorious fatwas were issued by an illegitimate authority. For example, in 1998, a fatwa issued by Osama Bin Laden and four other Islamic radicals called on Muslims to kill Americans and steal their money whenever and wherever they find it (Jerrold M. Post, personal communication, October 15, 2004). Although this fatwa has been rejected by the majority of the Muslim community, it has ignited acts of terror that have resulted in massive loss of life. However, when a fatwa is issued by a respectable Mufti council, such as the Al-Azhar Al-Sharif in Egypt, then the fatwa is greeted in Egypt and among the Muslim community throughout the world.

Islamic criminal law, on the other hand, is the most controversial section of Shariah because it applies stringent corporal punishments, such as flogging, amputation, stoning, or beheading for certain crimes (al-Omari & al-Ani, 2003). These corporal punishments and their divine sources have ignited a firestorm of controversy over their compatibility with international contemporary conceptions, such as human rights, freedom of religion, and the capacity to address new and emerging issues (Dalacoura, 2007; Peters, 2005).

In a manner similar to the Western world, the Islamic world has embraced cyberspace[3] and set up websites. There are hundreds, if not thousands, of Islamic websites in cyberspace; indeed, cyberspace has become a place for Muslims to interact, socialize, and, most importantly, propagate their own beliefs. It is not uncommon to find Islamic websites designed and optimized specifically to defend Islam from its enemies. For example, the website http://www.d-sunnah.net was established to defend Ahl al-Sunnah (Nation of Sunnah). Similarly, dozens of websites (see, e.g., http://www.islamtoday.net/pbuh.htm) were established to defend the Prophet of Islam, Mohammed, against European newspapers' publication of cartoons lampooning the Prophet. Hacktivism, the Muslim Hackers Group, is an Arabic hackers' group website that provides Muslim hackers with free hacking tools (translated by the author from http://groups.google.com.sa/group/mslamhaker?hl=ar).

---

[2] Saudi Arabia follows a very rigid form of Shariah known as *Wahhabism*.
[3] The term *cyberspace* was first coined by William Gibson in his novel *Neuromancer* (1984) to describe a fictional and visionary world experienced by millions of users in their everyday lives.

Negative Fatwa Ignites Cyber Vandalism

In July 2008, the Al-Azhar Al-Sharif issued a remarkable fatwa condoning cyber attacks against infidels' websites. The fatwa stated that "cyber vandalism 'jihad' is religiously permitted because it is a digital weapon used against the enemy of Islam who are defaming Islam, the prophet Mohammad, and Muslims" (Jihad, 2008, para. 4). According to this fatwa, hacktivism is legitimate and perceived as a sort of jihad against the enemy of Islam. This fatwa is too broad and motivational a tool for Muslim youths because it includes any website that a Sunni Muslim hacker might consider an adversarial website. For this reason, the fatwa of Al-Azhar Al-Sharif may have ignited what can be termed *cyber-sectarian conflict*. For example, in September 2008, Sunni hackers attacked more than 300 Shia websites, including the main website of the Grand Ayatollah Ali al-Sistani.[4] A group of Shia hackers called the Shia Digital Security Team responded by attacking more than 77 Sunni websites (translated from http://www.saudiyatnet.net). The fatwa also motivated a Saudi hacker known as "snipper Haks" to hack and bring down more than 55 websites in the Netherlands, in response to a video defaming the Prophet of Islam produced by Geert Wilders (n.d.; translated from http://www. arabianbusiness.com/arabic/516279), a Dutch politician and the leader of the Party for Freedom. Muslims hackers continuously attack nonbelievers' websites such as the Arabic atheist website http://www.ladeenyon.net, which has been the subject of repeated attacks. A member of the Arabic atheist "ladeenyon" commented that Al-Mujahedin cyber attacks against our website have not stopped since it was built, killing and sabotaging on earth and the Internet—they are not professionals but seek to kill and corrupt. They believe themselves to be intellectually superior, but they are not because they use what they believe to be the tools of the infidels, namely, hacking programs.... The website will survive (see http://www. forum.3almani.org/viewtopic.php?f=12&t=326).

In April 2009, a contradictory fatwa against hacktivism was issued by Sheikh Saleh Al Fozan, a member of the Saudi Higher Council of Clerics, forbidding hacking activities against Israeli websites (see http://www.lojainiat. com/?action=dnews&mid=13658). Although his fatwa has been the subject of hot debate on Arabic cyberworld blogs and has been condemned by the majority of cyberspace users, the fatwa is of enormous importance within a particular small group of Muslim hackers and Internet users because it was issued by a higher religious figure who plays a significant role in the Saudi Arabian community. This fatwa contradicts several previous fatwas

---

[4] Grand Ayotallah Ali al-Sistani is the supreme religious authority for millions of Shia, the second biggest branch of Islam after Sunni.

issued by different scholars permitting and praising Muslim hacking activities against Zionist and missionary websites as well as against the Al-Azhar Al-Sharif's fatwa.[5]

The harmful effects of the above fatwas are twofold: They radicalize Muslim youths using cyberspace, and they encourage Muslim users to learn hacking techniques and commit different forms of cyber vandalism, such as hacking, distribution of viruses, Trojans and worms, cyber defamation, and denial of service attack (DoS).[6] In this chapter, we attempt to shed some light on two key issues, as outlined in the paragraph that follows.

First, Muslim hackers do not believe in secular modern laws and, therefore, will not abide by them. This is simply because the majority of Muslims believe that Allah is the only legislator who can enact legislation, and those who do not adhere to His Law are infidels.[7] Shariah's role in cyber vandalism is significant because Muslim hackers consider Shariah to be the ultimate law system.

Second, although cyber vandalism is a new phenomenon, Shariah law is widely understood as a collection of ancient religious dogma that belongs to a time other than ours. Hence, how can Shariah respond to cyber vandalism?

This chapter first explores contemporary Muslim thoughts—both conservatives' and reformists'—and their role in shaping modern criminal law. The next sections examine (a) whether Shariah law is inflexible or nonresponsive to modern issues and (b) Islamic criminal law and its response to cyber vandalism. Finally, it examines conservative and reformist approaches to the criminalization of cyber vandalism.

---

[5] In October 2008, Sheikh Salman Al-Oda, a prominent and popular Islamic scholar, issued a fatwa condoning cyber vandalism against immoral websites. See http://www.brydah.com/ib/showthread.php?t=61641

[6] A *denial of service attack* (DoS) is one of the most recent types of cyber attacks committed through the use of hacking programs such as SYN Flood Attack. A DoS temporarily prevents legitimate network traffic, for example, by disrupting a connection between the client (Internet user) and the provider server (Internet provider). For more information about DoS attacks, see Jeremy Andrews' (2004) *Understanding TCP Reset Attacks* at http://kerneltrap.org/node/3072. See also Route's (1998) "Teardrops and Land Bugs Denial of Service Attacks Exploit TCP/IP Vulnerabilities" in *Software Magazine*.

[7] The Holy Qur'an contains several verses that can be referred to for guidance in this respect. For example, the Almighty said, "Let, then, the followers of the Gospel judge in accordance with what God has revealed therein: for they who do not judge in the light of what God has bestowed from on high-it is they, they who are truly iniquitous" (Al-Ma'idah 5: 47). Sheik Muhammad Bin al Uthaymeen, a prominent Saudi cleric, condemned Islamic countries that do not apply Shariah law and labeled anyone who does not apply or accept it a *Kafir* (nonbeliever).

Conservatives Versus Reformists

The Islamic world is not homogeneous in terms of religious perspective and theology; rather, it is heterogeneous, consisting typically of conservatives and reformists. The key difference between them is their understanding and interpretation of the Holy Scripture and the Prophet's traditions (Parrillo, 2008). Conservative views are held by those scholars who believe that Allah's commands and the Prophet's traditions (Sunnah) are infallible sources of law and therefore should be applied without modification or reinterpretation. Thus, they consider the Qura'n[8] and Sunnah[9] to be the ultimate sources of Shariah law. They argue that the four great Sunni scholars (Maliki, Hanbali, Hanafi, and Shafi) and their followers elucidated Shariah principles and purposes; therefore, the four Fiqh schools, which were established by the four Sunni scholars, are sufficient, and no further research in jurisprudence is needed. Conservatives maintain that the methods of Fiqh—such as *Ijtihad*[10] (reasoning), *Maslahah Mursalah* (considerations of public interest), *Qiyas* (juristic analogy), and *Fatwa* (religious decision)—are sufficient to solve contemporary issues (al-Akhdar, 2002).

In contrast to the conservatives, the reformists were recently formed by a group of scholars known as "the Quranic people."[11] They argue that God's commands revealed in the sacred Qur'an are the only infallible source of Shariah because the Qur'an established unequivocal and comprehensive principles and, therefore, there is no need for any sources other than the Qur'an to deduce the rules of Shariah. They reject the approaches formulated and applied by the four Sunni schools. Furthermore, they deny the Sunnah tradition as the second source of Shariah. They maintain their position upon the following grounds (Mansour, 2008):

- First, the Prophet Muhammad prohibited his followers from writing his traditions.

---

[8] The Qur'an is the primary text of Islam, and the literal word of Allah, revealed to the Prophet Muhammad over a period of 23 years. Allah means God in Arabic. It contains the commands of Allah, glimpses of the stories of previous Prophets, moral and legal injunctions.

[9] Sunnah is what the Prophet Muhammad did and said, known as *Hadith*. It was collected by different scholars nearly 200 years after the Prophet's death.

[10] *Ijtidhad* means "the exercise of independent judgment, whether on a specific case or on a rule of law, where the Qur'an and the tradition of the Prophet do not give explicit directions" (Lewis, 1991).

[11] Sheik Ahmed Subhy Mansour is the founder and spiritual leader of the Quranic Family. The reformation movement started in Egypt in 1977 to revive Egyptian society, inspired by the Imam Sheik Muhammad Abdou in 1905 (see http://www.alarabiya.net/articles/2008/03/11/46777.html). However, the Quranic family view differs from that of other Muslim reformists, such as Jamal al-Din Afghani (1839–1897) and Egyptian scholar Muhammad A'bduh (1849–1905). For more information, see Taji-Farouki and Nafi (2004).

- Second, the Qur'an has completed the divine religion.
- Third, the credibility of the Sunnah tradition is weak because Muslim started to collect it 2 centuries after the Prophet's era when Muslims began creating fake traditions for political reasons.
- Fourth, the contradiction between the Qur'an (the first source) and the Sunnah tradition makes the latter unauthentic because God promised to keep his words (the Qur'an) uncorrupted.

Although the Quranic people have been labelled by the Sunni scholars as *apostates* (Ismael, 2008), they were able to reinterpret the Quranic verses to bring them into harmony with contemporary international human rights—for example, freedom of religion and disavowal of harsh punishments such as stoning (Mansour, 1998).

Conservatives and Reformists' Fatwas on Cyber Vandalism

Although all the above fatwas have been issued by the conservatives, who advocate a radical return to Shariah law in ways that many people consider to be obsolete, none of the reformists issued a fatwa regarding the legitimacy or otherwise of hacking activities. This, of course, poses a potential risk to cyberspace because the Shariah principle of criminalization states that there is no crime without law. The Almighty said, "And nor shall we punishing until we had sent them an Apostle" (Qur'an 17:15). It can be understood from this that crimes and punishments should not be imposed retroactively.[12] If there is no positive fatwa from reformists, then the negative fatwas issued by conservatives will have a significant impact on Muslim hackers and Internet users—and, consequently, cyber criminals committing cyber vandalism can escape conviction. Therefore, the question that should be asked is why Muslim scholars—particularly, the reformists—have not yet formulated a fatwa forbidding cyber vandalism. Is it because Shariah is inflexible or obsolete?

Shariah Tends to Be Inflexible and Nonresponsive to Modern Issues

There are two opposing views expressed concerning the supposed inflexibility or rigidity of Shariah. Contemporary Muslim scholars argue vehemently that Shariah's principles are applicable in any place and at

---

[12]For example, the Prophet did not punish Muslims who got married according to the pre-Islamic system of marriage or had incestuous relationships before they became Muslims.

any time. This view is adopted by both conservatives and reformists. Conversely, secular Muslim scholars and some orientalists[13] describe it as being rigid, stagnant, and incapable of reflecting a society's developments (Al-Akhdar, 2007).

I presume that both of the above views are inaccurate and misleading. This can be explained through the examination of two different statements, respectively issued by Imam Ibn Timia (1263–1328) and Imam Ibn Qayyim (1292–1350). The former's statement centers on the spiritual meaning of Shariah. He stated, "Shariah is full of benefits, full of purposes and objectives, so anything unjust or harmful is not from Shariah" (translated by the author from Imam Ibn Timia). Imam Ibn Qayyim, on the other hand, stated that, "Fatwa is changeable according to the benefits, conditions, times, places and individuals' intentions" (Qayyim, 1968, p. 438). Another scholar added that Shariah, in all its judgments, must bring benefits and prevent corruption (al-Shak, n.d., p. 19). Indeed, the Prophet's companions had changed their fatwas and, most importantly, suspended God's commands on several occasions to meet a new situation they had encountered. For example, in two different incidents, Omar Bin Khattab, the second Caliph, applied the spiritual meaning of the Shariah through suspending a scriptural command. In the first instance, he suspended the punishment for theft during a famine year; and in the second incident, he terminated a Quranic command and a Prophetic tradition when he stopped paying alms to the nonbelievers who used to receive a share of assistance from the Prophet. In the first instance, Omar's argument was that applying Shariah in such a case would result in unjust treatment; and in the second instance, he claimed that the command had become obsolete—it was applied when Islam was weak, but once Islam had become strong, there was no need to solicit nonbelievers' support (Foda, 1986, p. 22). This is, of course, contrary to one of the most important principles of Shariah, which states that "no Ijtihad when an explicit text exists in the Holy Qur'an" (Ramadan, 2005). In other words, the exercise of independent judgment is constrained by the commands laid down by Allah.

From the above statements and examples, it can be concluded that the spiritual meaning of Shariah—that is, justice and full of benefits—is applicable in any place and at any time. Omar was able to apply Shariah and frame appropriate potential solutions to problems and to exercise appropriate Ijtihad. On the other hand, the Shariah scriptures formulated and developed by the four Sunni schools 12 centuries ago are quite rigid; in some cases, they were inflexible and incapable of responding to changing and emerging issues, such as cyber vandalism criminalization.

---

[13] The most prominent orientalist scholars in the twentieth century are Bernard Lewis, Elie Kedourie, Ignaz Goldziher, and Joseph Schacht.

Islamic Criminal Panel and Cyber Vandalism

Regarding the criminalization of acts and their punishment, the objective of Shariah law is to protect five important values: religion, human life, intellect, lineage, and property. Muhammad Mohyi Aldeen (n.d.) indicated that the process of criminalizing acts in the contemporary world is similar to that found in Shariah—that is, it is established to protect interests that are vital to human beings.

The system of criminalizing acts in Shariah law is divided into three categories to protect the five values mentioned above: Hudud,[14] Qisas, and Ta'azir.[15] The *Hudud* category is rigid. It specifically addresses six forms of physical crimes: apostasy, drinking wine, adultery, theft, defamation, and highway robbery. It protects all five pillars mentioned above through a narrow approach that focuses only on God's rights (Quraishi, 2005).[16] In other words, these actions are criminalized to meet the five objectives of the Lawgiver (Allah). The *Qisas* category is also specific, protecting human life against all forms of physical violence, such as murder and injury (Kusha, 2000). Cyber vandalism cannot be criminalized under the Hudud or Qisas categories because none of the cyber vandalism can be portrayed as a physical action against any one of the five values (religion, human life, intellect, lineage, and property). However, if cyber vandalism gradually scales up from being a cyber attack to causing actual physical harm or injury, it can be prosecuted under Qisas.

Lastly, the *Ta'azir* category deals with the least serious crimes (Vogel, 2000, p. 247). It is unspecific and flexible; therefore, all sorts of crimes that are not addressed under Hudud or Qisas can be punished under Ta'azir, including incomplete Hudud crimes (Peters, 2005, p. 65). For example, Hudud punishment for theft is amputation, but the punishment must be decreased to Ta'azir punishment if the proscribed amount of money stolen was not attained. The Prophet said that "The hand is not cut off for fruit or palm pith" (Maalik, 1989, p. 353). Unlike in Hudud and Qisas, in Ta'azir, the judge's

---

[14]*Hudud* literally means "borders or anything that God forbids us from doing"; however, not all of the Hudud offenses that are mentioned in the Qur'an require corporal punishments. Some Hudud offences impose religious punishment, such as fasting.

[15]*Ta' azir* is a punishment for the sake of Allah or for the sake of individuals for offenses not considered Hudud.

[16]The Arab tribes that dwelled in the Arabian Peninsula in the pre-Islamic era (Al-Jahellia), as well as the nations in different parts of the Middle East, had witnessed similar principles and practices. For example, the Hammurabi Code of Law, which was enacted around the eighteenth century B.C., addressed the concept "An eye for an eye" in Article 196, which stated, "If a man put out the eye of another man, his eye shall be put out" (Horne, 2007, p. 56). Indeed, several Quranic principles and practices have been derived from the monotheistic religions of Christianity and Judaism, which derived some beliefs and rituals from ancient religions and systems.

discretion is unrestricted, and he can impose the appropriate punishment for offenses committed against any of the five values. Furthermore, in the Ta'azir category, *Ijtihad* (Reasoning), *Maslahah Mursalah* (Considerations of public interest) and *Qiyas* (Juristic analogy) play critical roles in decision making. Nevertheless, cyber vandalism cannot be brought under this category unless Shariah itself criminalizes or otherwise prohibits such activities. Therefore, the main question addressed here is, "Does Shariah prohibit cyber vandalism?"

Shariah Prohibits Cyber Vandalism

Shariah does not explicitly criminalize any kind of cybercrime, but it does contain general rules of criminalization that can be applied by reformists to prohibit cyber vandalism. The above-mentioned scholars—conservatives and reformists—approach criminalization issues differently.

According to the conservatives, the second source of Shariah law (Prophet Tradition) provides significant support for the criminalization of modern crime. Scholars have quoted a number of Hadiths—for example, the Prophet, who said, "No harm shall be inflicted [on anyone] nor reciprocated [against anyone]"—to criminalize emerging crimes. The Hadith provides a legal basis for prohibiting cyber vandalism because it causes harm, either directly to the computer systems or indirectly to an individual's property—one of the five important values protected by Shariah. Nevertheless, Shariah's traditional sources are not sufficient to address cyber vandalism in detail; therefore, a secular criminal code is important to criminalize all forms of cyber crime, including cyber vandalism. The code aims to protect the five values and, therefore, meets the spiritual meaning of Shariah. For example, Saudi Arabia applies the traditional form of Shariah law, but it has also enacted a modern *Cybercrimes Act*, equivalent to that found in developed countries, to punish cyber criminals appropriately. It criminalizes acts of hacking, including cyber sabotage (Kornakov, 2007).

The second approach adopted by reformists interprets the Quranic injunctions liberally. Quranic commands provide some support for the criminalization of cyber vandalism. The Almighty said, in Sourat Al-A'raf, "hence, do not spread corruption on earth after it has been so well ordered" (Qur'an 7:56). Al-Baqara (The Cow), Verse 60, states, "Eat and drink the sustenance provided by God, and do not act wickedly on earth by spreading corruption." Another verse (Verse 206) states, "God does not love corruption." According to the classical interpretations, the word *corruption* has two meanings. One meaning is "religious disobedience," such as not believing in God (*Kuffar*), and the other is "sins or committing sins." According to *Webster's Online Dictionary* (n.d.), the word *sin* means an offense against God, religion, or good morals. In Shariah, *sin* is divided into two categories: *Kubra* (a supreme, mortal sin such as "Shirk"; i.e., associating someone else with God) and *Sugkra* (an inferior, venial sin and shortcoming) (Abd-UL-Massih, n.d.). The former sin incurs serious punishment, which falls under the Hudud or Qisas, whereas the latter category may incur Ta'azir punishment. Thus, it can be seen that both sins are associated with breaking God's will and have nothing to do with cyber vandalism, such as a DoS. Consequently, the word *sin* should be reinterpreted, going beyond the literal meaning of the scripture to include any mischievous corruption, including hacking and causing cyber-sectarian conflict. This objective could be attained by stretching the meaning of corruption to make it more appropriate to address digital corruption and hacktivism.

Conclusion

The Islamic world has populated cyberspace and established websites propagating Islamic rhetoric and ideology. Some of these websites are established to defend Islam and to teach hacking techniques to Muslim youths. Unfortunately, the growing Muslim presence in cyberspace has been accompanied by contradictory fatwas: (1) a prevailing fatwa that has affected cyberspace negatively and incited Muslim youths to commit cyber vandalism, and (2) an unpopular fatwa that condemned cyber vandalism against Israeli websites. Thus, it is not uncommon to find that Islamic and non-Islamic websites have been hacked and vandalized by Anti-Fitna Muslim Hackers or other hackers. Shariah and Islamic criminal laws were created and developed many years before the arrival of information technology. Muslim scholars, conservatives, and reformists face the toughest question of all: how to bring Shariah law in line with contemporary technological development and criminalization. Although conservatives always defend the capability of Shariah law to address contemporary issues, they appear unable to move one step forward and present a comprehensive legal response to these issues. Conversely, reformists have reshaped significant parts of Shariah to be more aligned with contemporary issues. However, neither has shaped a criminal code parallel to that of modern legal systems. This situation will give Muslim hackers and cyber terrorists justification to launch attacks in cyberspace. Shariah law is not only rich with general principles, but it also urges its followers to develop an efficient response to cyber vandalism.

References

Abd-UL-Massih. (n.d). *Understanding Islam.* Retrieved from http://www.arabicbible. com/christian/q_about_islam_practices.htm al-Akhdar, A. (2002). هستيريا جماعية:المثقفون والعمليات الانتحارية [Educated People and Suicide Operations: Mass Hysteria]. Retrieved from http://www.yassar.freesurf. fr/stoa/bal418.html

al-Akhdar, A. (2007). الميثاق العقلاني [Rational Charter]. Retrieved from http://www. elaph.com/ElaphWeb/ElaphWriter/2007/11/281513.htm

al-Fozan, A. (n.d.). المواقع اليهودية لا يجوز اختراق [Attacking Jewish Websites Is Prohibited]. Retrieved from http://www.lojainiat.com/?action=dnews&mid=13658

al-Odah, S. (2003.) من يملك حق الاجتهاد [Who Can Make Ijtihad]. Cairo, Egypt: Maktabat al-Nahat al-Islam.

al-Odah, S. (n.d.). مهاجمة المواقع الالكترونية السنية خير [Attacking Bad Websites Is Fine]. Retrieved from http://www.brydah.com/ib/showthread.php?t=61641

al-Omari, I., & al-Ani, M. (2003). فقة العقوبات في التشريعة الاسلامية, دراسة مقارنة [Punishment Fiqh: Islamic Criminal Law: Comparative Study T.] (2nd ed). Amman, Jordan: Dar Al-Massira.

al Shak, S. (n.d.). الشرعية مدخل لدرسة علم المقاصد [Introduction to the Science of Shariah Objectives T.].

Andrews, J. (2004). *Understanding TCP reset attacks: Part I*. Retrieved from http:// kerneltrap.org/node/3072

Dalacoura, K. (2007). *Islam, liberalism and human rights: Implications for international relations*. London, United Kingdom: I. B. Tauris.

Foda, F. (1986). الحقيقة الغائبة [The Absent Truth]. Damascus, Syria: Dār al-Fikr.

Gibson, W. (1984). *Neuromancer*. New York, NY: Ace.

Hasan, N. (2006). *Laskar jihad: Islam, militancy, and the quest for identity in postnew order Indonesia*. Ithaca, NY: Cornell Southeast Asia Program Publications.

Holy Qur'an 17:15.

Horne, C. F. (2007). *The code of Hammurabi*. Charleston, SC: Forgotten Books.

Ismael, F. (2008). يعقدون مؤتمر هم الأول بأمريكا لإلغاء السنة الكفار المسلمون [The Muslim Infidels Held The First Conference in United States To Abolish Al-Sunnah]. *Alarabiya News*. Retrieved from http://www.alarabiya.net/articles/2008/03/11/46777.html

Jihad, S. (2008). الازهر يجيز الجهاد الالكتروني و الفقهاء يؤيدون [Al-Azhar Permits the Electronic Jihad and Scholars support It]. Retrieved from http://islamonline.net

Kornakov, K. (2007). *Saudi Arabia tough stance on cybercrime*. Retrieved from http:// www.viruslist.com/en/news?id=208274060

Kusha, H. (2000). Iran: Developing nation-state. In G. Barak (Ed.), *Crime and crime control: A global view* (pp. 83–103). Westport, CT: Greenwood Publishing Group.

Maalik, I. A. (1989). *Maalik's muwatta* (A. Abdurrahman Bewley, Trans.) London, United Kingdom: Kegan Paul International.

Mansour, A. (1998). Penalty of apostasy. *Ahl AlQuran*. Retrieved from http://www. ahl-alquran.com/English/show_article.php?main_id=523

Mansour, A. (2008). Denying Sunnah on Saheh Muslim Introduction. *Ahl AlQuran*. Retrieved from http://www.ahl-alquran.com/arabic/show_article. php?main_id=2899

Parrillo, V. N. (Eds.). (2008). *Encyclopedia of social problems*. Thousand Oaks, CA: SAGE Publications, Inc.

Peters, R. (2005). *Crime and punishment in Islamic law*. Cambridge, United Kingdom: Cambridge University Press.

Qayyim, I. M. (1968). اعلام الموقعين عن رب العالمين [The Message of the Elite Informers About the God]. Cairo, Egypt: Maktabat al-Kullīyāt al-Azharīyah.

Quraishi, M. (2005). *Muslims and crime: A comparative study.* London, United Kingdom: Ashgate Publishing.

Ramadan, T. (2005). *Western Muslims and the future of Islam.* Oxford, United Kingdom: Oxford University Press.

Ramadan, T. (2006). The way (Al-Sharia) of Islam. In M. Kamrava (Ed.), *The new voices of Islam: Reforming politics and modernity: A reader* (pp. 68–83). London, United Kingdom: I. B. Tauris.

Route. (1998). Teardrops and land bugs. *Software Magazine, 18*(4), 16. Retrieved from http://findarticles.com/p/articles/mi_m0SMG/is_n4_v17/ai_20442603

Taji-Farouki, S., & Nafi, B. M. (2004). *Islamic thought in the twentieth century.* London, United Kingdom: I. B. Tauris.

Vogel, F. (2000). *Islamic law and legal system: Studies of Saudi Arabia.* Leiden, The Netherlands: Koninklijke Brill.

Webster's Online Dictionary. (n.d.). *Sin.* Retrieved from http://www.websters-online.com

Cyber Bullying
Legal Obligations and Educational Policy Vacuum

20

SHAHEEN SHARIFF
DIANNE L. HOFF

Contents

Introduction

On a seemingly normal Tuesday afternoon, an eighth grade girl walks out of school and steps into her mother's car, ashen and visibly shaken. Unsure of how to proceed, her mother waits—she does not ask, and she does not move the car. Finally, her daughter speaks, saying she received the following cyber message during class: "Bitch, I know where you live. You'd better sleep each night with one eye open, on your knees. If you don't . . . I'll be there to be sure you do! —The Avenger."

Scenes like this are playing out in schools around the world. Students, especially adolescent girls, are increasingly victims (and, sometimes, perpetrators) of degrading, threatening, and/or sexually explicit messages and images conveyed electronically via cell phones, e-mail, chat rooms, and personal online profiles (Barak, 2005; Blair, 2003; Campbell, 2005; Herring, 2002; Brown, Jackson, & Cassidy, 2006; Ybarra & Mitchell, 2004). As Harmon (2004) observed, the Internet has provided young people with an arsenal of weapons for social cruelty. The phenomenon is called *cyber bullying*, which Patchin and Hinduja (2006) define as "willful and repeated harm inflicted through the medium of electronic text" (p. 152). Cyber bullying has its roots in traditional bullying that takes place in the physical school setting; however, the medium of cyberspace allows it to flourish in distinct ways, creating numerous challenges.

Cyber bullying is especially insidious because of its anonymous nature. Moreover, it allows participation by an infinite audience. In the school context, it is dangerous because it most often takes place outside school hours on home computers—making it difficult, if not impossible, to supervise. In that regard, cyber bullying is a modern-day version of Golding's (1954) *Lord of the Flies*. In this classic tale, Golding places a small group of schoolboys on a deserted island, where the rule makers are removed, compelling the boys to deal with the resulting leadership vacuum. Their first thoughts are to look for adult authority figures: "'Where's the man with the megaphone?' ... 'Aren't there any grownups at all?' 'I don't think so.' The fair boy said this solemnly; but then the delight of a realized ambition overcame him" (Golding, 1954, p. 7).

The parallels between what happens on that island and what is happening today in schools are astounding. Left alone with no supervision, for example, Golding's boys harass, terrorize, and ultimately kill one another. Similarly, cyber bullying puts students on a virtual island with no supervision and very few rules, which allows bullying to escalate to dangerous, even life-threatening, levels. Further, the boys on the island realize that being evil is easier when they assume a different persona, and so they paint their faces for anonymity before they attack. Cyber bullies are no different; they hide behind pseudonyms (e.g., "The Avenger") and well-disguised Internet Protocol (IP) addresses, making it difficult—if not impossible—for the victim to determine the source of the threat. This anonymous nature of cyber bullying is perhaps the most troubling of all, for it leaves victims wondering which of their classmates might be "The Avenger." Indeed, the entire class might be involved. For a victim of cyber bullying, attending school—and, in so doing, confronting unknown perpetrators—is like being on an island: There is no escape.

Unlike in Golding's (1954) time, today's young people do not have to travel to a remote island to find such a world. It is as close as the cell phone or the family computer. Cyberspace has become a real locale without rules and without civilization. On the Internet, no one has yet found an acceptable and workable way to create and enforce the modicum of culture that allows people to get along with each other. Nowhere on the Internet is this more true than in the virtual space frequented by children, who often have the technological capacity and skill to run electronic circles around their elders but who lack the internal psychological and sociological controls to moderate their behavior.

Maintaining civilization and civil behavior is difficult enough in organized society, even where the rule of law is supposed to prevail and where order and authority exist to protect innocent citizens. But what happens—as in dystopian fiction—when the rules and the authority are removed? This is the dilemma that schools confront as they attempt to navigate the legal and moral challenges around responding to cyber bullying and, ultimately, aim to develop in students appropriate moral compasses for an electronic age.

Our chapter focuses on the legal responsibilities for schools in dealing with cyber bullying, although we recognize that adults in society (through Internet networks, media, and technology corporations) have provided the technological tools, condoned, and modeled many of the negative behaviors that evolve in the virtual islands of unsupervised cyberspace. American legislation, in fact, protects technology corporations at the expense of victims of cyber targeting, defamation, and harassment (Myers, 2006; Servance, 2003; Wallace, 1999). Further, although many aspects of cyber bullying are clearly criminal in nature and would most likely be subject to prosecution if brought before the courts (e.g., threats of violence, criminal coercion, terrorist threats, stalking, hate crimes, child pornography, and sexual exploitation), we focus greater attention on the institutional responsibilities of schools and ISPs as opposed to the criminal liability of students.

By reviewing established and emerging law relating to school obligations to prevent cyber bullying, in this chapter we draw attention to a need for guidelines that would help schools adopt educational means to prevent and reduce cyber bullying. We appreciate that legislative initiatives and judicial efforts are often designed to avoid the floodgates of litigation on cyber bullying and cyber targeting. Our chapter explains how, regrettably, initial judicial and school responses tacitly condone cyber bullying and perpetuate the problem. We suggest a policy approach that will move the dialogue toward educational and protective measures that might better enable children to learn in physical and virtual school environments without fear of cyber bullying, as unprecedented problems related to new technologies begin to surface. Ultimately, this shows greater promise of the floodgates to litigation than criminal liability and laws that protect ISPs.

In addition, we explore the challenges for schools in monitoring students' online discourses because cyber bullying typically occurs outside supervision boundaries. This raises important legal questions about the extent to which schools can be expected to intervene when their students cyber bully off campus and outside school hours from their home computers. The policy vacuum must be addressed because parents are often too busy with their own lives and careers to be aware of what their children are doing online. As Wallis (2006) observes, most family homes are wired with computers in each room, cell phones for each member of the family, iPods, CD players, and televisions, many of which are in use at the same time. Young people are far more adept at multitasking than their parents, and as they grow up, they become immersed in technology, making the lines between their virtual and "real" or physical lives increasingly blurred.

In this chapter, we draw on a body of emerging research about cyber bullying[1] and begin by providing background on the forms and conditions of bullying in general, followed by an explanation of how cyber bullying differs from the traditional notion of bullying. Next, we review and analyze relevant case law to identify applicable legal standards for schools, both in Canada and the United States. The international focus is intentional, considering that cyber bullying quickly crosses jurisdictional boundaries rarely encountered in other school challenges. We close with recommendations for the development of ontology of the legal boundaries in cyberspace as they relate to schools. We encourage the development of informed guidelines for the implementation of inclusive, educational, and legally defensible policy approaches to cyber bullying.

Bullying: Its Forms and Conditions

Cyber bullying is an extension of general bullying in schools. Therefore, it is important to define the most prevalent forms of bullying and the conditions

---

[1] Specifically, it draws on research related to the impact of cyber bullying on student safety and learning in U.S. and Canadian schools (Aftab, 2004; Belsey, 2005; Balfour, 2005; Myers, 2006; Servance, 2003; Willard, 2003). It builds on publications and ongoing work by Shaheen Shariff (Principal Investigator), Margaret Jackson and Wanda Cassidy (Co-Investigators), and Colleen Sheppard (Collaborator) under a grant funded by the Social Sciences and Humanities Research Council of Canada to research the legal and educational policy implications of cyber bullying (known as the *Cyber Bullying Project*). The project goal is to develop a profile of cyber bullying as it differs from general bullying; examine its prevalence and impact; review legal considerations related to freedom of expression, safety, and school liability; and contribute to international conventions relating to children's rights (Brown et al., 2006; Shariff, 2005; Shariff & Gouin, 2005; Shariff & Strong-Wilson, 2005).

under which bullying occurs before presenting a profile of its cyber counterpart.

Bullying typically adopts two forms: overt and covert. *Overt bullying* involves physical aggression, such as beating, kicking, shoving, and sexual touching. It can be accompanied by *covert bullying*, in which victims are excluded from peer groups, stalked, stared at, gossiped about, verbally threatened, and harassed (Olweus, 2001). Covert bullying can be random or discriminatory. It can include verbal harassment that incorporates racial, sexual, or homophobic slurs.

Several conditions are present when bullying occurs in schools. These conditions distinguish bullying from friendly teasing and horseplay. First, bullying is unwanted, deliberate, persistent, and relentless, creating a power imbalance between perpetrator(s) and victims. Second, victim blame is a key component, and it is used to justify social exclusion from the peer group (Katch, 2001). Victims might be excluded for looking different, for being homosexual or lesbian, or simply appearing to be gay (Shariff, 2004). They might be teased about their clothes, accent, or appearance; for being intelligent, gifted, and talented; or for having special needs and/or disabilities (Glover, Cartwright, & Gleeson, 1998).

Cyber Bullying as an Extension of Bullying

Cyber bullying is an insidious and covert variation of verbal and written bullying. It is conveyed by adolescents and teens through electronic media such as cell phones, websites, webcams, chat rooms, and e-mail (Harmon, 2004; Leishman, 2002). Students create personal online profiles (e.g., Xanga, MySpace) where they might list classmates they do not like. Xanga and MySpace are social networking sites in which students can create personal profiles. These profiles combine weblogs, pictures, audio, video, instant messaging (IM), bulletin boards, and other interactive capabilities. Cyber bullying can also take the form of sexual photographs (e-mailed in confidence to friends) that are altered and sent to unlimited audiences once relationships sour (Harmon, 2004).

Preliminary research has disclosed that in Canada, 99% of teens use the Internet regularly; 74% of girls aged 12–18 years spend more time on chat rooms or participating in IM than on doing homework; one in every 17 children is threatened on the Internet; and one in four youths aged 11–19 years is threatened via computer or cell phone (Leishman, 2002; Mitchell, 2004). A recent survey of 3,700 middle school students disclosed that 18% experienced cyber bullying (Chu, 2005). A similar Canadian study of 177 middle school students in Calgary, Alberta (Li, 2005) disclosed that bullying was inflicted upon 23% of respondents by e-mail, 35% by chat rooms, 41% by cell phone text messaging, 32% by known schoolmates, 11% by people outside their school, and 16% by multiple sources, including schoolmates.

A comparative review of cyber bullying incidents under the Cyber Bullying Project disclosed the following results (Brown et al., 2006). The review disclosed that Australia is the global leader in Short Message Service (SMS; text messaging), with approximately 500 million messages being sent each month as opposed to 10 million in 2000. The study disclosed that 12% of children between 6 and 9 years of age used text messaging at least once a day; it also disclosed that 49% of 10- to 14-year-olds and 80% of 15- to 17-year-olds used SMS daily. Moreover, 61% of Australian homes had computers, and 46% of those computers had Internet access. Finally, 46% of 14-year-old Australian youths, 55% of 15-year-olds, and 73% of 16-year-olds have their own cell phones.

Moreover, the study confirmed that in Japan, children are exposed to digital gadgets at a very early age. It is interesting to note that only about half of Japanese children at age 11 years use the Internet, and only 20% are regular users (Dickie et al., 2004). The authors further explained that more than 80% of children and adolescents in Great Britain have access to home computers and that 75% of children at age 11 years own a cell phone.

Furthermore, according to a study conducted by the National Children's Home and Tesco Mobile (NCHTM, 2005), approximately 16% of British children and adolescents reported receiving threatening text messages or being bullied over the Internet; one in four young people between the ages of 11 and 19 years were threatened via personal cell phone or personal computers; and approximately 29% of those surveyed had not reported the cyber bullying. Of those reporting cyber bullying, 42% confided to a friend, and 32% reported to parents.

In a recent study of more than 300 teens under age 18 years (Patchin & Hinduja, 2006), 60% reported they had been ignored by peers online, 50% said that they had been disrespected, 30% said that they had been called names, and 21% said that they had been threatened (p. 158). The students in the study also reported negative effects from being bullied, with 42.5% saying they were frustrated and 40% reporting feelings of anger. Nearly one third of the teens reported that cyber bullying had affected them at school (31.9%), and 26.5% said it had affected them at home (Patchin & Hinduja, 2006, p. 161.)

Disturbingly, the NCHTM study found that caregivers' knowledge of cyber bullying was minimal. The survey disclosed that 56% of parents are not concerned about their children being bullied electronically, and many are in denial as to the impact of such behavior. Nineteen percent believe that such incidents are rare. Paradoxically, British teachers are very concerned about such bullying, with 50% confirming that their students had experienced such bullying. Another distressing finding is that 67% of those teachers are elementary school teachers for children younger than 11 years of age.

The review also found that in the United States, approximately 70% of children between the ages of 4 and 6 years have used computers, and 68% of children under the age of 2 years have used screen media. Surprisingly, only 13% of 8- to 17-year-olds in the United States own cell phones, unlike their counterparts in the United Kingdom and Canada.

Anonymity, Lack of Supervision, and an Infinite Audience

In addition to the findings that caregivers may not realize the seriousness of cyber bullying, there are several aspects that make it a significant challenge for schools. As with Golding's (1954) boys, who hid their identities behind painted faces and masks, most cyber bullying is anonymous. First, anonymity in cyberspace adds enormously to the challenges for schools (Harmon, 2004). For example, in Li's (2005) study, 41% of the students surveyed did not know the identity of their perpetrators. Second, cyber bullying allows participation by an infinite audience and can originate anywhere, making the boundaries of supervision difficult for schools to determine. Third, sexual harassment is a prevalent aspect of cyber bullying, which subjects young adolescent girls, boys who might appear to be homosexual, and gay and lesbian students to increased vulnerability.

Although cyber bullying begins anonymously in the virtual environment, it affects learning in the physical school environment. The consequences can be psychologically devastating for victims and socially detrimental for all students (Gati, Tenyi, Tury, & Wildmann, 2002). Just as the immaturity of Golding's (1954) boys on that deserted island drove them to commit acts that they might never have endorsed under the watchful eye of adults, so, too, in cyberspace, young people who might otherwise be inclusive and respectful in face-to-face interactions are increasingly tempted to engage in negative online discourse without realizing the impact of their actions (Parks & Floyd, 1996; Willard, 2005). Ybarra and Mitchell (2004) explained that cyberspace provides adolescents with the ability to withhold their identity in cyberspace, providing them with a unique method by which to assert their dominance. Moreover, the computer keyboard provides the control and sense of power that some students cannot achieve in face-to-face relationships (Brown et al., 2006).

Young people in cyberspace lose their inhibitions in the absence of central power, clear institutional or familial boundaries, and hierarchical structures (Milson & Chu, 2002). As Bandura (1991) explained over a decade ago, physical distance provides a context in which students can ignore or trivialize their misbehavior, as easily as Golding's boys did on their distant island. In cyberspace, this form of disengagement is amplified.

Brown and colleagues (2006) also discussed the *social presence theory* (Rice, 1987; Rice & Love, 1987; Short, Williams, & Christie, 1976) and *social context cues theory* (Sproull & Kiesler, 1991) as they apply to social interactions in cyberspace. These theories posit that online social interactions become increasingly impersonal with the reduction of contextual, visual, and aural cues, reducing sensitivity to online patrons and becoming increasingly confrontational and uncharacteristic. Parks and Floyd (1996), for example, observed that cyberspace is "another life-world, a parallel universe" (p. 93). We observe the parallels with the island in *Lord of the Flies* (Golding, 1954), which provided the boys with a parallel universe in which no rules existed.

Lack of Rules and Supervision

Lack of institutional and parental rules in cyberspace have the effect of creating virtual islands similar to the physical islands in *Lord of the Flies* (Golding, 1954). The absence of adult supervision allows perpetrators free reign to pick on students who may not fit their definition of "cool" because of their weight, appearance, accent, abilities, or disabilities (Shariff & Strong-Wilson, 2005). Cyberspace provides a borderless playground that empowers some students to harass, isolate, insult, exclude, and threaten classmates. The Internet—unlike the school day—is open and available around the clock, empowering infinite numbers of students to join in the abuse. Without limits and clear codes of conduct, communication in cyberspace (even among adults) can rapidly deteriorate into abuse because of the knowledge and sense of security that comes with the limited possibility of being detected and disciplined.

This is illustrated in *Lord of the Flies* (Golding, 1954) when young Piggy (nearsighted and overweight) is excluded, isolated, harassed, and hunted down. His perpetrators take advantage of his disabilities, and these actions lead to his eventual death. The fear and isolation that Piggy experiences on that island is not far removed from that regularly experienced by victims of cyber bullying. Fear of unknown cyber perpetrators among classmates and the bullying that continues at school distracts all students (victims, bystanders, and perpetrators) from schoolwork. It creates a hostile physical school environment in which students feel unwelcome and unsafe. In such an atmosphere, equal opportunities to learn are greatly reduced (Devlin, 1997; Shariff & Strong-Wilson, 2005).

It is interesting to note that although Golding's *Lord of the Flies* was written in 1954, the author had tremendous foresight into what can happen when authority figures, caregivers, and parents are absent for long periods of time from any setting, including a virtual one. He might well have been predicting young people's social relations on the Internet. As we noted earlier, the Internet has provided young people with an arsenal of weapons for social cruelty (Harmon, 2004) without making allowances for supervision of their use. Not only is this similar to Golding's (1954) analysis of what might occur if adolescents were placed on a deserted island completely unsupervised, but it is also akin to providing them with weapons to help destroy each other.

The characteristics and conditions relating to the power shifts—and the behavioral and ethical breakdowns in cyberspace—suggest an obligation by the adults and public institutions that influence young people's lives (parents, teachers, school administrators, network providers, community stakeholders, and the courts) to work toward improved supervision, attention to adolescent online discourse, and increased accountability on the part of Internet service providers (ISPs).

Although school administrators and teachers argue that they cannot possibly be expected to supervise students on home computers, parents are increasingly beginning to sue schools and technology companies for failing to protect their children. One such example is illustrated in the plight of David Knight, a boy from Ontario, Canada, who was bullied persistently in the physical school setting from elementary through high school (by the same classmates). In high school, the bullying was magnified as cyber bullying took over. His classmates set up a website on which they described him as homosexual (which he was not), a drug trafficker, and a pedophile (both of which were also untrue). The website received millions of hits in which participants contributed insults and derogatory comments.

Unsupervised by school or parents (with the ISP refusing to close down the website for fear of being challenged as breaching free expression rights), David's nightmare continued for 6 months until he sued the school board and the ISP. International scholars of cyber bullying are awaiting the Canadian judicial decision in David's case, which continues to be postponed. Some of the issues raised in his case are nonetheless important, and we address them as part of our analysis of the legal considerations.

Although research suggests that bullying is reduced by 50% when young people are allowed to contribute to rule making (Olweus, 1997), a complete lack of supervision can result in enormous power differentials between dominant and weaker peers, resulting in anarchy and a total breakdown of social and ethical norms and structures. This is especially true when adolescents are involved because their social development is influenced by hormonal changes and social influences (Boyd, 2000; Tolman, Spencer, Rosen-Reynoso, & Porches, 2001).

Research on bullying finds that typically 30% of onlookers and bystanders support perpetrators instead of victims (Boulton, 1993; Salmivalli, Lagerspetz, Bjorqvist, Osterman, & Kaukianen, 1996). The longer it persists, the more bystanders join in the abuse, creating a power imbalance between victim and perpetrators. Isolation renders victims vulnerable to continued abuse, and the cycle repeats itself. What might begin as friendly banter among classmates at school can quickly turn into verbal bullying that continues into cyberspace as covert psychological bullying. The difference in cyberspace is that hundreds of perpetrators can get involved in the abuse, and, as in *Lord of the Flies* (Golding, 1954), peers who may not engage in the bullying at school can hide behind technology (similar to the masks and face paint used by Golding's boys, today's cyber bullies hide behind screen names) to inflict the most serious abuse (see, e.g., Shariff, 2004; Shariff & Strong-Wilson, 2005).

Consider another internationally known case of the "Star Wars Kid." Young Ghyzlain Reza (a slightly overweight boy from Quebec, Canada) had filmed himself playing out a Star Wars character. He mistakenly left the video in his school's film room. Two classmates found the tape and posted it on the Internet at http://www.jedimaster.net. This website attracted 15 million hits. One-hundred six clones of the video were made and redistributed. Wherever Ghyzlain went, his schoolmates would jump on desks and tables and imitate him. He finally withdrew from school and is now being home schooled. The case was to be heard on April 10, 2006, but was settled out of court.

These examples illustrate that even when frustrated parents turn to the courts for guidance, their claims are often delayed or settled out of court because of the lack of clear legal boundaries regarding freedom of expression, student privacy, and protection in cyberspace (Shariff & Johnny, 2005; Wallace, 1999). In cases where cyber perpetrators are known (as they were in the Star Wars Kid case), classmates are also being charged with criminal harassment. Although David and Ghyzlain have supportive parents to turn to, our concern is with victims of cyber bullying who, like Piggy in *Lord of the Flies* (Golding, 1954) cannot turn to parents or caregivers for emotional or financial support. This is confirmed in the NCHTM (2005) findings (noted earlier) regarding the lack of concern by caregivers relative to cyber bullying, making it a significant issue.

Research also suggests that victims are reluctant to report cyber bullying for fear that their own computer and cell phone privileges will be removed (see website of i-SafeAmerica at http://www.isafe.org). Lost computer privileges would ostracize them to an even greater extent from their peer groups, whose virtual relationships have become an integral aspect of their social relationships. In some cases, the isolation and ridicule becomes too much, resulting in suicide (for case examples, see Shariff, 2004, 2005).

Prior to moving on to a discussion of stakeholder roles and responsibilities, it is important to note that sexual and homophobic harassment have been found to be highly prevalent in cyber bullying.

Prevalence of Sexual and Homophobic Harassment

Preliminary research suggests that although both genders engage in cyber bullying, there are differences (Chu, 2005; Li, 2005). It has been argued that children who engage in any form of bullying are victims. However, studies (Dibbell, 1993; Evard, 1996) have shown that teenage girls are more often at the receiving end of cyber violence.

A review of the scholarly literature (Shariff & Gouin, 2005) finds that according to Herring (2002), 25% of Internet users aged 10–17 years were exposed to unwanted pornographic images in the past year, and 8% of the images involved violence in addition to sex and nudity. Mitchell and colleagues (2001, as cited in Barak, 2005), who conducted a survey of American teenagers, found that 19% of these youths (mostly older girls) had experienced at least one sexual solicitation online in the preceding year. According to Adam (2001), one in three female children reported online harassment in 2001. This fact is not surprising, given that girls aged 12 to 18 years have been found to spend at least 74% of their time in chat rooms or participating in IM (Berson, Berson, & Ferron, 2002).

Moreover, adolescent hormones rage and influence social relationships as children negotiate social and romantic relationships and become more physically self-conscious, independent, and insecure (Boyd, 2000). Research on dating and harassment practices at the middle school level (Tolman, 2001) shows that peer pressure causes males to engage in increased homophobic bullying of male peers and increased sexual harassment of female peers to establish their manhood. During this confusing stage of adolescent life, the conditions are ripe for bullying to take place. The Internet provides a perfect medium for adolescent anxieties to play themselves out.

Roles and Responsibilities: Schools or Parents?

Although its nebulous nature and ability to spread like wildfire are indeed challenging, cyber bullying does not elicit school responses that differ significantly from reported reactions to general forms of bullying (Harmon, 2004; Shariff, 2004). A review of emerging litigation on bullying (Shariff, 2003) disclosed common patterns in school responses to victim complaints. For example, plaintiffs explained that when they approached their school administrators and teachers for support, these authority figures put up a "wall of defense." According to some parents surveyed during that research, school administrators allegedly (a) assumed that the victims–plaintiffs invited the abuse; (b) believed that parents exaggerated the problem; and (c) assumed that written antibullying policies absolved them from doing more to protect victims. Despite well-meaning and seemingly sensible antibullying programs, this approach means that some educators tacitly condone negative and noninclusive attitudes, thus sustaining the power structures that exist in a discriminatory school environment. For example, some scholars argue that the tendency in schools to implement blanket zero-tolerance policies

(DiGiulio, 2001; Giroux, 2003; Skiba & Peterson, 1999) overlooks the various forms of oppression that marginalize some students in schools.

Not surprisingly, these responses have produced minimally effective results other than to criminalize young people and add a burden to the criminal justice system (DiGuilio, 2001; Giroux, 2003; Shariff & Strong-Wilson, 2005). To make matters worse, most ISPs refuse to close websites or block e-mails to avoid breaching free expression rights because they are protected from liability by legislation—at least, in the United States they are (Myers, 2006). This increases the danger to victims. Children's "behavior" cannot be the sole focus of policy—multidisciplinary attention to institutional context is crucial. This is where schools can—and, in our opinion, ought to—implement a mandate as educational leaders. Although parents undeniably have an obligation to monitor their children's activities on the Internet, teachers, school counselors, administrators, judges, and policymakers have no less a responsibility to adapt to a rapidly evolving technological society, address emerging challenges, and guide children to become civic-minded individuals.

It is reasonable to suggest that because schools use technology to deliver curriculum and assign homework (and increasingly provide laptops for students' use at home), it is also imperative that they pay attention to how their students use that technology. Schools need to recognize and establish standards and codes of conduct with respect to Internet and cell phone use and to define acceptable boundaries for their students' social relationships in cyberspace. Educators, in their valuable role of fostering inclusive and positive school environments, would benefit from scholarship and legally defensible policy guidelines. These should become part of teacher preparation programs, leadership programs, and professional development. The study of bullying and cyber bullying must be reconceptualized from an interdisciplinary, institutional, educational, and legal perspective. An interdisciplinary perspective would draw upon academic expertise in the fields of education, psychology, criminology, sociology, and law—all of which are relevant to the study of cyber bullying.

Legal Obligations

Before we move onto a discussion of the legal obligations for schools, it is worth seguing into a short discussion of the legal standards currently applied to technology companies. These corporations create and provide the nexus for cyber bullying, cyber harassment, cyber targeting, and other forms of online abuse. Although a comprehensive survey of the legislation covering technology companies is underway but not completed (Shariff, 2005), Myers (2006) undertook an in-depth evaluation of one relevant piece of legislation in the United States—the *Communications Decency Act of 1996*. Under this federal legislation, Congress granted broad immunity to ISPs. This legislation leaves no one legally accountable for cyber targeting (which includes cyber bullying, harassment, stalking, defamation, threats, and so forth). Section 230 of this Act provides, in part, the following stipulations:

(c) Protection for "Good Samaritan" blocking and screening of offensive material.

(1) Treatment of publisher or speaker. No provider or user of an interactive computer service shall be treated as the publisher or speaker of any information provided by another information content provider.

(2) Civil Liability. No provider or user of an interactive computer service shall be held liable on account of – (A) Any action voluntarily taken in good faith to restrict access to or availability of material that the provider or user considers to be obscene, lewd, lascivious, filthy, excessively violent, harassing, or otherwise objectionable, whether or not such material is constitutionally protect; or (B) any action taken to enable or make available to information content providers or others the technical means to restrict access to material described in paragraph (1).

Myers (2006) explains that one landmark case, *Zeran v. America OnLine, Inc.* (1997), is the general precedent used by American courts to rule on Internet abuse. This case resulted in leaving no one legally accountable for injuries caused by anonymous postings on the Internet. The case involved a series of anonymous postings on America OnLine's (AOL's) message board following the Oklahoma City bombings in April 1995. The messages claimed to advertise "naughty Oklahoma t-shirts." The captions on the t-shirts included "Visit Oklahoma ... It's a Blast!!!" and "Finally a Day Care Center That Keeps Kids Quiet—Oklahoma 1995" (*Zeran v. America OnLine, Inc.*, 1997). The individual who posted the messages identified himself as "Ken Z." and named Ken Zeran's as the person to call, posting his phone number to whoever wanted to order the offensive t-shirts. Zeran received abusive telephone calls and even death threats as a result and notified AOL, which in turn terminated the contract from which the messages originated. However, the perpetrator continued to set up new accounts with false names and credit cards. Zeran finally sued AOL, claiming negligence. The court ruled that Section 230 of the Communications Decency Act (CDA) provided absolute immunity to AOL, regardless of its awareness of the defamatory material.

The *Zeran* ruling, Myers notes, maintained the status of ISPs as "distributors" rather than "publishers." Publishers (e.g., book publishers) are liable for defamation by third parties using their services, especially if they are made aware of the behavior but fail to act to prevent it. Zeran followed a case in which an ISP was elevated to the status of "publisher" (*Stratton Oakmont v. Prodigy Services Co.*, 1995). The ISP, Prodigy, had decided to regulate the content of its bulletin boards (in part so that it could market itself as a "family-oriented" computer service). By taking on an editorial role, Prodigy opened itself up to greater liability than computer networks that do not edit content. Thus, ISPs argued that if they agree to monitor and edit online content, they in fact subject themselves to greater liability. This is why most ISPs ignore reports of abuse. Most are confident that they will not be held liable subsequent to *Zeran v. AOL* (1997). The irony of this, as Myers (2006) points out, is that the title of S.230 reads "Protection for 'Good Samaritan' blocking and screening of offensive material." The objective of the CDA was to protect pro-active ISPs and preserve competition between ISPs on the Internet.

Myers (2006) makes the point that if David Knight were bringing his lawsuit in the United States, S.230 might make it too difficult for him to argue that the ISP he is suing was aware of the website with his picture, labeling him as a homosexual pedophile and drug pusher. Nonetheless, he believes "the winds of change are stirring" (p. 672) for S.230 immunity. At the state level, he cites the common law case called *Bryson v. News America Publ'ns, Inc.* (1996). The case involved a fictional story titled "Bryson" written by Lucy Logsdon. Lucy wrote about being bullied at school by Bryson, whom she called a "slut." The real Bryson read the story and remembered living in the same town as Lucy Logsdon. Bryson sued News America for libel and won. The court stated that even though the story was labeled as fictional, it portrayed realistic characters responding in a realistic manner to realistic events and that a reasonable reader might logically conclude that the author of the story had drawn upon her teenage experiences to write it. If the courts rely on this case, David Knight's lawyers might well argue that the website with David's picture labeling him as a pedophile could reasonably be interpreted as true by those who visited the website, resulting in negligence and liability against the ISP.

Furthermore, in *John Doe v. GTE Corp.* (2003)—which involved the secret filming (and subsequent posting and selling on a website) of athletes showering in a changing room—the Seventh Circuit Court of Appeals upheld S.230 immunity, relying on *Zeran v. AOL* (1997), in favor of GTE corporation. However, Judge Easterbrook questioned the reasoning in *Zeran*, noting that S.230 is supposed to be the "Good Samaritan," blocking and screening offensive material, but, in fact, by eliminating liability for ISPs, it ends up defending abusers and defeating legitimate claims by victims of tortuous abuse on the Internet.

The law is slow to change, especially when judges are well aware of the floodgate of litigation that might be unleashed if ISPs are held liable. In the meantime, schools need guidelines that provide reasonable boundaries and direction as to the extent of their responsibility. This would alleviate their reluctance to breach freedom of expression guarantees or student privacy rights. Educators need to know the extent to which they have the authority to protect victims from abuse by their classmates—and their ultimate responsibility to foster inclusive school environments that encourage socially responsible discourse—on or off school grounds, in the physical school setting and in virtual space.

The Educational Policy Vacuum

Traditional responses to bullying are largely ineffective because of the anonymous nature of cyber bullying, its capacity for an infinite audience, and participation by large numbers of young people. In this regard, it is important to consider the emerging legal stance adopted by the courts toward cyber harassment. In the following section, we review the legal principles of Canada and the United States as they relate to cyber bullying: freedom of speech/expression, privacy, torts, and human rights/antidiscrimination law.

Freedom of Speech and Expression Rights

Canadian school officials and ISPs worry that if they intervene with student discourses in cyberspace, they might face challenges under Section 2(b) of the *Charter of Rights and Freedoms* ("the Charter") (Department of Justice, Canada, 1982) for infringement of student free expression rights. Freedom of expression, thought, and opinion are guaranteed to all Canadians, including students, under Section 2(b) of the Charter. These freedoms are limited only by Section 1 of the Charter, which helps the courts weigh and balance individual rights with the collective rights of the greater good in a democracy. Section 1 of the Charter states that the rights set out in it are subject "only to such reasonable limits prescribed by law as can be demonstrably justified in a free and democratic society" (para. 2). Any school policy that infringes on individual rights must, therefore, be justified by the policymaker as having a pressing and substantial objective to protect the greater good. The onus also rests with policymakers to establish that the rights in question will be infringed as minimally as possible (*R. v. Oakes*, 1986).

As MacKay and Burt-Gerrans (2005) pointed out, expression is constitutionally protected as long as it is not violent (see, e.g., *Irwin Toy Ltd. v. Québec* [A.G.], 1989). This means that any expression that intends to convey nonviolent meaning is typically safeguarded by the Canadian courts. This interpretation has been extended to the school setting. For instance, one of the best known cases of protected freedom of expression in schools involved a rap song that contained a message to students to reduce promiscuity. In a well-known Canadian freedom of expression case (*Lutes v. Board of Education of Prairie View School Division No. 74*, 1992), Chris Lutes sang a song by Queen Latifah titled "Let's Talk About Sex" even though a school district administrator objected to the song. He was suspended and sought judicial review. The court found that his freedom of expression rights under Section 2(b) had been violated and that the administrator's objection to the song did not reasonably justify the infringement of those rights. In fact, the court stated that this was an overreaction to an educational song about sexual abstinence.

This raises important legal questions as they relate to cyber bullying. Is online harassment considered to be a violent expression? Even though physical force cannot take place online, victims can (and do) perceive online sexual threats as very real. The impact on the victim is no different from the telephone threat that caused Canadian teenager Dawn Marie Wesley to commit suicide. The words "You're f . . . . . g dead!" by a classmate caused her to perceive that real harm would come to her. Her perpetrator was convicted of criminal harassment because the court observed that perceived harm by the victim amounts to the same thing as actual harm (Shariff, 2004). Herring (2002) explained that online harassment—which negatively affects the physical, psychological, or emotional well-being of a victim—constitutes a form of actual violence. Barak (2005) noted that harassers can use sexual coercion through several means—directly offensive sexual remarks that humiliate the victim; passive sexual harassment by using nicknames and online identities such as "wetpussy" or "xlargetool"; or graphic gendered harassment, which includes sending unwanted pornographic content, sexual jokes, and other graphic sexual context. These forms of online harassment make recipients feel powerless, demeaned, and threatened.

Some U.S. judges, however, have refused to acknowledge that online harassment contains a violent message. Consider some of the initial court rulings on cyber harassment cited by Wallace (1999). In one instance, a student set up a website denouncing the administrators and teachers at a university. The judge's response was as follows, "Disliking or being upset by the content of a student's speech is not an acceptable justification for limiting student speech" (as quoted in Wallace, 1999, p. 131).

Similarly, in *United States of America, Plaintiff v. Jake Baker* (1995, as cited in Wallace, 1999), Jake Baker posted a story to the "alt.sex.stories" newsgroup. His story graphically described the rape and torture of a university classmate. He also communicated (via e-mail to a friend) his plans to actually carry out the rape. Students who read the story were outraged and charged him with criminal harassment. The district court threw out the claim, holding that because there was no possibility of physical rape on the Internet, there could be no claim for harassment. Moreover, the court was reluctant to infringe on Baker's freedom of expression rights. The precedents set by these courts were followed in the *People v. B.F. Jones* (1886; cited in Wallace, 1999). The case involved sexual harassment of a female participant in a multi-user dimension (MUD) group by Jones, a male participant. The court explained its ruling as follows:

It is not the policy of the law to punish those unsuccessful threats which it is not presumed would terrify ordinary persons excessively; and there is so much opportunity for magnifying undefined menaces that probably as much mischief would be caused by letting them be prosecuted as by refraining from it. (Quoted in Wallace, 1999, p. 228)

In another case, *Emmett v. Kent School District No. 413* (2000), a boy placed mock obituaries on a website called "The Unofficial Kentlake High Home Page," which allowed visitors to vote on who should be "the next to die." The school, upon learning of the website, expelled the student (and then later reduced this to a 5-day suspension). The family brought suit, and the court ruled in favor of the student, stating that the school had not proven that the website "intended to threaten anyone" (para. 2).

This reluctance by the courts to avoid involvement in the quagmire of cyberspace is not surprising and not much different from their stance regarding Internet companies. The courts have typically adopted a hands-off approach in matters of educational policy. In the realm of physical violence in schools, for example, American courts have set a very high threshold for plaintiffs to bring claims for negligence against schools—in some cases, even when students have been shot or stabbed (Shariff, 2003, 2004; Shariff & Strong-Wilson, 2005).

The worrisome aspect regarding the failure of claims for criminal harassment is that pedophiles and predators gain significantly easier access to Internet "Lists of Hoes" (i.e., names of girls labeled as prostitutes), for example, and capitalize on them. This takes adolescent cyber bullying into the more dangerous adult realm of pornography. For example, in one case reported by Harmon (2004), photographs of a young girl who masturbated for her boyfriend were dispersed on the Internet once the relationship soured. The boundaries of this type of harassment need clarification. Laws against the distribution of pornography have been in existence for many years, but they need upgrading to address virtual infringements of privacy. Once in the hands of sexual predators, such photographs could result in life-threatening circumstances for teenage victims if they are contacted and lured into a physical relationship.

Moreover, Servance (2003) confirmed that when addressing cases of cyber bullying in the school context, American courts continue to apply a standard for protecting student free expression that goes back to the 1960s, when students protested against the Vietnam War. The courts continue to apply the standards established in three landmark cases (the "Triumvirate"): *Tinker v. Des Moines Independent Community School District* (1969), *Bethel School District #403 v. Fraser* (1986), and *Hazelwood School* District v. *Kuhlmeier* (1988). *Tinker v. Des Moines Independent Community School District* (1969) involved students' rights to wear black armbands as a form of silent protest against the Vietnam War. Despite warnings ahead of time not to engage in this activity, many students participated and were suspended. The students sued the school administration, and the court held in favor of the students—establishing the famous quotation that "students do not leave their free expression rights at the school house gate" (Servance, 2003). The court asserted that unless the speech materially and substantially disrupts learning, schools may not restrict it.

This point is illustrated in *Beidler v. North Thurston School District Number 3* (2000). The student in this case denounced the high school assistant principal as an alcoholic and Nazi. As a result, teachers complained about being uncomfortable having Karl Beidler (the student) in their classes. He was given emergency suspension and was transferred for the remainder of his junior year to an alternative setting within the district. Beidler brought suit against the school, saying that his website had caused "no substantial disruption," and the court agreed, ruling that the district had not met the *Tinker* standard regarding disruptive speech.

So far, cases such as *Beidler* and others (e.g. *Flaherty v. Keystone Oaks School District*, 2001) have usually involved students posting questionable material regarding the adults in the school. In the absence of school disruption or direct threats, courts have basically sent the message that schools may not limit student speech (posted online on personally owned computers) that is critical, even offensive, about adults. Still emerging are cases involving student-to-student cyber bullying, which, according to research (Devlin, 1997; Gati et al., 2002) has an impact on the emotional well-being of the victims in the school setting. Based on the research, a strong case could be advanced that cyber bullying materially and substantially disrupts learning for the victims and potentially for other students, as well.

A new standard was set in the second case in the Triumvirate in 1986. The Supreme Court held, in *Bethel School District #403 v. Fraser* (1986), that schools may prohibit speech that undermines their basic educational mission. In this case, student Matthew Fraser's campaign speech included "obscene, profane language" that contained insinuations to sexual and political prowess:

> I know a man who is firm – he's firm in his pants … [He] takes his pants and pounds it in…. He doesn't attack things in spurts—he drives hard, pushing and pushing until finally—he succeeds … [He] is a man who will go to the very end—even the climax for each and every one of you. (p. 1227)

The school suspended Fraser, and the courts upheld the school's action, noting that schools are not the arena for the type of vulgar expression in Fraser's speech. Of importance, the judge noted that schools should not have to tolerate speech that is inconsistent with school values. Although he acknowledged that it is crucial to allow unpopular speech, he emphasized that schools have a vital role in preparing students to participate in democratic society by teaching appropriate forms of civil discourse that are fundamental to democratic society.

Of significant relevance to cyber bullying today, this ruling also stated that schools must teach students the boundaries of socially acceptable behavior. The court stated that threatening or offensive speech has little value in a school setting and cannot be ignored by schools. Moreover, the court noted that the speech infringed on the rights of others (specifically, on the rights of female audience members, although that was not directly stated). The sexual insinuations to rape were clearly offensive and threatening to students.

The *Fraser* (1986) decision extends *Tinker* (1969) and is also, in our view, applicable to student freedom of expression in the cyber bullying context. As explained in the profile of cyber bullying, a substantial amount of the emerging research on Internet communications reveals the prevalence of sexual harassment, sexual solicitation, homophobia, and threats against women or female students. Not only does this form of cyber bullying materially disrupt learning and impede educational objectives, but it also creates power imbalances within the school environment and distracts female and gay or lesbian students from equal opportunities to learn. Consistent with the *Fraser* ruling, expression of this nature infringes their constitutional rights in an educational context and creates a hostile and negative school environment (physical and virtual).

The third American court decision, *Hazelwood vs. Kuhlmeier* (1988), involved the principal's decision to censor portions of the school newspaper. The principal was worried that two articles, one on teen pregnancy and the other on divorce, were too transparent to protect student identities. The students who worked on the articles sued, citing infringement of their First Amendment rights to free speech. The court in *Hazelwood* reasoned that because schools are entitled to exercise control over school-sponsored speech, they are not bound by the First Amendment to accept or tolerate speech that goes against the values held by the school system.

It is plausible that the reasoning in *Hazelwood* (1988) might be extended to cyber bullying that originates on school computers. First, it is important to note that unlike the *Tinker* (1969) case, which questioned whether a school should tolerate particular student speech, in *Hazelwood*, the courts questioned whether the First Amendment requires a school to promote student speech. They noted that "the standard articulated in *Tinker* (1969) for determining when a school may punish student expression need not also be the standard for determining when a school may refuse to lend its name and resources to the dissemination of student expression" (p. 509). Certainly, when a school allows students to use its computers for both classroom-related and extracurricular activities, it is providing students with resources and thereby becoming a tacit sponsor of such activities. Therefore, it would seem that educators do not violate First Amendment rights when they exercise control over inappropriate forms of communication disseminated using school computers.

Moreover, the courts noted that educators have authority over school-sponsored activities because these activities are considered part of the school's curriculum. This means that schools are not legally obliged to promote or allow school-sponsored speech that is incompatible with its educational goals. This point is firmly solidified in *Fraser* (1986), where, as previously noted, a student could be disciplined for speech that is "wholly inconsistent with the 'fundamental values' of public school education" (Servance, 2003, p. 1218). If we apply this logic to the cyber bullying context, it seems reasonable for schools to place limitations on any form of student expression (including digital forms) that either infringes upon the rights of others or is inconsistent with school values. Similarly, it could be argued that school computers are school property; therefore, any e-mails or correspondence between students—including websites created using those computers—could be censored. Schools may also impose disciplinary consequences for bullying behavior generated on school-owned equipment if schools have a policy regulating the type of content that may be sent or received from school computers.

The legal boundaries of supervision are murkier for schools, however, when students are engaged in bullying behavior from home on their personal computers. For example, in *Emmett v. Kent School District No. 413* (2000), the courts did not give schools the same authority to act as they have given for websites that are created on school computers. A key factor here was that the schools could not show that the off campus–created website would cause a "material and substantial disruption" (para. 4) in school. Similarly, in *Killion v. Franklin Regional School District* (2001), the court drew from the *Fraser* (1986), *Tinker* (1969), and *Hazelwood* (1988) cases (as well as the *Emmett v. Kent School District No 413* [2000] and *Beussink v. Woodland R-IV School District* [1988] cases) to determine that schools must be able to show substantial disruption in order to limit off-campus speech. In this case, a student used his website to denounce the high school athletic director and make attacks on his sex life and his obesity. The court noted that the school could provide no evidence that disruption to classes had occurred.

In contrast, if a website is clearly derogatory, profane, threatening, or disruptive, the schools may be supported in taking action, even when the website was created on a home computer. In *J.S., a Minor, v. Bethlehem Area School District* (2000), a student created a website "Teacher Sux," in which graphic pictures of severed heads, along with a statement to "send $20.00 to help pay for a hit man" was enough for a judge to uphold the expulsion of the student. The court relied on other cases (e.g., *Beussink v. Woodlands R-IV*

School District, 1998), holding that websites that are accessed at school, with an intended audience within the school community, can be dealt with as on-campus speech. The court further ruled that disciplining the student for off-school behavior was appropriate in this case because the action "caused actual and substantial disruption of the work of the school" (para. 6).

More recently, in *Layshock v. Hermitage School District* (2006), senior Justin Layshock created a parody of the principal on MySpace.com, which depicted him as, among other things, too drunk to remember his own birthday. School administrators placed Justin in an alternative school and banned him from participating in any Hermitage High School events, including graduation. The parents went to court, requesting a temporary restraining order to allow Justin to participate at school until the case could come to trial. In deciding whether to lift the restraining order, the court noted that the school was able to show substantial disruption to the work of school. In this case, so many students accessed the website that the school had to shut down its computer system, causing loss of instructional time and access for other students. Indeed, the school was "abuzz about the profiles, who created them, and how they could be accessed" (para. 13). Judge McVerry, therefore, refused to lift the restraining order, upholding the school's discipline. By the time the case can reach a full trial, the student will have long since graduated.

In regard to off-campus behavior and Canadian courts, the high court established in *Ross v. New Brunswick School District No. 15* (1996) that schools must maintain conditions that are conducive to leaning. Although the *Ross* case involved the free speech of a teacher who distributed anti-Semitic publications outside of school, the following statement from the ruling has been quoted in almost every Charter argument for a positive school environment:

> Schools are an arena for the exchange of ideas and must, therefore, be premised upon principles of tolerance and impartiality so that all persons within the school environment feel equally free to participate. As the board of inquiry stated, a school board has a duty to maintain a positive school environment for all persons served by it. (Para 42)

Even though Ross's anti-Semitic publications were distributed outside the school context, the court noted that he poisoned the school and classroom environment for his Jewish students within the classroom. They knew about his publications and felt threatened, fearful, and uncomfortable. This is highly applicable to the cyber bullying context. For example, schools often maintain that cyber bullying falls outside their realm of responsibility because it occurs after regular school hours. However, if we draw upon the rationale used in the preceding cases from both Canada and the United States, it would seem that the on-campus/off-campus (physical vs. virtual space) distinction is moot if the actions cause disruption to the learning environment. It is the effect (not location) of the harassment, bullying, and threats (despite the fact that they are made outside of the physical school setting) that is important. The key for schools is to determine a clear nexus between the cyber bullying act and the school. This can be established if the cyber bullying was accessed or displayed at school, if it caused substantial disruption to the learning environment, or if it created a poisoned or hostile environment for any student. Once the nexus is determined, school officials are justified, even obligated, to address it.

In sum, although U.S. courts lean toward supporting student free expression, they stress certain limits in the school context. Expressions that substantially or materially disrupt learning, interfere with the educational mission, or use school-owned technology to harass or threaten other students are not protected by the First Amendment and allow school intervention. The reasoning in these decisions does not substantially differ from that of a Supreme Court of Canada decision in *R. v. M.R.M* (1998) relating to the right of schools to restrict constitutional rights when school property and student privacy rights are involved.

Student Privacy and Cyber Bullying

Another legal issue that could arise in cyber bullying situations is the need for schools to search a computer. In Canada, under Section 8 of the Charter, everyone has the right to be free from unreasonable search and seizure. Hence, protection of privacy is guaranteed within reasonable limits in a free and democratic society. Furthermore, Section 7 of the Charter states that "everyone has the right to life, liberty, and security of the person" (para. 10). In the cyber bullying context, both of these sections are relevant. The boundaries with respect to the obligations on schools to override search and seizure rights to protect others must be balanced with the right to life, liberty, and security of the person. Furthermore, victims might argue that their rights to life, liberty, and security of the person are infringed under Section 7 when schools fail to intervene and protect them from cyber bullying.

Based on Section 1 considerations, the courts generally give priority to the safety of the greater number of stakeholders as justification for overriding privacy rights. In *R. v. M.R.M.* (1998), for example, the Supreme Court of Canada ruled that as long as a school principal is not acting as an agent of the police, he or she can search student lockers if there is a suspicion of hidden weapons or drugs. The high court held that school lockers are the property of schools. When there is a danger to safety and learning of the students, the infringement on student privacy rights can be reasonably justified under Section 1 of the Charter. Given the devastating psychological consequences of cyber bullying on victims and the entire school environment, it is quite possible that a Charter interpretation that requires a balancing of the victim's right to safety under Section 7 and the perpetrators' right to computer privacy under Section 8 and free expression under Section 2(b), the court might rule in favor of the victim.

The rationale used by the Supreme Court of Canada in *R. v. M.R.M.* (1998) was that students should already have a lowered expectation of privacy because they know that their school principals or administrators may need to conduct searches in schools and that safety ought to be the overriding concern to protect students. The high court explained its interpretation of a "safe and ordered school environment":

> Teachers and principals are placed in a position of trust that carries with it onerous responsibilities. When children attend school or school functions, it is they [the teachers and principals] who must care for the children's safety and well-being. It is they who must carry out the fundamentally important task of teaching children so that they can function in our society and fulfill their potential. In order to teach, school officials must provide an atmosphere that encourages learning. During the school day, they must protect and teach our children. (p. 394)

Similarly, in the United States, the Fourth Amendment of the Constitution guarantees protection from unreasonable searches and seizures. The legal cases involving schools have generally involved searches of lockers and backpacks, but recently, the principles of those cases are being applied to searches of computers. Courts have held that schools need only "reasonable suspicion" to search but caution, "A student's freedom from unreasonable search and seizure must be balanced against the school official's need to maintain order and discipline and to protect the health and welfare of all the students" (Alexander & Alexander, 2005, p. 154). Schools may search school-owned property, such as lockers, for routine maintenance or when they have reasonable suspicion that a student is harboring something illegal. In *People v. Overton* (1967), the courts noted that schools can issue policies regarding what may be stored in school lockers. Correspondingly, educators are entitled to conduct spot checks or involuntary searches of lockers to ensure that students comply with these regulations. In fact, the courts regard the inspection of student lockers not only as a right but also as a duty of schools when it is believed that a student is using school property to harbor illegal materials.

In terms of technology, it could be argued that, similar to lockers, e-mail addresses are owned by the school because they are transmitted using school property. Therefore, if a student is suspected of sending harassing comments via e-mail or has found such comments while browsing on school computers, the school should consider it their responsibility to monitor and discipline this activity. This point might be further justified by cases such as *Garrity v. John*

Hancock Mut. Life Ins. Co. (2002), where it was found that employers have a right to inspect employee e-mail accounts in cases where employees have been warned that their messages are accessible to the organization. With regard to school searches, we can also consider cases such as *New Jersey v. T.L.O.* (1985). In this ruling, it was found that although students have a legitimate expectation of privacy within the school setting, schools also have a right to search student property if there are reasonable grounds for suspecting that the student is violating either the law or school regulations. Since the land-mark T.L.O. case, courts have given schools even more latitude in conduct-ing searches. In *Veronia School District 47J v. Acton* (1995), for example, the constitutionality of conducting random drug testing among student athletes was upheld. This was expanded again in *Board of Education of Independent School District No. 92 of Pottawatomie County v. Earls* (2002), where Justice Thomas said that students in any extracurricular activity "implicitly have a lower expectation of privacy" (para. 4). Again, it would seem reasonable for schools to apply this rationale to technology, considering that students often use school-owned computers for purposes beyond the academic curriculum. If students are informed in advance that school equipment may be routinely searched (thus reducing their expectation of privacy), schools are likely to be upheld in random searches of their networks and school-owned equip-ment for purposes such as routine maintenance or when they have genuine concern for students' safety. Individual searches of computers or of a specific student's Internet use may be carried out if school administrators have rea-sonable suspicion that a student has acted in violation of district policy or has committed a criminal act.

Tort Law and Negligence

Constitutional claims are expensive and time consuming. When suing schools, parents often turn first to the law of torts and negligence because it is remedial and plaintiffs can seek compensation for *torts*, or "wrongs," by the institution. Negligence in the supervision of children at school is one form of a tort.

When a claim in negligence is brought against a school, the plaintiff must establish that there was a duty of care and tangible harm, that the tan-gible harm was foreseeable, and that the school official's actions or omis-sions either proximately or remotely caused the injury. Even though physical injuries are tangible and (in Canada) are easier to establish (MacKay & Dickinson, 1998), the threshold for claimants in the United States is very high. School law cases involving psychological harm are less common, but there are precedents. In *Spears v. Jefferson Parish School Board* (1994), for example, a kindergarten teacher scared one of his students by joking that he had killed another student. He even went so far as to put a rope around the child's neck and have him pretend to be dead. All of this caused considerable psychological damage to the student who was the brunt of joke, causing the court to find the school liable for the actions of the teacher that resulted in emotional harm to the child.

Courts have also supported claimants in cases involving suicide or psychological harm that could potentially result in suicide (Shariff, 2003). Bullying research and numerous media reports confirm that *bullycide* (suicide by victims of bullying) is on the rise (DiGuilio, 2001; Harmon, 2004). Similarly, courts in Britain have ruled that bullying is not only an educational problem but also a health problem, acknowledging the severe consequences on the emotional and, sometimes, physical health of victims (Shariff, 2003). Gradually, the courts are beginning to recognize emotional and psychological harm as "tangible," including mental shock and suffering (Linden & Klar, 1994, 1999). Therefore, claims for negligence against schools under tort law may be more successful than charges of criminal harassment against perpetrators.

Canadian Human Rights and U.S. Sexual Harassment and Discrimination Law

Another area of law that relates to cyber bullying (particularly with respect to sexual harassment in institutional settings) is Canadian human rights law, which has established an institutional obligation to protect sexual harassment victims. Two cases illustrate this point.

The first involved a Canadian case of sexual harassment by a co-worker, both inside and outside the workplace (*Robichaud v. Canada*, 1987). The Supreme Court of Canada ruled that institutions are responsible for providing safe environments for their employees even if the sexual harassment by a co-worker occurs outside of the workplace. The fact that the victim must face their tormentors in the workplace imposes an obligation on the employer to address the problem effectively. This case is highly relevant to cyber bullying because school officials often maintain they are not responsible for harassment by schoolmates that occurs outside of school grounds or before or after school hours. As the Supreme Court of Canada confirmed in *Robichaud*, if the victim has to face the perpetrator within the institution, the institution is responsible for correcting the problem no matter where the harassment actually takes place.

A second example involves the homophobic harassment of a male high school student of Iranian heritage in British Columbia, Canada (*Jubran v. North Vancouver School District*, 2002). Even though Azmi Jubran was not gay, his appearance caused the majority of students in his class to tease him as being gay for the duration of his 4 years at Handsworth Secondary School in North Vancouver. The British Columbia Human Rights Tribunal ruled that the school had created a negative school environment in failing to protect Jubran and failing to discipline the perpetrators. The tribunal ruled that they did an inadequate job of educating the students to be inclusive and socially responsible. Upon appeal by the school board and the high school, the British Columbia Supreme Court adopted a narrow construction of the case. The judge ruled that because the claim was brought under S.8 of the Human Rights Code (which protects homosexuals from harassment) and because Jubran claimed that he was not homosexual, he had no claim. The British Columbia Court of Appeals, however, rendered a more thoughtful and practical ruling, overturning the Supreme Court decision and reinstating the tribunal's decision. The court reiterated that Jubran had every right to a claim against the school and school board because they had fostered and sustained a negative school environment in which he was prevented from enjoying equal opportunities to an education free of discrimination and harassment (see Shariff & Strong-Wilson, 2005).

U.S. law provides protection from sexual harassment, and gender discrimination is provided under Title IX of the Education Amendments of 1972. Additional protection for all forms of discrimination is provided under the Equal Protection Clause of the 14th Amendment of the U.S. Constitution, along with specific federal laws (e.g., Titles VI and VII of the Civil Rights Act of 1964) and states' Human Rights Laws.

Title IX states that "No person in the United States shall, on the basis of sex, be excluded from participation in, be denied the benefits of, or be subjected to discrimination under any education program or activity receiving federal financial assistance" (para. 1). Schools are clearly included in this group, and courts have held that schools must take reasonable steps to intervene in sexual harassment issues.

Title IX guidelines suggest that it is the school's responsibility to take action when they know or should have known about harassment. However, the standard of "actual knowledge" versus "should have known" was tested in a landmark case on sexual harassment in schools. In *Gebser v. Lago Vista Independent School District* (1998), the Supreme Court of the United States, in a 5–4 decision, supported the "actual knowledge" standard. In this case, a student was suffering from abuse by her teacher. Some of it occurred on school grounds during an Advanced Placement class in which she was the only student. The plaintiffs argued that the school should have known about the abuse through proper supervision of the teacher. The court ruled that because the student had told no one about the abuse, the school could not be held liable. Although this ruling seems to relieve schools of some responsibility, the *Gebser* ruling made it clear that if the school had received any information about this misconduct and had failed to take immediate action, the court would have considered that "deliberate indifference." This premise was tested in a controversial landmark decision, also in 1998: The case of

Davis v. Munroe County Board of Education (1999) involved the persistent sexual harassment of a fifth grade female student, Lashonda Davis, whose parents informed the teachers and the school principal numerous times to no avail. Lashonda's grades dropped, and her health was negatively affected. In a majority 5–4 decision, the Supreme Court ruled that in failing to act to protect Lashonda, the school had created a "deliberately dangerous environment" that had prevented "equal opportunities for learning" (para. 1).

In *Nabozny v. Podlesny* (1996), the court relied on the protections guaranteed in the 14th Amendment of the U.S. Constitution in finding for the plaintiff when the school failed to protect him against relentless harassment that he had faced for being gay. The federal judge pointed out that it was the school's responsibility to protect gay students just as much as they would any other student.

The cases discussed in this chapter illustrate that schools will be held liable if they fail to act when students are being harassed at school. The logical next assumption is that schools must likewise protect students from cyber bullying, which creates a similarly dangerous environment for victims, engendering fear and distraction and preventing victims from enjoying equal opportunities to learn.

Conclusion and Implications

In this chapter, we have drawn attention to the complexities of cyber bullying, its insidious and anonymous nature, and the forms through which it is conveyed. We have explained that because it takes place mainly on home computers and personal cell phones, it becomes difficult to supervise by school personnel. We have provided the analogy of *Lord of the Flies* (Golding, 1954), which highlighted the social deterioration that occurs when adolescents remain unsupervised. We have explained that cyber bullying is most prevalent among adolescents and that it makes up a significant amount of gender-based harassment and homophobia. Our review of the legal considerations that arise with respect to defamation, freedom of expression, student safety, and privacy in the school context highlights that although online harassment occurs in virtual space, it nonetheless constitutes a form of "real" violence and ought to be understood and interpreted this way by schools and courts.

The United States constitutional cases covered in this chapter disclose that although courts continue to consider freedom of expression from a geographical perspective—namely, on-campus versus off-campus expression—*Tinker* (1969) is applicable to cyber bullying because it allows schools to intervene if such expression materially and substantially disrupts learning. Furthermore, *Fraser* (1986) confirms that schools are well within their rights to intervene when expression impedes the educational mission of the school. Finally, as *Kuhlmeier* (1988) and *R. v. M.R.M.* (1998) confirm, student privacy rights are subject to school authority in cases where student safety is concerned—justifying school locker searches. It can be argued that when cyber bullying is conducted on school computers, such communication can be confiscated and dealt with by school officials.

The right of schools to intervene to reduce cyber bullying is also related to their obligations to provide students with a safe school environment that provides equal opportunities to learn. Canadian constitutional decisions in *Ross* (1996) and *R. v. M.R.M.* (1998) support the need for schools to provide positive school environments, which, we have argued, extend to virtual space. Furthermore, human rights jurisprudence on sexual harassment in Canada and the United States has supported the institutional obligation to address harassment regardless of whether it takes place on or off school property.

Until the courts provide schools and ISPs with policy directions that specifically address cyber bullying, these rulings at least provide reasonable guidelines to inform educational policy and practice. In the meantime, it is important for schools to foster inclusive learning environments and attend to every complaint of cyber bullying through educational and communicative means. To do so, we propose a four-pronged approach, which involves (a) developing appropriate policies; (b) encouraging university research, teacher education, and professional development; (c) endorsing online educational programming; and (d) empowering young people to engage in critical thinking to promote positive online interaction.

Policy Development

As several scholars observed (Cassidy & Jackson 2005; Mackay & Burt-Gerrans, 2005), zero-tolerance policies, suspension, and criminal harassment charges against adolescents rarely solve school problems (DiGuilio, 2001; Giroux, 2003). In this regard, it is important that schools acknowledge their important role as educators and work with parents and relevant stakeholders to develop nonarbitrary policies that can be implemented through positive educational programs and critical thinking tools that provide students with beneficial Internet experiences. In 2005, a Canadian Internet organization that supports schools (Media Awareness Network) released its results on positive and negative uses of the Internet (Steeves & Wing, 2005). The website provides excellent programming options for students at all grade levels. In the United States, i-SAFE America—a nonprofit Internet safety foundation endorsed by the U.S. Congress—provides valuable resources to schools, students, parents, and law enforcement officials in protecting the online experiences of K–12 students. Our point is that schools cannot address this problem alone: They must inform their policies through collaboration with other stakeholders.

Research, Teacher Education, and Professional Development

University faculties of education can assist the efforts of policymakers by conducting further research, which can inform teacher education and professional development on this emerging and complex form of virtual harassment. They should also collaborate with the legal community to develop guidelines for schools and incorporate this knowledge into teacher education, leadership preparation, and professional development programs. By working together, Ministries/Departments of Education, law enforcement providers, the legal community, education and legal academics, Internet corporations, and community organizations can curtail cyber bullying and protect students. It will require considerable effort and a unified approach in order to delineate clearly the parameters of civil behavior and establish consequences for misbehavior. But only with such guidelines can we hope to rescue students from the virtual *Lord of the Flies* (Golding, 1954) island on which they now find themselves. The first step is to provide educators with the tools that they need to develop and implement inclusive, educational, and legally defensible policies and practices in a rapidly evolving age of new technologies.

Interactive Online Educational Programs

We also advocate the development of interactive online educational programs that would help students arrive at their own moral and ethical judgments about social relationships and discrimination. It is essential that students are empowered to take leadership and responsibility in fostering positive and inclusive virtual environments. A number of positive initiatives have been commenced by Media Awareness Network (Steeves & Wing, 2005), Willard (2005), and Balfour (2005), in which adult programming provides support and guidance on Internet and technology use and relationships. For example, in their recent study, Media Awareness Network (Steeves & Wing, 2005) found that children as young as 9 years of age were interested in knowing how to authenticate information on the Internet to avoid predators and harassment. Many of the students interviewed expressed an interest in finding educational resources and a desire to engage in responsible use of the resources available to them.

Student Empowerment and Critical Thinking

Finally, empowerment and student participation in learning, critical thinking, and rule making are critical to ensure that we do not abandon young people on the island of virtual reality. It is crucial that we engage young people in the rule-making aspects relating to responsible use of new technologies and work with these young people (on a consistent, supportive basis) to help them think critically about the consequences of their actions for the victims, their own education, and their families. In this regard, the international work of The Critical Thinking Consortium (TC2), directed by Roland Case (2005), would be highly applicable. The consortium works with schools and teachers to infuse critical thinking into the curriculum, whereby students are presented with problematic scenarios and taught the tools to help them to make reasoned judgments about their actions, attitudes, and responses in specific situations. As Willard (2005) suggests, in the cyber bullying context, it is of crucial importance that we provide the supports to help young people reconnect with their sense of ethics so that they can think critically about the impact of their online actions and attitudes.

In sum, now that the complexities and negative potential of new technologies have emerged, it is time to work collaboratively with students, parents, technology corporations, universities, law enforcement providers, and government to establish codes of conduct and guidelines. Although technology corporations are reluctant to monitor and edit online abuse because of the reverse effect of protective laws that might hold them liable in the United States, courts need to revisit their approach to liability and develop a more balanced approach that resembles the decision adopted by a British court in *Godfrey v. Demon Internet Ltd.* (1999). The court in that case held that once the ISP knows about the cyber bullying and fails to act, it is liable under the *Defamation Act of 1996*.

Regardless, we cannot rely on ISPs or the courts. We must monitor virtual discourse on a regular basis and act quickly to address complaints of cyber bullying before adolescent relationships deteriorate to the level that they did on that remote island in *Lord of the Flies* (Golding, 1954). If we can prevent even one child or teenager, like Piggy, from falling through the cracks and down the cliff of virtual reality, then we are well on our way to protecting and educating students and keeping schools out of court.

References

Adam, A. (2001). Cyberstalking: Gender and computer ethics. In E. Green & A. Adam (Eds.), *Virtual gender: Technology, consumption and identity* (pp. 209–224). New York, NY: Routledge.

Alexander, K., & Alexander, M. D. (2005). *American public school law* (6th ed.). Belmont, CA: Thomson West.

Balfour, C. (2005, September). *A journey of social change: Turning government digital strategy into cybersafe local school practices.* Paper presented at the International Conference on Cyber-Safety, Oxford University, Oxford, United Kingdom. Retrieved from http://www.oii.ox.ac.uk/cybersafety

Bandura, A. (1991). Social cognitive theory of moral thought and action. In W. M. Kurtines & J. L. Gewirtz (Eds.), *Handbook of moral behavior and development* (Vol. 1, pp. 45–103). Hillsdale, NJ: Erlbaum. Retrieved from http://www.des. emory.edu/mfp/BanSCTMoral.pdf

Barak, A. (2005). Sexual harassment on the Internet. *Social Science Computer Review*, 23(1), 77–92.

Beidler v. North Thurston School District Number 3, 99-2-00236-6 (Wash. Supr. Ct. 2000).

Berson, I. R., Berson, M. J., & Ferron, J. M. (2002). Emerging risks of violence in the digital age: Lessons for educators from an online study of adolescent girls in the United States. *Journal of School Violence*, 1(2), 51–71.

Bethel School District No. 403 et al. v. Fraser, a minor, et al., 478 U.S. 675 (1986).

Beussink v. Woodland R-IV School District, 30 F. Supp. 2d 1175 (E.D. Mo. 1988).

Blair, J. (2003). New breed of bullies torment their peers on the Internet. *Education Week*, 22(21), 6.

Board of Education of Independent School District No. 92 of Pottawatomie County v. Earls, 536 U.S. 822, 122 S. Ct. 2559 (2002). Retrieved from http://www.law. cornell.edu/supct/html/01-332.ZS.html

Boulton, M. J. (1993). A comparison of adults' and children's abilities to distinguish between aggressive and playful fighting in middle school pupils: Implications for playground supervision and behavior management. *Educational Studies*, 19, 193–203.

Boyd, N. (2000). *The beast within: Why men are violent*. Vancouver, British Columbia, Canada: Greystone Books.

Brown, K., Jackson, M., & Cassidy, W. (2006). Cyber-bullying: Developing policy to direct responses that are equitable and effective in addressing this special form of bullying. *Canadian Journal of Educational Administration and Policy*, 57, 1–37.

Bryson v. News America Publ'ns, Inc. 627 N.E. 2d. 1207 (Ill. 1996).

Campbell, M. (2005). Cyber bullying: An older problem in a new guise? *Australian Journal of Guidance and Counseling*, 15, 68–76.

Case, R. (2005). Bringing critical thinking to the main stage. *Education Canada*, 45(2), 45–49.

Cassidy, W., & Jackson, M. (2005, Fall). The need for equality in education: An inter-sectionality examination of labeling and zero tolerance practices. *McGill Journal of Education*, 40, 445–466.

Chu, J. (2005, August 8). You wanna take this online? Cyberspace is the 21st century bully's playground where girls play rougher than boys. *Time*, 166(6), 42–43.

Davis v. Monroe County Board of Education, 1107 91 F.3d 1418 (1999). Retrieved from http://www.law.cornell.edu/supct/html/97-843.ZS.html

Department of Justice, Canada (1982). *Canadian charter of rights and freedoms*. Retrieved from http://laws.justice.gc.ca/en/charter

Devlin, A. (1997). Offenders at school: Links between school failure and aggressive behaviour. In D. Tattum & H. Graham (Eds.), *Bullying: Home, school and community* (pp. 149–158). London, United Kingdom: David Fulton.

Dibbell, J. (1993, December 23). A rape in cyberspace. Retrieved from http://www. juliandibbell.com/texts/bungle_vv.html

Dickie, M., Merchant, K., Nakamoto, M., Nuttall, C., Terazono, E., & Yeager, H. (2004, April 13). Digital media. *Financial Times*, p. 8.

DiGiulio, R. C. (2001). *Educate, medicate, or litigate? What teachers, parents, and administrators must do about student behaviour.* Thousand Oaks, CA: Corwin Press.

Emmet v. Kent School District No 413, 92F. Supp. 2d 1088 (W.D. Wash. 2000). Retrieved from http://www2.bc.edu/~herbeck/cyberlaw.emmettvkent.html

Evard, M. (1996). So please stop, thank you: Girls online. In L. Cherny & E. R. Weise (Eds.), *Wired_women: Gender and new realities in cyberspace* (pp. 188–204). Toronto, Ontario, Canada: Seal Press.

Flaherty v. Keystone Oaks School District, 247F Supp. 2d 446 (W.D. Pa 2001).

Garrity v. John Hancock Mut. Life Ins. Co., 18 IER Cases 981 (D. Mass. 2002).

Gebser v. Lago Vista Independent School District, 524 U.S. 274 (1998).

Giroux, H. (2003). *The abandoned generation: Democracy beyond the culture of fear.* New York, NY: Palgrave MacMillan.

Glover, D., Cartwright, N., & Gleeson, D. (1998). *Towards bully-free schools.* Philadelphia, PA: Open University Press.

Godfrey v. Demon Internet Ltd. (1999). [2001] Q.B. 201.

Golding, W. (1954). *Lord of the Flies.* New York, NY: Penguin Putnam.

Harmon, A. (2004, August 26). Internet gives teenage bullies weapons . . . from afar. *New York Times*. Retrieved from http://www.nytimes.com./2004/08/26/education

Hazelwood School District v. Kuhlmeier, 484 U.S. 260 (1988).

Herring, S. C. (2002). Cyber violence: Recognizing and resisting abuse in online environments. *Asian Women, 14*, 187–212.

Irwin Toy Ltd. v. Québec (A.G.), 1 S.C.R. 927 (1989).

John Doe v. GTE Corp. 347. F.3d. 655 (7th Cir. 2003).

J.S., a Minor, v. Bethlehem Area School District, 757 A.2d 412 (Pa.Commw. 2000). Retrieved from http://www.departments.bucknell.edu/edu/ed370/ABSTRACTS%2001/harris.html

Jubran v. North Vancouver School District, BCHRT 10 (2002).

Katch, J. (2001). *Under deadman's skin: Discovering the meaning of children's violent play.* Boston, MA: Beacon Press.

Killion v. Franklin Regional School District, 136 F. Supp. 2d 446 (2001).

Layshock v. Hermitage School District, 2:06-cv-00116 TFM (2006). Retrieved from http://caselaw.findlaw.com/us-3rd-circuit/1506485.html

Leishman, J. (2002, October 10). Cyber bullying: The Internet is the latest weapon in a bully's arsenal. *CBC News*. Retrieved from http://cbc.ca/news/national/news/cyber bullying/index.html

Li, Q. (2005, April). *Cyber bullying in schools: The nature extent of adolescents' experience.* Paper presented at the American Education Research Association Conference in Montreal, Quebec, Canada.

Linden, A. M., & Klar, L. N. (Eds.) (1994). *Canadian tort law: Cases, notes & materials* (10th ed.). Markham, Ontario, Canada: Butterworths Canada.

Linden, A. M., & Klar, L. N. (Eds.) (1999) *Canadian tort law: Cases, notes & materials* (11th ed.). Vancouver, British Columbia, Canada: Butterworths Canada.

Lutes v. Board of Education of Prairie View School Division No. 74, S.J. No. 198, DRS 93-03792, Q.B. No. 1305 (1992).

MacKay, A. W., & Burt-Gerrans, J. (2005). Student freedom of expression: Violent content and the safe school balance. *McGill Journal of Education, 40,* 423–443.

MacKay, A. W., & Dickinson, G. M. (1998). Beyond the "careful parent": Tort liability in education. Toronto, Ontario, Canada: Emond Montgomery.

Milson, A., & Chu, B. W. (2002). Character education for cyberspace: Developing good netizens. *The Social Studies, 93*(3), 117–119.

Mitchell, A. (2004, January 24). Bullied by the click of a mouse. *The Globe and Mail.* Retrieved from http://www.cyber bullying.ca/globe-mail_January24.html

Myers, D. A. (2006, Winter). Defamation and the quiescent anarchy of the Internet: A case study of cyber-targeting. *Penn State Law Review, 110,* 667–686.

Nabozny v. Podlesny, 92 F.3d 446 (1996).

National Children's Home and Tesco Mobile. (2005). Putting U in the picture: Mobile bullying survey 2005. Retrieved from http://www.filemaker.co.uk/educationcentre/downloads/articles/Mobile_bullying_report.pdf

New Jersey v. T.L.O., 469 U.S. 325 (1985).

Olweus, D. (2001). Peer harassment: A critical analysis and some important issues. Introduction. In J. Juvonen & S. Graham (Eds.), *Peer harassment in school: The plight of the vulnerable and victimized* (pp. 3–20). New York, NY: Guilford Press.

Parks, M., & Floyd, K. (1996). Making friends in cyberspace. *Journal of Communication, 46,* 80–97.

Patchin, J., & Hinduja, S. (2006). Bullies move beyond the schoolyard: A preliminary look at cyber bullying. *Youth Violence and Juvenile Justice, 4,* 148–169.

People v. B.F. Jones, 62 Mich. 304, 28 NW 839 (1886).

People v. Overton, 20 N.Y. 360 (1967).

R. v. M.R.M, 3 S.C.R. 393 (1998).

R. v. Oakes, (1986) 1 S.C.R. 103, 26 D.L.R. 94th 200, 24 C.C.C. (3d) 321.

Rice, R. E. (1987). Computer-mediated communication and organizational innovation. *Journal of Communication, 37,* 65–94

Rice, R. E., & Love, G. (1987). Electonric emotion: Socioemotional content in a computer-mediated communication network. *Communication Research, 14,* 85–108.

Robichaud v. Canada, (Treasury Board), 2 S.C.R (1987).

Ross v. New Brunswick School District No. 15, 1 S.C.R. 826 (1996).

Salmivalli, C., Lagerspetz, K., Bjorqvist, K., Osterman, K., & Kaukianen, A. (1996). Bullying as a group process: Participant roles and their relations to social status within the group. *Aggressive Behavior, 25,* 81–89.

Servance, R. L. (2003). Cyber bullying, cyber-harassment, and the conflict between schools and the First Amendment. *Wisconsin Law Review, 6,* 1213–1215.

Shariff, S. (2003). *A system on trial: Identifying legal standards for educational, ethical and legally defensible approaches to bullying in schools* (Unpublished doctoral dissertation). Simon Fraser University, Burnaby, British Columbia.

Shariff, S. (2004). Keeping schools out of court: Legally defensible models of leadership to reduce cyber bullying [Educational Forum]. *Delta Kappa Pi, 68,* 222–233.

Shariff, S. (2005). Cyber-dilemmas in the new millennium: Balancing free expression and student safety in cyberspace. *McGill Journal of Education, 40,* 467–487.

Shariff, S., & Gouin, R. (2005, September). *Cyber-dilemmas: Gendered hierarchies, free expression and cyber-safety in schools.* Paper presented at the International Conference on Cyber-Safety, Oxford University, Oxford, United Kingdom. Retrieved from http://www.oii.ox.ac.uk/cybersafety

Shariff, S., & Johnny, L. (2005). The role of the charter in balancing freedom of expression, safety and equality in a virtual school environment. In M. Manley-Casimir (Ed.), *Courts, charter and the schools: The impact of judicial decisions on educational policy and practice* (pp. XX–XX). Toronto, Ontario, Canada: University of Toronto Press.

Shariff, S., & Strong-Wilson, T. (2005). Bullying and new technologies. In J. Kincheloe (Ed.), *Classroom teaching: An introduction* (pp. 219–240). New York, NY: David Lang.

Short, J., Williams, E., & Christie, B. (1976). *The social psychology of telecommunication.* London, United Kingdom: Wiley.

Skiba, R., & Peterson, R. (1999). The dark side of zero tolerance: Can punishment lead to safe schools? *Phi Delta Kappan, 80,* 372–376, 381–383.

Spears v. Jefferson Parish School Board, 646 So. 2d. 1104 (1994).

Sproull, L., & Kiesler, S. (1991). *Connections: New ways of working in the networked organization.* Cambridge, MA: MIT Press.

Steeves, V., & Wing, C. (2005). Young Canadians in a wired world. *Media Awareness Network.* Retrieved from http://www.media-awareness.ca

Stratton Oakmont v. Prodigy Services Co. (1995). N.Y. Misc. LEXIS 229 (N.Y. App. Div. 1995)

Tinker v. Des Moines Independent Community School District, 393 U.S. 503 (1969).

Tolman, D. L., Spencer, R., Rosen-Reynoso, M., & Porches, M. (2001, April). *"He's the man!" Gender ideologies and early adolescents' experiences with sexual harassment.* Paper presented at the American Educational Researchers Association Conference, Seattle, WA.

United States Department of Labor, Title IX, Education Amendments, 20 U.S.C. §1681-1688. Retrieved from http://www.dol.gov/oasam/regs/statutes/titleix.htm

Veronia School District 47J v. Acton, 515 U.S. 646, 115 S.Ct. 2386 (1995).

Wallace, P. (1999). *The psychology of the Internet.* Cambridge, United Kingdom: Cambridge University Press.

Wallis, C. (2006, March 27). The multitasking generation. *Time, 167,* 48–55.

Willard, N. (2005). *Educator's guide to cyber bullying: Addressing the harm caused by online social cruelty.* Retrieved from http://cyberbully.org

Ybarra, M., & Mitchell, K. (2004). Youth engaging in online harassment: Association with caregiver–child relationships, Internet use, and personal characteristics. *Journal of Adolescence, 27,* 319–336.

Zeran v. America Online, Inc. 129 F. 3d. 327 (4th Cir. 1997).

Human Rights Infringement in the Digital Age

21

RUSSELL G. SMITH[1]

Contents

Introduction

In this chapter, I consider the human rights implications of crime control in the digital age—that is, crime that involves information systems as instruments or as targets of illegality. The term *digital* simply refers to the fact that computerized systems operate by reducing information to streams of 1s and 0s. Thus, almost every type of information is able to be transmitted across telecommunications networks connected either by wires or by means of radio waves. Advances in information and communications technologies (ICT) not only have created a range of new crime problems but also have facilitated the prevention, detection, investigation, prosecution, adjudication, and punishment of crime. Examples include the use of encryption to ensure that data are held securely, neural networks to detect financial crime, biometric systems to identify suspects, hard drive imaging to secure

---

[1] The views expressed are those of the author alone and not the Australian government.

data from alteration or destruction, sharing of data held in official databases to identify suspects and risks, electronic courtrooms to present evidence clearly, and electronic monitoring of offenders to enhance surveillance during periods of home detention.

Although technology has assisted criminal justice agencies and offered many protections for suspects and offenders, risks of infringement of human rights have arisen from the ways in which legal reforms designed to deal with computer crime risks have been framed. As Arup and Tucker (1998) observed:

> Information technology has provided authoritarian states with capacity to monitor contain and discipline their subjects but information technology and the human rights associated with it have also done much to undermine their hold. (p. 245)

In this chapter, I identify some areas of human rights concern that legal reforms designed to address ICT-related crime have created, and I assess whether the achievements and benefits derived outweigh the potential and actual infringements of liberty that exist. I conclude that policymakers have sometimes been attracted by the novelty and efficiency of technology without having due regard to the sometimes covert infringements of human rights that can, and do, occur.

What Are Human Rights?

At present, there are no specific normative instruments that comprehensively set out human rights applicable in the digital age. Instead, developments in ICT have implications for the various existing international and local regimes that seek to protect human rights (see Weeramantry, 1990). These implications include the following:

- The Universal Declaration of Human Rights (1948; UDHR)
- The International Covenant on Civil and Political Rights (1966; ICCPR), to which Australia is a signatory
- The International Covenant on Economic, Social and Cultural Rights (1966; ICESCR), to which Australia is a signatory
- The Optional Protocol to the International Covenant on Civil and Political Rights (1966)

The UDHR sets out general principles concerning physical integrity (life, liberty, arrest, detention, torture, freedom of movement, asylum), social welfare (social security, the right to work, rest, leisure, education), health, adequate standard of living, the family, legal integrity (nationality, participation in government, recognition before the law, fair trial), and mental and moral integrity (dignity; freedom of thought, conscience, and religion; freedom of opinion and expression; freedom of peaceful assembly and association). These rights are described more fully in the covenants and protocols cited previously.

In addition, some countries and regions have developed their own Human Rights Conventions, such as the European Convention for the Protection of Human Rights and Fundamental Freedoms, the U.S. Constitution, and the Canadian Charter of Rights and Freedoms. There are also the British constitutional documents Magna Carta (1215) and the Declaration of Rights (1689), which—along with common law—has created a climate of respect for individual liberty in English common-law countries.

In Australia, there are numerous pieces of legislation that give effect to these human rights principles, although there is no national-level Human Rights Act. At the federal level, there numerous pieces of legislation that are relevant to the protection of human rights, including the Australian Human Rights Commission Act 1986 (Commonwealth), which protects certain specific rights such as freedom from various forms of discrimination. Additionally, a variety of state and territory acts protect human rights in various ways dealing with principles of antidiscrimination, freedom of information, equal opportunity, and adherence to the rules of natural justice, to mention a few (see http://www.humanrights.gov.au/about/legislation/index. html). In the Australian Capital Territory, various rights are also now protected under the Human Rights Act 2004 (Australian Capital Territory) and the Human Rights Commission Act 2005 (Australian Capital Territory), both of which are based on the ICCPR. In Victoria, since January 1, 2007, human rights are also protected under the Charter of Human Rights and Responsibilities Act 2006 (Victoria).

The purpose of the following discussion is not to assess whether legislation in Australia relevant to cyber crime complies with each convention or piece of legislation; rather, the aim is to indicate some areas in which human rights concerns have been identified and to point to potential areas of infringement if certain technological developments occur. Presently, Australia can be guided by what has occurred in various overseas countries that have enacted local human rights legislation or whose legislation has been challenged by Human Rights Commissions or higher courts.

What Rights Are at Risk From Crime Control in the Digital Age?

In the digital age, misuse of ICT can take place in relation to both government and private-sector activities. Most human rights principles are directed at identifying and preventing abuses by government agencies, although recently, we have seen an extension of privacy protections from the public sector to the private sector. In addition, human rights abuses can arise from the actions of individuals, which give rise to the need for governments to enact laws to protect citizens both from the acts of government agencies and of other individuals and corporations—a point recognized by Arup and Tucker (1998). The present discussion focuses on abuses that can occur in criminal justice contexts involving cyber crime; increasingly, these contexts are inclusive of private corporations as providers of investigative, judicial, and correctional services.

Weeramantry (1983) has identified various technological advances that could detract from basic human rights unless regulated by legislation. Over the last 20 years, many new issues have arisen, and Table 21.1 sets out those areas of concern that relate to the regulation of ICT in the context of criminal justice in the 21st century.

The technologies that are relevant to infringements of human rights include the Internet, DNA analysis techniques, biometric identification technologies, closed-circuit television (CCTV) and mobile phone cameras, listening devices, networked databases and neural networks for data analysis, voice recognition systems, and others. Many of these technologies were developed by the military and security industry in the 1940s during the Cold War for policing and national security purposes. Since the 1990s, their miniaturization and power has increased immensely. It needs to be emphasized that potential infringements of human rights most often arise following the introduction of legislative measures designed to regulate these new technologies rather than from the creation or usage of the technologies themselves.

With the advent of personal computers and wireless technologies in recent times, the capacity to carry out complete surveillance of people is astounding, although the idea of the "surveillance society" has its roots in much older times. In the late 18th century, Bentham designed his *Panopticon*—or "total institution"—in which those in charge could easily monitor the activities of inmates, be they prisoners or patients in hospitals, through the use of specially designed buildings (Semple, 1993). Foucault (1977) identified the societal implications of the power imbalance that would result in discipline and punishment. Unfortunately, technologies of surveillance have since developed, often with less than adequate controls over potential abuse.

Examples of Potential Human Rights Infringements From Crime Control in the Digital Age

Over the last 30 years, during which time cyber crime and its control have developed, society has witnessed many examples of the misuse of ICT—and

Table 21.1 Potential Human Rights Infringement in Connection With ICT and Its Regulation

Human Rights	Sources of Possible Denigration by ICT
Human freedom and dignity (UDHR Article 1, ICCPR Article 10)	Electronic surveillance (listening devices, CCTV)
	DNA analysis
	Data matching by government agencies
	Identity smart cards
	Electronic tagging of offenders
Freedom from discrimination (UDHR Article 2, ICCPR Article 26)	Cyber racism
	Computer addiction
Freedom of thought and expression (UDHR Article 18, 19; ICCPR Article 18, 19)	Maintenance of databases
	Surveillance devices
	Spam/Denial-of-service attacks
	Online content restrictions
Right to bodily security and freedom from inhuman punishments (UDHR Article 3, 5; ICCPR Article 7)	Electronic tagging of offenders
	Embedded computer chips in humans
	Biometric identification
Right to a fair trial, presumption of innocence, freedom from self-incrimination (UDHR Article 11; ICCPR Article 9, 14)	Disclosure of encryption keys/passwords
	Use of electronic evidence in court
	Co-mingling of electronic evidence
	Juror access to online information
Right to own property and protect intellectual property (UDHR Article 17, 27.1)	Digital piracy
	Computer hacking
	Electronic espionage
Right to privacy (UDHR Article 12, ICCPR Article17)	Electronic surveillance
	Maintenance of databases
	Data matching by government agencies
	Identity smart cards
	e-commerce marketing and spam
Right to life (UDHR Article 3, ICCPR Article 6)	Cyber terrorism
	Capital punishment for cyber crime
Right to participate in government and vote (UDHR Article 21, ICCPR Article 25)	Online indoctrination
	Electronic surveillance
	Digital monopolies
	Invasions of privacy
	Surveillance of electronic voting activities

Source: Adapted from Weeramantry, C. G., *The slumbering sentinels: Law and human rights in the wake of technology*, Penguin Books, Melbourne, Australia.
UDHR, articles of the Universal Declaration of Human Rights (1948); ICCPR, articles of the International Covenant on Civil and Political Rights (1966); ICT = information and communications technologies; CCTV, closed captioned television.

legislative responses to it—that could be said to have infringed human rights. The following are some illustrations that have been detected or that individuals have raised as potential infringements. Some relate to abuses of normative instruments in other countries—especially the U.S. Constitution—and so are not of direct relevance to Australia at present. Others relate to more universal human rights and so have particular importance in Australia. The following is not an exhaustive list but serves to illustrate the kinds of issues that exist in the 21st century. It can be anticipated that the years ahead will see an escalation in these and other potential forms of human rights abuses.

Privacy

One particular group of rights that has relevance to ICT concerns the protection of privacy. In Australia, the legislative protection of privacy came relatively late, in 1988, with the enactment of the Privacy Act 1988 (Commonwealth) and the more recent Privacy Amendment (Private Sector) Act 2000 (Commonwealth). There are also privacy laws in some states and territories, such as the Privacy and Personal Information Protection Act 1998 (New South Wales) and the Information Privacy Act 2000 (Victoria). However, Australian privacy laws are not particularly strong legislative instruments: Remedies for breach of privacy are generally by way of declaration rather than criminal punishment, and private-sector compliance is largely through voluntary codes of practice.

The protection of privacy in Australia arguably lags behind privacy protection in Europe, where various Privacy Directives have enabled legislators to implement protections under the European Convention for the Protection of Human Rights and Fundamental Freedoms. Recent measures include the Privacy Directive (95/46/EC) and the Privacy and Electronic Communications Directive (2002/58/EC; see Smith, Grabosky, & Urbas, 2004).

The ability to monitor computer usage creates a number of potential human rights concerns, including infringements of human freedom, freedom of thought and expression, and the right to privacy. Although the monitoring of e-mails and Internet usage by employers is usually undertaken with the knowledge of employees, informed and free consent is sometimes lacking.

Less certain are situations in which Internet service providers (ISPs) and telecommunications carriers monitor computer usage or provide logs to government agencies. Article 20 (Real-Time Collection of Traffic Data) and Article 21 (Interception of Content Data) of the Council of Europe's Convention on Cyber Crime, for example, have been criticized as involving breaches of human rights in requiring organizations to collect traffic data and the content of communications and make this available to law enforcement agencies (Taylor, 2001).

Recent moves toward the creation of electronic identity cards, e-passports, and data-matching also raise potential infringements of privacy that need to be addressed prior to the widespread implementation of such initiatives. Hong Kong, for example, has developed multi-use ID smartcards that contain basic biometric information such as thumbprints and a photograph, and these cards can perform multiple functions, including being used as drivers' licenses and library cards (Benitez, 2002). A pilot program for a biometric ID card has also been implemented in Great Britain, in relation to asylum seekers (McAuliffe, 2002).

Some of the main privacy concerns that affect biometrically enabled identity cards include fears that (a) information will be gathered without permission or knowledge or without explicitly defining the purpose for which it is required; (b) information will be used for a variety of purposes other than those for which it was originally acquired (known as *function creep*); (c) information will be shared without explicit permission; or (d) information will be used to track people across multiple databases to amalgamate information for the purpose of surveillance or social control.

In addition to complying with privacy principles and privacy legislation, additional measures may be needed to enhance privacy protections in the digital age. These include mandating the use of specified levels of encryption for the capture, storage, and transmission of data; limiting database matching except under close scrutiny by independent observers; preventing the reconstruction or retention of original biometric samples from encrypted biometric information; and preventing comparisons with reproductions of biometric information not obtained directly from individuals. Some of these aspects may require amendments to the Privacy Act 1988 (Commonwealth).

Search, Seizure, and Criminal Trials

Computer crime legislation is expanding the range of investigatory powers available to law enforcement agencies to deal with such problems as concealing electronic evidence through the use of encryption. Those countries, unconstrained by a Bill of Rights, have devised a simple solution to the challenge of encryption. They simply require individuals to disclose encryption keys or face criminal charges. In the United Kingdom, this can entail imprisonment for up to 2 years (Regulation of Investigatory Powers Act 2000 [England] ss. 49–55). In Europe, Article 6 of the Rome Convention could be a barrier to such compulsory disclosure, although the European Commission on Human Rights has restricted the scope of the article to oral statements. Nevertheless, European procedures for compulsory decryption would have to be formulated precisely in order to withstand judicial scrutiny (Smith et al., 2004, p. 67).

The Australian Cybercrime Act 2001 (Commonwealth) provides a maximum penalty of 6 months imprisonment for failure to comply with a magistrate's order to provide such information to investigating officials (see s. 3LA Criminal Code Act 1995 [Commonwealth] and s. 201A of the Customs Act 1901 [Commonwealth]). Arguably, this could infringe upon article 14(3) (g) of the ICCPR, which provides that a person shall not be compelled to testify against himself or to confess guilt.

The Council of Europe's Convention on Cyber Crime (2001) incorporates various provisions designed to safeguard human rights norms and privileges in connection with cyber crime investigations, such as requirements for judicial or other independent supervision, proportionality, and respect for and consideration of the rights of third parties. Given the strength of the provisions allowing search, seizure, and surveillance, however, these requirements have been criticized by some privacy advocates as being inadequate (Taylor, 2001).

Another particular area of concern relates to the use of "keystroke-logging" software, which can be installed remotely on computers to capture information such as passwords and decryption keys typed on keyboards. Some have argued that such activities infringe upon the U.S. Constitution's Fourth Amendment, which ensures every U.S. citizen's right against unreasonable search and seizure. In one case, Federal Bureau of Investigation (FBI) agents in the United States tricked a pair of suspected hackers out of passwords and account numbers and then downloaded evidence from their computers in Russia.

The U.S. District Court rejected several motions filed on behalf of the defendants, who sought to suppress the evidence obtained from their computers. They argued that the FBI agents had violated their Fourth Amendment right against unreasonable search and seizure by secretly obtaining the passwords and account numbers using a "sniffer" program that recorded their keystrokes when the FBI agents remotely accessed the computers in Chelyabinsk, Russia.

The court found that the defendants had no expectation of privacy when they sat down at computers at an FBI office that was set up to lure the suspects to the United States with offers of work in the computer security field. When they sat down at the networked computer, they knew that the systems administrator could and likely would monitor their activities.

The court also found that the Fourth Amendment applied to neither the computers (because they are the property of a nonresident and are located outside the United States) nor the data, at least until it was transmitted to the United States. The judge noted that investigators then obtained a search warrant before viewing the nearly 250 gigabytes of data. He rejected the argument that the warrant should have been obtained before the data were downloaded, noting that the agents had good reason to fear that if they did not copy the data, the defendants' co-conspirators would destroy the evidence or make it unavailable (*United States v. Gorshkov and Ivanov*, 2001).

Fairness in relation to the gathering and use of electronic evidence also can be placed in jeopardy because of the extent of electronic information that has been gathered. Often, it will be necessary for police to image an entire computer's hard drive when executing a search warrant, despite the fact that much of the data copied will be irrelevant to the investigation. If the irrelevant material contains evidence of unsuspected criminal activity by other persons, their rights may be adversely affected.

In relation to criminal trials, a number of human rights implications arise. The rights to a fair trial, presumption of innocence, and freedom from self-incrimination are all established rights (UDHR Article 11, ICCPR Articles 9, 14) that could be infringed upon where individuals use ICT to gather and to present evidence. Risks could arise where electronic evidence is presented in court proceedings that may be unduly prejudicial to the accused or where jurors undertake private online research into the background of an accused person contrary to directions from the judge. In both New South Wales and Queensland, it is an offense for a juror to undertake investigations on the Internet or otherwise (Jury Act 1977 [New South Wales] s. 68C; Jury Act 1995 [Queensland] s. 69A). The extent of online information is such that prejudicial material could easily be discovered by jurors during a trial, with few opportunities for the judge or defense counsel to learn of this potential problem (see Spigelman, 2005).

An example of this occurred recently in New South Wales. The accused had been convicted of murdering his first wife, but the Court of Criminal Appeal ordered a retrial. He had also been tried and acquitted of the murder of his second wife. Both wives were from the Philippines, and a website called The Solidarity Philippines Australia Network contained material that was prejudicial to the accused. During the retrial, a juror conducted Internet searches and inspected the website, discovering that the accused had been tried and convicted of murdering his first wife and charged and acquitted of murdering his second wife. The Court of Criminal Appeal set aside the conviction in the retrial because of the conduct of the juror in obtaining access to the information contained on the Internet. As a result, the court ordered a further retrial, of which the accused was convicted of murdering his first wife (*R. v. K*, 2003).

Discrimination

Potential infringement upon antidiscrimination laws in the digital age can arise in situations in which persons accused of illegal online activity claim to be acting because of some form of impairment. A Canadian civil case, for example, involved the dismissal of a university academic for using his employer's equipment to download child pornography (*Re Seneca College and Ontario Public Service Employees Union, Local 560*, 2002). The professor, who had pleaded guilty to criminal charges, was given a suspended sentence and placed on probation for 2 years.

He sought to challenge his discharge from the college on the grounds that it arose from a mental disorder that could be considered a disability under Ontario's Human Rights Code. Accordingly, it was argued that he had been discriminated against on the basis of mental disability. The professor, who lived under difficult circumstances with his aging parents, claimed to have used the Internet as an escape from the sadness and isolation that characterized his personal life. He claimed that he was unable to control his impulses.

The court held that the evidence did not support a conclusion that the professor was suffering from any form of medically recognized mental disorder. His inappropriate use of the college computers was both selective and controlled, and the depression for which he was temporarily hospitalized was brought about by his impending dismissal from the college as a result of his misconduct. These findings served to neutralize any justification for therapeutic use, or extenuation based on compulsive behavior. His dismissal from the college was upheld (see Smith et al., 2004, p. 79).

Freedom of Thought and Expression

The UDHR and the ICCPR establish rights to freedom of thought, conscience, religion, and expression. In the digital age, infringements could arise from both government agencies and business organizations and other individuals. In the case of organizations, surveillance of e-mail and mobile phone communications could entail infringements of freedom of expression. In the case of individuals, the dissemination of spam, racist material, or distributed denial-of-service attacks could infringe other people's human rights. Laws that restrict online content in various ways—including obscene or defamatory materials—could also involving breaches of freedom of expression.

These rights are obviously not unrestricted, and the conventions allow for limitations in order to protect the rights or reputation of others and for the protection of national security, public order, public health, and morals. Clearly, the Internet creates an environment in which these rights are difficult to balance.

In Australia, for example, several states and territories have enacted various criminal laws prohibiting racial and religious vilification, although at the Commonwealth level—as with privacy—the approach has been less punitive. In a case concerning Fredrick Toben's Adelaide Institute, for example, the Human Rights and Equal Opportunity Commission (HREOC) ordered a website questioning the historical occurrence of the Holocaust to be closed down, but there were no criminal penalties involved [*Jones v. Toben*, 2009; *Jones v. Toben (No. 2)*, 2009].

The issue of *cyber racism* has also recently been addressed by the Council of Europe. In May 2001, the Council's Convention on Cyber Crime was opened for signature—together with a First Additional Protocol concerning criminalization of racist and xenophobic propaganda over the Internet— aimed at a harmonized approach to the criminalization of such content as well as investigative issues and international assistance (Smith et al., 2004).

In the United States, it has been argued in some cases that the imposition of restrictions on the use of computers or monitoring of convicted offenders' online activities infringes upon the First Amendment of the Constitution concerning freedom of speech. It has been held, however, that restrictions should survive a First Amendment challenge if they are reasonably related to the offense and to the defendant's history and past conduct. They should also involve no greater deprivation of liberty than is reasonably necessary to achieve the ends of protecting the public and promoting rehabilitation of the defendant (Painter, 2001; *United States v. Ristine*, 2003; *United States v. Mitnick*, 1998).

The famous case involving Kevin Mitnick—who, in addition to being sentenced to almost 5 years' imprisonment and ordered to pay $4,125 in restitution and to assign to his victims any proceeds he may receive from selling the story of his conduct—was subject to stringent conditions during his 3-year period of parole. These conditions included a complete prohibition (without prior express written approval of the probation officer) on the possession or use (personally or through third parties), for any purpose, of the following: cell phones, computers, any computer software programs, computer peripherals or support equipment, personal information assistants, modems, anything capable of accessing computer networks, and any other electronic equipment presently available or new technology that becomes available that can be converted to, or has as its function, the ability to act as a computer system or to access a computer system, computer network, or telecommunications network. In addition, Mitnick was prohibited from acting as a consultant or advisor to individuals or groups engaged in any computer-related activity (*United States v. Kevin Mitnick*, 1998).

Mitnick appealed against this order on the basis that it involved a violation of his First Amendment rights and because it was said to be vague and overly restrictive. The Appeals Court held that the district court had not abused its discretion because the conditions imposed were reasonably related to legitimate sentencing goals and were no more restrictive than necessary. Conditions that restrict otherwise lawful activities are still legitimate when the defendant, by engaging in them, might be tempted to commit further crimes. Also, the fact that Mitnick may have engaged in otherwise prohibited conduct with his probation officer's approval made the conditions imposed less restrictive that an outright ban on such conduct.

The Appeals Court also rejected Mitnick's contention that the supervised release conditions impermissibly restricted the exercise of his First Amendment rights of freedom of speech. Despite the increasing pervasiveness and importance of the Internet as a communication tool, restrictions on access to such technology are proper if related to and reasonably necessary to promote the goals of sentencing (*United States v. Kevin Mitnick*, 1998). As long as the conditions were expressly related to preventing recidivism and did not go beyond what was reasonably necessary, they were valid. Mitnick also contended that the district court erred by imposing supervised release conditions that restricted his employment in the computer and telecommunications industries as well as employment in which Mitnick would have access to computers and computer-related equipment. The district court was held not to have abused its discretion because a reasonably direct relationship existed between Mitnick's possible occupation and his offenses (*United States v. Kevin Mitnick*, 1998).

The rights to participate in government and to vote by secret ballot or free voting procedures are specified in the UDHR and ICCPR (UDHR Article 21, ICCPR Article 25). Where electronic or online voting procedures are used, potential infringements could arise from individuals who do not have access to computers being disenfranchised, from surveillance of voting activities by citizens, or from manipulation of information provided to voters. Problems of the authentication of the identity of individuals will also arise (Smith, 2002).

Cruel and Unusual Punishment

Article 7 of the ICCPR provides that no one shall be subjected to torture or to cruel, inhuman or degrading treatment or punishment. Capital punishment is still employed in a number of countries—and, in some rare instances, in China, capital punishment has even been ordered for computer-related offenses. There was one case in which a 36-year-old computer hacker in Hangzhou Province was sentenced to death for embezzling 1.66 million yuan (about $200,000) by counterfeiting bank paper and misappropriating funds from bank customers' accounts (he was employed there as an accountant; People's Daily Online, 2000).

The use of electronic monitoring as a punishment—if sufficiently invasive—could also, arguably, infringe upon Article 7 of the ICCPR. Electronic monitoring is undoubtedly an invasive technology that involves the physical attachment of a device to a person. Modern technologies are also psychologically invasive in the sense that the person's every move can be tracked, other than when the device is programmed to be off. Fox (1987) reported that "those who have experienced the regime of [electronically] monitored home detention indicate that it is psychologically wearing and more onerous in terms of self discipline than the world of prison" (p. 142).

Generally, conditional orders that require the surveillance of offenders must not be unreasonable in their potential to interfere with the offender's life. In the Northern Territory case of *Dunn v. Woodcock* (2003), conditions were imposed on an offender convicted of unlawfully supplying cannabis, which required her to consent to any number of searches at any time during the day or night over a period of 12 months, regardless of whether the police had reasonable grounds for believing that there may be dangerous drugs concealed upon her premises and even if a search warrant had not been obtained. The court considered that the condition placed an unreasonable burden on the offender because it placed her in the power of the police who could exercise very substantial control over her life by the mere threat of exercising the power to search unreasonably or unfairly. The court struck out the condition on the grounds that it was unduly oppressive.

A more invasive development involves the use of computer chips embedded beneath the skin of offenders, albeit with their consent (Bright, 2002; The Economist, 2002). Miniature tracking devices can be implanted beneath the skin and can track an individual's location as well as monitor physiological signs. Although these may be removed using a simple surgical procedure, the potential for civil action for any adverse consequences of the surgery or the implant itself demands serious consideration before any such developments take place. Professional ethical issues also arise for doctors involved in the nontherapeutic implantation and removal procedures. In the United Kingdom, there have been indications that the government may consider the use of surgically implanted devices for convicted pedophiles (Bright, 2002).

Australia has recently enacted legislation (Criminal Code Act 1995) that enables, *inter alia*, control orders—that may include electronic monitoring—to be issued in situations where such orders will substantially assist in preventing a terrorist act or where it is suspected, on reasonable grounds, that a person has provided training to or received training from a listed terrorist organization.

In making an order, the judge must be satisfied on the balance of probabilities that the order to be imposed would substantially assist in preventing a terrorist act, or that the person has provided training to, or received training from, a listed terrorist organization, and that each of the obligations, prohibitions, and restrictions to be imposed on the person by the order is reasonably necessary and reasonably appropriate and adapted for the purpose of protecting the public from a terrorist act [see Criminal Code Act 1995 (Commonwealth) s.104.4(c)]. Such a control order can be made for up to 12 months, except in the case of 16- to 18-year-olds, in which case the control order can be made for only up to 3 months [see Criminal Code Act

1995 (Commonwealth) s.104.5]. Control orders cannot be made in respect to people less than 16 years of age. Failure to comply with a control order, such as by removing a tracking device, carries a maximum penalty of 5 years imprisonment [see Criminal Code Act 1995 (Commonwealth) s.104.27]. The attorney general must provide written consent prior to such orders being sought from a judge. Electronic monitoring is defined in the legislation as a "tracking device," which means any electronic device capable of being used to determine or monitor the location of a person or an object or the status of an object [see Criminal Code Act 1995 (Commonwealth) s.100.1(1)].

Although the use of electronic monitoring in this context would entail similar issues to its use in correctional settings, the manner in which the legislation has been framed in Australia has raised numerous legal and human rights concerns (see, e.g., Byrnes, Charlesworth, & McKinnon 2005). These questions relate principally to the legal protections that govern the making of orders, their constitutionality, and their compliance or otherwise with international human rights protections. Questions also arise concerning the effectiveness of such orders in enabling government agencies to gain useful information about terrorist threats. Clearly, if a suspect were required to wear an electronic device, he or she would no longer be included in terrorist activities, as the risks of detection would be substantial. It remains to be seen whether electronically monitored control orders will be used, and to what extent, and whether these human rights concerns will eventuate. Once again, it needs to be emphasized that these potential infringements for human rights arise from the legislative measures introduced rather than from the creation and use of the monitoring technologies themselves.

How Can We Prevent Human Rights Infringement in the Digital Age?

Ultimately, the prevention of human rights infringements in the digital age lies with individual legislatures, which should ensure that new legislation complies with current international and local normative instruments. In addition, the private sector could play a part in preventing abuses by designing new technologies in ways that prevent or minimize potential human rights abuses. Thus, the protection of human rights can best be achieved through an interaction between technological innovation and policy reform.

First, hardware and software developers could be persuaded to build into new products technological solutions to problems that concern human rights when developing new technologies. An example is the use of systems that prevent illegal copying of data to protect copyright.

Second, it is important for the human rights implications of new technologies to be examined before (not after) they are introduced. Fox (2001, p. 268) notes the need for academics to question the use of new technologies, and Kirby (1998, p. 331) has stressed the need for ongoing and informed debate about the social implications of new technologies as well as the desirability of establishing global principles to guide the use of new technologies.

The following cautionary observation of Casella (2003) is worth recalling in the present context:

> The longer a technology is used, the more entrenched in life it becomes. When technologies are new, or are used in newer ways … their uses are easier to modify and their consequences easier to control.… If we wish to question the unintended consequences of these developments, now is the time to do so. (p. 92)

Finally, rigorous evaluative research needs to be conducted once new technologies have been introduced in order to monitor their potential for denigration of human rights and infringements of international and national laws. The reporting requirements under international law should be taken seriously by governments, and individuals and organizations should be encouraged to report infringing practices immediately after they appear.

In the capitalist marketplace, where corporate reputations are important, having a link to new technologies that infringe upon human rights may be a powerful deterrent and a useful way of ensuring that some of the more egregious developments in the digital age are avoided. At the same time, the development of technologies to protect and to enhance human rights could be a powerful marketing feature. An example would be the use of biometric user authentication technologies to protect personal identity information. Ideally, those responsible for technological innovation should work closely with human rights advocates and policymakers to prevent potential problems from arising during the development phase of new technologies rather than devising solutions once problems have arisen and human rights have been infringed.

References

Arup, C., & Tucker, G. (1998). Information technology law and human rights. In D. Kinley (Ed.), *Human rights in Australian law* (pp. 243–266). Sydney, Australia: Federation Press.

Australian Human Rights Commission Act of 1986 (Commonwealth).

Benitez, M. A. (2002, February 27). ID card contract awarded. *South China Morning Post* (Hong Kong), p. 2.

Bright, M. (2002). Surgical tags plan for sex offenders. *The Observer*. Retrieved from http://society.guardian.co.uk/children/story/0,1074,842393,00.html

Byrnes, A., Charlesworth, H., & McKinnon, G. (2005, October 18). *Human rights implications of the Anti-Terrorism Bill 2005. Letter of advice to Mr. John Stanhope.* Retrieved from http://www.chiefminister.act.gov.au/docs/_20051018.pdf

Casella, R. (2003). The false allure of security technologies. *Social Justice, 30,* 82–93.

Charter of Human Rights and Responsibilities Act 2006 (Victoria).

Dunn v. Woodcock, NTSC 24 (S. Ct. of the Northern Territory, March 20, 2003).

The Economist. (2002, August 15). Something to watch over you: Surveillance. *The Economist.* Retrieved from http://www.economist.com/node/1280634

Foucault, M. (1977). *Discipline and punish: The birth of the prison* (Allan Sheridan, Transl.). London, United Kingdom: Penguin Books.

Fox, R. G. (1987). Dr Schwitzgebel's machine revisited: Electronic monitoring of offenders. *Australian and New Zealand Journal of Criminology, 20,* 131–147.

Fox, R. G. (2001). Someone to watch over us: Back to the panopticon? *Criminal Justice, 1,* 251–276.

Human Rights Act 2004 (Australian Capital Territory).

Human Rights Commission Act 2005 (Australian Capital Territory).

Information Privacy Act 2000 (Victoria).

Jones v. Toben, HREOCA 39 (October 5, 2000).

Jones v. Toben, FCA 1150 (September 17, 2002).

Jones v. Toben, FCA 354 (20 April 20, 2009).

Jones v. Toben (No. 2), FCA 477 (May 13, 2009).

Kirby, M. (1998). Privacy in cyberspace. *University of New South Wales Law Journal, 21,* 323–333.

McAuliffe, W. (2002, February 5). Asylum seekers get first UK biometric ID cards. *ZDNet Australia.* Retrieved from http://www.zdnet.com.au/asylum-seekers-get-first-uk-biometric-id-cards-120263301.htm

Painter, C. M. E. (2001). Supervised release and probation restrictions in hacker cases. *U.S. Department of Justice Executive Office for United States Attorneys United States Attorneys' USA Bulletin, 4*(2). Retrieved from http://www.usdoj.gov/criminal/cybercrime/usamarch2001_7.htm

People's Daily Online. (2000, June 13). Chinese hacker sentenced to death for embezzlement. *People's Daily Online.* Retrieved from http://english1.peopledaily.com.cn/english/200006/13/eng20000613_42866.html

Privacy Act 1988 (Commonwealth).

Privacy Amendment (Private Sector) Act 2000 (Commonwealth).

Privacy and Personal Information Protection Act 1998 (New South Wales).

Privacy Directive (95/46/EC) Directive 95/46/EC of the European Parliament and of the Council of 24 October 1995 on the protection of individuals with regard to the processing of personal data and on the free movement of such data. Retrieved from http://eur-lex.europa.eu/LexUriServ/LexUriServ.do?uri=CELEX:31995L0046:EN:HTML

Privacy and Electronic Communications Directive (2002/58/EC) Directive 2002/58/EC of the European Parliament and of the Council of 12 July 2002 concerning the processing of personal data and the protection of privacy in the electronic communications sector (Directive on privacy and electronic communications. Retrieved from http://eur-lex.europa.eu/LexUriServ/LexUriServ.do?uri=CELEX:32002L0058:EN:NOT

R v. K 59 NSWLR 431; 144 A Crim R 468; NSWCCA 406 (2003).

Re Seneca College and Ontario Public Service Employees Union, Local 560, 109 L.A.C. (4th) 334, 2002 L.A.C. Lexis 160, File No. MPA/Y200927 (2002).

Semple, J. (1993). *Bentham's prison: A study of the panopticon penitentiary.* Oxford, United Kingdom: Clarendon Press.

Smith, R. G. (2002). Electronic voting: Benefits and risks. In A. Graycar (Ed.), *Trends and Issues in Crime and Criminal Justice* (No. 224, pp. 1–6). Canberra, Australia: Australian Institute of Criminology.

Smith, R. G., Grabosky, P., & Urbas, G. (2004). *Cyber criminals on trial.* Cambridge, United Kingdom: Cambridge University Press.

Spigelman, J. J. (2005). The Internet and the right to a fair trial. *Criminal Law Journal, 29*, 331–339.

Taylor, G. (2001). The Council of Europe's Convention on Cybercrime and Australia: A civil liberties perspective. *Cyber Law Research, 30.* Retrieved from http://www.austlii.edu.au/au/other/CyberLRes/2001/30

United States v. Gorshkov and Ivanov, WL 1024026 (W.D. Wash. 2001).

United States v. Kevin Mitnick, No. 97-50365, WL 255343 (9th Circ. Central Ca, May 20, 1998).

United States v. Mitnick, 145 F.3d 1342 (9th Circ. Central Ca, May 14, 1998).

United States v. Ristine, 335 F.3d 692 (8th Circ., July 2, 2003).

Weeramantry, C. G. (1983). *The slumbering sentinels: Law and human rights in the wake of technology.* Melbourne, Australia: Penguin Books.

Weeramantry, C. G. (1990). Human rights. In J. Wallace & T. Pagone (Eds.), *Rights and freedoms in Australia* (pp. 240–255). Sydney, Australia: Federation Press.

Conclusion

K. JAISHANKAR

Internet technology and the development of cyberspace have taken society to the next level of evolution. Cyberspace has defied the boundaries and has made geography (or place) irrelevant. Cyberspace presents myriad potential opportunities for society in the new millennium. In the 1990s, a new era was ushered in, in which Internet technology reigned supreme. However, the increase in the netizens has dwarfed the technology to a mere medium. Additionally, the perpetrators who attacked machines through machines have started attacking real humans through the machines. This radical development led criminologists to address the need for a discipline to study and analyze criminal behavior in cyberspace. The crimes, offender behaviors, and victimization that occur in cyberspace needed to be studied from a social science versus a technological perspective. Thus, *cyber criminology* as an academic discipline was born with the launch of the *International Journal of Cyber Criminology* (http://www.cybercrimejournal.com), an online open-access journal, in 2007.

Since the launch of the *International Journal of Cyber Criminology*, the term *cyber criminology* has taken its academic roots in the online as well as offline academic circles (Jaishankar, 2007; Nhan & Bachmann, 2010). According to Nhan and Bachmann (2010), "Cyber criminology is slowly emerging from a niche area that is often marginalized by mainstream criminology to one of high importance" (p. 175). Although cyber criminology is gaining hold within the mainstream field of criminology, the big question is, "Will it evolve as a separate discipline?" There are many such criminologies that have not become separate disciplines (e.g., green criminology, biocriminology, environmental criminology). One reason could be that in spite of their research scope, they lacked content that could be taught. However, cyber criminology has the potential to become an independent discipline because of its dynamic expansion of exceptional interdisciplinary content in teaching and research.

If cyber criminology is to be established as a separate discipline, various challenges face the modern-day cyber criminologists. These challenges include (a) issues in teaching, (b) research in cyber criminology, and (c) professionalization of the discipline.

Issues in Teaching

Many of the universities in the United States and the United Kingdom offer criminology programs with a course in cyber crime. Recently, some universities in the United Kingdom—such as Canterbury Christ Church University; University College, Dublin; and University of Bedfordshire—have started offering master of science (MSc) courses in cyber crime forensics and forensic computing. The mushrooming courses on cyber forensics prove that universities are more interested in the practical investigative part of cyber crimes than the causation of cyber crimes. Although the practical part is important, neglecting the theoretical issues behind cyber crimes would not compliment a holistic understanding of cyber crimes. Hence, courses should be offered as an MSc in cyber criminology and forensics; this will enable a combination of both theoretical and practical aspects of cyber crimes.

Getting quality teachers to teach cyber crimes, laws, and investigation is one of the biggest challenges in developing programs in cyber criminology. The growth of Internet science, computer science, and information technology has a great impact on the development of the cyber criminology discipline. Conventional criminologists do not seem to be adapting to the growing needs of the expanding criminological discipline—they are not learning additional disciplines such as information technology and Internet science, both of which encompass the scope of cyber criminology. Without technical knowledge, conventional criminologists cannot move beyond teaching theoretical aspects of cyber crime. On the other hand, if technocrats were to be involved in teaching cyber criminology, they may be much less concerned with teaching the fundamentals of cyber criminology. They might be more inclined to speak about the technology than about the issues behind the cause of cyber crimes. Alternatively, if lawyers were to teach cyber criminology, they might focus only on cyber laws, thus leaving out other important components of cyber crimes. Such atomistic teaching by criminologists, technocrats, or lawyers will not help efforts to advance the formal discipline of cyber criminology. There is a strong need for holistic professionals who have a collective knowledge of cyber criminology, law, and forensics and who can take cyber criminology to the next level.

Conventional criminology departments could offer a multidisciplinary program of cyber criminology and forensics with assistance from other departments, such as departments of computer science, law, and information technology. Those professionals who complete their degrees in cyber criminology could then be further absorbed as research and teaching assistants to develop the discipline. This would create a pool of professionals who would serve as a repository, of sorts, with a blend of both theoretical and practical knowledge of cyber crimes, investigation, and laws; these professionals would be valuable in advancing the profession as well as assisting the criminal justice administration in the investigation of cyber crimes.

Research in Cyber Criminology

Current research in cyber criminology is highly encouraging. This book, which is a collection of selected research papers published in the *International Journal of Cyber Criminology*, is a good example. Articles published in the *International Journal of Cyber Criminology* were qualitative and quantitative and of high quality. The installation of a new International Cyber Crime Research Centre at the Simon Frazer University and the Centre for Cybercrime Research at the University of Ontario Institute of Technology—both in Canada—provides a good base for the development of research works in cyber criminology. Research centers such the Berkman Center for Internet and Society and the Centre for Cybercrime Studies at John Jay College of Criminal Justice are dedicated to contributing to the growth of cyber criminology. A cursory search on the Internet provides information about more such centers that are being developed and launched. This information gives me great hope that research in cyber criminology will be taken in an entirely new and exciting direction.

Because research in cyber criminology is new, it is not devoid of its own methodological flaws. In their recent work, Nhan and Bachmann (2010) highlighted certain methodological errors in cyber crime research. They feel that the "lack of a general definition, measurement issues, and survey problems such as bias and errors" (pp. 173) must be rectified by cyber criminologists in the future. Apart from these research issues, there is a dearth of researchers in the field of cyber criminology. Except for a few researchers in countries that include the United States, the United Kingdom, India, and Canada, there are no major researchers working in the field of cyber criminology. As pointed out earlier in the *Issues in Teaching* subsection, these lacunae can be overcome by creating more cyber criminologists. Research collaboration among various universities that conduct work in the field of cyber criminology can also fill this gap. Additionally, constant visits to the research centers by professionals from the industry would help in the development of research collaboration and transfer of expertise.

Professionalization of the Discipline

The major challenge that a new field of cyber criminology would face is the issue of the creation of jobs and the professionalization of the discipline. If cyber criminology remains a theoretical discipline, the creation of jobs would remain only at the level of theoretical research. As emphasized earlier, there is a need to grow cyber criminology as not only a theoretical but also a practical discipline. The amalgamation of cyber criminology, laws, and computer forensics can pave a new pathway for new jobs in the field of cyber criminology. Various universities and other bodies can create a certification program for cyber criminologists. These cyber criminologists can assist the police departments in the investigation of cyber crimes and start their own companies. Cyber criminologists also can evolve as cyber law specialists. Another significant area to which cyber criminologists can contribute is victim services. Cyber criminologists can become cyber victim counselors, who would counsel individuals who have fallen prey to cyber crimes and advise corporate bodies in the prevention of cyber victimization. Cyber criminologists also could act as a resource center on cyber crime victimization that would create awareness among the scholarly and lay public.

I sincerely believe that the challenges discussed herein can be overcome by current and future cyber criminologists, and I see a bright prospect for the growth of cyber criminology as an independent discipline.

References

Jaishankar, K. (2007). Cyber criminology: Evolving a novel discipline with a new journal. *International Journal of Cyber Criminology, 1*(1), 1–6.

Nhan, J., & Bachmann, M. (2010). Developments in cyber criminology. In M. Maguire & D. Okada (Eds.), *Critical issues in crime and justice: Thought, policy, and practice* (pp. 164–183). Thousand Oaks, CA: Sage.

Index